The DB2 Cluster Certification Guide

JONATHAN COOK ▪ CALENE JANACEK ▪ DWAINE SNOW

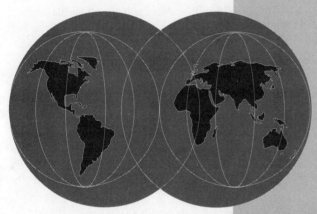

International Technical Support Organization
Austin, Texas 78758

ISBN 0-13-081900-X

90000

9 780130 819000

PRENTICE HALL PTR, UPPER SADDLE RIVER, NEW JERSEY 07458

Editorial/production supervision: *Maria Molinari*
Cover design director: *Jayne Conte*
Cover designer: *Bruce Kenselaar*
Manufacturing manager: *Pat Brown*
Marketing manager: *Kaylie Smith*
Acquisitions editor: *Mike Meehan*
Editorial assistant: *Bart Blanken*

Published by Prentice Hall PTR
Prentice-Hall, Inc.
A Simon & Schuster Company
Upper Saddle River, NJ 07458

Prentice Hall books are widely used by corporations and government agencies for training, marketing, and resale.
The publisher offers discounts on this book when ordered in bulk quantities.
For more information, contact Corporate Sales Dept.; Phone 800-382-3419; FAX: 201-236-7141
E-mail (Internet): corpsales@prenhall.com
Or write: Prentice Hall PTR, Corp. Sales Department, One Lake Street,Upper Saddle River, NJ 07458

10 9 8 7 6 5 4 3 2 1

ISBN 0-13-081900-X

Prentice-Hall International (UK) Limited, *London*
Prentice-Hall of Australia Pty. Limited, *Sydney*
Prentice-Hall Canada Inc., *Toronto*
Prentice-Hall Hispanoamericana, S.A., *Mexico*
Prentice-Hall of India Private Limited, *New Delhi*
Prentice-Hall of Japan, Inc., *Tokyo*
Simon & Schuster Asia Pte. Ltd., *Singapore*
Editora Prentice-Hall do Brasil, Ltda., *Rio de Janeiro*

Contents

Figures

Tables

Preface

This book is a complete guide to IBM's DB2 Universal Database Enterprise-Extended Edition. DB2 Universal Database (UDB) Enterprise-Extended Edition (EEE) is available on AIX, Windows NT, and Sun Solaris. This book, however, was written from a UNIX, specifically AIX operating system perspective. There may be some differences in the implementation of the DB2 UDB EEE product on these operating systems, but since they are not part of the certification testing for the IBM UDB for Cluster Exam, they are not covered in this publication. If you would like to become a Certified IBM Advanced Technical Expert on DB2 Universal Database V5, or you would simply like to understand the powerful DB2 UDB EEE product, then read on.

This guide helps you prepare for one of the tests in the the IBM Certified Advanced Technical Expert - DB2 Universal Database V5 program. The path to this level of certification involves the following:

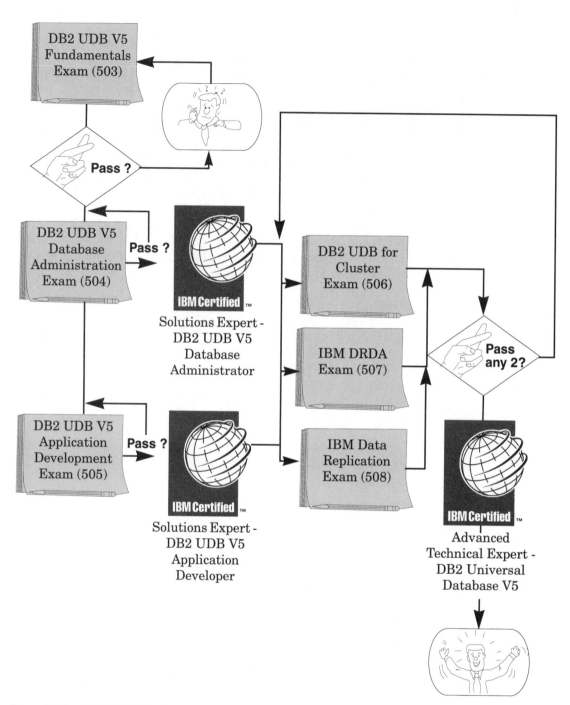

Figure 1. The Path to Certification

To become an IBM Certified Advanced Technical Expert - DB2 Universal Database V5, you must do the following:

1. Be either an IBM Certified Solutions Expert - DB2 UDB V5 Database Administrator or an IBM Certified Solutions Expert - DB2 UDB V5 Application Developer.

   To possess either of the IBM Certified Solutions Expert levels, you must have successfully passed:

   1. DB2 UDB V5 Fundamentals Exam (503)

   2. One or both of the following:

      • DB2 UDB V5 Database Administration Exam (504)

      • DB2 UDB V5 Application Development Exam (505)

2. Pass any two of the following three advanced exams:

   3. DB2 UDB for Cluster Exam (506)

   4. IBM DRDA Exam (507)

   5. IBM Data Replication Exam (508)

Those interested in taking the DB2 Universal Database V5 for Cluster Exam (506) should review the sample questions found in Appendix A, "Test Objectives and Sample Questions" on page 495. This test is one of the three advanced tests; passing any two of these tests along with the pre-requisites will give you the Advanced Technical Expert - DB2 Universal Database V5 certification.

As this guide is a follow-on to the existing *DB2 Universal Database Certification Guide*, for the most part, the information contained in that publication is not repeated in this guide.

The book is divided into the following areas:

• Overview - This chapter is a short introduction to the DB2 UDB Enterprise-Extended Edition product. It covers some features and functions and some of the terminology and conventions used throughout the book.

• Installation and Configuration - A partitioned database requires some specialized hardware setup and configuration. As such, there are numerous ways that the product can be installed and configured. This is explained in chapter two.

• Designing and Implementing a Database - When dealing with gigabytes or even terabytes of data, you need optimal logical and physical data placement. This chapter takes you through each logical step, explaining the relationship between the objects, followed by sections that help you to perform the activity with detail on the commands used.

- Loading Data - Chapter four discusses the methods available to get data into your cluster database, with discussion on each method so that you can choose the opimal method for your environment. Step by step detail is provided.

- Managing Data - This chapter covers activities that the database administrator must know. For example, there is a very detailed section covering what to do when your hardware configuration changes and how to rebalance your data. Also, how to efficiently back up and restore data is discussed.

- Performance Tuning and Problem Determination - These chapters look at the tuning parameters in a cluster environment. For complex queries, you need to understand what is happening during the execution of that query. The output from the explain facilities is detailed so that you not only understand what is happening during execution, but you can also learn how to influence the optimizer to improve performance.

How This Book was Created

This book was a joint effort between the Austin ITSO (International Technical Support Organization) and the IBM Toronto Lab. The ITSO is a group within IBM whose mission is to provide skill transfer on new products and emerging technology on a worldwide basis. We provide direct feedback to the IBM software labs as we gather input from various groups of DB2 users, including IBM support personnel, customers and business partners.

The ITSO provides a working envionment for interested individuals to work with new IBM software products. These individuals may include IBM employees and customers. Each team develops a workshop or book, known as a redbook.

┌─── **Web Site!!!!** ──────────────────────────────────────┐

Check out the ITSO web site for more information including a listing of available ITSO redbooks at: http://www.redbook.ibm.com/redbooks

└──┘

The DB2 Universal Database Enterprise-Edition Certification Guide was produced by many people from all over the world.

Figure 2. The Austin Team

Calene Janacek is the DB2 Project Leader for the International Technical Support Organization (ITSO) in Austin, Texas. She has been with IBM since 1989, working for the ITSO since 1993. Calene is responsible for producing technical manuals called "redbooks" that are used worldwide by support personnel and customers. She also develops workshops for new releases of DB2 that she teaches worldwide. She has presented at DB2 and AIX technical conferences.

Jonathan Cook is an Advisory Software Engineer at the International Technical Support Organization (ITSO), Austin Center. He has ten years of experience as a database specialist working in the areas of application development and database administration. He has been with IBM since 1992, working in both the United Kingdom and France before joining the Austin ITSO. He writes extensively and teaches IBM classes worldwide on DB2 for the UNIX and Intel platforms.

Dwaine Snow has worked with DB2 Universal Database and its predecessors for the past 8 years. During this time, he has written and designed applications using DB2. He has also worked in the DB2 UDB

Customer Service Team. Dwaine is currently the DB2 UDB Certification and Education coordinator. In this role, he is responsible for the DB2 Universal Database certification program and tests, as well as the availability of IBM courses required to develop DB2 UDB expertise. Dwaine has written a number of DB2-related articles and has contributed to a number of DB2 redbooks. He has presented at DB2 conferences and has taught DB2 UDB courses worldwide.

Diane DeVere Bullock has been a database administrator since 1986 working with DB2 and IMS. Diane currently provides database administration support to IBM's internal marketing database which consists of an on-line client/server configuration and a data warehouse that span 7 RISC AS/400's; the database appoximately 1 terabyte in size. Diane also provides consulting services in the areas of cross platform data replication and database tuning.

Eduardo Fontana is a Data Management Pre-Sales Technical Specialist who works for the Software Group in IBM Argentina. He has extensive experience of AIX, HACMP, RS/6000 SP, DB2 and Intel Operating Systems.

Frank Jeppesen is a Systems Engineer who works for IBM Denmark. Included in his responsibilities, is customer support on the DB2 products.

Luis Reina Julia works for IBM Global Services in Spain. He is an IBM Certified DB2 Specialist. He has been working with DB2 and data warehousing products for customers in Spain.

George Latimer is a Senior Availability Services Specialist who works for IBM Global Services based in Charlottesville, Virginia. His areas of speciality are ADSM, RS/6000 SP, DB2 and HACMP.

Clarence Sham has been working with DB2 products for ten years. After joining IBM in 1997 as an Advisory I/T Specialist, Clarence became a technical sales support for the Software Brand team in Hong Kong with responsibility for the Data Management products. Clarence gives technical presentations and product demos for customers in Hong Kong and China.

Tetsuya Shirai is an I/T specialist at IBM Japan. He has been been with IBM for six years, working the past two years with the DB2 products. Shirai-san works in the area of services with DB2, teaching classes to both customers and IBMers. He also provides consultanting services to DB2 customers worldwide. He is fluent in Japanese, Spanish, and English.

Guillermo F Unger joined IBM Argentina in 1988 where he has been involved with DB2 for MVS, VM, VSE, OS/400, OS/2, NT and AIX. He is a certified DB2 specialist and has also co-authored redbooks on DRDA and

Visualizer connectivity. He currently does DB2 technical support for Latin America South.

Fernando Ventura works for an IBM Business Partner in Buenos Aires Argentina. He has been supporting DB2 products for the last five years.

The following people were invaluable for their technical expertise and moral support:

Catherine Cook
IBM France

Bob Harbus
IBM Toronto Lab

Dale McInnis
IBM Toronto Lab

David L. Gray
Advanced Micro Devices, Austin, TX

A special thanks goes to the staff at the IBM Teraplex Center in Poughkeepsie, without whose help this project would never have been completed:

Joe Labriola, Joe Catucci, Gus Branish, Kurt Sulzbach and Paul Bildzok.

Chapter 1. Overview

This chapter introduces you to DB2 Universal Database (UDB) Enterprise-Extended Edition. We'll refer to it as DB2 UDB EEE or simply EEE for convenience. DB2 Universal Database Enterprise-Extended Edition is one of the DB2 Universal Database Server products.

DB2 UDB EEE is intended to be used in a partitioned database environment. A partitioned database environment is one where the data and processing are distributed among a cluster or group of machines. The use of partitioned database systems has developed out of an increase in the use of Relational Database Management Systems (RDBMS). As the popularity and use of database systems have increased, so too have users' expectations and needs. Users want to execute more queries with faster response times, even if scanning terabytes of data. Queries are structured to generate complex reports, searching gigabytes, or more of data. Queries have grown not only in the amount of data searched, but also in their complexity.

Based on the increase in the complexity of queries and volumes of data, it is has become increasingly unlikely that the processing capacity of any single processor, or even one system with multiple processors is sufficient to provide acceptable response times. Consider the example of scanning a table in a non-partitioned database. Let's say this table is scanned at a rate of 2.25 megabytes/second. If the table size is 10 GB, it would take this non-partitioned RDBMS over an hour to scan the 10 GB table. If that processing could be distributed evenly among 128 processors, the time required to scan the data in the table would drop to 35 seconds.

There are also architectural limits in terms of the number of disks that can be attached to a single processor. This limits the size of a database held on a single processor. The EEE product extends the functionality, reliability, and scalability of an RDBMS to a partitioned database environment. Using the EEE product in your environment, you can manage very large databases and execute applications where complex queries can be executed quickly while processing large amounts of data.

This chapter looks at some typical scenarios using DB2 UDB EEE, along with other products as needed to fit certain business needs. We'll also discuss some of the terminology used throughout this book. We'll introduce you to some of the user interfaces that you'll use in your UDB EEE environment, such as the Control Center and the Client Configuration Assistant and a text-based application called the Command Line Processor.

1.0.1 DB2 Family of Products

The term *universal* in DB2 Universal Database means the ability to store all kinds of electronic information. This includes traditional relational data as well as structured and unstructured binary information, documents and text in many languages, graphics, images, multimedia (audio and video), or information specific to operations like engineering drawings, maps, insurance claims forms, numerical control streams, or any other type of electronic information.

The DB2 database products are collectively known as the *DB2 Family*. The DB2 family is divided into two main groups:

- DB2 for midrange and large systems. Supported platforms are OS/400, VSE/VM and OS/390.
- DB2 UDB for Intel and UNIX environments. Supported platforms include OS/2, Windows NT, Windows 95, AIX, HP-UX, and Solaris.

The midrange and large system members of the DB2 Family are very similar to DB2 UDB, but due to operating system differences, their features and implementations sometimes differ.

DB2 UDB provides seamless database connectivity using the most popular network communications protocols, including NetBIOS, TCP/IP, IPX/SPX, Named Pipes, and APPC. The infrastructure (but not the protocol) that DB2 database clients use to communicate with DB2 database servers is provided by DB2.

1.1 DB2 Universal Database V5

Before we discuss DB2 UDB EEE, we'll look at the history of this product. DB2 UDB V5 represents the merger of two successful products: DB2 Parallel Edition V1.2 and DB2 Common Server V2.1.2, as shown in Figure 3. Both were based on DB2/6000 Version 1, but were developed in parallel to address specific customer needs.

- DB2 Parallel Edition addressed the need to query very large databases running on massively parallel processors and clusters and was developed to optimize parallel query capabilities on IBM's RS/6000 SP hardware.
- DB2 Common Server addressed the needs of the general database server market on UNIX, OS/2 and Windows NT.

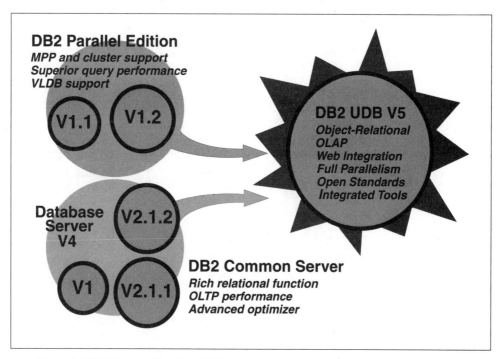

Figure 3. DB2 Universal Database Version 5

The merging of these two products results in a product capable of scaling from laptops to massively parallel systems and capable of supporting high-volume parallel transactions, using the rich function of DB2 Version 2. To this merged function, additional support for on-line analytical or OLAP processing is added. There is more Web integration in DB2 UDB V5, and Net.Data is packaged with the database server. Also included is more support for industry standards, such as greater DCE support, more SQL92 compliance, and integrated tools that include data replication, a governor and a job scheduler.

1.1.1 DB2 Universal Database - The Scalable Database

In Figure 4, all of the DB2 Universal Database Server products are shown. DB2 UDB is capable of supporting hardware platforms from laptops to massively parallel systems with hundreds of nodes. This provides extensive and granular growth. There are four different DB2 Database Server Products in Version 5. The subject of this book is DB2 Universal Database Enterprise-Extended Edition.

For simplicity, we will refer to the DB2 Universal Database family of products as DB2.

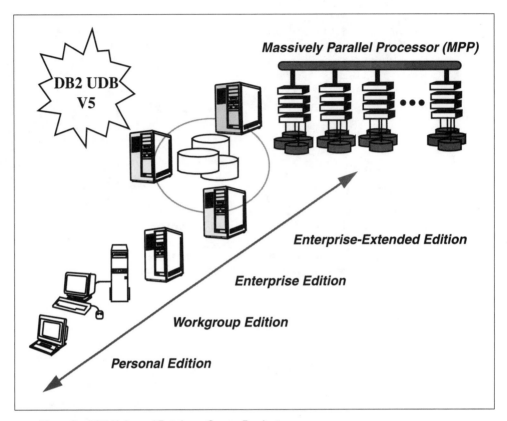

Figure 4. DB2 Universal Database Server Products

1.2 DB2 UDB Family of Products

All DB2 products require licensing. There are three main DB2 products, namely:

- **DB2 Universal Database** (UDB). There are four versions of the DB2 Universal Database product, as shown in Figure 4: DB2 Personal Edition, DB2 Workgroup Edition, DB2 Enterprise Edition, and DB2 Enterprise-Extended Edition.

- **DB2 Connect.** This provides the ability to access a host database using the Distributed Relational Database Architecture (DRDA). There are two versions of this product: DB2 Connect Personal Edition and DB2 Connect Enterprise Edition.

- **DB2 Developer's Edition**. This provides the ability to develop and test a database application for one user. There are two versions of this product: DB2 Personal Developer's Edition (PDE) and DB2 Universal Developer's Edition (UDE).

All DB2 products have a common component called the DB2 Client Application Enabler (CAE). Once a DB2 application has been developed, the DB2 Client Application Enabler component must be installed on each workstation where the application is executed. Figure 5 shows the relationship between the application, CAE and the DB2 Database Server. If the application and database are installed on the same workstation, the application is known as a *local client*. If the application is installed on a workstation other than the DB2 server, the application is known as a *remote client*.

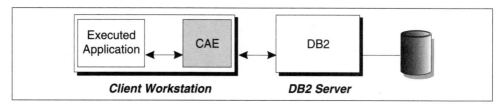

Figure 5. Remote Client Accessing DB2 Server Using CAE

The Client Application Enabler provides functions other than the ability to communicate with a DB2 UDB server or DB2 Connect gateway machine. From the CAE, you can do any of the following:

- Issue an interactive SQL statement on a remote client which accesses data on a remote UDB server.
- Graphically administer and monitor a UDB database server.
- Run applications that were developed to comply with the Open Database Connectivity (ODBC) standard.
- Run Java applications that access and manipulate data in DB2 UDB databases using Java Database Connectivity (JDBC).

There are no licensing requirements to install the Client Application Enabler (CAE) component. Licensing is controlled at the DB2 UDB server.

The version of the CAE that you need to install depends on the operating system on the client machine. For example, if you have a database application developed for AIX, you will need to install the Client Application Enabler for AIX.

There is a different CAE for each supported DB2 client operating system. The supported platforms are OS/2, Windows NT, Windows 95, Windows 3.x, AIX, HP-UX, MacIntosh, DOS and Solaris. The CAE component should be installed on all end-user workstations.

A complete set of CAEs is provided with Workgroup Edition, Enterprise Edition, Enterprise-Extended Edition, and with the DB2 Connect Enterprise products. This set of CAEs is provided on a CD-ROM, and is referred to as the *DB2 CAE Client Pack*.

1.2.1 DB2 Universal Database

DB2 Universal Database, or UDB, is a Relational Database Management System (RDBMS). It can be included in one of the following four database server products:

- **DB2 Personal Edition**

  An RDBMS engine that **will not** support remote clients. This is available on the Intel platform only.

- **DB2 Workgroup Edition**

  An RDBMS engine that **will** support remote clients. This is available on the Intel uniprocessor machines only.

- **DB2 Enterprise Edition**

  Similar to the Workgroup Edition, but is also available for SMP machines. In addition, this product allows remote client applications to access data on a host database using DRDA.

- **DB2 Enterprise-Extended Edition**

  Similar to the Enterprise Edition, with additional support for clusters of database servers in a partitioned database environment.

1.2.2 DB2 UDB Enterprise-Extended Edition

DB2 Universal Database Enterprise-Extended Edition contains all the features and functions found in the Enterprise Edition, such as:

- Powerful RDBMS
- Accessibility of applications from a wide range of client platforms, including DOS, Windows, Macintosh, OS/2, AIX, HP-UX, SCO, SINIX, and Solaris
- Support for Java, JDBC, ODBC, and CLI
- Web/database connectivity and Java integration

- Host connectivity, through DB2 Connect

- Extended GUI administration tools, such as the Control Center

- Object-relational support, using DB2 Extenders

DB2 UDB EEE has other features that help to satisfy the needs of decision support and data warehousing applications. These features include:

- Intelligent data distribution.

   DB2 UDB EEE supports parallel queries by using intelligent database partitioning. In an MPP (Massively Parallel Processor) or cluster configuration, DB2 UDB EEE distributes the data and database functions to multiple hosts. DB2 UDB EEE uses a hashing algorithm that enables it to manage the distribution (and redistribution) of data as required.

- A cost-based SQL optimizer.

   DB2's cost-based SQL optimizer makes use information about how the data is distributed to evaluate the different access paths for an SQL query. It will then use the access path with the estimated shortest elapsed execution time. The optimizer supports SQL query rewrite, On-Line Analytical Processing (OLAP), SQL extensions, Dynamic Bit-Mapped Indexing Anding (DBIA) and Star Joins. These features are commonly used in data warehousing applications.

- Parallel everything.

   DB2 UDB EEE's capabilities range from taking advantage of cluster hardware configurations, partitioning of data, access plans automatically created for parallel execution with standard SQL, and parallel execution of utilities. DB2's parallel execution applies to SELECT, INSERT, UPDATE and DELETE functions. Data scans, joins, sorts, load balancing, table reorganization, data load, index creation, indexed access, backup and restore are all performed simultaneously on all hosts in the DB2 cluster.

- Scalability.

   As your business grows, DB2 can accommodate more users and more data with predictably scalable performance. It uses a concept called shared nothing. (This is discussed in more detail in "Parallel Architecture and Processing" on page 14). Shared nothing architecture allows parallel queries to be processed with the minimum of contention for resources between the hosts in the DB2 cluster. Because the number of partitions of data has little impact on traffic between hosts, performance scales in an almost linear manner as you add more machines to your DB2 cluster.

DB2 UDB EEE product provides the ability for a database to be partitioned across multiple independent computers using the same operating system. To the end-user or application developer, the database appears to be a single logical entity. DB2 UDB Enterprise-Extended Edition is designed for applications where the database is simply too large for a single computer to handle efficiently. SQL operations can operate in parallel on the individual database partitions, thus improving the performance of a single query.

The next sections look at examples of how DB2 UDB EEE may be used in customer environments.

Configuration One - Distribution Scenario

This first scenario involves a distribution customer using DB2 UDB EEE to help determine buyer's decisions. They also have an inventory system that gives them "just-in-time" control over quantities of items. They had an existing DB2 MVS environment that they wanted to incorporate into the new system.

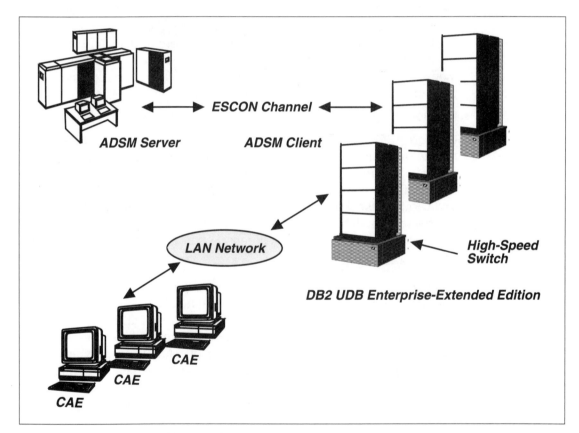

Figure 6. Configuration One - Distribution Scenario

Figure 6 shows a mixed hardware environment made up of a number of RS/6000 SP hosts, an MVS system, and a number of workstation clients. The mainframe here is used to store the backups of the DB2 UDB EEE databases. The ADSM (ADSTAR Distributed Storage Manager) server is located on the mainframe. The ADSM client is installed on each SP node where DB2 is installed. ADSM allows you to manage your recovery strategy by storing crucial backup files. The ESCON channel is used here by ADSM to improve the performance of backup and restore operations.

The SP nodes use the high-speed switch for internal DB2 communication between nodes. There is also an external token-ring network used by remote clients to access the DB2 UDB EEE database. Each remote client needs only the Client Application Enabler and a DB2-supported communication product, such as TCP/IP.

Configuration Two
In this example, DB2 UDB EEE is installed on a Windows NT cluster.

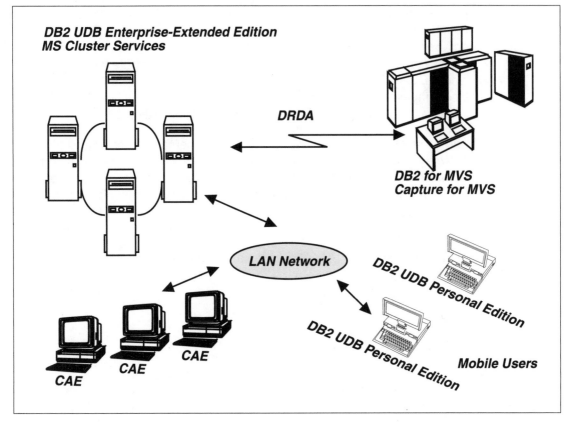

DB2 UDB Enterprise-Extended Edition
MS Cluster Services

DRDA

DB2 for MVS
Capture for MVS

LAN Network

DB2 UDB Personal Edition

DB2 UDB Personal Edition

CAE

CAE

CAE

Mobile Users

Figure 7. Configuration Two - Customer-Based System

This is an example of a business that is moving from an account-based system to a customer-based system. There are some users who are truly clients and perform operations only against the partitioned database on the NT cluster. The mobile users represent smaller offices where copies of the database are replicated from the MVS host to the NT cluster and then to the laptop users. Each laptop is running DB2 Universal Database Personal Edition, which allows them to store a copy of the database on their machines.

1.3 Terminology Used in DB2 UDB EEE

This section focuses on some of the terms and definitions we'll use for the remainder of the book. This includes some of the DB2 command and SQL statement syntax.

The terminology used can be sometimes confusing due to the history of the DB2 UDB EEE product. We'll focus on the current terms, but point out where some of the old terminology is still used.

A database is simply a collection of data. If you're familiar with DB2 or other RBDMSs, you'll know that data is stored in tables in a database, with tables having a certain number of columns and rows. In DB2 EEE, a database is divided into several parts that are called *database partitions*. A *database partition* is a part of the database that has its own portion of the user data, indexes, configuration files and transaction logs. Let's look at a simple environment where there is one database partition for every machine in your cluster.

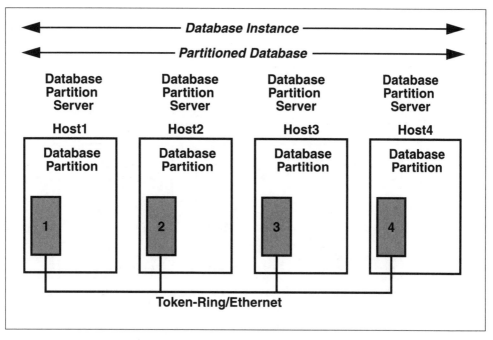

Figure 8. Database Partitions

Figure 8 shows an example of a simple four-host cluster. Each system or machine in the DB2 UDB EEE environment is referred to as a host. A configuration file determines which hosts will be part of the DB2 UDB EEE environment. This is covered in detail in Chapter 2, "Installation and Configuration" on page 27. A database partition server manages a partition of the database. Using TCP/IP, the DB2 hosts communicate via a token-ring or ethernet connection.

A database instance is a logical database manager environment. You can have several instances of the database manager product executing within the same group of hosts. You can use these instances to separate the development environment from the production environment, tune the database manager to a particular environment, and protect sensitive information from a particular group of people. A database is created within a database instance. The database may either be partitioned or non-partitioned. When you are using DB2 UDB EEE, this database will almost always be a partitioned database so that you can distribute the function and data among all the hosts in your DB2 cluster.

In addition, it is possible to have multiple database partitions on a single host.

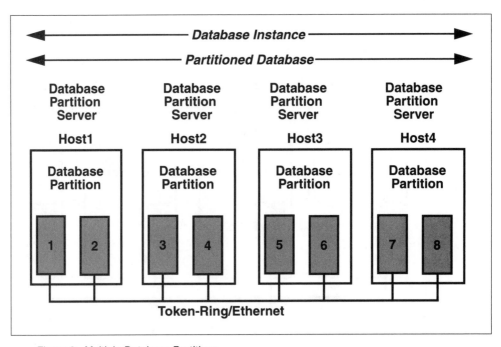

Figure 9. Multiple Database Partitions

Figure 9 uses the same four host DB2 cluster used in the last example (Figure 8 on page 11). Notice that each host has two database partitions. Quite often this type of configuration is used to take advantage of SMP (Symmetric Multi-Processor) hardware. You can distribute the database function and processing among different hosts and among processors on the same host.

It is desirable to have the same number of database partitions on each host, though there may be exceptions to this statement. For example, if your original cluster consisted of single CPU machines and you added new hardware to your DB2 cluster that included SMP machines, you might consider creating multiple database partitions on the new SMP hardware.

You might also want to keep one database partition reserved to store only the system catalogs and not contain any user data. The database partition that holds the system catalog tables is referred to as the *catalog partition*. You may also come into contact with the term *catalog node*. The term *node* was used in DB2 Parallel Edition and caused some confusion as it referred to both software and hardware. A node in DB2 terminology is a database partition. However, we also refer to uni-processor or symmetric multiprocessor machines as nodes. This book will try to avoid confusion in terminology. However, some of the DB2 commands and SQL statements use the old terminology.

1.3.1 DB2 Commands and SQL Statements

Let's look at a DB2 command to see both an example of terminology and how commands will appear in this book.

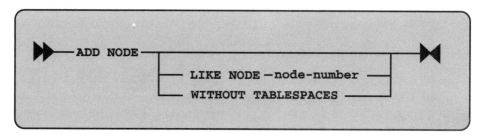

Figure 10. Example of a Command in DB2 UDB EEE

The **ADD NODE** command shown in Figure 10 is used in DB2 UDB EEE to add a database partition. The term *node* here means database partition. In our documentation, we use the term SDP to refer to an environment with a single database partition per host. Similarly, the term MDP refers to an environment with a multiple database partitions per host. Note that the **ADD NODE** command also has several options:

- **LIKE NODE** *node-number*. This means that you are adding a database partition that is similar to an existing one. Containers will be created for the temporary table space for that partition. These containers will be the same as the containers on the specified *node-number*.

- **WITHOUT TABLESPACES**. This option of the **ADD NODE** command means no containers will be created for the temporary table space for that partition. They will be created later.

A table space defines where table data is stored on disk. You'll also notice that in DB2 commands and SQL statements, table space appears as one word. Whereas, in our documentation, table space appears as two words.

The **ADD NODE** command is covered in detail in Chapter 5, "Managing Data" on page 251.

1.3.2 Parallel Architecture and Processing

This section explains some more terminology that is used in a partitioned database environment. We will show how DB2 UDB EEE uses this terminology.

DB2 UDB EEE is a product that takes advantage of *shared nothing architecture*.

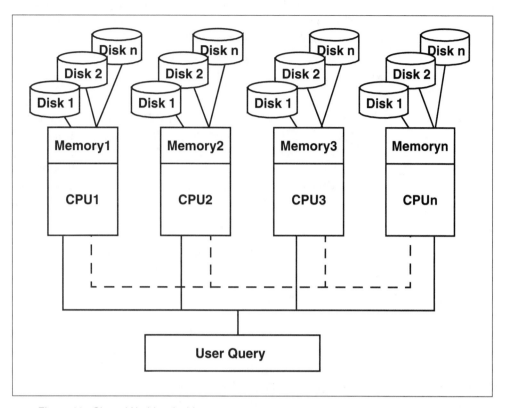

Figure 11. Shared Nothing Architecture

Figure 11 shows an example of shared nothing architecture. Here we see loosely coupled processors are linked by some high-speed interconnection. Each processor has its own memory and accesses its own disks. The advantages of this type of architecture are the following:

- Scalability in terms of database size and number of processors.

- Performance gains from not sharing resources across a network.

Total memory has a fixed capacity. By increasing the number of machines, you can exceed that fixed amount because the memory is shared among machines. The same is true for total disk capacity. The other advantage that could be gained is in the number of operations that are performed. Each machine only needs to do part of the work. So, processing is more distributed and the database can manage a larger amount of data.

Performance gains are assisted by the concept of function shipping. Function shipping assists in the reduction of network traffic because functions such as

SQL queries are shipped instead of data. Function shipping means that relational operators are executed on the processor containing the data whenever possible. So, the operation (or the SQL) is moved to where the data resides. Function shipping is well suited to the shared nothing architecture model.

The high-speed interconnection used between hosts is represented in Figure 11 on page 15 by the dotted lines. In an SP cluster, this would be the high-speed switch. The smoother lines represent another type of network. The user query issues an SQL statement. For example, an SQL select statement is issued. Every database partition receives the operation from one processor who works as a dispatcher. This dispatcher is sometimes referred to as the co-ordinator partition. Each database partition executes the operation on its own set of data. An exchange of information among the hosts may occur. The result from the operation is sent back to the coordinator partition. The coordinator partition assembles the data and returns it to the requestor.

1.3.2.1 Types of Parallelism
In DB2 Universal Database V5, parallelism support was extended to exploit the symmetric multi-processor (SMP) systems. This functionality will better exploit SMP shared memory architecture to speed up individual SQL queries and utilities. The utilities have also gained increased support for parallel I/O servers for driving multiple disk drives, similar to that already supported with SQL requests. The new SMP support builds upon the existing parallelism support that existed in prior versions of DB2 including:

- Parallel transactions. Each user's request could be run on a separate processes or threads.

- Parallel computers. Using DB2 Parallel Edition to support MPP machines with multiple parallel database nodes

- Parallel I/O. The ability to define multiple processes or threads to manage the I/O activity for different physical drives.

- Parallel disks. DB2 would allow databases to be created over many disk drives allowing concurrent physical access to data.

Many database tasks can be executed in parallel in both a partition and non-partitioned database. The result is that the task will be executed faster. There are many factors that contribute taking advantage of executing in parallel, such as the type of task, the database configuration and the hardware environment. This section discusses parallelism with respect to DB2. You'll find the following types of parallelism supported in DB2:

- I/O
- Query
- Utility

I/O parallelism is achieved for some operations when DB2 can take advantage of storing your table data on separate physical disks on one host. The DB2 database manager can read from or write to two or more disks in parallel, thus reducing overall executing time.

Query parallelism can be broken down further into three types:

- **Inter-Transaction**

  DB2 has always supported inter-transaction parallelism. With DB2, you are able to have multiple applications query a database at the same time. Each of those queries may execute independently of the others, but DB2 can execute all of them at the same time. You may also hear the term inter-query used to refer to inter-transaction parallelism. This is the ability to execute more than one transaction at a time.

- **Inter-Partition**

  The SQL statement is broken into a number of subset queries. Each subset query works on a subset of the data.

- **Intra-Partition**

  A single SQL statement is broken down into separate tasks, like scan, join or sort. These separate tasks are performed in parallel.

Let's take a closer look at inter- and intra-partition query parallelism by discussing an example of each.

Inter-Partition Parallelism
When DB2 uses inter-partition parallelism, a single query is split across many processors.

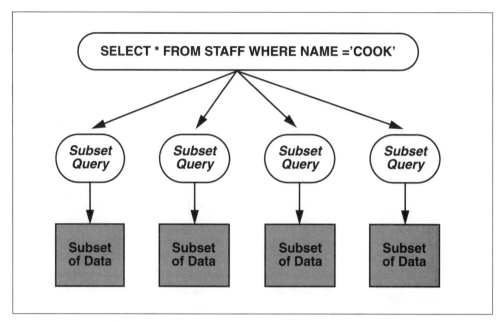

Figure 12. Inter-Partition Parallelism

Figure 12 is an example of inter-partition parallelism. A single query, in this example a **SELECT** statement with a **WHERE** predicate, is decomposed into four subset queries. Each subset query works on 25% of the data in the staff table. Each subset query finds all the qualifying rows in its subset of the data and returns only the desired columns in these rows to the application.

This kind of parallelism is sometimes referred to as *data parallelism*. This reflects the fact that the data is divided into parts to be processed. There are two types of division of data:

- Static

  The data is divided into parts when it is loaded or inserted into the table. This is the case for the data in each database partition in a EEE database.

- Dynamic

  The data is divided into parts for the duration of the query, based on data ranges (if using index access), or page ranges (if using table access). This is the case for a non-partitioned database on an SMP machine, where it is usual to see each subset query running on a different processor.

Intra-Partition Parallelism
An example of intra-partition parallelism is shown in Figure 13.

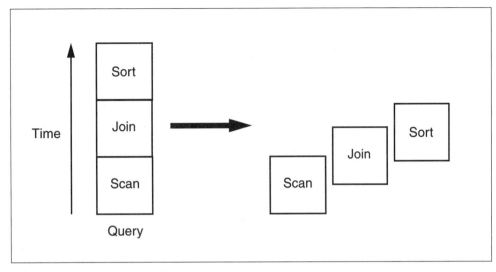

Figure 13. Intra-Partition Parallelism

On on left side of the diagram, we see an SQL query which consists of a scan, a join and a sort. Without some form of parallel processing, these tasks are performed serially, one after the other. When DB2 uses intra-partition parallelism, these tasks are performed in parallel, as shown at the right. For example, the join task is started before the scan task has finished.

This kind of parallelism is also referred to as *pipeline parallelism*, as the output from one task is piped into another task as its input.

1.3.2.2 Combining Inter- and Intra-Partition Parallelism
It is possible to combine both inter- and intra-partition parallelism in a single SQL query. Figure 14 shows an example of this.

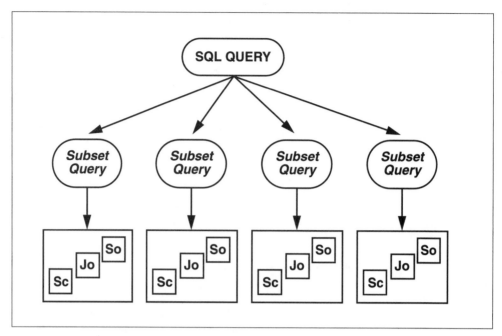

Figure 14. Combining Intra- and Inter-Partition Parallelism

The combination of these two types of parallelism results in a very efficient way to execute complex SQL queries against large databases. A typical hardware configuration which benefits greatly from executing queries in this way is a cluster of SMP machines. Typically, in this case, a subset query is sent to each SMP machine in the cluster. Then, at each SMP machine, intra-partition (or pipeline) parallelism is performed against the subset of data at that machine.

1.3.2.3 Parallelism in DB2 Utilities
DB2's utilities have also been enhanced to take advantage of parallelism. The LOAD utility has been enhanced to support the parsing and formatting of the input data in parallel. Also, the LOAD now can use parallel I/O servers to write the data to the containers in parallel.

During index creation, the scanning and subsequent sorting of the data can now occur in parallel. This speeds up index creation during a **CREATE INDEX** statement, during restart processing (if an index is marked invalid) and also during **REORG** processing.

During backup and restore processing, DB2 can also take advantage of running buffer manipulators in parallel to read/write data to/from the database. In DB2 Common Server Version 2, backup/restore could take advantage of disk parallelism but it can now also take advantage of multiple CPUs by assigning the buffer manipulators among the CPUs.

1.4 DB2 User Interfaces

This section discusses some of the user interfaces that are provided with the DB2 product. Currently, you can monitor your DB2 UDB EEE cluster from an Intel-based operating system such as Windows NT or OS/2. We'll look at some of the GUI tools that are used throughout this book, the Control Center, the Client Configuration Assistant (CCA) and the Command Center.

We'll also cover the Command Line Processor (CLP), which is a text-based tool that you can use to enter DB2 commands and SQL statements.

1.4.1 The Control Center

The Control Center is the central point of administration for DB2 Universal Database Version 5. The Control Center enables the user to perform typical database administration tasks. It gives a clear overview of the entire system, enables remote database management and provides step-by-step assistance for complex tasks.

Figure 15 shows an example of the information available from the Control Center. The Systems object represents both local and remote machines. To display all the DB2 systems that your system can access, expand the object tree by clicking on the plus sign (+) next to Systems. The left portion of the screen lists available systems (local and remote) with DB2 installed.

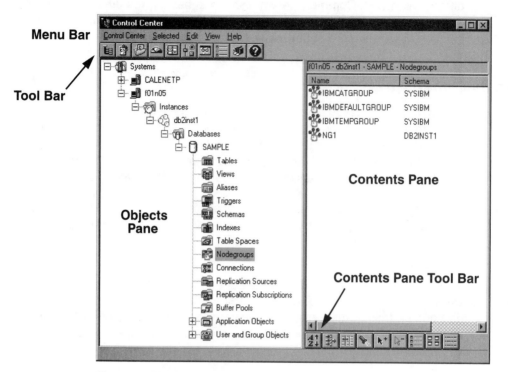

Figure 15. The Control Center

We can see from the figure that the system f01n05 contains a DB2 instance, db2inst1, in which the database SAMPLE is located. The nodegroups for the SAMPLE database are highlighted. A nodegroup is a defined set of one or more database partitions in a database.

The main components of the Control Center are listed below:

- **Menu Bar**. This is used to access Control Center functions and online help.

- **Tool Bar**. These icons are used to access the other administration tools.

- **Objects Pane**. This is found on the left-hand side of the Control Center window. It contains all the objects that can be managed from the Control Center as well as their relationship to each other.

- **Contents Pane**. This is found on the right side of the Control Center window and contains the objects that belong to or correspond to the object selected on the Objects Pane.

- **Contents Pane Toolbar**. These icons are used to tailor the view of the objects and information in the Contents pane. These functions can also be selected in the View menu.

Hover Help is also available in the Control Center, providing a short description for each icon on the tool bar as you move the mouse pointer over the icon.

1.4.2 Client Configuration Assistant

The Client Configuration Assistant (CCA) helps you to configure a DB2 client system in order to access a remote DB2 server system. There are a number of ways to enable a client to access a remote database. You do not need to know the syntax of commands, however when trying to access a DB2 UDB EEE server, it is helpful to know how the remote database server is defined on your network. One of the options in the CCA is to search the network for valid DB2 servers. This is called the *search* method. Alternatively, when you use the *known* method, you specify the database server you want to access.

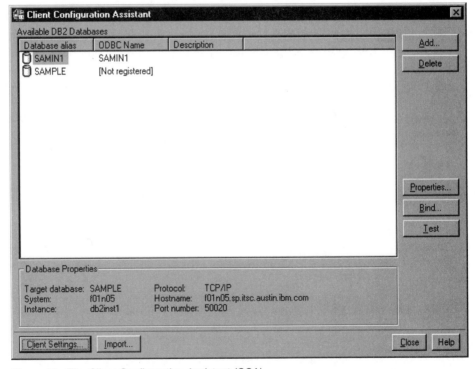

Figure 16. The Client Configuration Assistant (CCA)

Figure 16 shows the initial window of the CCA. From here, you can add or delete remote databases, choose your client settings and import client profiles. Client profiles are a way to copy all of a client's configuration information to another system so that you can avoid having to entering the same information more than once.

In this example, two databases are cataloged. The SAMIN1 database is highlighted. Properties about the SAMIN1 database are found in the gray-shaded area. The name of the database on the server, the host, the instance in which the database is located, the protocol used to connect to the database, and the port number used for the TCP/IP connection are all displayed.

1.4.3 The Command Center

The Command Center provides an interactive window that lets the user perform tasks such as executing SQL statements, DB2 commands and operating system commands. The execution result for one or more SQL statements and DB2 commands can be seen in the result window.

Using the Help provided in the Command Center, you can access the syntax of DB2 commands. You can access the other DB2 GUI tools, such as Control Center and Script Center, by using the main icons bar.

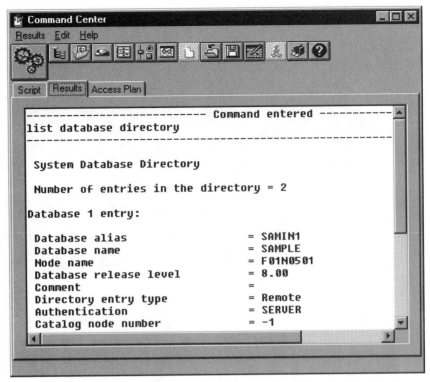

```
 Command Center                                           _ □ ×
 Results  Edit  Help
  [gears]  [toolbar icons]

  Script │ Results │ Access Plan │

  ┌──────────────────────────────────────────────────────┐
  │ ------------------------- Command entered -----------▲ │
  │ list database directory                                │
  │ ------------------------------------------------------ │
  │                                                        │
  │                                                        │
  │   System Database Directory                            │
  │                                                        │
  │   Number of entries in the directory = 2               │
  │                                                        │
  │ Database 1 entry:                                      │
  │                                                        │
  │   Database alias              = SAMIN1                 │
  │   Database name               = SAMPLE                 │
  │   Node name                   = F01N0501               │
  │   Database release level      = 8.00                   │
  │   Comment                     =                        │
  │   Directory entry type        = Remote                 │
  │   Authentication              = SERVER                 │
  │   Catalog node number         = -1                   ▼ │
  │ ◄                                                   ►  │
  └──────────────────────────────────────────────────────┘
```

Figure 17. The Command Center

In our example, we executed the **LIST DATABASE DIRECTORY** command to show the databases cataloged on our system. To execute the command, you can either click on the gears in the top left-hand corner or on the **Results** tab.

The execution plan and the statistics associated with an SQL statement before execution can be displayed. Enter the SQL, then select **Script** from the menu bar, then select **Create Access Plan**.

This GUI version of Command Line Processor uses the same options as traditional CLP for autocommit, SQLCA and SQLCODE display, output file, stop on error, and so on.

1.4.4 The Command Line Processor (CLP)

The Command Line Processor or CLP is a component common to all DB2 products. It is a text-based application used to execute SQL statements and DB2 commands. For example, if we issue to same command (**LIST DATATBASE DIRECTORY**) as we used in the Command Center:

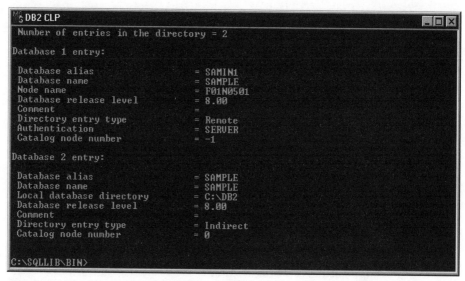

```
DB2 CLP                                                                    ▬□✕
 Number of entries in the directory = 2

Database 1 entry:

  Database alias                    = SAMIN1
  Database name                     = SAMPLE
  Node name                         = F01N0501
  Database release level            = 8.00
  Comment                           =
  Directory entry type              = Remote
  Authentication                    = SERVER
  Catalog node number               = -1

Database 2 entry:

  Database alias                    = SAMPLE
  Database name                     = SAMPLE
  Local database directory          = C:\DB2
  Database release level            = 8.00
  Comment                           =
  Directory entry type              = Indirect
  Catalog node number               = 0


C:\SQLLIB\BIN>
```

Figure 18. The Command Line Processor (CLP)

Figure 18 shows two entries, SAMIN1, which is a remote database and
SAMPLE, which is local to the machine.

Chapter 2. Installation and Configuration

This chapter discusses the planning, installation and configuration of DB2 Universal Database Enterprise-Extended Edition in an RS/6000 SP cluster environment. We'll break the chapter into three main sections:

- Planning or pre-installation tasks
- Installation of the software
- Post-installation tasks

Each section is by no means complete in its description. Our goal in this chapter is to provide you with enough information before you have to perform a task, such as installing the DB2 UDB EEE software or creating special users for DB2. There are many tasks that need to be performed. Also, be aware that the DB2 UDB EEE product may be installed on AIX, NT and Sun Solaris operating systems. We focus on installing in an AIX environment on an RS/6000 SP machine. However, the procedures we follow for the tasks can be applied to other environments.

When setting up DB2 UDB EEE on your cluster system, you need to fully understand what your options are and which method is best suited for your environment. The correct setup of your environment is crucial. You do not want to have to reinstall six months later when you realize that a crucial planning step was not considered. To assist you, we provide check points in these sections so that you can prevent an installation disaster. We start each section with a list of activities that must be considered. If you understand each of those activities fully, you can skip the detail in that section.

2.1 Pre-Installation Tasks and Planning

When installing the DB2 UDB EEE product, you need to take into consideration certain basic requirements. These are not the requirements for creating and storing a database. This is a list of points to check before beginning the installation of DB2 UDB EEE:

- Which hardware supports DB2 UDB EEE?
- How much memory is required to install and use the product?
- How much disk space is needed for installation?
- What are the software pre-requisites, if any?
- Are there any special users that must exist before installing DB2 UDB EEE?

- Are there any tasks to complete at the AIX level (creation of the file system for the instance owner's home directory, for example) before installing the product?

We'll look at these considerations over the next several pages. For additional information, refer to the *DB2 UDB EEE for AIX Quick Beginnings*, S72H-9620-00.

2.1.1 Hardware Requirements

DB2 UDB EEE for AIX can be installed on any of the following hardware:

- IBM RS/6000 SMP machines
- IBM RS/6000 SP machines with thin nodes, wide nodes and/or high nodes, connected through internal Ethernet, external token-ring and/or a high-performance switch.

2.1.1.1 Memory

The amount of real memory required depends on the configuration that you'll be using. If there are less than 32 database partition servers in an instance, a minimum of 256 MB real memory per machine is recommended. If there are more than 32 database partition servers per instance, or more than 30 clients, it is recommended to have a minimum of 512 MB real memory per machine. This assumes one database partition server per machine. Remember, these are guidelines, and you may need more memory if you have more database partition servers, more users, or if you have specific performance requirements.

2.1.1.2 Disk Space

The following describes the *minimum* amount of disk space that is required to install the DB2 UDB EEE Server product. It does not include the disk requirements necessary for the creation and storage of a database, operating system, application development tools, and communication products. Consult each product manual for disk space requirements.

DB2 Universal Database Extended - Enterprise Edition for AIX	Recommended Minimum Disk (MB)
Server Code	55 MB
On-line documentation in html format (English)	72 MB
Far-East Code Page Conversion Support	5 MB

Table 1. Storage Requirements for DB2 UDB EEE Product and Components

---

Online Documentation

If you plan to install the on-line documentation in HTML format (English), make sure you have at least twice the recommended space available because the component will be installed in compressed format and you need the extra disk space temporarily for the de-compression to be successful.

2.1.2 Software Prerequisites

This section outlines the software required to run DB2 UDB EEE Server on an RS/6000 SP machine.

- Operating System

  AIX Version 4.1.4 or later.

- Communication Software

  To support two-phase commit using APPC, you need IBM Communications Server Version 4.1 or later, which supports the LU6.2 Syncpoint Manager function. If you do not need to support two-phase commit, IBM SNA Server/6000 Version 1.x or later is sufficient.

  To support remote clients using IPX/SPX, you can use IBM NetBIOS and IPX/SPX for AIX Version 2.1, IBM NetWare for AIX Version 3.11B, or the AIX Connections feature of AIX 4.1.4.

  TCP/IP is provided by the AIX base operating system. However, only Version 4.1.4 or later supports two-phase commit over TCP/IP.

- Other Software

  If you need to use the DRDA Application Server function of DB2, you must install the Syncpoint Manager (SPM) and its prerequisites in order to use two-phase commit.

If you plan to use the ADSTAR Distributed Storage Manager (ADSM) facilities to backup and restore your databases, you require ADSM Client Version 2.1.0.6.

2.1.3 Choice of User Management Systems

Before actually installing DB2 UDB EEE, the system administrator should create some new users:

1. DB2 (or Database) instance owner. You may have multiple database instances in your environment. However, for the installation of the product, you need only one instance owner.

2. Owner of fenced User-Defined Functions (UDFs) and stored procedures. This user executes user-defined functions and stored procedures in an area of memory not used by DB2.

3. Database Administration Server (DAS) instance owner. Using DB2 Discovery, the DAS instance allows clients to connect to DB2 servers using DB2 Discovery, and to do remote administration.

These three special users need access to all the database partitions in your cluster. For this reason, these three users should be created on all the hosts in your cluster. You can manually create the three users on all the hosts in your cluster; however, this is not recommended. You should create the three users once on one host and use file collections and/or Network Information Services (NIS) to propagate the user information to the remaining hosts in your cluster. The next section discusses file collections and Network Information Services (NIS).

2.1.3.1 File Collections

File Collections form an integral part of the SP system of management tools. A File Collection is a mechanism for easily maintaining copies of important files across the nodes in an SP system. By default, File Collections are enabled when you install the AIX operating system on the SP nodes.

A File Collection is simply a set of defined files that is managed and controlled by the supper program. The supper program propagates your File Collections among the hosts in your SP. A special File Collections directory is used to store the lists of files and directories that you want to replicate, and the rules which control them. These files do not need to be physically in the File Collections directory, but may be located anywhere on the system. There is only one master copy of these files. When they are updated, the changes are replicated to other hosts that contain the duplicate files. Updates to the duplicate files in the other hosts are, by default, overwritten by the supper program at predefined intervals.

One of the File Collections that is automatically installed on an SP is user.admin, which contains the files that hold information about the users defined on the system.

2.1.3.2 Network Information Services (NIS)

Network Information Services (NIS) is a distributed database containing system configuration files. By using NIS, these files will look the same throughout the SP machine. NFS and NIS are packaged together. Since the SP install image includes NFS, NIS is available as well. The most common implementation of NIS is based upon the distributed maps containing the information from the /etc/hosts file and the user-related files: /etc/passwd, /etc/group and /etc/security/passwd.

2.1.3.3 Comparison of File Collections and NIS

Enabling File Collections by default causes the replacement of the /usr/bin/passwd by a dummy command, indicating that you must update your password on the Control Workstation.

Where to Create Users

If you want to create a new user, you should do this on the Control Workstation and the user will be propagated to the other SP nodes . If you create the new user on any SP node (not the Control Workstation), the newly created user will be overwritten by the File Collections propagation at the time of the next propagation cycle.

On the other hand, NIS allows an administrator to maintain system configuration files in any of the nodes within the SP machine. When any of these files are changed on any node, the changes are automatically propagated to all the other nodes.

You can choose to have both File Collections and NIS running on the SP machine. When doing so, the File Collections should exclude the user administration files and the /usr/bin/passwd command should be restored (the original `passwd` command is stored as /usr/bin/passwd.orig).

2.1.3.4 User Management Summary

- If File Collections is enabled but not NIS, you should create the AIX users on the master server (the node that contains the master copy of /etc/passwd, which is normally the Control Workstation), and let File Collections propagate the changes for you.

- If File Collections and NIS are enabled, File Collections should exclude the propagation of user administration files. Under this set up, you can create an AIX user on any node of your choice, and NIS will propagate the changes to all the other nodes in the system.

- If File Collections and NIS are not enabled, you can create AIX users manually on all nodes. You can either manually issue the same command on all nodes, or use the `dsh` or `rsh` commands to help you distribute the create user command to all nodes.

File Collections and NIS provide the ability to change user information only once, and then have the changes replicated to the other SP nodes. The manual replication of user information should be avoided if possible.

2.1.4 Creating Users for DB2 UDB EEE

In the previous section, we mentioned three DB2 UDB EEE users that should exist. It is recommended to create those users and groups for those users before installing the DB2 UDB EEE product. You'll need three users:

1. DB2 instance owner

2. User who can execute fenced UDFs or stored procedures

3. Database Administration Server (DAS) instance owner

This section discusses creating groups, users and the environment.

2.1.4.1 Creating the DB2 Instance Owner

The DB2 instance owner user must exist in AIX before you create the DB2 instance.

This section discusses creating the group for the DB2 instance owner, the DB2 instance owner user, the home directory for this user, and making the home directory accessible to all the hosts in the cluster. In our example, the environment is an RS/6000 SP with AIX. If you are using File Collections to propagate the user administration files, log in as root at the Control Workstation. If you are using NIS to propagate the user administration files, you can log in as root at any of the hosts where DB2 will be used.

Creating the Group

You must be logged in as the root user to create this group. A group ID is associated with the group.

The following rules apply to the *group* for the DB2 instance owner:

- The group ID must be the same on all hosts in your cluster.

- The group must be defined as the primary group for the DB2 instance owner.

- Any user in this group will have DB2 system administrative (SYSADM) privileges.

The following is the command to create a group in AIX:

```
cws1:/ > mkgroup id=999 dbadmin2
```

This command will create a group in AIX called dbadmin2 (a name we have chosen ourselves) with a group ID of 999. You can also use SMIT to do this task.

Creating the DB2 Instance Owner User
You should be logged in as the root user to create the DB2 instance owner. The following rules apply to the name of this user:

- Must be between 1 to 8 characters

- Cannot be any of the following:
    - USERS
    - ADMINS
    - GUESTS
    - PUBLIC
    - LOCAL

- Cannot begin with
    - IBM
    - SQL
    - SYS

- Cannot include accented characters

This user should be created as an AIX user, not an SP user. SP users use AMD to manage their home directories, which is unsuitable for the DB2 instance owner. AMD can cause mounting or locking problems.

The following is the command for creating the DB2 instance owner and assigning an initial password:

```
cws1:/ > mkuser id=1004 pgrp=dbadmin2 groups=dbadmin2
home=/home/db2inst2 db2inst2
cws1:/ > passwd db2inst2
Changing password for "db2inst2"
db2inst2's New password:
Enter the new password again:
cws1:/ >
```

The DB2 instance owner in our example is db2inst2. The ID associated with db2inst2 is 1004. The primary group for db2inst2 is db2admin9. The home directory is /home/db2inst2.

A password must be initially set by the AIX root user. It is recommended to log in as the DB2 instance owner and change the password before the DB2 UDB EEE product is installed and DB2 commands are issued across the hosts in your cluster.

To change the password of the newly created DB2 instance owner from the screen where the root user created the DB2 instance owner, use the AIX login command. You will be prompted to change the password because this is the first login for this user. After setting the password, type exit once to return to root login screen.

```
cws1:/ > login db2inst2
db2inst2's Password:
3004-610 You are required to change your password.
        Please choose a new one.

db2inst2's New password:
Enter the new password again:
cws1:/home/db2inst2 > exit
cws1:/ >
```

Replicate the User Information to the SP Nodes

If you are using File Collections to propagate the user administration files to the SP nodes, use the following command from the Control Workstation:

```
dsh -a /var/sysman/supper update user.admin
```

If you don't enter this command, by default an automatic cron job will run the command every hour at 10 minutes past the hour.

Create the Home Directory for the Instance Owner

The home directory will contain all the files (or links to files) necessary to run the database instance. For DB2 UDB EEE, you must create the home directory for the DB2 instance owner so that it can be shared among the hosts in your cluster. For performance reasons, it is recommended to create the home directory on an SP host (not the Control Workstation) to take advantage of the high-performance switch. You will then use NFS (Network File System) to remotely mount the file system and make it available to all the hosts in your DB2 cluster.

It is also recommended that the home directory be a separate file system so that you can better control the allocation of space. The following steps outline the process to create a separate file system for the DB2 instance owner's home directory:

- Add a new file system at the SP node you have chosen to hold the home directory for the DB2 instance owner.

- Mount the file system (locally).

- Change ownership of the home directory to the DB2 instance owner.

- NFS export the home directory.

- From all other hosts, mount the file system via NFS.

We look at this process in detail in the next few pages.

Add a New File System

We'll use the AIX system management tool, SMIT. Note that you can also use the command line. As the root user, use this SMIT path:

System Storage Management->File Systems->Add/Change/Show/Delete File Systems->Journaled File Systems->Add a Journaled File System.

After selecting the volume group, you should see a screen similar to the following:

```
                    Add a Standard Journaled File System

Type or select values in entry fields.
Press Enter AFTER making all desired changes.

                                                    [Entry Fields]
  Volume group name                               dbvg
* SIZE of file system (in 512-byte blocks)        [60000]                    #
* MOUNT POINT                                      [/home/db2inst2]
  Mount AUTOMATICALLY at system restart?           yes                       +
  PERMISSIONS                                      read/write                +
  Mount OPTIONS                                    []                        +
  Start Disk Accounting?                           no                        +
  Fragment Size (bytes)                            4096                      +
  Number of bytes per inode                        4096                      +
  Allocation Group Size (MBytes)                   8                         +



F1=Help          F2=Refresh        F3=Cancel          F4=List
F5=Reset         F6=Command        F7=Edit            F8=Image
F9=Shell         F10=Exit          Enter=Do
```

Here, the /home/db2inst2 file system is created in the dbvg volume group. The initial size is 60,000 512-byte blocks, which is about 29 MB. The option to have the file system automatically mounted when the system is restarted has been selected. The remaining fields can be left to default values.

Mount the File System Locally

As the root user, enter the following command:

```
mount /home/db2inst2
```

Change Ownership of the Home Directory

The DB2 instance owner must be able to write to the home directory. As the AIX root user, to change ownership, do the following:

```
f01n05:/ > chown db2inst2.dbadmin2 /home/db2inst2
f01n05:/ > ls -ld /home/db2inst2
drwxr-xr-x   2 db2inst2 dbadmin2      512 Feb 20 10:00
/home/db2inst2
```

NFS Export the Home Directory

To make the home directory available to other hosts, you must export it using NFS. From the host where the file system was created, the following command was used to go directly to the NFS mount screen:

    smitty nfs

Select **Network File System (NFS), Add a Directory to Exports List** and press **Enter**. Your screen should be similar to the following:

```
                    Add a Directory to Exports List

Type or select values in entry fields.
Press Enter AFTER making all desired changes.

                                              [Entry Fields]
* PATHNAME of directory to export            [/home/db2inst2]
* MODE to export directory                    read-write          +
  HOSTS & NETGROUPS allowed client access    []
  Anonymous UID                              [-2]
  HOSTS allowed root access                  [f01n06,f01n07]
  HOSTNAME list. If exported read-mostly     []
  Use SECURE option?                          no                  +
* EXPORT directory now, system restart or both  both              +
  PATHNAME of alternate Exports file         []



F1=Help           F2=Refresh        F3=Cancel         F4=List
F5=Reset          F6=Command        F7=Edit           F8=Image
F9=Shell          F10=Exit          Enter=Do
```

You must enter the pathname of the directory to export. For the field entitled HOSTS allowed root access, enter the names of the other hosts where DB2 will be used. In our example, f01n06 and f01n07 require root access. If you do not complete this field, you will not be able to start DB2 EEE.

NFS Mount the Directory on Other Hosts

From all remaining hosts (that is, hosts in the cluster other than the one where the home directory was created and exported), log in as root and enter:

    smitty nfs

Do not use AMD

You should not mount the remote directory by using the AMD or the automounter utilities. These utilities can cause mounting or locking problems.

You should see a screen similar to the following:

```
                        Add a File System for Mounting

Type or select values in entry fields.
Press Enter AFTER making all desired changes.

                                                    [Entry Fields]
* PATHNAME of mount point                           [/home/db2inst2]         /
* PATHNAME of remote directory                      [/home/db2inst2]
* HOST where remote directory resides               [f01n05s]
  Mount type NAME                                   []
* Use SECURE mount option?                          no                       +
* MOUNT now, add entry to /etc/filesystems or both?  both                    +
* /etc/filesystems entry will mount the directory   yes                      +
  on system RESTART.
* MODE for this NFS file system                     read-write               +
* ATTEMPT mount in foreground or background         background               +
  NUMBER of times to attempt mount                  []                       #
  Buffer SIZE for read                              []                       #
  Buffer SIZE for writes                            []                       #
  NFS TIMEOUT. In tenths of a second                []                       #
  Internet port NUMBER for server                   []                       #
* Mount file system soft or hard                    soft                     +


F1=Help            F2=Refresh        F3=Cancel          F4=List
F5=Reset           F6=Command        F7=Edit            F8=Image
F9=Shell           F10=Exit          Enter=Do
```

Every field with an asterisk is required. The fields for which we entered values in our example were:

- PATHNAME of mount point. This is the home directory of the DB2 instance owner, /home/db2inst2.

- PATHNAME of remote directory. The same path name should be selected. Here, it is /home/db2inst2.

- HOST where remote directory resides. This is the name of the host where the remote export was done.

- MOUNT now. By selecting both, an entry in /etc/filesystems will be added.

- Mount the directory on system RESTART. Set to yes.

- MODE for this NFS file system. Select read-write.

- Hard or Soft mount. A soft mount means that the host will not try for an infinite period of time to remotely mount the directory if that host is not available.

Mounting over the Switch

When using an RS/6000 SP system with a High Performance Switch, consider using the Switch for the NFS mount of the instance owner's home directory to improve performance. In this case, specify the network interface name of the switch (in our example, f01n05s) rather than the hostname (in our example, f01n05, the ethernet network interface). However, bear in mind that if the Switch becomes unavailable, then the SP nodes will lose access to the instance owner's home dircetory.

2.1.4.2 Creating a Group and User for the Fenced User

It is recommended to create a separate AIX group and user for the *Fenced User*. Fenced UDFs and stored procedures will execute under this user and group. The group must be the primary group of the user. Using the same method as for the DB2 instance owner, we executed the following commands:

```
cws1:/ > mkgroup id=991 db2fadm2
cws1:/ > mkuser id=1001 pgrp=db2fadm2 groups=db2fadm2
home=/home/db2fenc2 db2fenc2
cws1:/ > passwd db2fenc2
Changing password for "db2fenc2"
db2fenc2's New password:
Enter the new password again:
cws1:/ >
cws1:/ > login db2fenc2
db2fenc2's Password:
3004-610 You are required to change your password.
        Please choose a new one.

db2fenc2's New password:
Enter the new password again:
cws1:/home/db2fenc2 > exit
cws1:/ >
```

- The `mkgroup` command creates a group named db2fadm2 with GID 991.

- The `mkuser` command creates a user named db2fenc2 with UID 1001, who belongs to group db2fadm2 and has a home directory of /home/db2fenc2.

- The home directory (/home/db2fenc2) is also created on the Control Workstation.

- The `passwd` command lets you enter an initial password for the user db2fenc2.

- The `login` command is used to stop the system from asking for password again at the next logon.

Replicate the User Information to the SP Nodes

If you are using File Collections to propagate the user administration files to the SP nodes, use the following command from the Control Workstation:

```
dsh -a /var/sysman/supper update user.admin
```

If you don't enter this command, by default an automatic cron job will run the command every hour at 10 minutes past the hour.

2.1.4.3 Creating the DAS Instance Owner

The DB2 Administration Server (DAS) is a special DB2 instance for managing DB2 servers. The DB2 Administration Server instance on a DB2 server machine provides a remote client the ability to administer and detect the instances and databases at the server.

You can think of the DAS instance as being global to a machine. The environment of the DAS instance is separate and different from that of the DB2 instance owner. The DAS instance owner should have a different group and user ID from that of the DB2 instance owner. The home directory for the DAS instance owner should be NFS-mounted across all nodes in your DB2 cluster.

In an EEE environment, you should first configure a DAS instance on one machine. Clients that use DB2 Discovery to connect to the EEE database will then all use the same machine as their coordinator node, that is, as their point of entry to the database. If you need to distribute this function across more machines for performance reasons, you can do this as a subsequent step. Bear in mind also that the DAS instance consumes resources. If you are using the machine (or database partition) which hosts the catalog partition for data as well, you may need to locate the DAS instance to another machine for optimal performance.

DAS Instance and Coordinator Partition

If you decide to hold a coordinator partition on a particular SP node, you do not have to create a DAS instance on that SP node. You only have to create a DAS instance if you want to use DB2 Discovery to allow client connections.

Creating an AIX Group and User for DAS Instance Owner

Create an AIX group and user for the DAS instance owner. Use the same method as when creating the AIX Group and User for the DB2 instance owner:

```
cws1:/ > mkgroup id=990 db2asgp2
cws1:/ > mkuser id=1000 pgrp=db2asgp2 groups=db2asgp2
home=/home/db2as2 db2as2
cws1:/ > passwd db2as2
Changing password for "db2as2"
db2as2's New password:
Enter the new password again:
cws1:/ >
cws1:/ > login db2as2
db2as2's Password:
3004-610 You are required to change your password.
        Please choose a new one.

db2as2's New password:
Enter the new password again:
cws1:/home/db2as2 > exit
cws1:/ >
```

- **The mkgroup** command creates a group named db2asgp2 with GID 990.

- The **mkuser** command creates a user named db2as2 with UID 1000, who belongs to group db2asgp2 and has a home directory of /home/db2as2.

- The home directory (/home/db2as2) is created on the Control Workstation.

- The **passwd** command lets you create an initial password for the user db2as2.

- The **login** command is used to stop the system from asking for password again at the next logon.

Replicate the User Information to the Other Nodes

If you are using File Collections to propagate the user administration files to the other SP nodes, use the following command from the Control Workstation:

```
dsh -a /var/sysman/supper update user.admin
```

If you don't enter this command, by default an automatic cron job will run the command every hour at 10 minutes past the hour.

Create the Home Directory for the DAS Instance Owner

The home directory will contain all the files (or links to files) necessary to run the DAS instance. You should create the home directory for the DAS instance owner so that it can be shared among the hosts in your cluster. It is recommended that the home directory be a separate file system so that you can better control the allocation of space. The following steps outline the process to create a separate file system for the DAS instance owner's home directory:

- Add a new file system at the SP node you have chosen to hold the DAS instance.
- Mount the file system (locally).
- Change ownership of the home directory to the DAS instance owner.
- NFS export the home directory.
- From all other hosts, mount the file system via NFS.

DB2 and DAS Instance Owner's Home Directories

If you are using the same host to hold the DB2 and DAS instance's home directories, you can simplify the configuration by making a single file system to hold both users' home directories. You will then only have to create a single filesystem and configure NFS for this single filesystem.

We'll look at this process in detail in the next few pages.

Add a New File System

We'll use the AIX system management tool, SMIT. Note that you can also use the command line. As the root user, use this SMIT path:

System Storage Management->File Systems->Add/Change/Show/Delete File Systems->Journaled File Systems->Add a Journaled File System.

After selecting the volume group, you should see a screen similar to the following:

```
                    Add a Standard Journaled File System

Type or select values in entry fields.
Press Enter AFTER making all desired changes.

                                                  [Entry Fields]
    Volume group name                             dbvg
  * SIZE of file system (in 512-byte blocks)      [60000]                    #
  * MOUNT POINT                                    [/home/db2as2]
    Mount AUTOMATICALLY at system restart?         yes                       +
    PERMISSIONS                                    read/write                +
    Mount OPTIONS                                  []                        +
    Start Disk Accounting?                         no                        +
    Fragment Size (bytes)                          4096                      +
    Number of bytes per inode                      4096                      +
    Allocation Group Size (MBytes)                 8                         +


F1=Help              F2=Refresh         F3=Cancel           F4=List
F5=Reset             F6=Command         F7=Edit             F8=Image
F9=Shell             F10=Exit           Enter=Do
```

Here, the /home/db2as2 file system is created in the dbvg volume group. The initial size is 60,000 512-byte blocks which is about 29 MB. The option to have the file system automatically mounted when the system is restarted has been selected. The remaining fields can be left to default values.

Mount the File System Locally
As the root user, enter the following command:

```
mount /home/db2as2
```

Change Ownership of the Home Directory
The DB2 instance owner must be able to write to the home directory. As the AIX root user, to change ownership, issue the following:

```
f01n05:/ > chown db2as2.dbasgp9 /home/db2as2
f01n05:/ > ls -ld /home/db2as2
drwxr-xr-x 2 db2as2 db2asgp2 512 Feb 20 9:00 /home/db2as2
```

NFS Export the Home Directory

To make the home directory available to other hosts, you should export it using NFS. From the host where the file system was created, the following command was used to go directly to the NFS mount screen:

```
smitty nfs
```

Select **Network File System (NFS), Add a Directory to Exports List** and press **Enter**. Your screen should be similar to the following:

```
                        Add a Directory to Exports List

Type or select values in entry fields.
Press Enter AFTER making all desired changes.

                                                      [Entry Fields]
  * PATHNAME of directory to export                   [/home/db2as2]
  * MODE to export directory                           read-write         +
    HOSTS & NETGROUPS allowed client access           []
    Anonymous UID                                     [-2]
    HOSTS allowed root access                         [f01n06, f01n07]
    HOSTNAME list. If exported read-mostly            []
    Use SECURE option?                                 no                 +
  * EXPORT directory now, system restart or both      both               +
    PATHNAME of alternate Exports file                []




F1=Help            F2=Refresh         F3=Cancel          F4=List
F5=Reset           F6=Command         F7=Edit            F8=Image
F9=Shell           F10=Exit           Enter=Do
```

You must enter the pathname of the directory to export. For the field entitled HOSTS allowed root access, enter the names of the other hosts (in this example, f01n06 and f01n07) where DB2 will be used.

NFS Mount the Directory on Other Hosts

From all remaining hosts (that is, hosts in the cluster other than the one where the home directory was created and exported), log in as root and enter:

```
smitty nfs
```

Do not use AMD

You should not mount the remote directory by using the AMD or the automounter utilities. These utilities can cause mounting or locking problems.

You should see a screen similar to the following:

```
                         Add a File System for Mounting

Type or select values in entry fields.
Press Enter AFTER making all desired changes.

                                                  [Entry Fields]
* PATHNAME of mount point                        [/home/db2as2]           /
* PATHNAME of remote directory                   [/home/db2as2]
* HOST where remote directory resides            [f01n05s]
  Mount type NAME                                []
* Use SECURE mount option?                       no                      +
* MOUNT now, add entry to /etc/filesystems or both?  both                +
* /etc/filesystems entry will mount the directory    yes                 +
  on system RESTART.
* MODE for this NFS file system                  read-write              +
* ATTEMPT mount in foreground or background      background              +
  NUMBER of times to attempt mount               []                      #
  Buffer SIZE for read                           []                      #
  Buffer SIZE for writes                         []                      #
  NFS TIMEOUT. In tenths of a second             []                      #
  Internet port NUMBER for server                []                      #
* Mount file system soft or hard                 soft                    +



F1=Help            F2=Refresh         F3=Cancel          F4=List
F5=Reset           F6=Command         F7=Edit            F8=Image
F9=Shell           F10=Exit           Enter=Do
```

Every field with an asterisk is required. The fields for which we entered values in our example were:

- PATHNAME of mount point. This is the home directory of the DB2 instance owner, /home/db2as2.

- PATHNAME of remote directory. The same path name should be selected. Here, it is /home/db2as2.

- HOST where remote directory resides. This is the name of the host where the remote export was done.

- MOUNT now. By selecting both, an entry in /etc/filesystems will be added.

- Mount the directory on system RESTART. Set to yes.

- MODE for this NFS file system. Select read-write.

- Hard or Soft mount. A soft mount means that the host will not try for an infinite period of time to remotely mount the directory if that host is not available.

2.2 Installing DB2 UDB EEE

This section covers the installation of the DB2 UDB EEE product. You have some decisions to make before installation, depending on your environment. These decisions include:

- Where to install the product

- How to perform the install

This section discusses each installation method in detail. Then, we present a summary section with guidelines to help you determine the method or combination of methods that is appropriate for your environment.

2.2.1 Choice of Code Installation

You can choose to install DB2 UDB EEE either on every host or on only one host and make it available via NFS to the other hosts. In terms of performance, it is advisable to install the DB2 code on all hosts. However, maintenance (applying fixes or doing software upgrades, for example), is easier if DB2 installed only on one host.

You have several options for installing the DB2 software. They are:

- The DB2 Installer program supplied with the product.

- A system management tool (if provided with the operating system), for example, SMIT on AIX.

- The `installp` command (on AIX). This command can be run using `dsh`, which causes an application to execute on all hosts in a defined environment.

We cover all three methods. The DB2 Installer program is intended for those users not familiar with DB2 UDB EEE and AIX in an SP environment. If you use SMIT or `installp` then the instances must be created manually. If you have a large number of hosts in the DB2 Cluster, then you can automate the installation process by using the `installp` command under `dsh`. The method you use depends on the number of hosts in your DB2 cluster and your level of experience.

2.2.1.1 Making the CD-ROM Drive Available
Whichever method you use to install DB2 UDB EEE, you should first make sure that the CD-ROM drive is mounted and available. If not, the following steps should be done:

1. Log in as root.

2. Insert the DB2 UDB EEE CD-ROM into the drive.

3. Create a directory by entering the following command:

```
mkdir /cdrom
```

4. Allocate a CD-ROM file system either using a command or SMIT.

   From the command prompt:

```
crfs -v cdrfs -p ro -d cd0
```

   Or from SMIT, select the following path:

   FileSystems ->Add/Change/Show/Delete FileSystems->CD-ROM FileSystems ->Add CDROM FileSystems.

   Enter the DEVICE Name, for example, cd0.

5. Mount the CD-ROM file system using the following command (Our file system name is /dev/cd0):

```
mount -v cdrfs -r /dev/cd0 /cdrom
```

2.2.2 Using DB2 Installer

This method involves running the DB2 Installer, a menu-based program delivered with the DB2 UDB EEE product that allows the user to:

- Install the DB2 UDB EEE product
- Configure a DB2 Instance
- Configure a DAS Instance

In the following section, we outline the steps necessary to install the DB2 UDB EEE on a single host. These steps should be repeated on all the hosts in the DB2 Cluster. We cover the creation of the DB2 and DAS instances later in this chapter.

Log in as root on a host that is not the Control Workstation (normally the first node in the DB2 Cluster). Change to the CD-ROM device directory and invoke the DB2 Installer program by entering the db2setup command:

```
f01n05:/ > cd /cdrom
f01n05:/cdrom/ >./db2setup
```

You should see the following initial screen. The DB2 Installer program scans your system to check for prerequisite software:

```
T+------------------------- DB2 Installer --------------------------+
|                                                                   |
|   Select Install to select products and their components to install, or |
|   select Create to create the DB2 services.                       |
|                                                                   |
|                                                                   |
|   To select products and their components, select       [ Install... ] |
|   Install.                                                        |
|                                                                   |
|   To create a +--- Please Wait ----------------------------+[ Create... ] |
|   Server, sele|                                             |     |
|               |    Scanning your system for information...  |     |
|               |                                             |     |
|               |                                             |     |
|               +---------------------------------------------+     |
|                                                                   |
|                                                                   |
|                                                                   |
|                                                                   |
|                                                                   |
|                                                                   |
|   [  Close  ]                                        [  Help  ]   |
+-------------------------------------------------------------------+
```

If no DB2 product has been installed in your system, you'll see the following screen:

```
+------------------------- Install DB2 V5 -------------------------+
|                                                                  |
|   Select the products you are licensed to install. Your Proof of |
|   Entitlement and License Information booklet identify the products for |
|   which you are licensed.                                        |
|                                                                  |
|   To see the preselected components or customize the selection, select |
|   Customize for the product.                                     |
|   [ ] DB2 Client Application Enabler              : Customize... : |
|   : : DB2 UDB Workgroup Edition                   : Customize... : |
|   : : DB2 UDB Enterprise Edition                  : Customize... : |
|   : : DB2 Connect Enterprise Edition              : Customize... : |
|   [ ] DB2 UDB Extended Enterprise Edition         : Customize... : |
|   [ ] DB2 Software Developer's Kit                : Customize... : |
|                                                                  |
|   To choose a language for the following components, select Customize for |
|   the product.                                                   |
|      DB2 Product Messages                         [ Customize... ] |
|      DB2 Product Library                          [ Customize... ] |
|                                                                  |
|                                                                  |
|   [  OK  ]                   [ Cancel ]              [  Help  ]   |
+------------------------------------------------------------------+
```

This screen shows the products available on the CD-ROM. The brackets [ ] next to a product indicate that you are able to select that product for installation. To do so, press the tab key to position the cursor over the product name. The double ellipse : : next to a product indicates that it is not available for installation.

```
+----------------------------- Install DB2 V5 ----------------------------+
|                                                                         |
|    Select the products you are licensed to install. Your Proof of       |
|    Entitlement and License Information booklet identify the products for |
|    which you are licensed.                                              |
|                                                                         |
|    To see the preselected components or customize the selection, select  |
|    Customize for the product.                                           |
|    [ ] DB2 Client Application Enabler              : Customize... :     |
|    : : DB2 UDB Workgroup Edition                    : Customize... :     |
|    : : DB2 UDB Enterprise Edition                   : Customize... :     |
|    : : DB2 Connect Enterprise Edition               : Customize... :     |
|    [*] DB2 UDB Extended Enterprise Edition          [ Customize... ]     |
|    [ ] DB2 Software Developer's Kit                 : Customize... :     |
|                                                                         |
|    To choose a language for the following components, select Customize for|
|    the product.                                                         |
|       DB2 Product Messages                          [ Customize... ]     |
|       DB2 Product Library                           [ Customize... ]     |
|                                                                         |
|                                                                         |
|                                                                         |
|    [   OK   ]                  [ Cancel ]                 [  Help  ]    |
+-------------------------------------------------------------------------+
```

Move the cursor to DB2 UDB Extended Enterprise Edition and press either the space bar or the return key to select it. There should now be an asterisk inside the brackets [*], indicating that you have chosen to install this product.

To see what will be installed automatically with the DB2 UDB Extended Enterprise Edition product, move the cursor to [Customize...] and press **Enter**. You should see the following:

```
+--- DB2 Universal Database Extended Enterprise Edition --------------------+
|                                                                          |
|  Required:      DB2 Client                                               |
|                 DB2 Run-time Environment                                 |
|                 DB2 Engine                                               |
|                 DB2 Communication Support - TCP/IP                       |
|                 DB2 Communication Support - IPX/SPX                      |
|                 DB2 Communication Support - SNA                          |
|                 DB2 Communication Support - DRDA Application Server       |
|                 Administration Server                                    |
|                 DB2 Connect Support                                      |
|                 DB2 Parallel Extension                                   |
|                 License Support                                          |
|  Optional:      [*] Open Database Connectivity (ODBC)                    |
|                 [*] Java Database Connectivity (JDBC)                     |
|                 [*] Replication                                          |
|                 [*] DB2 Sample Database Source                           |
|                 Code Page Conversion Support:                            |
|                     [*] Japanese      [*] Simplified Chinese             |
|                     [*] Korean        [*] Traditional Chinese            |
|                                                                          |
|  [ Select All ]               [ Deselect All ]            [ Default ]    |
|  [  OK   ]                        [ Cancel ]              [  Help  ]     |
+--------------------------------------------------------------------------+
```

The required components listed will be installed by the DB2 Installer program.
You cannot deselect them. The optional components are, by default, all
selected to be installed. If you do not want to install an optional component,
deselect it by pressing the tab key to move the cursor over the option and
then press the space bar or the return key. The asterisk inside the bracket
should be removed [ ].

Tab to [**OK**] and press **Enter**. You will return to the Install DB2 V5 screen.

```
+----------------------------- Install DB2 V5 -----------------------------+
|                                                                          |
|  Select the products you are licensed to install. Your Proof of          |
|  Entitlement and License Information booklet identify the products for   |
|  which you are licensed.                                                 |
|                                                                          |
|  To see the preselected components or customize the selection, select    |
|  Customize for the product.                                              |
|  :*: DB2 Client Application Enabler                  [ Customize... ]    |
|  : : DB2 UDB Workgroup Edition                       : Customize... :    |
|  : : DB2 UDB Enterprise Edition                      : Customize... :    |
|  : : DB2 Connect Enterprise Edition                  : Customize... :    |
|  :*: DB2 UDB Extended Enterprise Edition             [ Customize... ]    |
|  [ ] DB2 Software Developer's Kit                    : Customize... :    |
|                                                                          |
|  To choose a language for the following components, select Customize for |
|  the product.                                                            |
|      DB2 Product Messages                            [ Customize... ]    |
|      DB2 Product Library                             [ Customize... ]    |
|                                                                          |
|                                                                          |
|                                                                          |
|  [  OK   ]                    [ Cancel ]                  [ Help  ]      |
+--------------------------------------------------------------------------+
```

The DB2 Product Messages are by default installed in English. If you require another language, you must select it for installation.

2.2.2.1 Installing the Online Documentation

The online documentation in HTML format is not installed by default. Because this component takes over 70 MB of disk space, you should install it on only one node in the DB2 cluster.

Disk Space Requirements for Online Docs

Remember to check that you have enough disk space in the file system to uncompress and install the DB2 Product Library. You'll need approximately 150 MB.

To install the online documentation, use the tab key and place the cursor over the [Customize...] option for the DB2 Product Library. Press **Enter**. The following screen appears:

```
+----------------------------- Install DB2 V5 -----------------------------+
|                                                                          |
|   Select the products you are licensed to install. Your Proof of         |
|   Entitlement and License Information booklet identify the products for   |
|   which you are licensed.                                                 |
|+--- DB2 Product Library --------------------------------------------------+|
||                                                                        ||
||  Required:                                                             ||
||  Optional:     DB2 Product Library (HTML):                             ||
||                       [ ] en_US       [ ] fr_FR       [ ] de_DE        ||
||                       [ ] es_ES       [ ] pt_BR       [ ] ja_JP        ||
||                       [ ] ko_KR       [ ] zh_CN       [ ] Zh_TW        ||
||                       [ ] da_DK       [ ] fi_FI       [ ] no_NO        ||
||                       [ ] sv_SE       : : cs_CZ       : : hu_HU        ||
||                       : : pl_PL       : : ru_RU       : : bg_BG        ||
||                       : : sl_SI                                        ||
||                                                                        ||
||   [ Select All ]             [ Deselect All ]          [ Default ]     ||
||   [   OK   ]                   [ Cancel ]              [  Help  ]       ||
|+--------------------------------------------------------------------------+|
|                                                                          |
|                                                                          |
|   [   OK   ]                   [ Cancel ]              [  Help  ]         |
+--------------------------------------------------------------------------+
```

In our example, we will install the DB2 Product Library in English (en_US). Use the tab key to move the cursor to en_US and press the space bar or **Enter**. Select [**OK**] and press **Enter** to go back to the initial DB2 Installer screen. Select [**OK**] and press **Enter** to proceed to the next screen:

```
+------------------------- Create DB2 Services -------------------------+
|                                                                        |
|   Select the items you want to create, and select OK when finished.    |
|                                                                        |
|                                                                        |
|   A DB2 Instance is an environment where you store data and run        |
|   applications. An instance can contain multiple databases.            |
|                                                                        |
|   [ ] Create a DB2 Instance.                        : Customize... :   |
|                                                                        |
|   An Administration Server provides services to support client tools that |
|   automate the configuration of connections to DB2 databases.          |
|                                                                        |
|   [ ] Create the Administration Server.             : Customize... :   |
|                                                                        |
|                                                                        |
|                                                                        |
|                                                                        |
|                                                                        |
|                                                                        |
|                                                                        |
|   [   OK   ]                  [ Cancel ]               [  Help  ]       |
+------------------------------------------------------------------------+
```

You will see the Create DB2 Services screen. You have the option to create a DB2 instance and/or a DAS instance. You can create either one of these instances now or by running the DB2 Installer program later. "Creating a DB2 Instance" on page 83 and "Creating the DAS Instance" on page 102 discuss using the DB2 Installer as well as the command line to create DB2 and DAS instances.

We are only installing DB2 and not creating any instances (DB2 or DAS) at this point. So, select [**OK**] and press **Enter**. You you will see a pop-up window asking you if you want to continue the installation. At the completion of the installation, you'll receive a status report as to the success or failure of the installation of the DB2 components. Your screen will be similar to the following:

```
+------------------------------ DB2 Installer --------------------------------+
|                                                                             |
|  +-- Status Report ------------------------------------------------------+  |
|  |                                                                      |  |
|  |                                                                      |  |
|  |  Installation                                                        |  |
|  |  ------------                                                        |  |
|  |                                                                      |  |
|  |    DB2 Client                                            SUCCESS     |  |
|  |    DB2 Run-time Environment                              SUCCESS     |  |
|  |    DB2 Engine                                            SUCCESS     |  |
|  |    DB2 Communication Support - TCP/IP                    SUCCESS     |  |
|  |    Administration Server                                 SUCCESS     |  |
|  |    DB2 Connect Support                                   SUCCESS     |  |
|  |    DB2 Parallel Extension                                SUCCESS     |  |
|  |    DB2 Communication Support - SNA                       SUCCESS     |  |
|  |    DB2 Communication Support - DRDA Application Server   SUCCESS     |  |
|  |    DB2 Communication Support - IPX/SPX                   SUCCESS     |  |
|  |    License Support for DB2 UDB Extended Enterprise Edition SUCCESS   |  |
|  |                                                                      |  |
|  |                                                        [ More... ]   |  |
|  +----------------------------------------------------------------------+  |
|  [ View Log ]                                               [   OK   ]     |
+-----------------------------------------------------------------------------+
```

You can see the DB2 products and components that were installed. The DB2
components that support communication protocols are installed even if the
communication products are not detected on the system (for example SNA
and IPX/SPX).

One of the options on this screen is to view the contents of the installation
log, /tmp/db2setup.log. You can either view the log or use an editor to view its
contents.

At this point, DB2 UDB EEE has been successfully installed on one of the
hosts. You should repeat the steps to install DB2 UDB EEE on the other hosts
in the DB2 cluster.

2.2.3 Using SMIT

When installing using SMIT, you can install DB2 from either of the following
commands:

```
smitty install_latest
```

or:

```
smitty easy_install_bundle
```

Either method can be used to install the DB2 UDB EEE product. In this section, we also discuss how to use SMIT to install on one host and on multiple hosts.

2.2.3.1 Installing on One Host

Log in as root on a host that is not the Control Workstation (normally the first node in the DB2 cluster). From the system prompt, enter:

```
smitty install_latest
```

You'll be prompted for the input device or directory. In our example, this is /cdrom/db2. The following screen should appear:

```
                Install and Update from LATEST Available Software

Type or select values in entry fields.
Press Enter AFTER making all desired changes.

                                                    [Entry Fields]
* INPUT device / directory for software            /cdrom/db2
* SOFTWARE to install                               [_all_latest]           +
  PREVIEW only? (install operation will NOT occur)  no                      +
  COMMIT software updates?                          yes                     +
  SAVE replaced files?                              no                      +
  AUTOMATICALLY install requisite software?         yes                     +
  EXTEND file systems if space needed?              yes                     +
  OVERWRITE same or newer versions?                 no                      +
  VERIFY install and check file sizes?              no                      +
  Include corresponding LANGUAGE filesets?          yes                     +
  DETAILED output?                                  no                      +


F1=Help            F2=Refresh         F3=Cancel          F4=List
F5=Reset           F6=Command         F7=Edit            F8=Image
F9=Shell           F10=Exit           Enter=Do
```

Tab to the SOFTWARE to install field and press <**F4**> to get a list of the contents of the CD-ROM. Be careful not to press **Enter** here, because doing so will cause all the DB2 software on the CD to be installed. The following list should be displayed:

```
                  Install and Update from LATEST Available Software
Ty+-------------------------------------------------------------------------+
Pr|                       SOFTWARE to install                               |
  |                                                                         |
  | Move cursor to desired item and press F7. Use arrow keys to scroll.     |
* |    ONE OR MORE items can be selected.                                   |
* | Press Enter AFTER making all selections.                               |+
  |                                                                         |+
  | [TOP]                                                                   |+
  |    #-------------------------------------------------------------------- |+
  |    #                                                                    |+
  |    # KEY:                                                               |+
  |    #   @ = Already installed                                           |+
  |    #   + = No license password required                                |+
  |    #                                                                    |+
  |    #-------------------------------------------------------------------- |+
  |                                                                         |
  |    DB2V5CAE.Bnd                                                    ALL |
  |      + 5.0.0.1  DB2 Client Application Enabler Software Bundle          |
  |                                                                         |
  |    DB2V5EEE.Bnd                                                    ALL |
  |      + 5.0.0.1  DB2 Ext Ent Software Bundle                             |
  |                                                                         |
  |    DB2V5SDK.Bnd                                                    ALL |
  |      + 5.0.0.1  DB2 SDK Software Bundle                                 |
  |                                                                         |
  |    db2_05_00.adt                                                  ALL |
  |      + 5.0.0.1  DB2 ADT Sample Programs                                 |
  |      + 5.0.0.1  DB2 Application Development Tools (ADT)                 |
  |                                                                         |
  |    db2_05_00.client                                               ALL |
  |      + 5.0.0.1  DB2 Client Application Enabler                          |
  |                                                                         |
  |    db2_05_00.cnvucs                                               ALL |
  |      + 5.0.0.1  Code Page Conversion Tables - Uni Code Support          |
  |                                                                         |
  |    db2_05_00.conn                                                 ALL |
  |      + 5.0.0.1  DB2 Connect                                             |
  |                                                                         |
  |    db2_05_00.conv                                                 ALL |
  |      + 5.0.0.1  Code Page Conversion Tables - Japanese                  |
  |      + 5.0.0.1  Code Page Conversion Tables - Korean                    |
  | [MORE...74]                                                             |
  |                                                                         |
  | F1=Help              F2=Refresh            F3=Cancel                    |
F1| F7=Select            F8=Image              F10=Exit                     |
F5| Enter=Do             /=Find                n=Find Next                  |
F9+-------------------------------------------------------------------------+
```

Software products and updates are comprised of installable units called filesets. You can select all or some of a software product's filesets. There are also software bundles as indicated by a Bnd extension, for example, DB2V5CAE.Bnd. If you select this product, all the DB2 components that comprise the bundle will be installed on your system.

You can select the components that you want to install by moving the cursor to the fileset name and pressing <**F7**>. To install the minimum required components for DB2 UDB EEE, select the fileset **db2_05_00.xrsv**, which is the License Support for DB2 UDB EEE:

```
              Install and Update from LATEST Available Software

Ty+-----------------------------------------------------------------------+
Pr|                        SOFTWARE to install                            |
  |                                                                       |
  | Move cursor to desired item and press F7. Use arrow keys to scroll.   |
* |     ONE OR MORE items can be selected.                                |
* | Press Enter AFTER making all selections.                             |+
  |                                                                       |+
  | [MORE...74]                                                           |+
  |   db2_05_00.html.ko_KR                                          ALL   |+
  |     + 5.0.0.1  DB2 Product Document (HTML) - Korean                   |+
  |                                                                       |+
  |   db2_05_00.html.no_NO                                          ALL   |+
  |     + 5.0.0.1  DB2 Product Document (HTML) - Norwegian                |+
  |                                                                       |+
  |   db2_05_00.html.pt_BR                                          ALL   |+
  |     + 5.0.0.1  DB2 Product Document (HTML) - Portuguese               |
  |                                                                       |
  |   db2_05_00.html.sv_SE                                          ALL   |
  |     + 5.0.0.1  DB2 Product Document (HTML) - Swedish                  |
  |                                                                       |
  |   db2_05_00.html.zh_CN                                          ALL   |
  |     + 5.0.0.1  DB2 Product Document (HTML) - Simplified Chinese       |
  |                                                                       |
  |   db2_05_00.jdbc                                                ALL   |
  |     + 5.0.0.1  Java Database Connectivity (JDBC) Support              |
  |                                                                       |
  |   db2_05_00.odbc                                                ALL   |
  |     + 5.0.0.1  Open Database Connectivity (ODBC) Support              |
  |                                                                       |
  |   db2_05_00.pext                                                ALL   |
  |     + 5.0.0.1  DB2 Parallel Extension                                 |
  |                                                                       |
  |   db2_05_00.repl                                                ALL   |
  |     + 5.0.0.1  DB2 Replication                                        |
  |                                                                       |
  | > db2_05_00.xsrv                                                ALL   |
  |     + 5.0.0.1  License Support for DB2 UDB Extended Enterprise Edition|
  |                                                                       |
  |   ifor_ls.client                                               ALL   |
  |     + 4.2.0.0  SystemView License Use Management Client GUI           |
  |     @ 4.2.0.0  SystemView License Use Management Client Runtime       |
  | [BOTTOM]                                                              |
  |                                                                       |
  | F1=Help              F2=Refresh            F3=Cancel                  |
F1| F7=Select            F8=Image              F10=Exit                   |
F5| Enter=Do             /=Find                n=Find Next                |
F9+-----------------------------------------------------------------------+
```

Once you have selected the db2_05_00.xsrv fileset, it is marked with >. Press **Enter** to proceed. You will return to the install screen.

```
                   Install and Update from LATEST Available Software

Type or select values in entry fields.
Press Enter AFTER making all desired changes.

                                                          [Entry Fields]
* INPUT device / directory for software                   /cdrom/db2
* SOFTWARE to install                                     [db2_05_00.xsrv       '> +
   PREVIEW only? (install operation will NOT occur)        no                      +
   COMMIT software updates?                                yes                     +
   SAVE replaced files?                                    no                      +
   AUTOMATICALLY install requisite software?               yes                     +
   EXTEND file systems if space needed?                    yes                     +
   OVERWRITE same or newer versions?                       no                      +
   VERIFY install and check file sizes?                    no                      +
   Include corresponding LANGUAGE filesets?                yes                     +
   DETAILED output?                                        no                      +


F1=Help           F2=Refresh        F3=Cancel            F4=List
F5=Reset          F6=Command        F7=Edit              F8=Image
F9=Shell          F10=Exit          Enter=Do
```

When the installation completes, you should see a report similar to the following:

```
                            COMMAND STATUS

Command: OK              stdout: yes            stderr: no

Before command completion, additional instructions may appear below.

[TOP]

( installp -acgNqQwXd /cdrom/db2 -f File 2>&1 )  ◄───  Command used
                                                        to install DB2
File:                                                   UDB EEE
    db2_05_00.xsrv              5.0.0.1

+------------------------------------------------------------------------+
                    Pre-installation Verification...
+------------------------------------------------------------------------+
Verifying selections...done
Verifying requisites...done
Results...

SUCCESSES
---------
  Filesets listed in this section passed pre-installation verification
  and will be installed.

  Selected Filesets
  -----------------
  db2_05_00.xsrv 5.0.0.1                    # License Support for DB2 UDB ...

  Requisites
  ----------
  (being installed automatically;  required by filesets listed above)
  db2_05_00.client 5.0.0.1                    # DB2 Client Application Enabler
  db2_05_00.cnvucs 5.0.0.1                    # Code Page Conversion Tables ...
  db2_05_00.cs.drda 5.0.0.1                   # DB2 Communication Support fo...
  db2_05_00.cs.ipx 5.0.0.1                    # DB2 Communication Support fo...
  db2_05_00.cs.rte 5.0.0.1                    # DB2 Communication Support fo...
  db2_05_00.cs.sna 5.0.0.1                    # DB2 Communication Support fo...
  db2_05_00.das 5.0.0.1                       # Administration Server
  db2_05_00.db2.engn 5.0.0.1                  # DB2 Engine
  db2_05_00.db2.rte 5.0.0.1                   # DB2 Run-time Environment
  db2_05_00.db2.samples 5.0.0.1               # DB2 Sample Database Source
  db2_05_00.pext 5.0.0.1                      # DB2 Parallel Extension

  << End of Success Section >>
[MORE...182]

F1=Help         F2=Refresh         F3=Cancel         F6=Command
F8=Image        F9=Shell           F10=Exit          /=Find
n=Find Next
```

Note the command used to install DB2. Page down to the end of the report,
and you see what components were successfully installed:

```
                              COMMAND STATUS

Command: OK            stdout: yes           stderr: no

Before command completion, additional instructions may appear below.
[MORE...182]

.... . << Copyright notice for db2_05_00.das >> . . . . . . .

Licensed Materials - Property of IBM

  5648A3200

  (C) Copyright International Business Machines Corp. 1993, 1997.

All rights reserved.
US Government Users Restricted Rights - Use, duplication or disclosure
restricted by GSA ADP Schedule Contract with IBM Corp.
. . . . . << End of copyright notice for db2_05_00.das >>. . . .

Finished processing all filesets.  (Total time:  2 mins 10 secs).

+-----------------------------------------------------------------------------+
                              Summaries:
+-----------------------------------------------------------------------------+

Installation Summary
--------------------
Name                        Level        Part        Event        Result
-----------------------------------------------------------------------------
db2_05_00.xsrv              5.0.0.1      USR         APPLY        SUCCESS
db2_05_00.pext              5.0.0.1      USR         APPLY        SUCCESS
db2_05_00.db2.samples       5.0.0.1      USR         APPLY        SUCCESS
db2_05_00.cs.sna            5.0.0.1      USR         APPLY        SUCCESS
db2_05_00.cs.ipx            5.0.0.1      USR         APPLY        SUCCESS
db2_05_00.cs.drda           5.0.0.1      USR         APPLY        SUCCESS
db2_05_00.client            5.0.0.1      USR         APPLY        SUCCESS
db2_05_00.db2.rte           5.0.0.1      USR         APPLY        SUCCESS
db2_05_00.db2.engn          5.0.0.1      USR         APPLY        SUCCESS
db2_05_00.cs.rte            5.0.0.1      USR         APPLY        SUCCESS
db2_05_00.cnvucs            5.0.0.1      USR         APPLY        SUCCESS
db2_05_00.das               5.0.0.1      USR         APPLY        SUCCESS


[BOTTOM]


F1=Help           F2=Refresh        F3=Cancel        F6=Command
F8=Image          F9=Shell          F10=Exit         /=Find
n=Find Next
```

Install on Remaining Nodes Using SMIT

When the SMIT tool executes, it saves the commands it uses and the
messages it generates in a file called smit.log. The smit.log file is in the home
directory of the root user.

Edit smit.log using the vi text editor and locate the `installp` command used to install DB2:

```
installp -acgNqQwXd /cdrom/db2 -f File 2>&1

File:
    db2_05_00.xsrv                      5.0.0.1
```

Change the `-F File` parameter to `db2_05_00.xsrv` and save this command into a file called, for example, db2.install:

```
installp -acgNqQwXd /cdrom/db2 db2_05_00.xsrv
```

Change the permissions of the file so that it can be executed. For example:

```
chmod 755 db2.install
```

Depending on the number of nodes on which you must install DB2, you can either copy db2.install to all the remaining nodes or NFS mount a directory where you have placed the file. Ensure that the CD-ROM is mounted and then from each of the remaining nodes in turn, log in as root, change directory to where the db2.install script is located, and issue the following command:

```
./db2.install
```

2.2.4 Using the installp Command

You can choose to install DB2 either on all nodes in your DB2 cluster or a subset of nodes. If you use the `installp` command under `dsh`, the install will run in parallel and unattended on a number of machines. You should still log into each host and check that the DB2 UDB EEE product has been successfully installed.

The format of the `installp` command is:

```
▶▶ installp -options input_directory packagename1 [packagename2...]▶◀
```

where:

- `-options` are the various option(s) of the `installp` command.
- `input_directory` is the device or directory where the products to be installed are located.
- `packagename1 packagename2` are the names of the packages you choose to install. Note that there is a space between the package names.

2.2.4.1 Installing On A Single Host Using installp

To install DB2 UDB EEE on a single host, enter the following command logged in as root:

```
installp -qagXd /cdrom/db2 db2_05_00.xsrv
```

where:

- `-qagXd` are the various options:
  - q stops the system for prompting for the device
  - a is the option to apply one or more software products or updates. This is the default action. This flag can be used with the -c option to apply and commit DB2 UDB EEE when installed.
  - g indicates to automatically install any pre-requisite products or updates that are needed by DB2.
  - x will expand file systems needed by DB2, if necessary.
  - d is followed by the device name to specify where the installation medium can be found. For DB2 UDB EEE, this can only by a CD-ROM device.
- `/cdrom/db2` is the name of the directory where the DB2 install images are located on the CD-ROM.
- `db2_05_00.xsrv` is the License Support for DB2 UDB Extended Enterprise Edition fileset.

2.2.4.2 Installing on Multiple Hosts Using dsh installp

There are two ways that you can use the `installp` command under `dsh` to install DB2 UDB EEE on multiple hosts simultaneously:

1. Execute the install on all the hosts at the same time.

2. Execute the install on a subset of the hosts at the same time.

Let's look at these two methods in detail.

Install on All Hosts via dsh installp

To run `installp` on all the nodes in the RS/6000 SP, as root from the Control Workstation, issue the following command:

```
dsh -a installp -qagXd /cdrom/db2 db2_05_00.xsrv
```

Installing on a Subset of Hosts

In order to install using dsh installp on only a subset of hosts in your cluster, you first have to specify the hosts in the subset. This list of hosts in known as the working collection.

1. On the SP Control Workstation, create a file that lists the host names of the subset of machines where you want to install DB2 UDB EEE. For example, we have created a file of four systems. The file is named hosts.txt, and its contents are as follows:

```
f01n05
f01n06
f01n07
```

2. On the Control Workstation, issue the following command:

```
export WCOLL=/hosts.txt
```

3. Issue the hostlist and dsh -q commands to verify that the names in the working collection are the correct hostnames:

```
cws1:/ > hostlist
f01n05
f01n06
f01n07
cws1:/ > dsh -q
Working collective file /hosts.txt:
f01n05
f01n06
f01n07
Fanout: 64
```

4. NFS-Mount the CD-ROM drive to the same directory (for example, /cdrom) on all the machines listed in your hosts.txt file.

5. Issue the following command from the Control Workstation to install the DB2 products and components:

```
dsh installp -qagXd /cdrom/db2 db2_05_00.xsrv
```

By default, the output from each host will be presented back to the issuing
terminal in the order specified in the working collection. In our example, we
first see output from f01n05:

```
cws1:/ > dsh installp -qagXd /cdrom/db2 db2_05_00.xsrv
f01n05: SUCCESSES
f01n05: ---------
f01n05:   Filesets listed in this section passed pre-installation verification
f01n05:   and will be installed.
f01n05:
f01n05:   Selected Filesets
f01n05:   -----------------
f01n05:   db2_05_00.xsrv 5.0.0.1                         # License Support for DB2...
f01n05:
f01n05:   Requisites
f01n05:   ----------
f01n05:   (being installed automatically;  required by filesets listed above)
f01n05:   db2_05_00.client 5.0.0.1                       # DB2 Client Application ...
f01n05:   db2_05_00.cnvucs 5.0.0.1                       # Code Page Conversion .
f01n05:   db2_05_00.cs.drda 5.0.0.1                      # DB2 Communication Supp ...
f01n05:   db2_05_00.cs.ipx 5.0.0.1                       # DB2 Communication Supp ...
f01n05:   db2_05_00.cs.rte 5.0.0.1                       # DB2 Communication Supp ...
f01n05:   db2_05_00.cs.sna 5.0.0.1                       # DB2 Communication Supp ...
f01n05:   db2_05_00.das 5.0.0.1                          # Administration Server
f01n05:   db2_05_00.db2.engn 5.0.0.1                     # DB2 Engine
f01n05:   db2_05_00.db2.rte 5.0.0.1                      # DB2 Run-time Environment
f01n05:   db2_05_00.db2.samples 5.0.0.1                  # DB2 Sample Database Source
f01n05:   db2_05_00.pext 5.0.0.1                         # DB2 Parallel Extension
f01n05:
f01n05:   << End of Success Section >>
f01n05:
```

When the installation has finished on all the machines, the last output we see
is from the last host in the working collection, f01n07:

```
f01n07: Finished processing all filesets.  (Total time:  1 mins 35 secs).$
f01n07: $
f01n07: +----------------------------------------------------------------------+$
f01n07:                              Summaries:$
f01n07: +----------------------------------------------------------------------+$
f01n07: $
f01n07: Installation Summary$
f01n07: --------------------$
f01n07: Name                        Level        Part      Event      Result$
f01n07: --------------------------------------------------------------------------$
f01n07: db2_05_00.xsrv              5.0.0.1      USR       APPLY      SUCCESS$
f01n07: db2_05_00.pext              5.0.0.1      USR       APPLY      SUCCESS$
f01n07: db2_05_00.db2.samples       5.0.0.1      USR       APPLY      SUCCESS$
f01n07: db2_05_00.cs.sna            5.0.0.1      USR       APPLY      SUCCESS$
f01n07: db2_05_00.cs.ipx            5.0.0.1      USR       APPLY      SUCCESS$
f01n07: db2_05_00.cs.drda           5.0.0.1      USR       APPLY      SUCCESS$
f01n07: db2_05_00.client            5.0.0.1      USR       APPLY      SUCCESS$
f01n07: db2_05_00.db2.rte           5.0.0.1      USR       APPLY      SUCCESS$
f01n07: db2_05_00.db2.engn          5.0.0.1      USR       APPLY      SUCCESS$
f01n07: db2_05_00.cs.rte            5.0.0.1      USR       APPLY      SUCCESS$
f01n07: db2_05_00.cnvucs            5.0.0.1      USR       APPLY      SUCCESS$
f01n07: db2_05_00.das               5.0.0.1      USR       APPLY      SUCCESS$
```

2.2.5 Verifying the Installation

DB2 UDB EEE is located in /usr/lpp/db2_05_00 where 5 is the version
number. You should have a db2_05_00 directory created in /usr/lpp with the
following subdirectories:

```
f01n05:/usr/lpp/db2_05_00 > ls
.rtelib    bin         function    map        samples
.rtelib2   bnd         install     misc       security
Readme     cfg         instance    msg
adm        conv        java        netls
adsm       doc         lib         odbclib
f01n05:/usr/lpp/db2_05_00 >
```

Using the lslpp command, you can see the DB2 components (filesets) that
were installed. In this example, we have installed DB2 UDB EEE with the
online documentation in English, support for ODBC and JDBC, replication
and the sample code.

```
f01n05:/ > lslpp -l db2_05_00*
  Fileset                      Level   State      Description
--------------------------------------------------------------------------
Path: /usr/lib/objrepos
  db2_05_00.client             5.0.0.1 COMMITTED  DB2 Client Application Enabler
  db2_05_00.cnvucs             5.0.0.1 COMMITTED  Code Page Conversion Tables -
                                                  Uni Code Support
  db2_05_00.conn               5.0.0.1 COMMITTED  DB2 Connect
  db2_05_00.cs.drda            5.0.0.1 COMMITTED  DB2 Communication Support for
                                                  DRDA Application Server
  db2_05_00.cs.ipx             5.0.0.1 COMMITTED  DB2 Communication Support for
                                                  IPX/SPX
  db2_05_00.cs.rte             5.0.0.1 COMMITTED  DB2 Communication Support for
                                                  TCP/IP
  db2_05_00.cs.sna             5.0.0.1 COMMITTED  DB2 Communication Support for
                                                  SNA
  db2_05_00.das                5.0.0.1 COMMITTED  Administration Server
  db2_05_00.db2.engn           5.0.0.1 COMMITTED  DB2 Engine
  db2_05_00.db2.rte            5.0.0.1 COMMITTED  DB2 Run-time Environment
  db2_05_00.db2.samples        5.0.0.1 COMMITTED  DB2 Sample Database Source
  db2_05_00.html.en_US         5.0.0.1 COMMITTED  DB2 Product Document (HTML) -
                                                  English
  db2_05_00.jdbc               5.0.0.1 COMMITTED  Java Database Connectivity
                                                  (JDBC) Support
  db2_05_00.odbc               5.0.0.1 COMMITTED  Open Database Connectivity
                                                  (ODBC) Support
  db2_05_00.pext               5.0.0.1 COMMITTED  DB2 Parallel Extension
  db2_05_00.repl               5.0.0.1 COMMITTED  DB2 Replication
  db2_05_00.xsrv               5.0.0.1 COMMITTED  License Support for DB2 UDB
                                                  Extended Enterprise Edition
f01n05:/ >
```

Using the du -k command, we can see that these DB2 product components
take approximately 63 MB. The DB2 Product Library requires about 71 MB
after installation. However, during the installation of the DB2 Product Library
you need about twice that amount (150 MB) because the files are
decompressed during installation.

2.2.6 How to Choose an Installation Method

Let's review the three installation methods and discuss the advantages and
disadvantages of each.

- Using the DB2 Installer program

  This method is the simplest because the DB2 Installer is a menu-driven
  program provided with the product. It can be used to configure some of the
  DB2 communication environment and to create the DB2 and DAS
  instances and the DB2 instance owner user and group, the DAS instance
  owner user and group and the fenced user and group. However, you will
  have to repeat the installation on every host. If your configuration is small

(8 hosts or less), you could establish a session on each host and perform the installation in this way. If your DB2 Cluster has a large number of hosts, this will be a time-consuming process.

- Using SMIT

  You must manually create the DB2 instance and the DAS instance and configure all DB2 communication after installation using SMIT. If you are not experienced in setting up client/server communication in DB2, this may not be the best method for you.

  However, using SMIT, you can save the `installp` command used to install DB2 UDB EEE. You can then execute this `installp` command on the other hosts, either from a separate session for each host, or using `dsh` to automate the process.

- Using the installp command under `dsh`.

  The dsh program executes an application on all hosts in a defined environment. This is probably the easiest method to use if you have many hosts in your DB2 cluster. You must still manually create the DB2 and DAS instance, the fenced user and configure all DB2 communication. You should also check that the installation was successful on each host.

2.3 Post-Installation Tasks

There are certain steps that must be done in order to use the DB2 UDB EEE product in a cluster environment. There are also optional steps depending on the function you want to use. For example, you must perform some configuration to allow communication between hosts in your cluster. However, it is not mandatory to use the graphical tools in a DB2 UDB EEE environment. We provide a checklist of the required activities in each section.

Post-installation tasks include the following:

1. Configuring DB2 communications between nodes

   This includes making entries into the /etc/services file and making sure that DB2 commands can be executed across all nodes either by using a .rhosts file in the DB2 instance owner's directory or an /etc/hosts.equiv file.

2. Creating a DB2 instance

   You create and administer your database within a DB2 instance. You will specify (in the db2nodes.cfg file) the hosts that make up the DB2 Cluster.

3. Modifying the environment

   This section has various tasks, some of which are required and others which are optional. One of the required tasks is to make sure that the DB2 instance owner can execute DB2 commands and create database objects.

4. Starting and testing the DB2 instance

   In this section we will discuss how to start the DB2 instance. We will also test the instance by creating the sample database and selecting data from this database.

5. Configuring the DAS instance (optional)

   If you want to administer your DB2 UDB EEE environment using the graphical tools (for example the Control Center) from a client workstation you will need to create a DAS instance at the server. You will also need to execute the `db2cclst` process, and make sure that administration server commands can be executed by the DAS instance owner.

6. Configure client/server communication using the graphical tools (optional)

   This section looks at how to enable communication between the DB2 UDB EEE server and a remote client using either the graphical tools or the DB2 command line processor.

7. Manually configure DB2 client/server communications (Optional)

This section looks at how to enable communication between the DB2 UDB EEE server and a remote client without using the graphical tools.

2.3.1 Configuring DB2 Communication between Nodes

There are a number of tasks to complete in order to enable communication between the hosts in your DB2 cluster. Here's a checklist of these tasks:

1. Make sure that all hosts can communicate with each other through TCP/IP.

   From each host, you should ensure that the hostnames of the other nodes can be resolved, through either /etc/hosts or a name server.

2. Reserve ports for the DB2 instance in the /etc/services file.

   You must reserve ports in the /etc/services file. These ports are used by DB2 UDB EEE to communicate between the nodes (or partitions). This section discusses the use of these ports.

3. Make sure that the DB2 instance owner can execute remote commands using the `rsh` command on all hosts to be used in the DB2 Cluster.

This section discusses two important files, db2nodes.cfg and /etc/services. The db2nodes.cfg file is a configuration file that defines the database partitions in a DB2 instance. We discuss the db2nodes.cfg file and its relationship to the /etc/services file.

2.3.1.1 Verify the TCP/IP Configuration on All Hosts

From each host, you should ensure that the hostnames of the other hosts can be resolved through either /etc/hosts or a name server and that all the network interfaces are functioning. This should be done for all network interfaces to be used by the DB2 instance (for example, the high-speed switch network interface).

2.3.1.2 The db2nodes.cfg Configuration File

The db2nodes.cfg file contains information about the database partitions in a DB2 instance. The file must be placed in the sqllib directory in the DB2 instance owner's home directory ($INSTHOME/sqllib). There is one file for every DB2 instance on your system. The file contains one entry for each database partition for that particular DB2 instance.

Before you create a DB2 instance, you must decide (as a minimum) how many database partitions will be defined per host so that you can reserve the correct number of ports in the /etc/services file. We actually complete the db2nodes.cfg file after DB2 Instance creation.

You can update the db2nodes.cfg configuration file with any text editor. The file is locked when you issue the `db2start` command and unlocked after the database manager is stopped using the `db2stop` command. When the file is locked, it can only be updated by the `db2start` command (for example, by using the `db2start restart` or `db2start addnode` commands).

There are four fields in the db2nodes.cfg configuration file: nodenum, hostname, logical port, and netname (Figure 19). Depending on your environment, the logical port and netname fields may be optional.

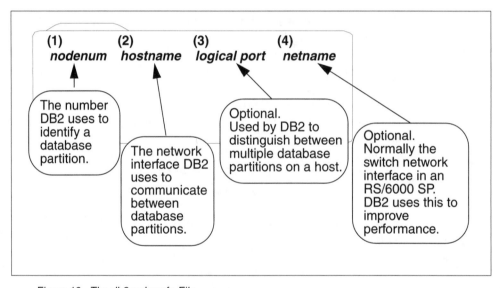

Figure 19. The db2nodes.cfg File

We'll look at each of the fields in the db2nodes.cfg file in detail. We will change the order of discussion because the hostname and netname in the db2nodes.cfg are related. So, we discuss those two fields together.

Nodenum (1)
The nodenum is a required field in the db2nodes.cfg file. It identifies database partitions in a particular DB2 instance. It must satisfy the following conditions:

- Each entry must be unique.
- The range of values is from 0 to 999.
- The first value for nodenum does not have to be 0.
- The entries must be in ascending order.
- Gaps can exist in the sequence.

Let's look at some examples of the db2nodes.cfg file that illustrate some of the rules about assigning the nodenum field.

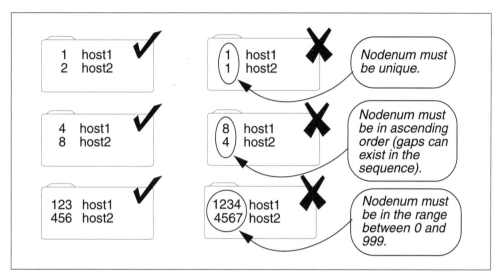

Figure 20. The Nodenum Field in the db2nodes.cfg File

Figure 20 shows some examples of the usage of the nodenum field in the db2nodes.cfg file. We only show two fields: nodenum and hostname. The files on the left side are examples of correct usage, but those on the right are incorrect according to the rules for nodenum. Note that nodenum and hostname do not have any naming relationship; however, a naming scheme is recommended, especially in large cluster systems that may involve using a switch and multiple database partitions on one SP node. For example, on a host whose hostname is tp3an05, consider using a value of 5 for the nodenum.

Logical Port (3)
The logical port in the db2nodes.cfg file is used by DB2 to distinguish between multiple database partitions on a single host. The logical port field must satisfy the following conditions:

- If not specified, it defaults to 0.
- Each entry must be unique per host.

- If using a single database partition per host, if the logical port is specified then it must be zero.
- If using multiple database partitions on a single host, the logical port number must start at 0 and continue 1, 2, 3, 4 and so on for each host.
- If using multiple database partitions on a single host, the number of logical ports required is the maximum number of database partitions defined on one particular host. An example is shown in "Configuration Scenarios" on page 77.
- A range of ports must be reserved in /etc/services, with one port for each database partition per host.

Let's look at some examples of the db2nodes.cfg file that illustrate some of the rules about assigning the logical port field.

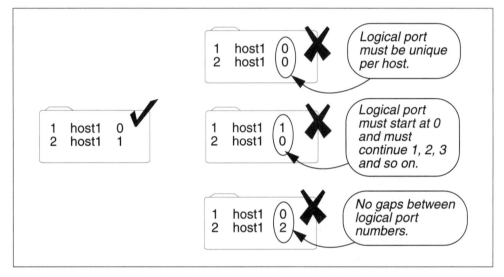

Figure 21. The Logical Port Field in the db2nodes.cfg File

Figure 21 shows correct entries for the logical port in the db2nodes.cfg file. This is indicated by the file on the left. The examples on the right side of the diagram show invalid values for the logical port field.

Let's look at some examples that show the relationship of the logical port field to the /etc/services file. Figure 22 shows the db2nodes.cfg file and a portion of the /etc/services file for a two-host cluster with one database partition per host.

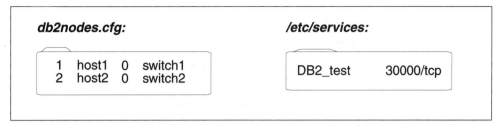

Figure 22. Logical Port and Single DB Partition per Machine

In Figure 22, we use 0 as the logical port since there is only one database partition per host. The /etc/services file here shows only one port needs to be reserved. The name of the reserved port is DB2_test, where test is the name of the DB2 instance. See "Reserving Ports in /etc/services" on page 74 for further details.

The next example illustrates multiple database partitions on a single physical node.

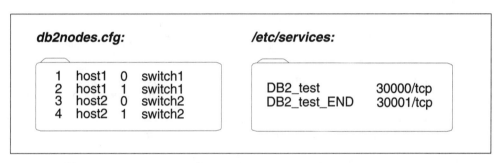

Figure 23. Logical Port and Multiple Database Partitions per Machine

Figure 23 shows two hosts. Each host has two database partitions defined on it, so we must then reserve two ports in /etc/services.

Hostname (2) and Netname (4)
The second field in the db2nodes.cfg is the hostname. The hostname specifies the network interface used by DB2 for communication between hosts. Typically, the hostname is an Ethernet or token-ring network interface. The fourth field is the netname. The netname is also a network interface used for DB2 for communication between hosts. The netname is usually specified as the switch network interface available on an RS/6000 SP.

If netname (also known as the switch name) is specified in the db2nodes.cfg file, then:

- Hostname is used for **db2start**, **db2stop** and **db2_all** commands.
- Netname is used for all other DB2 communication between nodes.
- A logical port must be specified.
- Netname defaults to hostname if not specified.

Interfaces for Hostname and Netname

One of the advantages in using a token-ring or Ethernet network interface for hostname and the switch interface for netname is that if the switch interface fails, you will still be able to stop DB2 gracefully and then later restart DB2. This is because the hostname (not the netname) is used for db2start and db2stop processing.

Let's look at a simple example of a db2nodes.cfg file which illustrates the usage of hostname and netname.

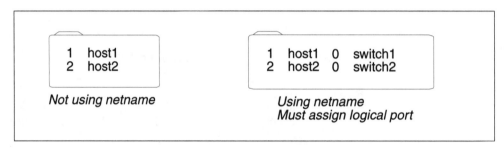

Figure 24. The Netname Field in the db2nodes.cfg File

Figure 24 shows a two-host cluster. The db2nodes.cfg on the left uses only a token-ring or Ethernet network interface for all of the DB2 communication between hosts. Therefore, netname is not assigned. However, the file on the right has values assigned for both hostname and netname. In this case, the logical port must be specified.

2.3.1.3 Reserving Ports in /etc/services
You must reserve ports in the /etc/services file to enable DB2 instance communication between database partitions.

You must set up the ports for DB2 instance communication between database partitions before the DB2 instance is created, or the instance creation will not be successful. You can change the entries if your configuration changes, but you must initially know the number of ports that you need in your environment to enable DB2 communication between nodes.

These are the rules for the entries in /etc/services which are used for communication between database partitions:

- The same ports must be reserved on all hosts to be used in the DB2 instance.

- The total number of ports reserved should be equal to the number of database partitions per host. If some hosts have more database partitions than others, then use the larger number.

Configuring /etc/services for a Single Database Partition per Host
Let's look at the fields that you need in the /etc/services file for a cluster environment with one database partition per host:

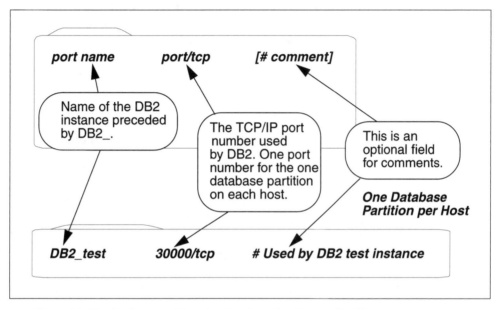

Figure 25. The /etc/services File - One Database Partition per Machine

Figure 25 is an example of the DB2 instance, test. In this instance, there is one database partition per host. The port number 30000 is reserved for the test instance. In order to avoid conflict with other applications it is recommended to use high values for DB2 port numbers. Port numbers of 1024 and below (well-known ports) are reserved for use with other programs.

These are the rules for each of the fields in the /etc/services file for the DB2 instance communication entries:

- Port name:
  - The instance name prefixed by DB2_ .

- The instance name must be entered as it exists in the operating system. In our example, the instance name (test) is in lower case.
- Port number:
  - Identifies the TCP/IP port number to reserve on each host for the database partition.
  - The same port must be reserved on all hosts.
  - Must be followed by /tcp.
- Comment:
  - An optional field:
  - Must be prefixed by #.

Configuring /etc/services for Multiple Database Partitions per Host

If you have more than one database partition per host, you must define a range of ports in the /etc/services with the following syntax:

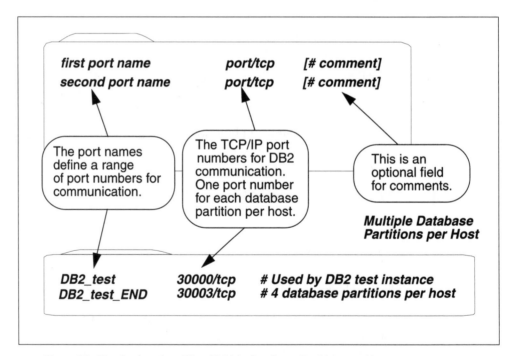

Figure 26. The /etc/services File - Multiple Database Partitions per Host

Figure 26 shows the entries for the /etc/services file when using multiple database partitions on a single host. You must reserve a range of port numbers, one for each database partition.

Some additional considerations apply to the services entries when using multiple database partitions per host:

- For the first port entry:

  - The port name must be the name of the instance preceded by DB2_. In our example, this is DB2_test.

  - The port number identifies the initial TCP/IP port number to reserve for the database partitions on each host.

- For the second port entry:

  - The port name must be the name of the instance preceded by DB2_ and suffixed by _END. In our example, this is DB2_test_END.

  - The port number identifies the last TCP/IP port number to reserve for the database partitions on each host.

- The number of ports reserved (last port number - initial port number + 1) must be greater than or equal to the maximum number of database partitions on any individual host.

- The same ports must be reserved on all hosts.

2.3.1.4 Configuration Scenarios

This section discusses one hardware configuration that can have multiple DB2 configurations. We look at an SP cluster of four hosts, with only one network interface and using both a token-ring or ethernet and switch interface. We show the contents of the db2nodes.cfg and the /etc/services file for each configuration.

Configuration One

The first example has one database partition per host.

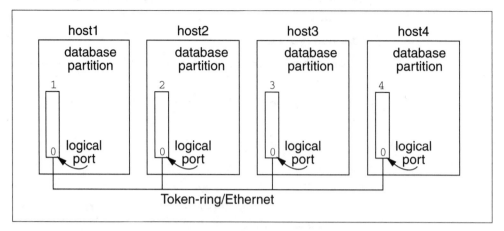

Figure 27. Cluster of Four Hosts, One Database Partition per Host

Figure 28 shows the db2nodes.cfg and /etc/services entries for this example:

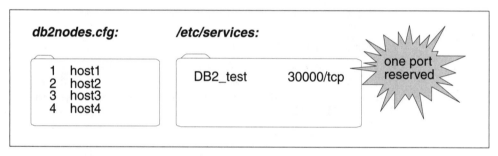

Figure 28. Configuration One - db2nodes.cfg and /etc/services

There are four hosts, and each host has only one database partition. You'll notice that the nodenum field and hostnames are related. This is not necessary, but is recommended, especially if there are a large number of hosts in your cluster. Because it is not specified, the logical port number defaults to 0. A switch is not being used; so there is no entry for netname. Only one entry in the /etc/services file is needed for this DB2 instance. The instance here is named test.

Configuration Two
The next scenario is the same physical hardware with two database partitions defined on every physical machine.

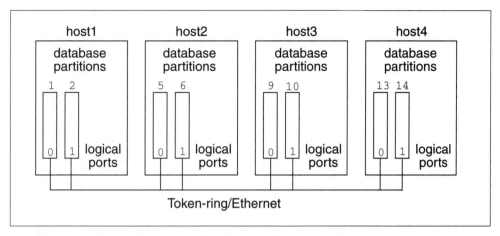

Figure 29. Cluster of Four Hosts - Two Database Partitions per Host

Figure 29 uses the same hardware configuration as Figure 28. However, there are two database partitions per host. The db2nodes.cfg and /etc/services contain:

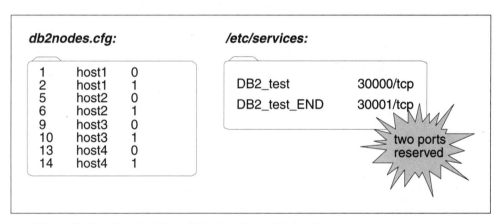

Figure 30. Configuration Two - db2nodes.cfg and /etc/services

In this example, you need to reserve two ports for the database partitions for the test instance in the /etc/services file on each host. Note that the nodenum field has gaps between some of its values. This is to allow growth should we need to add database partitions on each of the hosts. Also, you must specify the logical port numbers. The first logical port number on each host is 0.

Configuration Three

In the last example, we add two more database partitions on each node, bringing the total number of database partitions per node to four. We will also use the high-speed switch:

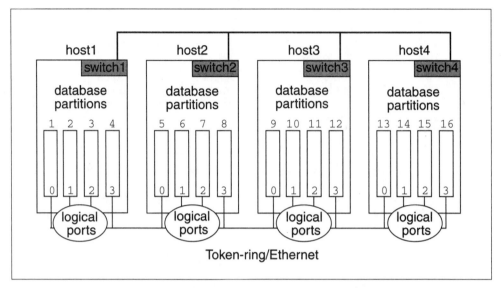

Figure 31. Cluster of Four Hosts - Four Database Partitions per Host

The db2nodes.cfg and /etc/services entries for this example are:

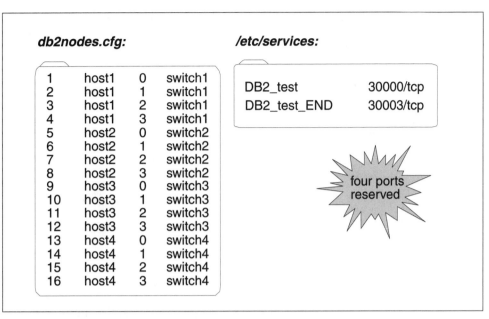

db2nodes.cfg:

1	host1	0	switch1
2	host1	1	switch1
3	host1	2	switch1
4	host1	3	switch1
5	host2	0	switch2
6	host2	1	switch2
7	host2	2	switch2
8	host2	3	switch2
9	host3	0	switch3
10	host3	1	switch3
11	host3	2	switch3
12	host3	3	switch3
13	host4	0	switch4
14	host4	1	switch4
15	host4	2	switch4
16	host4	3	switch4

/etc/services:

DB2_test	30000/tcp
DB2_test_END	30003/tcp

four ports reserved

Figure 32. Configuration Three - db2nodes.cfg and /etc/services

This time, we need to reserve four ports for the four database partitions in the /etc/services file on each host. Note that we have entered a value for netname (switch0 - switch4) because we want DB2 UDB EEE to use the high-performance switch to communicate between the SP nodes instead of the token-ring or Ethernet interfaces.

2.3.1.5 Enabling the Execution of Remote Commands

In a DB2 UDB EEE instance, each host must have the authority to perform remote commands on the other hosts that make up the instance. This can be done by creating an .rhosts file in the home directory of the instance owner. The home directory of the instance owner is NFS mounted to all the other hosts. Therefore, a single copy of the .rhosts file is accessible from all the hosts. Alternatively, you can create a /etc/hosts.equiv file on every host in the instance. However, this may be more difficult to maintain because any change requires a change on every host.

The .rhosts file is easy to create. You can control the level of security between the hosts by the format of the entries in this file.

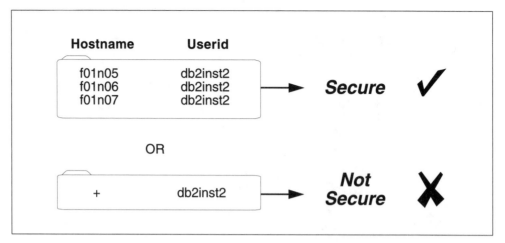

Hostname	Userid
f01n05	db2inst2
f01n06	db2inst2
f01n07	db2inst2

➡ *Secure* ✓

OR

+	db2inst2

➡ *Not Secure* ✗

Figure 33. Format of the .rhosts File

In the example marked Secure in Figure 33, all hosts and the users that can issue remote commands on a given host are listed. Alternatively, you can create the .rhosts file with only a plus sign and the name of the user that can execute the remote commands, as shown in the example marked Not Secure in the diagram. In this case, the db2inst2 user can issue remote commands from any host (including hosts not in the DB2 cluster).

Make sure that the IP addresses of the hosts can be resolved using either the the /etc/hosts file or a name server if you are using one.

2.3.2 Creating a DB2 Instance

This section discusses the creation of a DB2 instance. You create and store databases in DB2 instances. You may have more than one DB2 instance in your DB2 cluster.

These are the tasks involved in creating a DB2 instance:

1. The same user with the same user ID, group and group ID must exist on all hosts in your DB2 cluster.

2. The home directory of the DB2 instance owner should exist on one host and be NFS-mounted on all remaining hosts in the cluster.

3. Create the instance only on one DB2 host. This host should be the host where the home directory for the DB2 instance exists. Even if your DB2 cluster involves multiple database partitions on the same host, you create the DB2 instance only once on one host. You can create the DB2 instance by one of the following methods:

   1. Using the DB2 Installer program, or

   2. Using the db2icrt command.

   If you use the DB2 Installer program to create a DB2 instance, the utility will also configure the host for client/server communication. (This is not the same as configuring communication between database partitions).

DB2 instance, /etc/services, and db2nodes.cfg file

Remember that the entries for communicating between database partitions in the /etc/services file must be done before the DB2 instance is created, or the DB2 instance creation will fail. Once the instance is successfully created, you should configure the db2nodes.cfg file for your environment.

2.3.2.1 Using DB2 Installer

Log in as root, change to the DB2 UDB EEE install directory, and invoke the DB2 Installer program:

```
f01n05:/ > cd /usr/lpp/db2_05_00/install
f01n05:/usr/lpp/db2_05_00/install/ >./db2setup
```

You should see the following screen:

```
+----------------------- DB2 Installer -----------------------+
|                                                             |
|   Select Install to select products and their components to install, or   |
|   select Create to create the DB2 services.                 |
|                                                             |
|   To select products and their components, select        [ Install... ]   |
|   Install.                                                  |
|                                                             |
|   To create a DB2 Instance, or the Administration         [ Create... ]   |
|   Server, select Create.                                    |
|                                                             |
|                                                             |
|                                                             |
|                                                             |
|                                                             |
|                                                             |
|                                                             |
|                                                             |
|   [  Close  ]                                    [  Help  ]  |
+-------------------------------------------------------------+
```

Pressing tab or the arrow keys will move the cursor between the selectable fields. The position of the cursor is shown in reverse video. Pressing spacebar or Enter will select the field where the cursor is positioned.

Select the option to create a DB2 instance by pressing tab and then press **Enter**. The following screen is displayed:

```
+------------------------- Create DB2 Services -------------------------+
|                                                                       |
|  Select the items you want to create, and select OK when finished.    |
|                                                                       |
|                                                                       |
|  A DB2 Instance is an environment where you store data and run        |
|  applications. An instance can contain multiple databases.            |
|                                                                       |
|  [ ] Create a DB2 Instance.                         : Customize... :  |
|                                                                       |
|  An Administration Server provides services to support client tools that |
|  automate the configuration of connections to DB2 databases.          |
|                                                                       |
|  [ ] Create the Administration Server.              : Customize... :  |
|                                                                       |
|                                                                       |
|                                                                       |
|                                                                       |
|                                                                       |
|                                                                       |
|                                                                       |
|  [  OK   ]                    [ Cancel ]                    [ Help  ] |
+-----------------------------------------------------------------------+
```

Select the option to create a DB2 instance by pressing either **Enter** or the space bar. The following pop-up window is displayed:

```
+------------------------- Create DB2 Services -------------------------+
|                                                                       |
|+--- DB2 Instance ----------------------------------------------------+|
||                                                                     ||
||   Authentication:                                                   ||
||      Enter User ID, Group ID and Password that will be used for     ||
||      the DB2 Instance.                                              ||
||      User Name          [db2inst2]                                  ||
||      User ID            :        :          [*] Use default UID     ||
||      Group Name         [dbadmin2]                                  ||
||      Group ID           :        :          [*] Use default GID     ||
||      Password           [              ]                            ||
||      Verify Password    [              ]           [ Default ]      ||
||                                                                     ||
||   Protocol:                                                         ||
||      Select Customize to change the default      [ Customize... ]   ||
||      communication protocol.                                        ||
||                                                                     ||
||   [*] Auto start DB2 Instance at system boot.                       ||
||   [ ] Create a sample database for DB2 Instance.                    ||
||                                                                     ||
||   [  OK   ]                 [ Cancel ]                  [ Help  ]   ||
|+---------------------------------------------------------------------+|
+-----------------------------------------------------------------------+
```

You should enter the name of the user and group you created in "Creating the DB2 Instance Owner" on page 32. This user and group have already been defined on all hosts. If you enter a different user and group, then you must make sure that this user and group exist on all hosts and have identical user and group IDs.

File Collections

If you are using File Collections for user management, then any user created at the SP node that is hosting the DB2 instance will be automatically overwritten by the user information that exists at the Control Workstation. By default, this happens once an hour. You should create users and groups at the Control Workstation and then replicate the user information to the SP nodes, either by using the supper program, or waiting for the automatic replication to occur.

Notice that there is an asterisk in the field to auto-start DB2. This means that every time the system is re-started, DB2 will also start. You can de-select this by pressing **Enter** or the space bar over the field.

Using the tab key, move to the option that allows you to change the default communication protocol. Once Customize is highlighted, press **Enter**.

```
+-------------------------- Create DB2 Services ----------------------------+
|                                                                           |
|+--- DB2 Instance -------------------------------------------------------+ |
||                                                                        | |
||   Authentication:                                                      | |
||       Enter User ID, Group ID and Password that will be used for       | |
||       the DB2 Instance.                                                | |
||   +--- DB2 Instance Protocol ---------------------------------------+  | |
||   |                                                                 |  | |
||   |   Select protocols and then select Properties to modify the     |  | |
||   |   protocol values.                                              |  | |
||   |                                                                 |  | |
||   |   [*] TCP/IP    Detected                    [ Properties... ]   |  | |
||   |   [ ] IPX/SPX   Detected                    : Properties... :   |  | |
||   |                                                                 |  | |
||   |   [   OK   ]              [ Cancel ]              [  Help  ]     |  | |
||   +-----------------------------------------------------------------+  | |
||                                                                        | |
||   [*] Auto start DB2 Instance at system boot.                          | |
||   [ ] Create a sample database for DB2 Instance.                       | |
||                                                                        | |
||   [   OK   ]                  [ Cancel ]                  [  Help  ]    | |
|+------------------------------------------------------------------------+ |
+---------------------------------------------------------------------------+
```

This pop-up window shows the communication protocols that have been detected by the DB2 Installer program. Here, only TCP/IP has been selected. If you select **Properties**, you can see the values used by DB2 for communication between the DB2 servers and clients.

```
  +-------------------------- Create DB2 Services --------------------------+
  |                                                                         |
  |+--- DB2 Instance ------------------------------------------------------+|
  ||                                                                       ||
  ||   Authentication:                                                     ||
  ||       Enter User ID, Group ID and Password that will be used for      ||
  ||       the DB2 Instance.                                               ||
  ||   +--- +--- TCP/IP -------------------------------------------+---+   ||
  ||   |    |                                                      |   |   ||
  ||   | S|    Enter the Service Name and Port Number that will    |   |   ||
  ||   | p|    be used for TCP/IP connection.                      |   |   ||
  ||   |    |                                                      |   |   ||
  ||   | [|    Service Name      [db2cdb2inst2  ]            |]    |   |   ||
  ||   | [|    Port Number       [50000]          [ Default ] |:   |   ||
  ||   |    |                                                      |   |   ||
  ||   | [|    [   OK   ]        [ Cancel ]        [ Help ]   |]   |   |   ||
  ||   +----+--------------------------------------------------+---+   ||
  ||                                                                       ||
  ||   [*] Auto start DB2 Instance at system boot.                         ||
  ||   : : Create a sample database for DB2 Instance.                      ||
  ||                                                                       ||
  ||   [   OK   ]                   [ Cancel ]                 [ Help ]   ||
  |+---------------------------------------------------------------------+|
  +-------------------------------------------------------------------------+
```

The DB2 Installer has reserved port number 50000 and 50001 in the /etc/services file for communicating with clients. The service name for TCP/IP is **db2cdb2inst2**. This value will be used to update the database manager configuration file. You can use the values selected by the DB2 Installer program or supply your own.

┌─ **Ports Used for Client/Server Communications** ────────────────────┐

These ports are used for communications between DB2 Servers and Clients. They are unrelated to the ports used for communications between database partitions discussed in "Configuring DB2 Communication between Nodes" on page 69.

└──┘

Select **OK** until you are taken to the screen where you can create the fenced user. A fenced user can create and execute stored procedures and UDFs in an area of memory not used by DB2. The following screen allows you to create a fenced user with the DB2 Installer utility.

The default group and user for the User-Defined Functions are staff and db2fenc1. You should enter the user and group you created in "Creating a Group and User for the Fenced User" on page 39. In our case, we use **db2fenc2** as the user name and **db2fadm2** as the group name:

```
+-------------------------- Create DB2 Services --------------------------+
|                                                                          |
|+--- User-Defined Functions --------------------------------------------+|
||                                                                        ||
||   Fenced User-Defined Functions enable application developers to       ||
||   create their own suite of functions specific to their application    ||
||   or domain.                                                           ||
||                                                                        ||
||   Authentication:                                                      ||
||      Enter User ID, Group ID and Password that will be used for        ||
||      the fenced User-Defined Functions.                                ||
||      User Name         [db2fenc2]                                      ||
||      User ID           :       :            [*] Use default UID        ||
||      Group Name        [db2fadm2]                                      ||
||      Group ID          :       :            [*] Use default GID        ||
||      Password          [           ]                                   ||
||      Verify Password   [           ]               [ Default ]         ||
||                                                                        ||
||   Note: It is not recommended to use the DB2 Instance user ID for      ||
||         security reasons.                                              ||
||                                                                        ||
||   [   OK   ]              [ Cancel ]                   [  Help  ]       ||
|+------------------------------------------------------------------------+|
+--------------------------------------------------------------------------+
```

Select **OK** until the DB2 Installer displays a message warning you that you have not created a DAS instance. Ignore the warning for now (we will create the DAS instance in the next section) and select **OK** to continue. You will see a summary report:

```
+----------------------------- DB2 Installer -----------------------------+
|                                                                          |
|   +-- Summary Report ---------------------------------------------+      |
|   |                                                               |      |
|   |                                                               |      |
|   |   DB2 Services Creation                                       |      |
|   |   ---------------------                                       |      |
|   |                                                               |      |
|   |   DB2 Instance                                                |      |
|   |                                                               |      |
|   |     Group Name                                   dbadmin2     |      |
|   |     Group ID                                          999     |      |
|   |     User Name                                    db2inst2     |      |
|   |     User ID                                          1004     |      |
|   |     Service Name                              db2cdb2inst2     |      |
|   |     Port Number                                     50000     |      |
|   |     Update DBM configuration file for TCP/IP                  |      |
|   |                                                               |      |
|   |   User-Defined Functions                                      |      |
|   |                                                               |      |
|   |                                                  [ More... ]  |      |
|   +---------------------------------------------------------------+      |
|                              [ Continue ]                                |
+--------------------------------------------------------------------------+
```

The summary report shows that DB2 Installer is about to create a DB2 instance called db2inst2. The primary group for db2inst2 is dbadmin2. The TCP/IP port number to be used for communication is 50000 with a service name of db2cdb2inst2. Select **Continue** and then **OK** at the confirmation and the next screen showing the DB2 instance being created will be displayed:

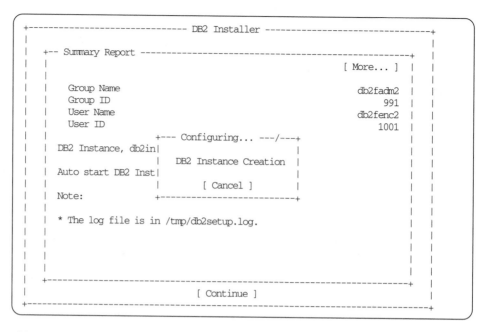

```
+------------------------------ DB2 Installer ------------------------------+        |
|                                                                           |        |
|  +-- Summary Report ----------------------------------------------------+ |        |
|  |                                                         [ More... ]  | |        |
|  |                                                                      | |        |
|  |    Group Name                                          db2fadm2      | |        |
|  |    Group ID                                                 991      | |        |
|  |    User Name                                           db2fenc2      | |        |
|  |    User ID                                                 1001      | |        |
|  |                           +--- Configuring... ---/---+                | |        |
|  |  DB2 Instance, db2in|                              |                  | |        |
|  |                     |         DB2 Instance Creation |                 | |        |
|  |  Auto start DB2 Inst|                              |                  | |        |
|  |                     |            [ Cancel ]         |                 | |        |
|  |  Note:              +------------------------------+                  | |        |
|  |                                                                      | |        |
|  |  * The log file is in /tmp/db2setup.log.                             | |        |
|  |                                                                      | |        |
|  |                                                                      | |        |
|  |                                                                      | |        |
|  |                                                                      | |        |
|  +----------------------------------------------------------------------+ |        |
|                           [ Continue ]                                    |        |
+---------------------------------------------------------------------------+        |
```

Messages are stored in the db2setup.log file in the /tmp directory.

The next section details how to create a DB2 instance using the `db2icrt` command. If you have already created a DB2 instance using the DB2 Installer you should pass over the next section and go to "Configuring the db2nodes.cfg File" on page 92.

2.3.2.2 Using the db2icrt Command
Alternatively, you can use the **db2icrt** command to create a DB2 instance. The command syntax is as follows:

```
db2icrt [-h|-?] [-d] [-aAuthType] [-uFencedID] InstName
```

where:

- `-h|-?` displays the usage information.

- `-d` turns debug mode on.

- `-aAuthType` defines the authentication type (SERVER, CLIENT, or DCS) for the instance.

- `-uFencedID` defines the name of the user under which fenced UDFs and fenced Stored Procedures will be run.

- **InstName** is the name of the instance.

You have to create entries in the /etc/services file for communications between the database partitions before you actually create the instance. See "Reserving Ports in /etc/services" on page 49 if you not done this already.

The **db2icrt** command is located in the /usr/lpp/db2_05_00/instance directory. To run this command, log in as root, and enter:

```
f01n05:/ > cd /usr/lpp/db2_05_00/instance
f01n05:/usr/lpp/db2_05_00/instance > ./db2icrt -u db2fenc2 db2inst2
DBI1070I Program db2icrt completed successfully.
```

This will create a DB2 instance called db2inst2 with a fenced user called db2fenc2. The authentication type, which is not specified, defaults to server.

After the successful completion of the **db2icrt** command, you must run additional commands to prepare the environment for the DB2 instance:

1. Still logged in as root, edit the /etc/services file and add two entries for communication between the DB2 server and remote clients:

```
db2cdb2inst2    50000/tcp # DB2 port for remote clients
db2idb2inst2    50001/tcp # interrupt ports for DB2 V1.x clients
```

   In this example, we have 50000 and 50001 as port numbers. You can choose any consecutive pair of unused numbers over 1024.

2. Switch user to the DB2 instance owner, and execute the db2profile file. This will setup some of the environment variables, and make sure that the instance owner can execute DB2 commands.

```
su - db2inst2
cd $HOME
. sqllib/db2profile
```

3. Make sure that the db2profile is executed whenever the instance owner logs into the system. Edit the .profile file of the instance owner and add the following line:

```
. sqllib/db2profile
```

4. Update the database manager configuration file with the service name of the TCP/IP port used for remote client access:

```
db2 update dbm cfg using SVCENAME db2cdb2inst2
```

5. Set up the default communication protocol by setting the instance level profile registry parameter DB2COMM:

```
db2set -i db2inst2 DB2COMM=TCPIP
```

6. If required, set auto-start for the instance:

```
db2set -i db2inst2 DB2AUTOSTART=TRUE
```

2.3.2.3 Configuring the db2nodes.cfg File

After you have successfully created a DB2 instance, you should configure the db2nodes.cfg file that is used for DB2 communication between database partitions. The format and usage of the db2nodes.cfg is explained in "The db2nodes.cfg Configuration File" on page 69.

Here are the items to consider when setting up the db2nodes.cfg file:

1. After a DB2 instance has been successfully created, a default db2nodes.cfg will be created in the sqllib directory of the DB2 instance owner ($INSTHOME/sqllib). It will initially contain one entry. For example:

```
0 f01n05 0
```

2. Using an editor (vi, for example) modify the db2nodes.cfg file so that it contains one entry for each database partition for the DB2 instance. For example, in a three-host system with one database partition per host:

```
1 f01n05
2 f01n06
3 f01n07
```

Note that once the instance has been started using the `db2start` command, the permission on this file will be set to read-only. To edit the file you should stop the instance using `db2stop`. If for any reason the DB2 instance is stopped ungracefully (such as a SP node failure), the db2nodes.cfg file may be left in a read-only state. In this case, you will have to manually reset the permissions using the `chmod` command.

2.3.3 Modifying the Environment

This section discusses the tasks to be completed after the DB2 UDB EEE product is installed and a DB2 instance has been created. The following is a list of tasks:

1. Increase the number of processes for the DB2 instance owner.

2. Check for sufficient paging space.

3. Configure TCP/IP network parameters.

2.3.3.1 Increasing Maxuproc

The DB2 UDB EEE instance owner executes a large number of processes in AIX. The maximum number of processes allowed for one user is defined by maxuproc and is by default 40. Use the following command to increase the value of maxuproc for the DB2 instance owner to 1000:

```
f01n05:/ > chdev -l sys0 -a maxuproc=1000
sys0 changed
f01n05:/>
```

2.3.3.2 Checking Paging Space

You have to make sure that you have enough paging space for DB2 to run. To check the available paging space, enter the following command:

```
f01n05:/ > lsps -a
Page Space   Physical Volume   Volume Group   Size   %Used   Active   Auto   Type
paging04     hdisk2            dbvg           80MB    5       yes      yes    lv
paging03     hdisk2            dbvg           80MB    38      yes      yes    lv
paging02     hdisk3            dbvg           80MB    42      yes      yes    lv
paging01     hdisk1            dbvg           80MB    42      yes      yes    lv
paging00     hdisk0            rootvg         48MB    61      yes      yes    lv
hd6          hdisk0            rootvg         80MB    56      yes      yes    lv
f01n05:/ >
```

If you do not have sufficient paging space to start DB2, AIX will by default kill the process that is using the most virtual memory. This is likely to be one of the DB2 processes.

To give you an idea of the paging space requirements of DB2 UDB EEE, we noticed that to start two database partitions per host, DB2 required around 40 MB in paging space to start. This figure varies depending on the communication protocols enabled, the database configuration parameter values and so on.

2.3.3.3 Tuning TCP/IP Network Parameters

When installing DB2 UDB EEE on an RS/6000 SP machine, there are a number of TCP/IP network parameters that need to be set correctly on all SP nodes. These are the recommended values for the TCP/IP parameters:

```
thewall       = 16384
sb_max        = 1310720
rfc13223      = 1
tcp_sendspace = 655360
tcp_recvspace = 655360
udp_sendspace = 65536
upd_recvspace = 655360
```

These parameters may be viewed or changed by using the AIX command, `no`. For example, to change the value of `thewall`:

```
no -a thewall=16384
```

In addition, if the high-performance switch is being used by DB2, the spoolsize and rpoolsize for css0 should be increased. To view the current settings, use the `lsattr -l css0 -E` command:

```
f01n05:/ > lsattr -l css0 -E
bus_mem_addr    0x04000000 Bus memory address     False
int_level       15         Bus interrupt level    False
int_priority    3          Interrupt priority     False
dma_lvl         10         DMA arbitration level  False
spoolsize       524288     Size of IP send buffer True
rpoolsize       524288     Size of IP receive buff True
adapter_status  css_ready  Configuration status   False
f01n05:/ >
```

The recommended values for the spoolsize and rpoolsize are:

```
spoolsize        8388608
rpoolsize        8388608
```

To update the network-related parameters, a sample script is provided called /usr/lpp/db2_05_00/misc/rc.local.sample. To run this script, first check that there is no rc.local file in the /etc/directory, then copy the file to the /etc directory and change the ownership and authorities as follows:

```
f01n05:/ > cp /usr/lpp/db2_05_00/misc/rc.local.sample
/etc/rc.local
f01n05:/ > chown root:sys /etc/rc.local
f01n05:/ > chmod 744 /etc/rc.local
f01n05:/ >
```

To run /etc/rc.local when the system is booted, use the `mkitab` command to add an entry in /etc/inittab:

```
mkitab "rclocal:2:wait:/etc/rc.local > /dev/console 2>&1"
```

To update the network parameters without rebooting the machine, issue the `/etc/rc.local` command.

2.3.4 Starting the DB2 Instance

You must start the DB2 instance before you can create a database.

To start the DB2 instance, log in as the instance owner and run the `db2start` command.

If the DB2 instance is started successfully, you'll receive messages similar to the following:

```
f01n05:/ > db2start
03-19-1998 15:32:21   1   0   SQL1063N  DB2START processing was successful.
03-19-1998 15:32:21   2   0   SQL1063N  DB2START processing was successful.
03-19-1998 15:32:22   3   0   SQL1063N  DB2START processing was successful.
SQL1063N  DB2START processing was successful.
f01n05:/ >
```

Note that the number after the timestamp is the nodenum of the database partition as defined in the db2nodes.cfg file.

To stop the DB2 instance, log in as the instance owner and run the `db2stop` command.

If the DB2 instance is stopped successfully, you'll receive messages similar to the following:

```
f01n05:/ > db2stop
03-19-1998 15:09:40   1   0   SQL1064N  DB2STOP processing was successful.
03-19-1998 15:09:40   2   0   SQL1064N  DB2STOP processing was successful.
03-19-1998 15:09:41   3   0   SQL1064N  DB2STOP processing was successful.
SQL1064N  DB2STOP processing was successful.
f01n05:/ >
```

2.3.4.1 Creating the Sample Database (Optional)

To verify that DB2 is correctly installed, you can create the sample database (called SAMPLE) that is supplied with the DB2 UDB EEE product.

In order to store DB2 EEE databases, you must create a separate file system that is locally mounted on each host, for example, /database. This file system can function as the mount point for other database files in the file system.

Consult "Add a New File System" on page 36 for detailed instructions on how to create a new file system; then see "Mount the File System Locally" on page 36. You must also make sure that the DB2 instance owner has write permission for the file system.

Filesystems for Databases

Databases must be created on locally mounted disks, and not on NFS-mounted file systems. Creating databases on an NFS-mounted file system is not supported.

The sample database is automatically cataloged with the database alias SAMPLE when it is created. By default, the database is created in the path specified by the `DFTDBPATH` database manager configuration parameter.

To create the sample database, perform the following steps:

1. Log in as the instance owner.

2. Change the default database path to /database. This is the name of the filesystem you created locally on each host in the DB2 instance.

   ```
   db2 update dbm cfg using DFTDBPATH /database
   ```

3. Create the sample database by issuing the following command:

   ```
   db2sampl
   ```

Catalog Partition

The host where you issue the create database command holds the catalog partition for the database. The system catalog tables are stored at this single partition.

Once the database has been created successfully, you should test that you can connect and select data from it:

```
f01n05:/ > db2 connect to sample

   Database Connection Information

 Database product      = DB2/6000 5.0.0
 SQL authorization ID  = DB2INST2
 Local database alias  = SAMPLE

f01n05:/ > db2 list database directory

 System Database Directory

 Number of entries in the directory = 1

Database 1 entry:

 Database alias                = SAMPLE
 Database name                 = SAMPLE
 Local database directory      = /database
 Database release level        = 8.00
 Comment                       =
 Directory entry type          = Indirect
 Catalog node number           = 0

f01n05:/ > db2 "select * from org"

DEPTNUMB DEPTNAME         MANAGER DIVISION   LOCATION
-------- --------------- ------- ---------- -------------
      10 Head Office         160 Corporate  New York
      15 New England          50 Eastern    Boston
      20 Mid Atlantic         10 Eastern    Washington
      38 South Atlantic       30 Eastern    Atlanta
      42 Great Lakes         100 Midwest    Chicago
      51 Plains              140 Midwest    Dallas
      66 Pacific             270 Western    San Francisco
      84 Mountain            290 Western    Denver

  8 record(s) selected.

f01n05:/ >
```

2.3.5 Configuring the DAS Instance to Enable The Graphical Tools

In order to use the graphical tools that are included in DB2 UDB Version 5 (such as the Control Center), we first have to do some configuration on the server side.

The DB2 Administration Server (DAS) is a special DB2 instance that provides a remote client the ability to administer and detect the instances and databases on a UDB database server. In a DB2 UDB EEE environment, you can choose to run a DAS instance on one or many hosts. Normally, you would start by configuring a single DAS instance on the host that you wish to hold the coordinator partition for the remote clients. (The coordinator partition is the partition to which remote clients connect). If you wish to share the coordinator function among several hosts (for reasons of performance), and you also wish to exploit the functions offered by the DAS instance on these hosts (such as DB2 Discovery), then you should consider configuring additional DAS instances on these hosts.

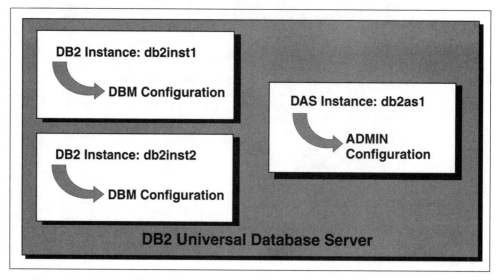

Figure 34. DB2 and DAS Instances

The DAS instance is similar to a DB2 instance in that the DAS instance also has a configuration file. Figure 34 shows a DB2 UDB EEE database server with one DAS instance, db2as1, and two DB2 instances, db2inst1 and db2inst2. Note that there is only one DAS instance on a machine. However, multiple DB2 instances may exist and be active on one database server machine. Databases can only be created within a DB2 instance.

In general, the tasks performed by the DAS instance are to:

- Query the operating system configuration information.

- Query the operating system for user and group information.

- Start and stop DB2 instances.

- Attach to a DB2 instance to perform administration at the database level, such as altering values in the database manager configuration, create, drop, backup, or recover a database.

- Provide a scheduler that is used to execute jobs locally and remotely. The scheduled jobs are user-defined and may include operating system commands.

- Provide a mechanism for DB2 Discovery to return DB2 UDB server information to remote clients.

The DAS instance can be used to perform administrative tasks from a remote client for the database server. All remote DB2 administration tasks will be sent to the DAS instance for local execution at the server. DB2 Discovery, a function provided by the DAS instance, returns server information to remote clients to allow communication to DB2 UDB databases.

2.3.5.1 Configuring a DAS Instance
In the next several sections, we'll describe the tasks that you need to perform set up the DAS instance on a DB2 UDB server so that an Intel-based client can administer the system using the graphical tools. These tasks are as follows:

1. Reserve ports for the DAS instance.

2. Create the DAS instance on the host chosen to hold the DAS instance.

3. Set up the environment for the DAS instance owner.

4. Set up the communications configuration for remote clients to communicate with the DAS instance.

The DAS Instance Owner user was created and configured in the pre-installation section. If you have not done this, see "Creating the DAS Instance Owner" on page 40.

2.3.5.2 Reserve Ports for the DAS instance
Logged in as root, edit the /etc/services file and add two entries for communication between the database partitions to be used by the DAS instance:

```
DB2_db2as2        40000/tcp # DB2 port for remote clients
DB2_db2as2_END    40003/tcp # interrupt ports for DB2 V1.x clients
```

You need to reserve enough ports to support the number of database partitions that the host is running. For example, if you have four database partitions running on the host, you need to reserve four ports.

In this example, we have used 40000 as the starting port number and 40003 as the last port number. You can choose any consecutive pair of unused numbers over 1024.

2.3.5.3 Creating the DAS Instance

As the root user, you create the DAS instance either by using the DB2 Installer utility or the `dasicrt` command. This section describes both methods.

Using DB2 Installer

Log in as root, change to the DB2 UDB EEE install directory, and invoke the DB2 Installer program:

```
f01n05:/ > cd /usr/lpp/db2_05_00/install
f01n05:/usr/lpp/db2_05_00/install/ >./db2setup
```

The following screen is displayed:

```
+----------------------------- DB2 Installer -----------------------------+
|                                                                          |
| Select Install to select products and their components to install, or    |
| select Create to create the DB2 services.                                |
|                                                                          |
|                                                                          |
| To select products and their components, select          [ Install... ] |
| Install.                                                                 |
|                                                                          |
| To create a DB2 Instance, or the Administration          [ Create... ]  |
| Server, select Create.                                                   |
|                                                                          |
|                                                                          |
|                                                                          |
|                                                                          |
|                                                                          |
|                                                                          |
|                                                                          |
|                                                                          |
|                                                                          |
|    [  Close  ]                                           [  Help  ]      |
+--------------------------------------------------------------------------+
```

Using the tab key, move the cursor to the option that allows you to create either the DB2 instance or the Administration Server (DAS) instance and press **Enter**.

```
+-------------------------- Create DB2 Services --------------------------+
|                                                                          |
| Select the items you want to create, and select OK when finished.        |
|                                                                          |
|                                                                          |
| A DB2 Instance is an environment where you store data and run            |
| applications. An instance can contain multiple databases.                |
|                                                                          |
| [ ] Create a DB2 Instance.                          : Customize... :     |
|                                                                          |
| An Administration Server provides services to support client tools that  |
| automate the configuration of connections to DB2 databases.              |
|                                                                          |
| [ ] Create the Administration Server.               : Customize... :     |
|                                                                          |
|                                                                          |
|                                                                          |
|                                                                          |
|                                                                          |
|    [  OK   ]                  [ Cancel ]                 [  Help  ]      |
+--------------------------------------------------------------------------+
```

Select the option to create the Administration Server (DAS) instance.

```
+------------------------- Create DB2 Services --------------------------+
|                                                                        |
|+--- Administration Server ---------------------------------------------+|
||                                                                      ||
||   Authentication:                                                    ||
||       Enter User ID, Group ID and Password that will be used for     ||
||       the Administration Server.                                     ||
||       User Name           [db2as2 ]                                  ||
||       User ID             :         :              [*] Use default UID ||
||       Group Name          [db2asgrp2]                                ||
||       Group ID            :         :              [*] Use default GID ||
||       Password            [              ]                           ||
||       Verify Password     [              ]            [ Default ]    ||
||                                                                      ||
||   Protocol:                                                          ||
||       Select Customize to change the default        [ Customize... ]  ||
||       communication protocol.                                        ||
||                                                                      ||
||   Note: It is not recommended to use the DB2 Instance user ID for    ||
||         security reasons.                                            ||
||                                                                      ||
||   [   OK   ]                        [ Cancel ]              [ Help ]  ||
|+----------------------------------------------------------------------+|
+------------------------------------------------------------------------+
```

You should enter the name of the user and group you created in "Creating an AIX Group and User for DAS Instance Owner" on page 41. This user and group have already been defined on all hosts.

As in the creation of the DB2 instance, the communication protocols that are installed and configured on the system are detected by the DB2 Installer and set up for use with the DAS instance. If you select **Customize** against **Protocol**, and then **Properties** against **TCP/IP**, the following screen is displayed. Note that the DAS instance always uses port 523 for client/server communications.

```
+------------------------- Create DB2 Services -------------------------+
|                                                                       |
|+--- Administration Server ------------------------------------------+|
||                                                                    ||
||  Authentication:                                                   ||
||      Enter User ID, Group ID and Password that will be used for    ||
||      the Administration Server.                                    ||
||  +--- +--- TCP/IP --------------------------------------+----+     ||
||  |    |                                                 |    |     ||
||  | S|   Enter the Service Name and Port Number that will |    |     ||
||  | p|   be used for TCP/IP connection.                   |    |     ||
||  |    |                                                 |    |     ||
||  | [|    Service Name       :              :          |]   |     ||
||  | [|    Port Number        :523  :            [ Default ] |:   |     ||
||  |    |                                                 |    |     ||
||  | [|   [   OK   ]         [ Cancel ]        [  Help  ] |]   |     ||
||  +----+--------------------------------------------------+----+     ||
||                                                                    ||
||  Note: It is not recommended to use the DB2 Instance user ID for   ||
||        security reasons.                                           ||
||                                                                    ||
||  [   OK   ]                  [ Cancel ]              [  Help  ]     ||
|+--------------------------------------------------------------------+|
+-----------------------------------------------------------------------+
```

The DAS instance always uses port 523 for TCP/IP connections. Select **OK** until the following screen appears:

```
+------------------------- Create DB2 Services -------------------------+
|                                                                       |
|+--- Administration Server ------------------------------------------+|
||                                                                    ||
||  Authentication:                                                   ||
||      Enter User ID, Group ID and Password that will be used for    ||
||      the Administration Server.                                    ||
||      User Name          [db2as2  ]                                 ||
||      User ID            :238   :              [*] Use default UID  ||
||      Group Na+--- Notice --------------------------------+         ||
||      Group ID|                                           | default GID ||
||      Password|   (!) DB2SYSTEM will be set to "f01n05".  |         ||
||      Verify P|                                           | [ Default ] ||
||              |                 [   OK   ]                |         ||
||  Protocol:   +-------------------------------------------+         ||
||      Select Customize to change the default       [ Customize... ] ||
||      communication protocol.                                       ||
||                                                                    ||
||  Note: It is not recommended to use the DB2 Instance user ID for   ||
||        security reasons.                                           ||
||                                                                    ||
||  [   OK   ]                  [ Cancel ]              [  Help  ]     ||
|+--------------------------------------------------------------------+|
+-----------------------------------------------------------------------+
```

The DB2 environment variable DB2SYSTEM is set to f01n05. This is the host where the DAS instance was created. Select **OK** until the Summary Report window is displayed:

```
+------------------------------- DB2 Installer -------------------------------+
|                                                                             |
|  +-- Summary Report ------------------------------------------------------+ |
|  |                                                                        | |
|  |                                                                        | |
|  |  DB2 Services Creation                                                 | |
|  |  ---------------------                                                 | |
|  |                                                                        | |
|  |  Administration Server                                                 | |
|  |                                                                        | |
|  |    Group Name                                        db2asgrp2         | |
|  |    Group ID                                                220         | |
|  |    User Name                                           db2as2          | |
|  |    User ID                                                 238         | |
|  |    Port Number                                             523         | |
|  |    Update DBM configuration file for TCP/IP                            | |
|  |                                                                        | |
|  |  Administration Server, db2as2, will be created.                       | |
|  |                                                                        | |
|  |  Note:                                                                 | |
|  |                                                      [ More... ]       | |
|  +------------------------------------------------------------------------+ |
|                              [ Continue ]                                   |
+-----------------------------------------------------------------------------+
```

Select **Continue** and **OK** at the confirmation. When the creation of the DAS instance has completed, the DAS instance is started. You can verify the commands that are issued by browsing the DB2 Installer log file, /tmp/db2setup.log.

The next section details how to create the DAS instance using the `dasicrt` command. If you have already created the DAS instance using the DB2 Installer, you should pass over the next section and go to "Starting the DAS Instance" on page 108.

Using the dasicrt Command

Alternatively, to create a DAS instance using the `dasicrt` command, change to the /usr/lpp/db2_05_00/instance directory and enter the following command when logged in as root:

```
f01n05:/usr/lpp/db2_05_00/instance > dasicrt ASName
```

where `ASName` is the name of the DAS instance owner.

To create a DAS instance named db2as2, we used the following commands:

```
f01n05:/ > /usr/lpp/db2_05_00/instance/dasicrt db2as2
DBI1070I Program db2icrt completed successfully.

DBI1070I Program dasicrt completed successfully.

f01n05:/ >
```

(It is normal to see two messages which report successful completion).

After the successful completion of the `dasicrt` command, you must run additional commands to prepare the environment for the DAS instance:

1. Switch user to the DAS instance owner, and execute the db2profile file. This will setup some of the environment variables, and make sure that the instance owner can execute DB2 commands.

```
su - db2as2
cd $HOME
. sqllib/db2profile
```

2. Make sure that the db2profile is executed whenever the instance owner logs into the system. Edit the .profile file of the instance owner and add the following line:

```
. sqllib/db2profile
```

3. Set up the default communication protocol by setting the instance level profile registry parameter DB2COMM:

```
db2set -i db2as2 DB2COMM=TCPIP
```

4. If required, set auto-start for the instance:

```
db2set -i db2as2 DB2AUTOSTART=TRUE
```

2.3.5.4 Starting the DAS Instance

To start the DAS Instance, use the following command logged in as the DAS instance owner:

```
f01n05:/home/db2as2 > db2admin start
SQL4406W  The DB2 Administration Server was started
successfully.
```

Using the `db2_local_ps` command you can now see six new AIX processes have been started:

```
f01n05:/home/db2as2 > db2_local_ps
Node 0
       UID     PID    PPID   C    STIME    TTY   TIME CMD
     db2as2  14338   55800   0  10:42:27    -   0:00 db2tcpdm
     db2as2  34044   55800   0  10:42:27    -   0:00 db2ipccm
     db2as2  41978   55800   0  10:42:27    -   0:00 db2gds
     db2as2  43776   55800   0  10:42:27    -   0:00 db2tcpcm
     db2as2  55800   19190   0  10:42:27    -   0:00 db2sysc
     db2as2  55860   41978   0  10:42:27    -   0:00 Scheduler
```

2.3.5.5 Starting the Control Center Listener Daemon

To enable you to use the Control Center graphical tool to manage partitioned databases, you must have a Control Center listener daemon running on each machine in the DB2 cluster. This daemon is called **db2cclst**, and is used by all instances that are on the host. The listener daemon is used by the Control Center to retrieve status, connection and snapshot information from each database partition server. The daemon is not associated with a specific instance; instead it functions as a global server for the machine.

On all hosts in the DB2 cluster, you must reserve a port called **db2ccmsrv** in the /etc/services for use by the db2cclst daemon. The number you reserve must be the same on all the hosts. To start the listener daemon, first log in as the DAS instance owner, then enter:

```
f01n05:db2as2 > db2cclst
```

Repeat this command on the other hosts in the DB2 cluster.

You should set up the db2cclst daemon to start at reboot time on all hosts. You can do this by using the `mkitab` command to modify the /etc/inittab file (logged in as root) as follows:

```
mkitab "db2cclst:2:once:su - db2as2 -c "db2cclst"
```

You can use the AIX **ps** command to check if the listener daemon is running. Error information for the db2cclst daemon is returned to the AIX syslog daemon log file.

2.3.5.6 Summary of the TCP/IP Ports Used by DB2 UDB EEE

In "Configuring the db2nodes.cfg File" on page 92, we discussed the usage of the db2nodes.cfg and the /etc/services files by DB2 UDB EEE. This section summarizes the ports used by DB2 UDB EEE:

- For communication between database partitions
- For communication between a DB2 UDB EEE instance and remote clients
- To enable DB2 Discovery
- To enable the graphical tools

Let's consider the example shown in Figure 35:

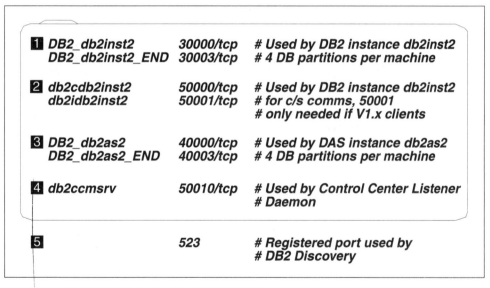

Figure 35. TCP/IP Ports Used by DB2 UDB EEE

There are a maximum of four database partitions on each of the hosts in the DB2 cluster. The usage of the ports in the diagram is as follows:

1. Port entries for communication between database partitions. There should be one port for every database partition that is defined on a host.

2. You need at least one port to be used by remote clients to communicate with the DB2 instance. Here, port number 50000 is reserved for the DB2 instance, db2inst2. The port name associated with 50000, here db2cdb2inst2, is used as the SVCENAME parameter in the database manager configuration file for the inst1 instance. If you have any V1.x clients, you must also reserve the next port, here 50001, as an interrupt port for V1.x clients. This second port is only needed if V1.x clients need to access your DB2 UDB EEE instance.

3. For every host in the DB2 cluster, you need to reserve one port for every database partition that is defined per host for use by the DAS instance.

4. For every host in the DB2 cluster, you need a port for the **db2cclst** process. This port is used by the Control Center for remote administration. The port number is arbitrary. It must be the same for all hosts in the DB2 cluster. The port name must be **db2ccmsrv**.

5. Port 523 is a registered or well-known port reserved for use by DB2. It is used by the DAS instance. It is configured when creating the DAS instance. It is shown here outside of the /etc/services file because no entry is made (by DB2) in the /etc/services file.

2.3.6 Using the Graphical Tools to Configure DB2 Clients

This section discusses how to configure a Windows NT DB2 client to access a DB2 UDB EEE database server using the graphical tools. The recommended way to do this is by using the Client Configuration Assistant. For details on how to install DB2 UDB on Windows NT, see *DB2 UDB for Windows NT Quick Beginnings*, S10J-8149.

2.3.6.1 Client Configuration Assistant

The Client Configuration Assistant (or CCA) can be used to configure your client workstation to access remote DB2 EEE servers. The Client Configuration Assistant provides three methods of configuration:

1. Search the local network for databases by using DB2 Discovery

2. Through an access profile

3. Manual Configuration

In this section, we will take you through the steps necessary to use the CCA to configure a client workstation to access a DB2 UDB EEE database.

We will use the first method listed above (Search the local network). The name of this method can be misleading because in fact, we use a "Directed Search". We will specify the hostname of the DB2 EEE Server (actually one of the SP nodes), and the client node and database directories will be set up automatically using DB2 Discovery. We found this method to be the most practical and efficient way to enable a client to access a DB2 UDB EEE database. Once the configuration is completed using the CCA, you can then access the remote database using the other graphical tools (for instance, the Control Center).

The CCA can easily be started from the desktop of any supported platform. For Windows 95 or Windows NT, click on **Start** and select **Programs->DB2 for Windows->Client Configuration Assistant**:

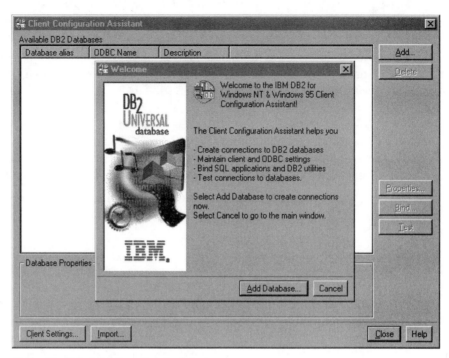

Figure 36. Client Configuration Assistant

- Click on the **Add Database** or **Add** push-button to configure connections using the Add Database SmartGuide.

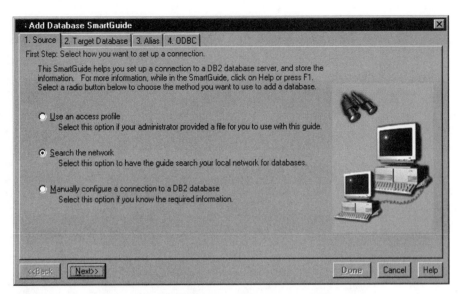

Figure 37. Methods to Add a Database

Figure 37 shows the Add Database SmartGuide window where you can choose the method to set up the client. From this window, do the following:

- Select the **Search the network** radio button.

- Click on **Next**.

The screen where you can choose between Known or Search methods of Discovery will appear.

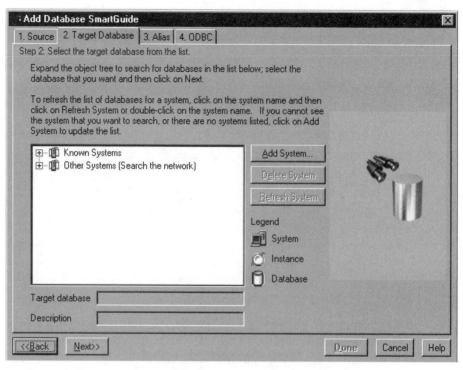

Figure 38. Methods of Discovery: Known and Search

When using the *Known* method, the remote client must provide some information about the DB2 Administration Server instance that is running on the remote DB2 UDB V5 server to be searched. This information consists of the following items:

- A protocol that is configured on the server where the DAS instance is running.
- The identifying name of the server according to the protocol chosen.

In Figure 38, you may choose between *Known* and *Search* methods. To use the *Known* method to configure a database connection to a DB2 server, follow the steps below:

- Click on the **[+]** sign beside the Known Systems icon, to list all the systems known to your client.
- If the system that contains the database you want is not listed:
  - Click on the **Add System** push-button.

- Enter the communication protocol and server identification. For TCP/IP, this is the hostname or IP address. If you enter a hostname, make sure that the hostname is pingable from an MS-DOS window before clicking on OK.

- Click on the **OK** push-button.

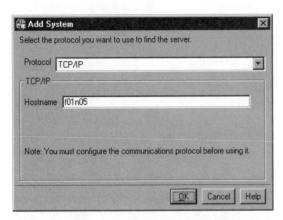

Figure 39. Using TCP/IP to Add a DB2 Server

If a remote DB2 UDB V5 server is found, the name of the server will appear in the list of known systems.

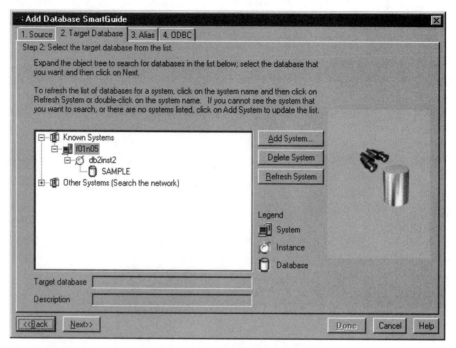

Figure 40. Known System Showing Instances and Databases

- Select the database that you want to access.

- Click on **Next**.

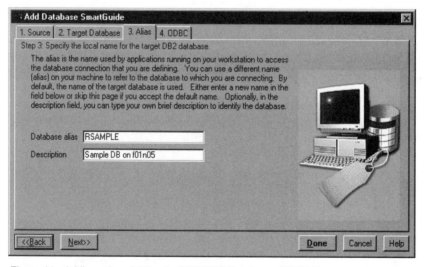

Figure 41. Adding a Local Alias for DB2 EEE Database SAMPLE

- You should then enter a local database alias, and optionally a description.
- Click on **Next**.

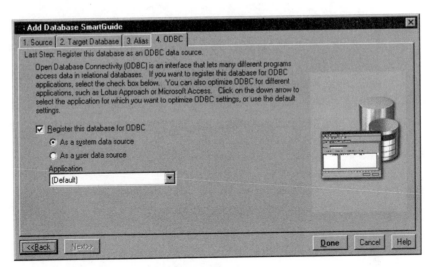

Figure 42. Register the Database for ODBC

- By default, the database will be registered for ODBC applications. If you do not want this to happen, click in the checkbox marked **Register this database for ODBC** to deselect this option.

- Click on the **Done** push-button.

You can now test the connection to the database. If the remote database has been configured to perform its authentication at the server, you will be prompted for a valid server username and password.

2.3.6.2 Control Center
Now that the CCA has set up the client workstation to access the remote DB2 EEE database, it is relatively simple to use the Control Center against the database. These are the steps you should follow:

- Start the Control Center and click on **[+] Systems.**

- Click on the **[+]** next to the system name.

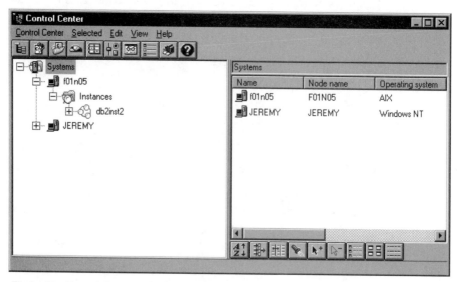

Figure 43. Control Center - List of Instances

- Click on the **[+]** next to the instance name.
- Our database SAMPLE is now accessible from the Control Center and ready to use.

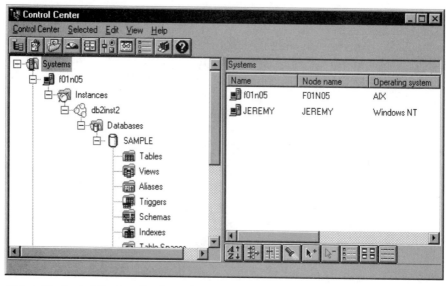

Figure 44. Control Center - Database Objects

2.3.7 Manually Configuring DB2 Client/Server Communications

This section gives details of the steps necessary to manually configure communication using TCP/IP between a DB2 UDB EEE database server on AIX and a DB2 client on Windows NT. For a complete discussion on DB2 UDB client/server connectivity using TCP/IP, APPC, NetBIOS, IPX/SPX and Named Pipes, refer to *The DB2 Universal Connectivity Guide to DB2, SG24-4894-00.*

We use the term *manual configuration steps* to mean the steps one would do to enable communication when not using the Client Configuration Assistant (CCA) or other DB2 UDB Version 5 graphical tools. This information is useful if:

- You have problems setting up client/server communication using the CCA.

- You need to set up a client which does not support the CCA (such as a UNIX client).

While our example covers configuring a Windows NT client, since we are not using the graphical tools, the same procedure can be applied to any supported DB2 client.

2.3.7.1 Configuring a DB2 UDB EEE Server on AIX Using TCP/IP

Figure 45 shows the basic steps for configuring a DB2 UDB EEE server on AIX using TCP/IP as a communication protocol. Note that the installation and configuration of the protocol stack to enable remote client connections is not detailed in this document.

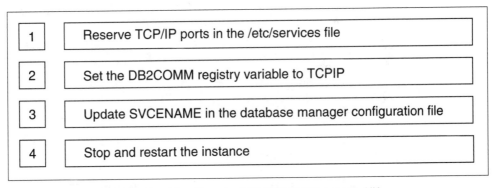

Figure 45. TCP/IP Configuration Steps for DB2 UDB EEE Server on AIX

1. Reserve TCP/IP ports in the /etc/services file

You must be logged in as root to update the /etc/services file. This file should contain two entries for each DB2 UDB EEE instance in order to provide

TCP/IP support for remote clients. The second entry is required to support TCP/IP interrupts from DB2 V1.x clients. For example, the entries to provide support for one DB2 instance could be:

```
db2cdb2inst2  30000/tcp  # DB2 connection service port (DB2 V1 or later)
                         # Also serves as an interrupt connection service
                         # port for DB2 V2 or later clients.
db2idb2inst2  30001/tcp  # DB2 interrupt connection service port for
                         # DB2 V1.x clients.
```

The name of the first port, **db2cdb2inst2**, can be chosen by the user. We update the value of the SVCENAME parameter in the database manager configuration file to this name. The port numbers, 30000 and 30001, are used for the connection and interrupt ports. These port numbers can be chosen by the user, but must not already exist in the /etc/services file. The second port number must equal to the first number plus one.

2. Set the DB2COMM Registry Variable to TCPIP

The registry variable DB2COMM determines which protocols will be enabled when the database manager is started. You can use the db2set command to set this variable to multiple values, separated by commas. For example, if your DB2 server is configured to start TCP/IP, the variable would be set to TCP/IP.

```
$ db2set DB2COMM=TCPIP
```

You can verify this setting by using the db2set command at the server:

```
$ db2set -all
[i] DB2COMM=TCPIP
[g] DB2SYSTEM=f01n05
[g] DBADMINSERVER=db2as2
```

If DB2COMM is undefined or set to null, no remote communication protocol support is started at the server.

3. Update SVCENAME in the Database Manager Configuration File

You tell the database manager which service name to *listen to* by updating the SVCENAME parameter in the database manager configuration file for the instance with the service name that you assigned in the first step. You will need SYSADM authority.

```
f01n05:/ > db2 update dbm cfg using SVCENAME db2cdb2inst2
DB20000I The UPDATE DATABASE MANAGER CONFIGURATION command
completed successfully.
DB21025I Client changes will not be effective until the next
time the application is started. Server changes will not be
effective until the next DB2START command.
```

4. Stop and Restart the DB2 Instance

You need to stop and restart the instance so that:

- The DB2 server processes which support remote clients over TCP/IP can be started.

- The change to SVCENAME can take effect.

```
f01n05:/ > db2stop
03-19-1998 15:09:40   1   0   SQL1064N  DB2STOP processing was successful.
03-19-1998 15:09:40   2   0   SQL1064N  DB2STOP processing was successful.
03-19-1998 15:09:41   3   0   SQL1064N  DB2STOP processing was successful.
SQL1064N  DB2STOP processing was successful.
f01n05:/ > db2start
03-19-1998 15:32:21   1   0   SQL1063N  DB2START processing was successful.
03-19-1998 15:32:21   2   0   SQL1063N  DB2START processing was successful.
03-19-1998 15:32:22   3   0   SQL1063N  DB2START processing was successful.
SQL1063N  DB2START processing was successful.
f01n05:/ >
```

Configuration Verification

You can verify that the database manager configuration file has been updated by querying the database manager configuration file:

```
f01n05:/ > db2 get dbm cfg | grep SVCENAME
TCP/IP Service name (SVCENAME) = db2cdb2inst2
```

You can verify that the DB2 server processes for TCP/IP have been started by running the db2_local_ps command:

```
f01n05: > db2_local_ps
Node 1
      UID    PID   PPID   C    STIME    TTY  TIME CMD
db2inst2   22090  20552   0  10:33:54    -   0:00 db2sysc 1
db2inst2   13136  22090   0  10:33:54    -   0:00 db2tcpcm 1
db2inst2   23116  22090   0  10:33:54    -   0:00 db2gds 1
db2inst2   25934  22090   0  10:33:54    -   0:00 db2ipccm 1
db2inst2   26194  22090   0  10:33:54    -   0:00 db2tcpim 1
db2inst2   18260  23116   0  10:33:55    -   0:00 db2resyn 1
```

The two processes to look for are db2tcpcm and db2tcpim.

2.3.7.2 Configuring a DB2 Client on Windows NT Using TCP/IP

Figure 46 shows the basic steps for configuring a Windows NT DB2 Client using TCP/IP as the communication protocol. Note that the installation and configuration of the TCP/IP protocol stack is not detailed in this document. This method does not use the graphical tools. To perform this function using the graphical tools, see "Using the Graphical Tools to Configure DB2 Clients" on page 111.

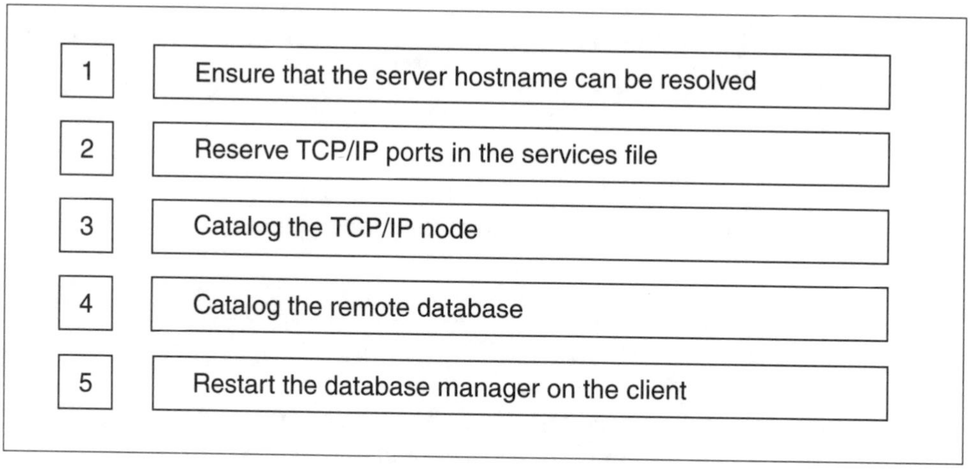

1	Ensure that the server hostname can be resolved
2	Reserve TCP/IP ports in the services file
3	Catalog the TCP/IP node
4	Catalog the remote database
5	Restart the database manager on the client

Figure 46. TCP/IP Configuration Steps for DB2 Client on Windows NT

1. Ensure that the server hostname can be resolved

You must make sure that the hostname of your DB2 server can be resolved from the client. You can test this using ping hostname. If your system does not use a name server and a hosts file does not exist, you can create it manually and place it in the C:\WINNT\SYSTEM32\DRIVERS\ETC directory, where C: is the Windows NT drive. An example of some entries in the hosts file might be:

```
9.3.1.245                      f01n05
9.3.1.246                      f01n06
9.3.1.247                      f01n07
```

where `9.3.1.xxx` is the IP address and `f01n0x` is the hostname.

2. Reserve TCP/IP ports in the services file

The services file should have at least one entry to communicate with the DB2 UDB EEE server. A second entry is required if you are using a DB2 V1.x client. For example, the entries to provide support for one DB2 instance could be:

```
db2cdb2inst2  30000/tcp # DB2 connection service port (DB2 V1 or later)
                        # Also serves as an interrupt connection service
                        # port for DB2 V2 or later clients.
db2idb2inst2 30001/tcp  # DB2 interrupt connection service port for
                        # for DB2 V1.x clients.
```

The name of the first port, **db2cdb2inst2**, and its number, 30000, should match the values at the DB2 server. Similarly, if you are using a DB2 V1.x client, the name and number of the second port should match the values used at the DB2 server.

3. Catalog the TCP/IP Node

This section discusses cataloging a remote TCP/IP node at the DB2 client. To catalog the remote server, execute the following command from a DB2 command window (you will need SYSADM or SYSCTRL authority):

```
C:> db2 catalog tcpip node NODE5 remote f01n05 server db2cdb2inst2
DB20000I The CATALOG TCPIP NODE command completed successfully.
DB21056W Directory changes may not be effective until the directory
cache is refreshed.
```

Where:

- **NODE5** is a name we chose to represent the server node (it must be unique in the node directory list)
- `f01n05` is the TCP/IP hostname of the server
- `db2cdb2inst2` is the service name defined in the services file (on both the client and the server).

You may also catalog the TCP/IP node by using the IP address instead of the hostname of the remote server node. To verify that the node directory has been updated, from a DB2 command window, query the node directory:

```
C:\> db2 list node directory

 Node Directory

 Number of entries in the directory = 1

 Node 1 entry:

 Node name                     = NODE5
 Comment                       =
 Protocol                      = TCPIP
 Hostname                      = f01n05
 Service name                  = db2cdb2inst2
```

4. Catalog the Remote Database

To catalog the remote database, execute the following command from a DB2 Command Window (you will need SYSADM or SYSCTRL authority):

```
C:\> db2 catalog database SAMPLE as RSAMPLE at node NODE5
DB20000I The CATALOG DATABASE command completed successfully.
DB21056W Directory changes may not be effective until the
directory cache is refreshed.
```

Where:

- SAMPLE is the name of the remote database on the DB2 server

- RSAMPLE is the alias (at the client) for this remote database

- NODE5 is the name of the node that we used in the CATALOG NODE command

To verify that the database directory has been updated, from a DB2 Command Window query the database directory:

```
C:\> db2 list database directory

System Database Directory

Number of entries in the directory = 1

Database 1 entry:

Database alias              = RSAMPLE
Database name               = SAMPLE
Node name                   = NODE5
Database release level      = 8.00
Comment                     =
Directory entry type        = Remote
Authentication              = SERVER
Catalog node number         = -1
```

5. Stop and Restart the Instance

To make sure that the changes to the node and database directories take effect for all client sessions, you should stop and restart the client instance. From a DB2 command window:

```
C:\> db2stop
SQL1064N  DB2STOP processing was successful.
C:\> db2start
SQL1063N  DB2START processing was successful.
```

Configuration Verification

To check that the configuration has been correctly completed, you should connect to the remote database:

```
C:\> db2 connect to rsample user db2inst2 using db2inst2

   Database Connection Information

Database product       = DB2/6000 5.0.0
SQL authorization ID   = DB2INST2
Local database alias   = RSAMPLE
```

Note that in this case, because the remote database was cataloged on the client with the default server authentication, a valid server username and password must be supplied when connecting to the database.

Chapter 3. Designing and Implementing a Database

A database is an organized collection of related objects. In order to be able to design and implement a database, it is important to understand the roles of the different objects and how they relate together.

Before you do the physical design and implementation of a database ask the following question: What is the logical design of the data you must represent?

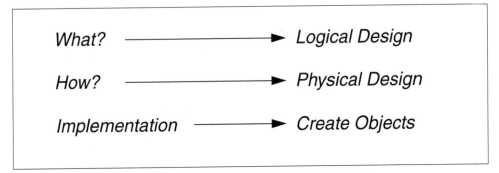

Figure 47. Steps to Create a Database

You must address the *what* question first; that is, what is the logical design of a database. It is important to have a complete understanding of the data before mapping it to a logical design. This will lead to an entity-relationship diagram.

After the logical design is complete, you can map it to the physical design.This step addresses the *how* question. How much space is required to store the data or files that will be created? Once the physical design is understood and itemized, you can create the database and the objects within it.

In this chapter, we discuss the different database objects in DB2 UDB EEE. This information is designed to aid you in the physical design of a database and its implementation.

3.1 Database Terminology

Let's look at an overview of the basic elements needed to create a DB2 UDB EEE database.

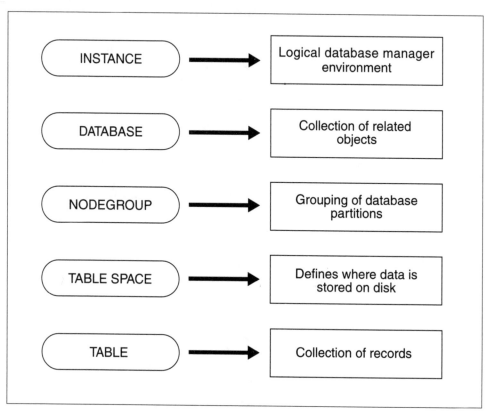

Figure 48. Database Terminology

Figure 48 shows some objects that you need to understand in designing a DB2 UDB EEE database:

- **Instance**: A logical database manager environment. You can have several instances of the database manager product on the same machine. Instances consist of one or many database partitions. Databases are created within an instance. You can have multiple databases within an instance.

- **Database**: A collection of related objects. These objects include tables, columns, data types, schemas, nodegroups, table spaces, views, indexes, packages, buffer pools, log files, transactions and locks.

- **Nodegroup**: A grouping of one or more database partitions.

- **Table Space**: The layer between the database and the disk storage. The table spaces define where data is physically stored on disk.

- **Table**: A set of data records formed by a specific number of columns. A table uses one or more table spaces to store its data.

In the sections that follow, we discuss these objects and the relationships between them.

3.1.1 Instances, Databases Partitions and Databases

Once you have successfully installed and configured DB2 UDB EEE (see Chapter 2) the following steps must be completed before you create a database:

- An instance must exist for the database. You should have created an instance as part of the installation of the DB2 software. You can use the db2icrt command to create an instance.

- The database partitions for the instance must be defined. The db2nodes.cfg configuration file determines the database partitions for your environment. Each database partition may be defined on a different host.

Figure 49 shows the relationship between instances, databases and database partitions.

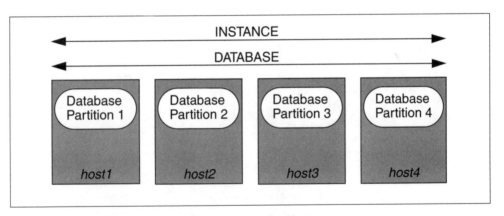

Figure 49. Instances, Databases and Database Partitions

The database will span all the database partitions defined in the instance. Note that you can have multiple database partitions defined on any one host.

3.2 DB2 Instances

A DB2 UDB EEE instance is defined as a logical database manager environment. Every instance is owned by an instance owner, and it is distinct from other instances. The username of the instance owner is the name of the

DB2 UDB EEE instance. Each instance can manage multiple databases; however, a single database can only belong to one instance.

It is possible to have multiple instances defined on a host. There are several reasons why you may wish to generate more than one instance:

- To maintain a separation between test and production environments
- To use different software levels
- To keep separate SYSADM access on different databases
- To keep separate sets of database manager configuration parameters for performance reasons

Figure 50 shows multiple instances. Two instances are defined, INSTANCE1 and INSTANCE2, each one having more than one database. Notice that the instances are completely independent. You can have, in separate instances, different databases with the same name.

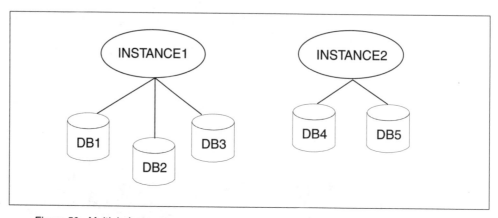

Figure 50. Multiple Instances

Each instance is related to an AIX user, the instance owner. The instance owner has complete control over the instance, and has SYSADM authority over the databases belonging to that instance. There is one-to-one correspondence between an instance and the ownership of the instance. An AIX user cannot be the owner of more than one instance, and an instance must be owned by one AIX user.

When an instance is created, the following directory structure is created:

```
$INSTHOME/sqllib
```

where $INSTHOME is the home directory of the instance owner. The $INSTHOME directory should be created on one of the hosts and shared with the rest of the hosts using NFS.

The instance is activated executing the db2start command from an AIX command line. You can type this command from any of the hosts that belong to the instance and DB2 will automatically start the instance on all hosts associated with that instance. The following is the output of the db2start command in an instance with four database partitions. The db2start command is issued from one host and executed on all the database partitions defined in the db2nodes.cfg file. The first and second column are the start date and time. The third column shows the database partition number where DB2 was started.

```
host1 > db2start
02-26-1998 18:39:04 1 0 SQL1063N DB2START processing was successful.
02-26-1998 18:39:05 2 0 SQL1063N DB2START processing was successful.
02-26-1998 18:39:06 3 0 SQL1063N DB2START processing was successful.
02-26-1998 18:39:07 4 0 SQL1063N DB2START processing was successful.
SQL1063N DB2START processing was successful.
```

To stop the instance, you have to end all the DB2 connections in all of the database partitions and the issue the db2stop command. If any DB2 connections exist in any of the database partitions, the instance will not be stopped in those database partitions. You'll have to disconnect all the DB2 connections and issue the db2stop command again.

```
host1 > db2stop
03-23-1998 09:26:53 1 0 SQL1064N DB2STOP processing was successful.
03-23-1998 09:26:54 2 0 SQL1064N DB2STOP processing was successful.
03-23-1998 09:26:53 1 0 SQL1064N DB2STOP processing was successful.
03-23-1998 09:26:54 2 0 SQL1064N DB2STOP processing was successful.
SQL1064N DB2STOP processing was successful.
```

3.2.1 Database Partitions

A database partition is a collection of data and system resources that are managed by a single database manager. The database partitions in an instance form a shared-nothing architecture and communicate through messages. Table data is not duplicated across the database partitions; rather each database partition holds a part of each table's data.

After creating an instance, you specify the mapping between the hosts and the database partitions.This mapping is defined the db2nodes.cfg file.

We can map several database partitions to each host, or we can map a single database partition to each host. A database partition can be only associated with a single host.

If one database partition is mapped to each host, we refer to this configuration as an SDP (single database partition on a host) configuration. If multiple database partitions are mapped to each host, we refer to this configuration as an MDP (multiple database partitions on a host) configuration.

Figure 51 is an example of an SDP configuration. There are four database partitions and four hosts. There is a one-to-one relationship between database partitions and hosts.

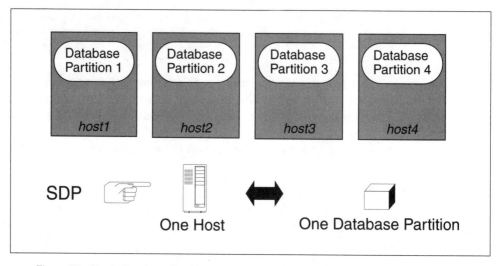

Figure 51. Single Database Partition per Host (SDP) Configuration

In Figure 52, shows an example of an MDP configuration.

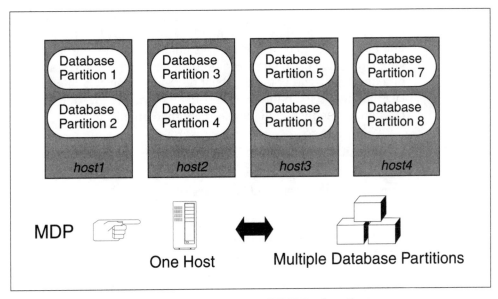

Figure 52. Multiple Database Partition per Host (MDP) Configuration

Each host is associated with two database partitions. There is a one-to-many relationship of between hosts and database partitions. If you plan to use an MDP configuration, your hosts would usually be SMP machines, so that the workload of each database partition could be shared among the multiple processors. DB2 UDB EEE is a partitioned database product. If you need only one database partition in your database, you should use DB2 UDB Enterprise Edition.

3.3 Partitioned Databases

A database is a collection of objects including tables, columns, data types, schemas, nodegroups, table spaces, views, indexes, packages, buffer pools, log files, transactions, and locks. A partitioned database is a database with two or more database partitions. Data in user tables can be located in one or more database partitions. When a table is distributed among multiple partitions, some of its rows are stored in one database partition, and others are stored in other database partitions.

After a DB2 UDB EEE instance is created and a `db2start` command has been issued, a database can be created. You create a database using the DB2 `create database` command. You must have SYSADM or SYSCTRL authority to create a database. This command is not part of the SQL language since each database product has a different syntax for the creation of a database. The database must be given a name to reference it. In DB2 UDB the database name can be 1 to 8 characters in length. Once you have created a database, you can start creating objects in it.

3.3.1 Considerations for Creating DB2 UDB EEE Database

Before you create a database using DB2 UDB EEE, there are a few considerations you should be aware of:

Define a Local File System to Store the Database

It is recommended to define a local file system (non-NFS) in all of the hosts that belong to the instance, and then create the database on that file system. You cannot create the database on a remote file system. When you issue the `create database` command. DB2 will automatically create the database on all of the database partitions defined in the instance.

Designating the Catalog Partition

In an SDP configuration, to designate a database partition as the catalog partition, you must first log into the host that holds that database partition and execute the `create database` command.

In an MDP configuration, there are multiple database partitions per host. To designate the catalog partition, you must first set the `DB2NODE` environment variable to the database partition number you wish to be the catalog partition. Issue a `db2 terminate` command first to end any DB2 background process that could be using another value for DB2NODE. For example, if you want the first database partition to be the catalog partition on host1, issue:

```
host1 > db2 terminate
host1 > db2set DB2NODE=1
host1 > db2 "create database SAMPLE on /database"
```

Consider Not Storing User Data on the Catalog Partition

The host on which you create the database will hold the catalog partition. It stores the system catalog tables for the database. For improved backup/restore performance, you should consider not storing user data on the catalog partition.

When you issue a DB2 backup database command, the backup of the catalog partition must complete before the other database partitions can start to be backed up. If you have no user data at the catalog partition, the backup will execute in less time.

We will now discuss some of the considerations to bear in mind when creating a database, specifically in relation to the nodegroups and table spaces that are created. If you need clarification on nodegroups and table spaces you should see "Nodegroups" on page 148 and "Table Spaces" on page 161 before starting this next section.

3.3.2 Creating Databases in an SDP Configuration

This section discusses some of the issues to consider when creating a partitioned database in an SDP configuration. At database creation, DB2 by default creates a number of initial nodegroups and table spaces. Figure 53 shows a database with four database partitions:

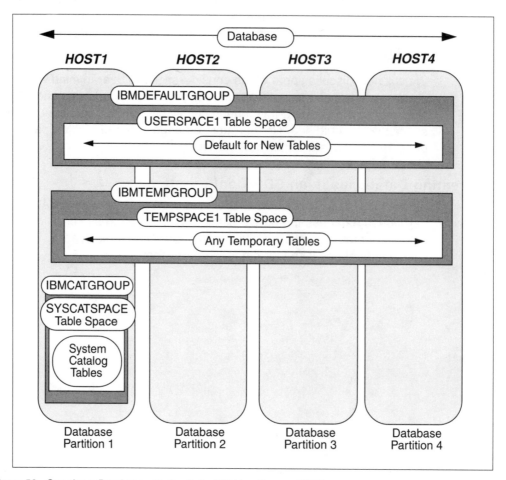

Figure 53. Creating a Database with the Default Tables Spaces (SDP)

From the diagram, we note that:

- The IBMDEFAULTGROUP nodegroup includes all the database partitions in the database. It contains the USERSPACE1 table space, which will be used by user tables if no table space is specified in the create table command.

- The IBMTEMPGROUP nodegroup also includes all the database partitions in the database. It contains the TEMPSPACE1 table space. Temporary data will be stored in this table space.

- The IBMCATGROUP nodegroup includes only the single partition where the database was created. This partition is known as the catalog partition. It contains the SYSCATSPACE table space, which is used by the system catalog tables.

While the nodegroup definitions are fixed, there are a number of ways to control the definitions of these table spaces:

1. Use the Default Settings
For example, if we want to create a database named sample on the path /database, with the default definitions for the three initial table spaces and the catalog tables in database partition one, log into the first host as a user with either SYSADM or SYSCTRL authority (user1) and execute the following command:

```
host1 > db2 "create database SAMPLE on /database"
```

The `create database` command will create the database in all of the database partitions in the instance (as defined in db2nodes.cfg).

2. Override the Default Settings
You can optionally specify user-defined table spaces in the syntax of the create database command.

For example, suppose you have an instance with four database partitions and want to create a database called sample on the path /database. You'd like the USERSPACE1 table space to be a DMS table space with one 1024-page raw container on each database partition. Issue the following database command from one of the hosts (the catalog database partition):

```
host1 > db2 "create database SAMPLE on /database user tablespace
managed by database using (device'/dev/rdata' 1024)"
```

Note that, before you execute the above command, you must create the /dev/rdata logical volume on each host used in the database. So there will be four /dev/rdata logical volumes, one on each host.

After the execution of the `create database` command, four containers will be created, one for each database partition. The same container name will be used in each database partition. In an SDP configuration, this will pose no problem because each database partition resides on a different host. However, in an MDP configuration, this form of the create database command will fail because the multiple database partitions on each host cannot share the same logical volume.

3. Use the Default Settings and Redefine the Table Spaces

For example, suppose you create a database called sample on the path /database in a four-database partioned database with the default table spaces definitions. From the catalog database partition, execute the following command:

```
host1 > db2 "create database sample on /database"
```

Connect to the database and drop the USERSPACE1 table space. Log into any host and issue the following statement. The table space will be dropped from all of the database partitions:

```
host1 > db2 connect to sample
host1 > db2 drop tablespace userspace1
```

Create a new table space USERSPACE1, using the `create tablespace` command and a container definition for the table space:

```
host1: > db2 "create tablespace userspace1 managed by
database using (device '/dev/rdata' 1024)"
```

If you want to change the definition of the temporary table space you must first create a new one, and then drop TEMPSPACE1. A database must always have a temporary table space defined. You will receive an error if you try to drop TEMPSPACE1 and have not defined another temporary table space:

```
host1 > db2 drop tablespace tempspace1
DB21034E The command was processed as an SQL statement because it
was not a valid Command Line Processor command. During SQL processing it
returned:
SQL0283N Temporary table space "TEMPSPACE1" cannot be dropped
because it is the only temporary table space in the database.
SQLSTATE=55026
```

Note that once SYSCATSPACE is created, you cannot change its definition without dropping the database and then re-creating it using the `create database` command, specifying the parameters for SYSCATSPACE as options.

3.3.2.1 Creating Databases in an MDP Configuration

In an MDP configuration, each host holds more than one database partition. Figure 54 shows how a database in an MDP configuration spans four database partitions on two hosts:

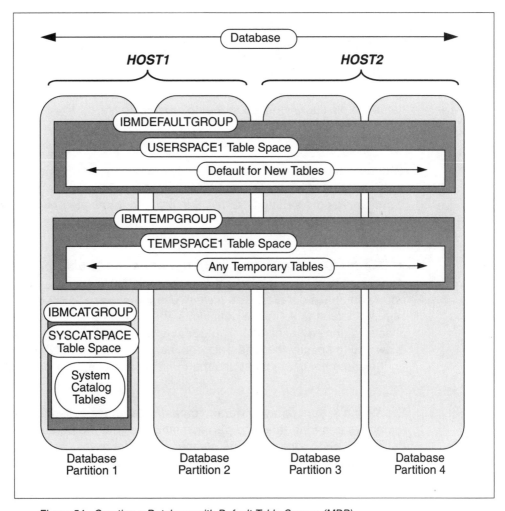

Figure 54. Creating a Database with Default Table Spaces (MDP)

In this enviroment, only two choices exist for defining tables spaces at database creation:

1. Use the Default Settings

For example, if we want to create a database named db1 on the path /database, with the default definitions for the three initial table spaces and the catalog tables in database partition one, execute the following commands:

```
host1 > db2 terminate
host1 > db2set DB2NODE=1
host1 > db2 "create database sample on /database"
```

The `create database` command will create the database in all of the database partitions defined in the db2nodes.cfg file.

Setting DB2NODE

DB2 uses the value of DB2NODE to determine the active database partition in an MDP configuration. You must issue the db2 terminate command before setting DB2NODE in order to terminate any background connection processes.

---

2. Use the Default Settings and Redefine the Table Spaces

If you want to change the definition ot the initial table spaces, you cannot do it during database creation. You have to use the `create database` command with the default table space definitions and then drop and re-create the table spaces with new definitions. The `create database` command does not allow you to specify the different containers for multiple database partitions on the same host. You must use the `create tablespace` command to do this.

For example, suppose you want to create a database called sample on /database in a four database partition instance with the default table space definitions. Set DB2NODE to the number of the database partition that is to be the catalog partition and execute these commands:

```
host1 > db2 terminate
host1 > db2set DB2NODE=1
host1 > db2 "create database sample on /database"
```

Then connect to the database and drop the USERSPACE1 table space. Issue the following statement to drop the table space:

```
host1 > db2 connect to sample
host1 > db2 drop tablespace userspace1
```

Re-create USERSPACE1 with new container definitions:

```
host1 > db2 "create tablespace userspace1 managed by database
using (device '/dev/dbp1/rdata' 1024 on node 1,3)
using (device '/dev/dbp2/rdata' 1024 on node 2,4)"
```

Database partitions 1 and 2 are on the same host so their containers cannot share the same name. The same is true for database partitions 3 and 4. (See "Creating Table Spaces" on page 169 for more details.)

3.3.3 Database Physical Directories and Files

When you create a database, several AIX directory structures and files are created in your system. In this section we briefly look at some of these structures. After you create the first database for an instance, two directory structures exists in all of the database partitions defined in the db2nodes.cfg file:

- /path/$DB2INSTANCE/NODEnnnn/sqldbdir
- /path/$DB2INSTANCE/NODEnnnn/SQL00001

where:

- **path** is the directory specified in the `create database` command. To assist in the management of your database, it is recommended that before you create a database, a separate file system (/path) be created and mounted on each host used by the database. This file system will hold control files for the database and will be the default location for the initial tables spaces and tables that are created at create database time. It must have the same name in all of the database partitions.

- **$DB2INSTANCE** is a subdirectory created within the previous filesystem with the same name as the name of instance owner. This will be the same name in all of the database partitions.

- **NODEnnnn** is a subdirectory created for each database partition that belongs to the database, where **nnnn** is the number of the database partition as defined in the db2nodes.cfg file. (For example, NODE0001, NODE0002, NODE0003, and so on.) This directory enables multiple database partitions to exist on the same host.

- **SQL00001** is a subdirectory that will contain various files used by this database. In this case, the name is SQL00001 because it is the first database in this instance. The next database created will be named SQL00002 and so on. This subdirectory will exist in all of the database partitions used by this database.

Example Showing the Directory Structures in Databases

Let's look at an example of which shows the different physical files that are created in each database partition when a database is created.

We have an instance called db2inst1 that has n database partitions. The home directory of db2inst1 is /home/db2inst1. Next, we create the first database, using the `create database` command:

```
db2 create database sample on /database
```

At the host where database partition 1 is defined, the following directory structures are created:

- /database/db2inst1/NODE0001/sqldbdir
- /database/db2inst1/NODE0001/SQL00001

At the host where database partition 2 is defined, the following directory structures are created:

- /database/db2inst1/NODE0002/sqldbdir
- /database/db2inst1/NODE0002/SQL00001

Directory Structures

So, in general, at the host where database partition n is defined, the following directory structures are created for the first database in the instance:

- /database/db2inst1/NODE000n/sqldbdir
- /database/db2inst1/NODE000n/SQL00001

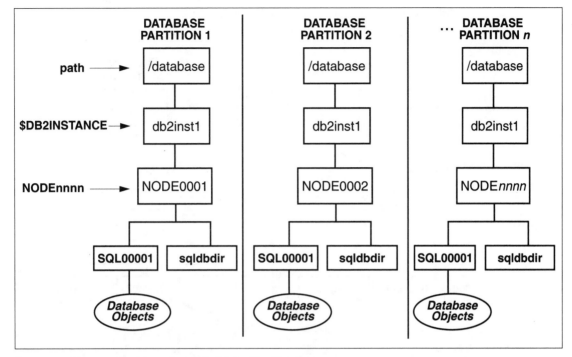

Figure 55. Directory Structures Created with the First Database

Figure 55 shows the directory structures that are created at each database partition after the creation of the first database.

If we now create another database in the same instance with the command:

```
db2 create database sample2 on /database
```

At the host where database partition 1 is defined the following directory structure is created:

- /database/db2inst1/NODE0001/SQL00002

Directory Structures

So, in general, at the host where the database partition *n* is defined, the following directory structure is created for the second database in the instance:

- /database/db2inst1/NODE000*n*/SQL00002

Figure 56 shows the directory structures that are created at each database partition after the creation of the second database:

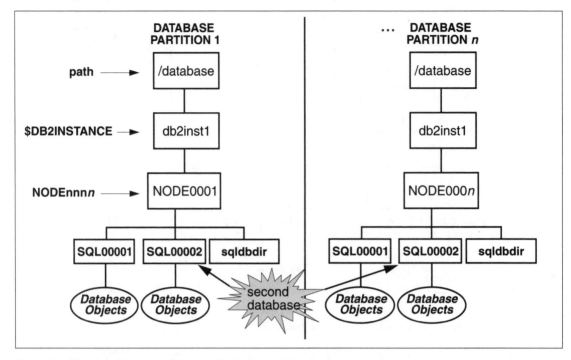

Figure 56. Directory Structures Created with the Second Database

3.3.4 Database Objects

We've looked at some of the physical directory structures that are created when you create a database. Next, we will provide an overview of the database objects created within those directories. These objects are created in the SQL00001 and SQL00002 directories shown in Figure 56.

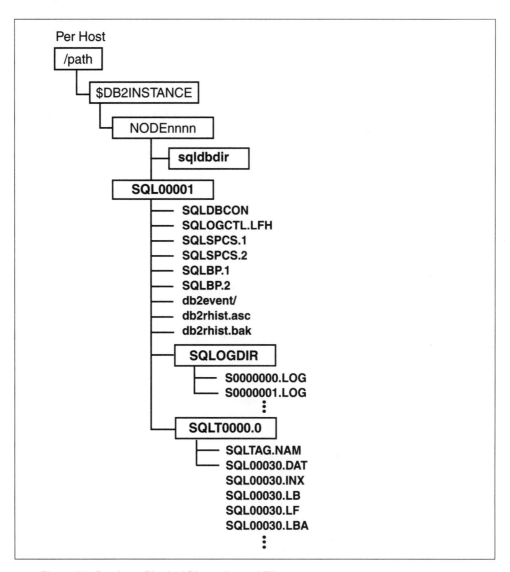

Per Host

```
/path
  └── $DB2INSTANCE
        └── NODEnnnn
              ├── sqldbdir
              └── SQL00001
                    ├── SQLDBCON
                    ├── SQLOGCTL.LFH
                    ├── SQLSPCS.1
                    ├── SQLSPCS.2
                    ├── SQLBP.1
                    ├── SQLBP.2
                    ├── db2event/
                    ├── db2rhist.asc
                    ├── db2rhist.bak
                    ├── SQLOGDIR
                    │     ├── S0000000.LOG
                    │     └── S0000001.LOG
                    │           ⋮
                    └── SQLT0000.0
                          ├── SQLTAG.NAM
                          └── SQL00030.DAT
                              SQL00030.INX
                              SQL00030.LB
                              SQL00030.LF
                              SQL00030.LBA
                                ⋮
```

Figure 57. Database Physical Directories and Files

Figure 57 on page 145 shows some of the files and directories that are associated with a DB2 UDB EEE database. You should not directly edit or alter these files.

From this figure, we can see how DB2 names certain database objects. When the first database is created, a local database directory (sqldbdir) is created. In addition, the database manager creates a separate subdirectory to store the database objects associated with that database. We've mentioned the naming scheme that is used by the database manager, /path/$DB2INSTANCE/NODEnnnn/SQL00001, where SQL00001 contains the objects associated with the first database created in the instance.

In the **SQL00001** directory, we see the following files and directories:

- The **SQLDBCON** file stores the tuning parameters and flags for the database.

- The **SQLOGCTL.LFH** file is used to help track and control all database log files.

- **SQLSPCS.1** contains the definition and current state of all table spaces in the database.

- **SQLSPCS.2** is a copy of SQLSPCS.1 and is created for protection in the event that SQLSPCS.1 fails. Without one of these files, you will not be able to access your database.

- The **SQLBP.1** and **SQLBP.2** files are used to manage buffer pools.

- The **db2event** directory is where event monitor files are created.

- The **db2rhist** files are where the recovery history file information is stored.

- **SQLOGDIR** holds the log files. These files are named Snnnnnnn.LOG where nnnnnnn ranges from 0000000 to 9999999.

- **SQLT0000.0** is a directory container of the SYSCATSPACE SMS table space. This table space contains the system catalog tables. We will discuss table spaces and containers in much more detail in "Table Spaces" on page 161.

Let's look at the various files that are found within this directory.

- The **SQLTAG.NAM** file is used by the database manager when you connect to the database to verify that the database is complete and consistent.

- **SQLnnnnn.DAT** is a table file for all columns of a table with the exception of long data (LONG VARCHAR or LONG VARGRAPHIC) and large object data (CLOB, BLOB, or DBCLOB).

- **SQLnnnnn.INX** is an index file for a table. All indexes for the corresponding table are stored in this single file. It is only created if indexes have been defined.

- **SQLnnnnn.LB** contains large object data (BLOB, CLOB or DBCLOB). This file is only created if BLOB, CLOB or DBCLOB column(s) exist.

- **SQLnnnnn.LF** contains LONG VARCHAR or LONG VARGRAPHIC data. This file is only created if long field column(s) exists.

- **SQLnnnnn.LBA** contains allocation and free space information about the SQLnnnnn.LB files.

Each table is stored in its own file adhering to the SQLnnnnn.DAT naming scheme, if stored in an SMS table space. You can determine the value of this integer by querying the values of tableid and tbspaceid in the SYSCAT.TABLES and SYSCAT.TABLESPACES system catalog tables.

3.3.5 Instance and Database Configuration

When a DB2 instance is created, parameters that control the instance are stored in a file $INSTHOME/sqllib/db2systm. This file is known as the database manager configuration file. Parameters for database configuration are stored in the SQLDBCON file shown in Figure 57 on page 145. This file is known as the database configuration file for a particular database. These two files cannot be edited directly with a text editor. The Command Line Processor, Control Center or Command Center may be used to view or change the values of the parameters in these two files.

3.3.5.1 Instance Configuration

Parameters that control the DB2 instance are kept in an NFS-shared file called db2systm. To change a parameter in the database manager configuration file, you must have SYSADM authority and use the `update dbm cfg` command from any of the hosts.

To Change the DBM Configuration File

When you make a change in the database manager configuration file for an instance, you must stop and start the instance to have the changes become effective.

3.3.5.2 Database Configuration

This configuration information is kept in a file that physically resides in each database partition. Its parameters specify the amount of resources to be allocated to that database; these parameters can be changed to improve performance or increase capacity. Different changes may be required depending on the type of activity in the specific database. You must have SYSADM, SYSCTRL or SYSMAINT authority to issue the `update db cfg` command. Because this file is kept at the database partition level, when you change a parameter it only changes the parameter for that database partition. If you want to have the database configuration parameters for all the database partitions updated, you should use the `db2_all` command. For example, suppose your database consisted of two database partitions:

```
host1 > db2_all db2 update db cfg for sample using sortheap 300

rah: host1
DB20000I The UPDATE DATABASE CONFIGURATION command completed successfully.
DB21026I All applications must disconnect from this database before the
changes become effective.

host1: db2 update db cfg... completed ok

rah: host2
DB20000I The UPDATE DATABASE CONFIGURATION command completed successfully.
DB21026I All applications must disconnect from this database before the
changes become effective.

host2: db2 update db cfg... completed ok
host1 >
```

Using `db2_all` followed by the `update db cfg` command will change the database configuration parameters for the database in all the database partitions.

> **To Change a Parameter Value in the DB Configuration File**
>
> When you make a change in the database configuration file, you must disconnect all applications from the database before the changes become effective.

3.4 Nodegroups

A nodegroup is a grouping of database partitions within a database. We use nodegroups to specify which set of database partitions a table's data will reside on.

Once a database has been created, nodegroups can be defined within the database. Each database partition must already be defined in the instance through the db2nodes.cfg configuration file. A nodegroup may contain from one to the entire number of database partitions defined in the db2nodes.cfg file.

You can create or drop a nodegroup using the CREATE NODEGROUP and DROP NODEGROUP statements. You can also create or drop a nodegroup from the Control Center.

When a nodegroup is created or modified, a partitioning map (see "Partitioning Maps" on page 154) is associated with it. A partitioning map in conjunction with other elements is used by the database manager to determine which database partition in the nodegroup will store a given row of data.

3.4.1 Nodegroup Classifications

We can establish two classifications for nodegroups: one based on the number of database partitions in the nodegroup and another based on how the nodegroup is created.

3.4.1.1 Single and Multi-Partition Nodegroups

Depending on the number of database partitions of a nodegroup, there are two types:

- *Single-partitition nodegroups*: Nodegroups that contain only one database partition.

- *Multi-partition nodegroups*: Nodegroups that contain more than one database partition.

Figure 58 on page 150 shows three nodegroups, NG123, NG3 and NG1234. Nodegroup NG3 is a single-partition nodegroup, because only database partition 3 is contained in it. NG123 and NG1234 are multi-partition nodegroups. NG123 spans partitions 1, 2, and 3, and NG1234 spans all four database partitions.

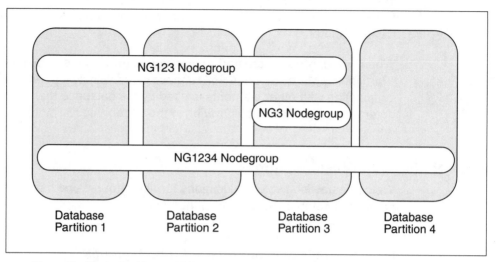

Figure 58. Single-Partition and Multi-Partition Nodegroups

Partitions in Nodegroups

Note that database partitions can be in more than one nodegroup. For example, database partition 3 is found in all three nodegroups, NG123, NG3 and NG1234.

3.4.1.2 User-Defined and System-Defined Nodegroups

Nodegroups can also be classified by the way they were created:

- *User-defined nodegroups.* These nodegroups are created by the user with either SYSADM or SYSCTRL authority after the database has been created using the CREATE NODEGROUP SQL statement. (See "Creating Nodegroups" on page 151 for more details.)

- *System-defined nodegroups.* These nodegroups are created when the database is created. There are three: IBMDEFAULTGROUP, IBMCATGROUP and IBMTEMPGROUP.

Let's discuss some of the characteristics of system-defined nodegroups.

- IBMDEFAULTGROUP:
  - Spans all database partitions listed in db2nodes.cfg
  - Default nodegroup for the CREATE TABLE SQL statement
  - Initially empty
  - Can be altered to add or remove database partitions

- Cannot be dropped using the DROP NODEGROUP SQL statement
- IBMTEMPGROUP:
    - Spans all database partitions listed in db2nodes.cfg
    - Holds temporary tables created during database processing
    - Cannot be dropped using the DROP NODEGROUP SQL statement
- IBMCATGROUP:
    - Restricted to a single database partition consisting of the catalog partition. The catalog partition is the partition where the CREATE DATABASE command is executed
    - Contains all of the system catalog tables
    - Cannot be altered to span more partitions
    - Cannot be dropped using the DROP NODEGROUP SQL statement

Let's look at an example of a database showing the three system-defined nodegroups (Figure 59 on page 151). The database is distributed among four database partitions. IBMDEFAULTGROUP and IBMTEMPGROUP include all the database partitions. IBMCATGROUP includes only the first database partition; this means than the CREATE DATABASE command was executed from the first database partition.

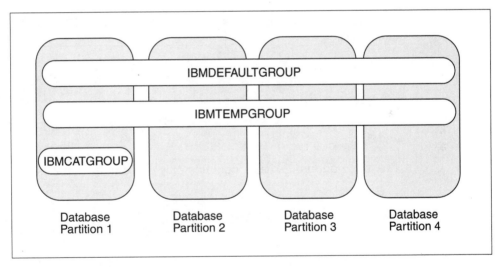

Figure 59. System-Defined Nodegroups

3.4.2 Creating Nodegroups

In order to be able to create a nodegroup:

- You must have SYSADM or SYSCTRL authority.

- You must be connected to the database where the nodegroup is to be created.

- The database partitions forming the nodegroup must have been defined in the database (via the db2nodes.cfg file).

If you satisfy the above requirements, you can create a nodegroup with the `create nodegroup` SQL statement. This statement does the following:

- Creates a partitioning map (for more details, see "Partitioning Maps" on page 154).

- Inserts rows in certain system catalog tables. These system catalog tables are SYSCAT.NODEGROUP, SYSCAT.PARTITIONMAPS and SYSCAT.NODEGROUPDEF (see "System Catalog Views Relating to Nodegroups" on page 158).

Let's look at the commands necessary to create the three nodegroups shown in Figure 58 on page 150. The first nodegroup, NG123 consists of three database partitions (1,2 and 3):

```
db2 create nodegroup NG123 on nodes (1,2,3)
```

The second nodegroup, NG1234, contains all of the partitions of the database:

```
db2 create nodegroup NG1234 on all nodes
```

Note that nodegroups NG123 and NG1234 share database partitions 1, 2, and 3.

The third nodegroup, NG3, contains only one database partition:

```
db2 create nodegroup NG3 on node (3)
```

3.4.3 Dropping Nodegroups

Before you can drop a nodegroup from a database, you must have:

- A connection to the database in which the nodegroup is defined
- SYSADM or SYSCTRL authority

You use the DROP NODEGROUP SQL statement to drop a nodegroup from a database. This statement will do the following:

- Delete the partitioning map
- Delete rows from certain system catalog tables

For example, to remove the NG123 nodegroup:

```
db2 drop nodegroup NG123
```

When you drop a nodegroup, all the tables spaces belonging to the nodegroup will also be dropped and therefore all tables in those table spaces.

3.4.4 Displaying Nodegroup Information

To display information about the nodegroups in a database, you should use the LIST NODEGROUPS command. For example, to display the names of the nodegroups in a database, connect to the database and issue the following command:

```
db2 list nodegroups
```

You will receive output similar to the following:

```
NODEGROUP NAME
------------------------------
IBMCATGROUP
IBMDEFAULTGROUP
IBMTEMPGROUP
NG123
NG3
NG1234

  6 record(s) selected.
```

Here, we see six nodegroups; the first three are the system-defined nodegroups (IBMCATGROUP, IBMDEFAULTGROUP and IBMTEMPGROUP), and the last three have been user-defined using the create nodegroup SQL statement.

If you use SHOW DETAIL parameter of the list nodegroups command, three more columns of information are displayed:

```
host1 > db2 list nodegroups show detail

NODEGROUP NAME                 PMAP_ID      NODE_NUMBER    IN_USE
----------------------------   -------   -----------------  ------
IBMCATGROUP                       0                    1       Y
IBMDEFAULTGROUP                   1                    1       Y
IBMDEFAULTGROUP                   1                    2       Y
IBMDEFAULTGROUP                   1                    3       Y
IBMDEFAULTGROUP                   1                    4       Y
NG123                             3                    1       Y
NG123                             3                    2       Y
NG123                             3                    3       Y
NG3                               4                    3       Y
NG1234                            5                    1       Y
NG1234                            5                    2       Y
NG1234                            5                    3       Y
NG1234                            5                    4       Y

13 record(s) selected.
```

These additional three columns are:

- PMAP_ID. This indicates the partitioning map associated with the nodegroup.

- NODE_NUMBER. The database partition number (node number) as defined in the db2nodes.cfg file.

- IN_USE. The status of the database partition.

The output that follows shows that there is one row for each database partition to which the nodegroup belongs. Also notice that IBMTEMPGROUP is not displayed in the output when using the SHOW DETAIL parameter.

You can also query the system catalog tables that hold nodegroup information using the SELECT SQL statement. See "System Catalog Views Relating to Nodegroups" on page 158 for more details.

3.4.5 Partitioning Maps

Partitioning maps form an important part of the process used by the database manager to allocate the rows of a table across the database partitions in a database. To understand why DB2 UDB EEE uses partitioning maps, we must first understand this process.

3.4.5.1 How DB2 UDB EEE Determines Where to Store Rows

DB2 UDB EEE uses a hashing algorithm to assign a given row of a table to a corresponding database partition. When a table is created, a partitioning key is defined for that table. This partitioning key consists of one or many columns. (See "Partitioning Keys" on page 189 for more details.) The database manager uses the value of the partitioning key for a given row as the input for the hashing function. The output of this function is a number between 0 and 4095 which is used as a displacement into the partitioning map. We use the term *index* for this displacement. The partitioning map contains a value at this displacement. This value is the database partition where the row is to be stored. Figure 60 shows an example of this process:

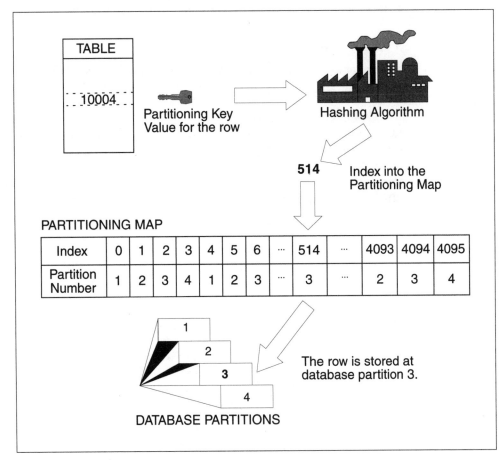

Figure 60. How DB2 EEE Determines where to Store Rows

In order to find out in which database partition a given row of a table is stored, DB2 does the following:

- Suppose a row is to be inserted in a table. We use the partitioning key value of the row (in this example, 10004) as input for the hashing algorithm. This algorithm transforms the partition key value into a number between 0 and 4095 that is the index into the partitioning map.

- The partitioning map contains a value at that index that indicates the database partition number where the row is to be stored.

Now let's consider partitioning maps in more detail.

A partitioning map is a sequential list (or vector) of 4096 database partition numbers. Each partitioning map corresponds to only one nodegroup and is created when the nodegroup is created (or when data is redistributed).

┌─ **Tables in a Nodegroup** ──────────────────────────────────┐

All the tables within a nodegroup use the same partitioning map.

└──┘

Let's look at some examples of partitioning maps and how they relate to nodegroups. Figure 61 shows three examples of partitioning maps. In the first and third examples, the partitioning map consists of a vector of 4096 elements (starting at index 0). We often represent partitioning maps as being formed of two rows. The first row represents the index, which ranges from 0 to 4095. The second row is the value at that index, which is a database partition number.

1. create nodegroup NG123 on nodes (1,2,3)

Index	0	1	2	3	4	5	6	7	...	...	...	4093	4094	4095
Partition Number	1	2	3	1	2	3	1	2	...	...	...	3	1	2

2. create nodegroup NG3 on node (3)

Index	0
Partition Number	3

3. create nodegroup NG1234 on all nodes

Index	0	1	2	3	4	5	6	7	...	...	...	4093	4094	4095
Partition Number	1	2	3	4	1	2	3	4	...	...	...	2	3	4

Figure 61. Partitioning Map Examples

1. In the first example, nodegroup NG123 is created using database partitions 1, 2 and 3; a default partitioning map is created containing only these database partitions.

2. In the second example, a single-partition nodegroup is created. The partition map has only one entry because all the data will be stored in the same database partition. In this example this is database partition 3.

3. In the third example, a nodegroup is created spanning all partitions of the database, database partitions 1,2,3 and 4. The partitioning map associated with the nodegroups will contain all of these database partition numbers.

A default partitioning map is created when a nodegroup is created. The map is stored in the SYSIBM.SYSPARTITIONMAPS system catalog table.

The default partitioning map contains the database partition numbers of the nodegroup assigned in a round-robin fashion as shown in Figure 61. It is also possible to use partitioning maps which do not use this round-robin system:

these maps are known as customized partitioning maps. Sometimes, you may need to generate a customized map before loading data to achieve an even distribution of a table's data across the database partitions used by the table. For more details, see "Loading Data" on page 199.

3.4.5.2 Displaying the Contents of a Partitioning Map

There is a utility, called *db2gmap*, that can extract the partitioning map of a nodegroup from the SYSIBM.SYSPARTITIONMAPS system catalog table.

For example, if you have a nodegroup called NG123 that consists of the database partitions 1,2 and 3 in a database called sample and you want the partitioning map of this nodegroup to be written to a file called NG123map.txt, issue the following command:

```
db2gpmap -d sample -g NG123 -m NG123map.txt
```

Here are the first eight lines of the output file (NG123map.txt) generated from the db2gpmap utility:

```
1 2 3 1 2 3 1 2 3 1 2 3 1 2 3 1 2 3 1 2 3 1 2 3 1 2 3 1 2 3
1 2 3 1 2 3 1 2 3 1 2 3 1 2 3 1 2 3 1 2 3 1 2 3 1 2 3 1 2 3
1 2 3 1 2 3 1 2 3 1 2 3 1 2 3 1 2 3 1 2 3 1 2 3 1 2 3 1 2 3
1 2 3 1 2 3 1 2 3 1 2 3 1 2 3 1 2 3 1 2 3 1 2 3 1 2 3 1 2 3
1 2 3 1 2 3 1 2 3 1 2 3 1 2 3 1 2 3 1 2 3 1 2 3 1 2 3 1 2 3
1 2 3 1 2 3 1 2 3 1 2 3 1 2 3 1 2 3 1 2 3 1 2 3 1 2 3 1 2 3
1 2 3 1 2 3 1 2 3 1 2 3 1 2 3 1 2 3 1 2 3 1 2 3 1 2 3 1 2 3
1 2 3 1 2 3 1 2 3 1 2 3 1 2 3 1 2 3 1 2 3 1 2 3 1 2 3 1 2 3
```

Here we see the default partitioning map for the NG123 nodegroup that spans database partitions 1, 2 and 3. The upper-left corner corresponds to the value at index 0 of the partitioning map. Moving to the right and down line-by-line, you can find the values at each index.

3.4.6 System Catalog Views Relating to Nodegroups

Three system catalog views store information about nodegroups and partitioning maps:

- SYSCAT.NODEGROUPDEF
- SYSCAT.NODEGROUPS
- SYSCAT.PARTITIONMAPS

3.4.6.1 SYSCAT.NODEGROUPDEF View

This view contains a row for each database partition that belongs to the nodegroup. It has the following columns:

- NGNAME: Name of the nodegroup. The name is defined when you create the nodegroup with the `create nodegroup` statement.

- NODENUM: Database partition number defining the database partitions that belong to the nodegroup. Each database partition has a unique database partition number as defined in the db2nodes.cfg file.

- IN_USE: Shows the status of the database partition. It can takes the following values:

  - A: Indicates that the newly added database partition is not in the partitioning map, but the containers for the table spaces in the nodegroup are created. The database partition is added to the partitioning map when a redistribute nodegroup operation is successfully completed.

  - D: Indicates that the database partition will be dropped when a redistribute nodegroup operation is completed.

  - T: Indicates that the newly added database partition is not in the partitioning map, and it was added using the `WITHOUT TABLESPACES` clause. Containers must be specifically added to the table spaces for the nodegroup using the `ALTER TABLESPACE` SQL statement.

  - Y: The database partition is in the partition map.

Here is an example of the contents of the SYSCAT.NODEGROUPDEF view:

```
host1 > db2 "select * from SYSCAT.NODEGROUPDEF"

NGNAME                   NODENUM IN_USE
------------------------ ------- ------
IBMCATGROUP                    1      Y
IBMDEFAULTGROUP                1      Y
IBMDEFAULTGROUP                2      Y
IBMDEFAULTGROUP                3      Y
IBMDEFAULTGROUP                4      Y

 5 record(s) selected.
```

We can see that IBMCATGROUP is defined in database partition 1 and is in use. IBMDEFAULTGROUP is defined in database partitions 1, 2, 3 and 4 and is also in use.

3.4.6.2 SYCAT.NODEGROUPS View

This view contains a row for each nodegroup defined in the database. It has the following columns:

- NGNAME: Name of the nodegroup. The name is defined when you create the nodegroup with the `create nodegroup` statement.

- DEFINER: Authorization ID of the creator of the nodegroup.

- PMAP_ID: Identifier of the partitioning map.

- REBALANCE_PMAP_ID: Identifier of the partitioning map created during redistribution.

- CREATE_TIME: Date and time of the nodegroup creation.

- REMARKS: Comments about the nodegroup.

The following is an example of the contents of the first four columns of this table:

```
host1 > db2 "select NGNAME, DEFINER, PMAP_ID, REBALANCE_PMAP_ID
from SYSCAT.NODEGROUPS"

NGNAME               DEFINER PMAP_ID REBALANCE_PMAP_ID
------------------------------------------------------------
IBMCATGROUP          SYSIBM      0              -1
IBMDEFAULTGROUP      SYSIBM      1              -1
IBMTEMPGROUP         SYSIBM      2              -1

 3 record(s) selected.
```

3.4.6.3 SYSCAT.SYSPARTITIONMAPS View

This view contains a row for each partitioning map created in a database. It has the following columns:

- PMAP_ID: Identifier of the partitioning map.

- PARTITIONMAP: The actual partitioning map stored as a binary large object. This is a vector of 4096 integers for a multiple partition nodegroup. For a single partition nodegroup, there is one entry denoting this one partition number.

3.4.7 Nodegroups Summary

Let's summarize some of the main characteristics of nodegroups:

- A nodegroup is a subset of database partitions.

- A nodegroup is owned by a single database.

- Database partitions of a nodegroup belong to the same database.
- A database may contain both single-partition and multi-partition nodegroups.
- A database partition can be a member of several different nodegroups.
- Three system-defined nodegroups are created by default when the `create database` command is issued: IBMDEFAULTGROUP, IBMTEMPGROUP and IBMCATGROUP.
- Users with SYSADM authority can create nodegroups that span a given set of partitions.
- There is only one partitioning map for each nodegroup (except during redistribution).
- The maximum number of nodegroups in a database is 32768.

3.5 Table Spaces

Table spaces exist in DB2 to provide you with a logical layer between your data and the storage devices. They define where table data is physically stored on disk. All DB2 tables reside in table spaces. You can use different kinds of table spaces to store different kinds of portions of a table, such as the data portion and the index portion. This gives you the ability to control the assignment of database objects to storage devices. For example, you can choose slower disks to store less-used data and faster disks to store indexes or frequently accessed data. You can also specify a particular table space for the system catalog tables, user tables or temporary tables.

Table spaces are created in nodegroups. When you create a table space, you can choose the nodegroup in which the table space will be created. The table space will span all the database partitions where the nodegroup is defined. If you don't specify a nodegroup, the default nodegroup, IBMDEFAULTGROUP, is used. This nodegroup includes all the database partitions in the database.

One table space can only belong to one nodegroup, but one nodegroup can contain more than one table space. In Figure 62, we can see that the relationship between nodegroups and table spaces is one-to-many:

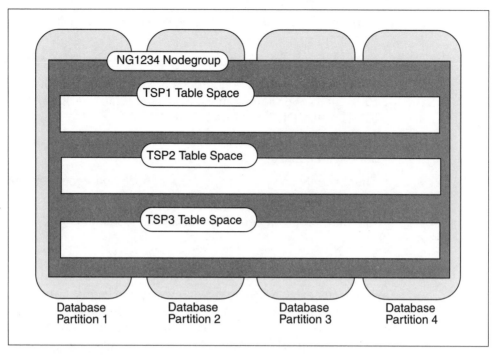

Figure 62. Relationship between Nodegroups and Table Spaces

Nodegroup NG1234 spans four database partitions. Three table spaces TSP1, TSP2 and TSP3 are defined in the nodegroup.

> **Table Space Backup and Recovery**
>
> Backup and recovery operations can be made at the table space level. This allows you to backup or restore table spaces individually, depending on your requirements.

3.5.1 Containers

A container is a generic term used to describe the allocation of physical space.

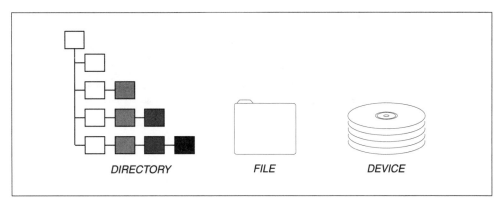

Figure 63. DB2 Containers

As shown is Figure 63, a container can be any of the following:

- Directory
- File
- Device

The type of container depends on the type of table space and the operating system being used. For example, in AIX, a logical volume is used as a device container. In this next section, we will detail the relationship between table spaces and containers.

3.5.2 The Relationship between Table Spaces and Containers

There is a one-to-many relationship between table spaces and containers. Multiple containers may be defined for a single table space. However, a container can only be assigned to one table space. Figure 64 shows this one-to-many relationship.

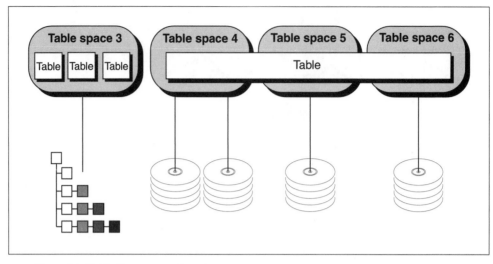

Figure 64. Table Spaces and Containers.

Table space 3 has only one container assigned to it, a directory. Table space 4 has two containers assigned to it. The containers for table space 4, table space 5 and table space 6 are devices. A mixture of containers is possible within a database. You may also mix container types and sizes within a table space, though it is not recommended for performance reasons. For example, if you use a mixture of fast and slow disks as the containers of a single table space, performance will be constrained by the slower disks. Notice that a table can use multiple table spaces (these can only be DMS table spaces). In Figure 64, one table uses table space 4, table space 5 and table space 6 to store its data.

3.5.3 Types of Tables Spaces

DB2 supports two kinds of table spaces:

- System Managed Storage (SMS) table spaces
- Database Managed Storage (DMS) table spaces

Both types of table spaces may be used in the same database. SMS table spaces are called System Managed because the Database Manager uses the operating system's mechanism to manage the files it requires.

3.5.3.1 SMS Table Spaces

System Managed Storage table spaces are based on the storage model where storage is acquired as needed. The space for the data of the tables created within an SMS table space is managed by the operating system.

SMS table spaces have the following characteristics:

- An SMS table space can only use directory containers. It cannot use file or raw containers.

- A container in an SMS table space does not pre-allocate its storage. A small amount of space is allocated during table space creation.

- Containers cannot be dynamically added to an SMS table space after the table space is created.

- The total number of containers in an SMS table space must be specified when creating the table space.

3.5.3.2 DMS Table Spaces

Database Managed Storage (DMS) table spaces are characterized by table spaces that are built on pre-allocated portions of storage. These areas of storage, known as containers, can be either raw devices or files. The space for the data of the tables created within a DMS table space container is managed by the database manager.

The database manager controls the storage space and allocates all the space when the container is created. When working with DMS table space containers, the following statements apply:

- If the container is a file, it is created when the table space is created and dropped when the table space is dropped.

- If the container is a device, such as a logical volume in AIX, the logical volume must exist before creating the table space. After dropping the table space, the device still exists and must be removed.

- Disk storage is pre-allocated to a container when a container is created.

- Containers can be added to a DMS table space after the table space is created.

3.5.3.3 Choosing the Type of a Table Space

When you create a table space, you have to choose the table space type (SMS or DMS), so it is important to understand the benefits and restrictions of the two types.

Let's first take a look at the benefits of using DMS table spaces:

- You can distribute a table across several table spaces for performance:

  One of the biggest advantages of using DMS table spaces, compared to SMS table spaces, is the ability to span a table over multiple table spaces. When creating a table in a DMS table space, you can decide to place certain table objects in different table spaces. DMS table spaces give you the flexibility to store data, indexes, and long/large object data in separate table spaces. All the table spaces used by the table are defined when the table is created.

For example, this allows you to store the data and indexes of a table on separate disks to improve performance. You can also control the placement of less frequently accessed items, like large objects (LOBs). This leads to more flexibility in administration tasks such as backup and restore operations. For example, if you have a certain amount of static data, you can place this data in a separate table space, and back it up much less frequently than the rest of the database.

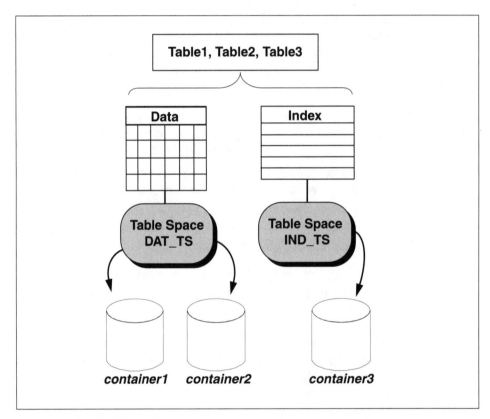

Figure 65. DMS Table Spaces

Figure 65 shows an example of three tables using two DMS table spaces. The regular table data is placed in the table space DAT_TS. Indexes for these tables are placed in the table space IND_TS. We can see from Figure 65 that the table space DAT_TS is created with two containers.

These containers do not have to be on separate disks. However, for performance reasons, it is better to assign the containers to different physical devices if you can.

- DMS table spaces can be expanded by adding new containers while the table space is being used.

- There may be performance benefits in using DMS table spaces because DB2 has more knowledge of the placement of the data. In addition, if you are using raw device containers, you can avoid the overhead of using the operating system's file system.

- When you create a DMS table space, you specify the size of the containers and the necessary disk space is pre-allocated. After this, the database manager does not have to compete with other applications for this disk space.

SMS tables spaces may be more suitable in the following cases:

- You have very small tables where even the smallest possible extent size (2 pages) would involve wasting space. If your database is going to grow a lot, use DMS table spaces.

- You are doing tests where the optimum performance is not required.

- You have migrated from a DB2 PE for AIX Version 1 database.

- To store temporary data.

3.5.4 Table Spaces Created by Default

When a database is created, three table spaces are created by default. If you do not specify any table space parameters with the db2 CREATE DATABASE command, the database manager will create these three SMS table spaces:

- SYSCATSPACE

  The system catalog tables are created in this table space when a database is created. This table space is defined in the IBMCATGROUP nodegroup, which includes only one database partition.

- USERSPACE1

  This is the table space used when you do not specify any table spaces when creating a table. This table space is defined in the IBMDEFAULTGROUP nodegroup, which includes all the database partitions in the database.

- TEMPSPACE1

This is used for temporary data. You must always have at least one temporary table space defined in your database. Even though it is not recommended, you can have more than one temporary table space (only one is used at the same time). The only reason for having two temporary table spaces is that when you want to change your temporary table space definition, you create the new temporary table space and then drop the original one. The TEMPSPACE1 table space is defined in the IBMTEMPGROUP nodegroup, which includes all the database partitions in the database.

Figure 66 shows the table spaces created by default when you create a database:

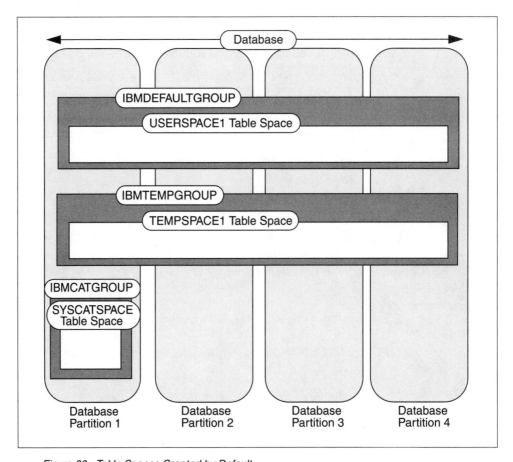

Figure 66. Table Spaces Created by Default

3.5.5 Creating Table Spaces

You can use the `CREATE TABLESPACE` SQL statement or the Control Center to create a table space. (You can also create table spaces using the `create database` command.)

Before you create a table space, you must:

- Be connected to the database (unless also creating the database)
- Have SYSADM or SYSCRTL authority

The `CREATE TABLESPACE` SQL statement creates a new table space within the database, assigns containers to the table space, and records the table space definition and attributes in the system catalog tables.

Figure 67 shows part of the syntax for the `CREATE TABLESPACE` SQL statement:

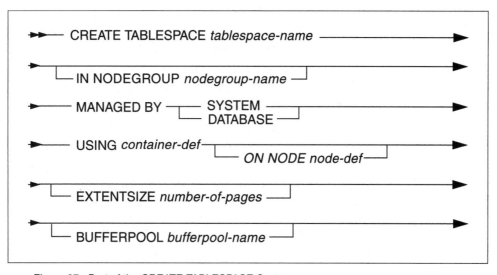

Figure 67. Part of the CREATE TABLESPACE Syntax

When you create a table space, you can specify:

- The nodegroup where the table space is to be created. The table space will be created in all of the database partitions that the nodegroup spans.

This is specified using the IN NODEGROUP *nodegroup-name* clause in the CREATE TABLESPACE statement.

- The type of table space. As explained before there are two types:

  - System Managed Storage (SMS) table spaces: The MANAGED BY SYSTEM clause is used to specify a SMS table space.

  - Database Managed Storage (DMS) table spaces: The MANAGED BY DATABASE clause is used to specify a DMS table space.

- The containers for each database partition with their description (USING *container-def* in Figure 67):

  - For SMS table spaces: You specify the containers using the clause USING (*'container-string'*,...) that identifies one or more containers that will belong to the table space and in which the table space's data will be stored. The *container-string* is the path to the directory that will be the container for the SMS table space.The name of this path cannot exceed 240 bytes in length. The only type of container possible for SMS table spaces is directories. The directories will be created if they do not exist.

  - For DMS table spaces: You have two choices for the containers:

    - FILE container: You use the clause USING (FILE *'container-string' number-of-pages*,...).

    - DEVICE container: You use the clause USING (DEVICE *'container-string' number-of-pages*,...).

    The *container-string* is the path to the FILE or DEVICE that will be the container for the DMS table space. The *number-of-pages* is the size in 4KB pages that will be pre-allocated for the container.

    A mixture of FILE and DEVICE containers can be specified. The *container-string* cannot exceed 254 bytes in length.

- The database partition(s) where the containers are to be created. You specify this using the ON NODE *node-def* clause. The reason for this clause is that you may want to have different container definitions in each or some of the database partitions defined for the nodegroup. See the example "Creating an SMS Table Space in a MDP Configuration" on page 171 for more details.

  If the ON NODE clause is not used in the CREATE TABLESPACE statement, each database partition in a DMS table space will have the same description, name and size of containers.

- The extent size. For table spaces with more than one container, the extent size is a value that specifies how many pages (4 KB) are written to a container before writing to another container. The `EXTENTSIZE` *number-of-pages* clause is used to specify this value.

- The buffer pool to use for the table space. The `BUFFERPOOL` *bufferpool-name* clause is used to specify a buffer pool for the table space (see "Buffer Pools" on page 178 for more information).

Let's look at some examples of creating table spaces for SDP (single database partition per host) and MDP (multiple database partitions per host) configurations.

3.5.5.1 Creating an SMS Table Space in a SDP Configuration

Let's create an SMS table space named TSP1 using a directory container /db/cont1. This directory will be created in all of the database partitions. Because this is an SDP configuration, we can use the same container name in each database partition. As the `IN NODEGROUP` parameter is not used, the table space will be created in the IBMDEFAULTGROUP nodegroup.

```
host1 > db2 "create tablespace TSP1 managed by system
using ('/db/cont1')"
DB20000I The SQL command completed successfully.
```

3.5.5.2 Creating an SMS Table Space in a MDP Configuration

This is an example of creating an SMS table space in an MDP configuration.

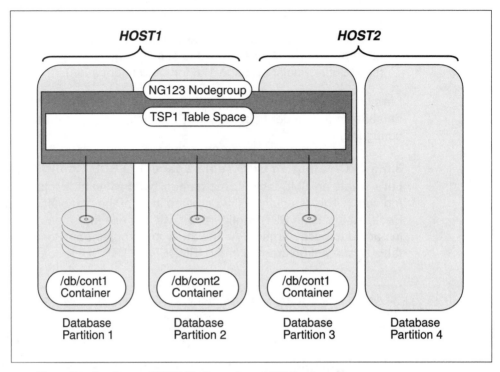

Figure 68. Creating an SMS Table Space in an MDP Configuration

In Figure 68, nodegroup NG123 spans three database partitions (1, 2 and 3) and database partition 1 and 2 are on the same host.

In this example, we must use different container names in database partitions 1 and 2. This is because the two database partitions belong to the same host (host1) and share the same disks. The statement to create the TSP1 table space is as follows:

```
host1 > db2 "create tablespace TSP1 managed by system
using ('/db/cont1') on node (1,3)
using ('/db/cont2') on node (2)"
DB20000I The SQL command completed successfully.
```

Note the ON NODE clause of the CREATE TABLESPACE statement is used to assign a specific container name to each database partition in an MDP configuration.

3.5.5.3 Creating a DMS Table Space in an SDP Configuration

We will look at two examples, one using file containers and the other using device containers.

File Containers

In the first example, a DMS table space is created in the NG1234 nodegroup. In each database partition, two file containers of 80 MB (20000 4KB pages) each called /db/file1 and /db/file2 are created.

```
host1 > db2 "create tablespace TSP1 in nodegroup NG1234
managed by database
using (file '/db/file1' 20000,
file '/db/file2' 20000)"
DB20000I The SQL command completed successfully.
```

Device Containers

In the second example, a DMS table space is created in the NG1234 nodegroup with two containers for each database partition. "Raw" device containers (AIX logical volumes) are used. We define two device containers of 80 MB in each database partition. The logical volumes must be created in each database partition before creating the table space.

```
host1 > db2 "create tablespace TSP1 in nodegroup NG1234
managed by database
using (device '/dev/rlv1' 20000,
device '/dev/rlv2' 20000)"

DB20000I The SQL command completed successfully.
```

Raw (Device) Containers

Logical volumes to be used for device containers must be created before executing the CREATE TABLESPACE SQL statement.

3.5.5.4 Creating a DMS Table Space in an MDP Configuration

Figure 69 shows an example of an MDP (multiple database partitions per host) configuration.

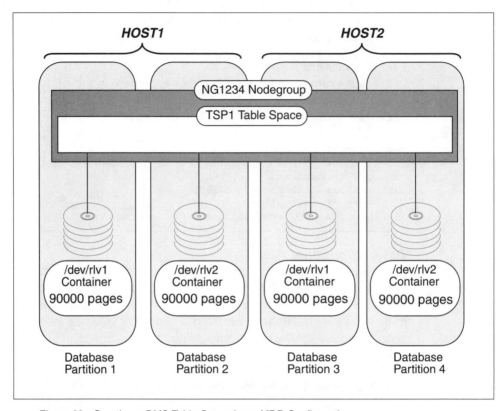

Figure 69. Creating a DMS Table Space in an MDP Configuration

On a two-host system, there is a four database partition nodegroup, NG1234. A table space, TSP1, is created in this nodegroup. The same container name is used (/dev/rlv1) on database partitions 1 and 3, and another name on database partitions 2 and 4 (/dev/rlv2). We cannot use the same container name for all the database partitions, as partitions which co-exist on the same host share the same disks.

Note that the containers have the same size on all four database partitions. In most scenarios, all the containers in a table space should be created with the same size.

When using logical volumes for a container, the container size should be set to size of the logical volume. (This is also true in an SDP environment.) If the size of the container is smaller than the logical volume, the remaining space will be wasted. The containers will be approximately 350 MB each, that is 90000 4KB pages, in each database partition. Since a nodegroup was not specified, IBMDEFAULTGROUP is used.

> **Defining Containers in an MDP Configuration**
>
> In an MDP configuration, table space containers for database partitions that are on the same host must have different names. This is because all the database partitions on the same host share the same physical resources. If you try to give the same name to containers in different database partitions on the same host, the CREATE TABLESPACE statement will fail.

The statement to create the TSP1 table space is as follows:

```
host1 > db2 "create tablespace TSP1 managed by database
using (device '/dev/rlv1' 90000) on node (1,3)
using (device '/dev/rlv2' 90000) on node (2,4)"
DB20000I The SQL command completed successfully.
```

3.5.6 Querying Tables Space and Container Definitions

There are two commands you can use to get information about your table spaces and containers:

- `list tablespaces`

This command will list the tablespace-id, name, type (SMS or DMS), type of contents (data/index, temporary or long) and the state of all the defined table spaces.

- `list tablespace containers for tablespace-id`

This command will list the container-id, name and type of all the containers for table space identified by the tablespace-id.

In DB2 UDB EEE, when you use the `list tablespaces` and `list tablespace containers` commands, only the table spaces and containers defined on the current database partition are listed. You should use `db2_all` to see information for all database partitions.

In an MDP configuration, if you need to get information at one particular database partition, follow these steps:

- End any connection background process by issuing the `db2 terminate` command.
- Set the `DB2NODE` registry variable to the database partition number.
- Connect to the database where the table spaces belongs.

> **Terminating Background Sessions**
>
> It is very important to terminate any existing DB2 sessions using the `db2 terminate` command before setting `DB2NODE`. Otherwise, the changes to `DB2NODE` will not take effect.

The following output is an example of the `list tablespaces` command. Notice that only the table spaces for the database partition referenced by the value of `DB2NODE` are listed. (Not all table spaces are shown).

```
host1 > db2 terminate
DB20000I The TERMINATE command completed successfully.
host1 > db2set DB2NODE=1
host1 > db2 connect to SAMPLE

   Database Connection Information

Database product        = DB2/6000 5.0.0
SQL authorization ID    = USER1
Local database alias    = SAMPLE

host1 > db2 list tablespaces

          Tablespaces for Current Database

Tablespace ID                           = 0
Name                                    = SYSCATSPACE
Type                                    = System managed space
Contents                                = Any data
State                                   = 0x0000
  Detailed explanation:
    Normal


.............................

DB21011I In a partitioned database server environment, only the table
spaces on the current node are listed.
```

> **Using DB2NODE**
>
> The value of DB2NODE determines the database partition number to be used when displaying table space information.

If you want to list the table spaces for all the database partitions, you should use the `db2_all` command. In the example that follows, there are two database partitions (1 and 2). A connection is made in all of the database partitions, and a `list tablespaces` command is issued. First, DB2 will list the table spaces for the SAMPLE database in database partition 1 and then the table spaces for database partition 2 are shown. (Not all table spaces are shown).

```
host1 > db2_all "db2 connect to SAMPLE; db2 list tablespaces"

rah: host1

   Database Connection Information

 Database product      = DB2/6000 5.0.0
 SQL authorization ID  = USER1
 Local database alias  = SAMPLE

         Tablespaces for Current Database

 Tablespace ID                        = 0
 Name                                 = SYSCATSPACE
 Type                                 = System managed space
 Contents                             = Any data
 State                                = 0x0000
   Detailed explanation:
     Normal

 ...........................

 DB21011I In a partitioned database server environment, only the table spaces
 on the current node are listed.

rah: host2

   Database Connection Information

 Database product      = DB2/6000 5.0.0
 SQL authorization ID  = USER1
 Local database alias  = SAMPLE

 Tablespaces for Current Database

 Tablespace ID                        = 1
 Name                                 = TEMPSPACE1
 Type                                 = System managed space
 Contents                             = Temporary data
 State                                = 0x0000
   Detailed explanation:
     Normal

 ...........................

 DB21011I In a partitioned database server environment, only the table spaces
 on the current node are listed.
```

3.5.6.1 System Catalog Tables Related to Table Spaces

SYSCAT.TABLESPACES is a view that contains a row for each table space defined in the database.

These are the columns in this view:

- TBSPACE: The name of the table space.
- DEFINER: ID of the table space definer.

- CREATE_TIME: Creation time.
- TBSPACEID: ID for the table space.
- TBSPACETYPE: Indicates the table space type. It can have two values:
  - S: for SMS table spaces
  - D: For DMS table spaces
- DATATYPE: Indicates the type of the data contained in the table space. It can have three values
  - A: all types
  - L: long data
  - T: temporary data
- EXTENTSIZE: Size of extent in 4 KB pages.
- PREFETCHSIZE: Number of pages to read for prefetch.
- OVERHEAD: Controller overhead and disk seek and latency time in milliseconds.
- TRANSFERRATE: Time to read one page into the buffer.
- PAGESIZE: Size in bytes of pages in table space.
- NGNAME: Name of the nodegroup where the table space belongs.
- BUFFERPOOLID: ID of the buffer pool assigned to the table space.
- REMARKS: Any comments.

There is another view, SYSCAT.TABLES (containing one row for each table) which contains four columns that indicate the table space where the table belongs. This columns are:

- TBSPACEID: ID of the primary table space for that table.
- TBSPACE: Name of the primary table space.
- INDEX_TBSPACE: Name of the index table space.
- LONG_TBSPACE: Name of the long table space.

3.5.7 Buffer Pools

A buffer pool is an area of memory used as a cache for the database manager. DB2 UDB EEE supports multiple buffer pools. Each buffer pool can have one or many table spaces assigned to it, but one table space can only be associated with one buffer pool.

Let's first look at how to manage buffer pools. Advice is given on how to use buffer pools to improve performance in "Performance Improvements Using Multiple Buffer Pools" on page 184.

All table spaces are assigned to a buffer pool. This assignment can be made with the `create tablespace` or `alter tablespace` SQL statements or via the Control Center. A buffer pool must exist in order to be referenced in the `create tablespace` or `alter tablespace` statements.

For example, if you want to create the table space TSP1 in the nodegroup NG1234 and specify that this table space will use the BP1 bufferpool:

```
host1 > db2 "create tablespace TSP1 in nodegroup NG1234
managed by system using ('/db/cont1')
bufferpool BP1"
DB20000I The SQL command completed successfully.
```

A table space can have its association with its buffer pool changed to a different buffer pool by using the `alter tablespace` statement. This change does not become effective until the next first connect or activate against this database. For example, if you want table space TSP1 to use buffer pool BP2, use the following:

```
host1 > db2 alter tablespace TSP1 bufferpool BP2
DB20000I The SQL command completed successfully.
```

If during the creation of a table space a buffer pool is not specified, then the default buffer pool IBMDEFAULTBP is used. The default buffer pool definition is specified for each database partition, with the capability to override the size on specific database partitions. During database creation, the three system-defined table spaces that are created (SYSCATSPACE, USERSPACE1 and TEMPSPACE1) are assigned to the IBMDEFAULTBP buffer pool.

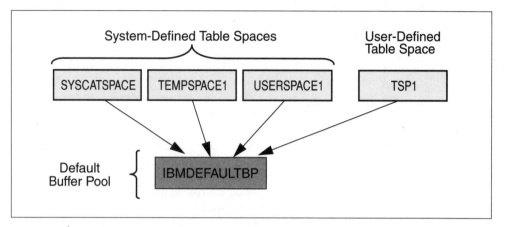

Figure 70. IBMDEFAULTBP Buffer Pool

Figure 70 shows that the three system-defined table spaces are associated with the default buffer pool, IBMDEFAULTBP. There is also a user-defined table space, called TSP1, that is also using the default buffer pool because when creating TSP1, no buffer pool was specified. This example also illustrates that the relationship between buffer pools and table spaces is one-to-many.

During the creation of a table space, you can specify that a user-defined buffer pool be used instead of the default IBMDEFAULTBP.

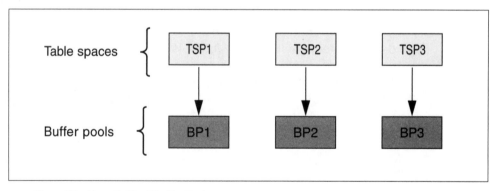

Figure 71. User-Defined Buffer Pools

Figure 71 shows three user-defined buffer pools (BP1, BP2 and BP3) each associated with a table space (TSP1, TSP2 and TSP3).

When you create a buffer pool, it is defined on all database partitions unless one or more nodegroups are specified. If nodegroups are specified, the buffer pool will only be created on the database partitions that are in those nodegroups.

Figure 72 shows buffer pool BP2 which has been created for nodegroup NG123:

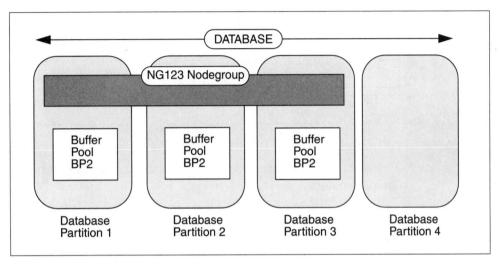

Figure 72. Bufferpool Defined for Nodegroup

If a table space is dropped, the buffer pool to which it was assigned remains as an object within the database. This is true even if no table spaces are now assigned to this buffer pool. The memory remains allocated for the buffer pool. You must explicitly drop the buffer pool to free up this memory.

3.5.7.1 Creating Buffer Pools

You can create a buffer pool using the CREATE BUFFERPOOL SQL statement. There are several decisions you have to make when creating a buffer pool, for example in which nodegroup(s) you want the buffer pool to be created.

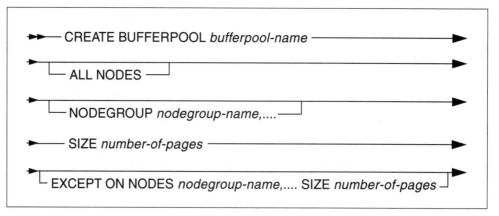

Figure 73. Part of the CREATE BUFFERPOOL Syntax

Figure 73 shows a part of the CREATE BUFFERPOOL SQL statement. Some of the parameters are:

- **ALL NODES**: If you use this clause, the buffer pool will be created on all database partitions in the database, and any table space can use the buffer pool.

- **NODEGROUP** *nodegroup_name,...*: Identifies the nodegroup or nodegroups to which the buffer pool definition is applicable. If this is specified, this buffer pool will only be created on partitions in these nodegroups.

- **SIZE**: Specifies the number of 4 KB pages for the buffer pool.

- **EXCEPT ON NODES**: Specifies the database partitions for which the size of the buffer pool will be different than the default. If this clause is not specified, then all partitions will have the same size buffer pool.

Examples of Creating Buffer Pools

Let's look at some examples of creating buffer pools. In the first example buffer pool BP1 is defined in all of the database partitions of the database. Each database partition is 4 MB (1000 4KB pages).

```
host1 > db2 create bufferpool BP1 all nodes size 1000
DB20000I The SQL command completed successfully.
```

The next example shows buffer pool BP2 associated only with nodegroup NG123. The buffer pool will be created in all of the database partitions where the NG123 nodegroup is defined.

```
host1 > db2 create bufferpool BP2 nodegroup NG123 size 1000
DB20000I The SQL command completed successfully.
```

In this example, buffer pool BP3 is associated with nodegroups NG2 and NG3:

```
host1 > db2 create bufferpool BP3 nodegroup NG2, NG3 size 1000
DB20000I The SQL command completed successfully.
```

If you create a buffer pool for a nodegroup, then only the tables spaces in that nodegroup can use the buffer pool. For example, the BP2 bufferpool is created for use with nodegroup NG123. If we try to create a table space TSP2 in the NG2 nodegroup and specify the BP2 buffer pool, we will receive an error because the NG2 nodegroup is not defined for the BP2 buffer pool.

```
host1 > db2 create bufferpool BP2 nodegroup NG123 size 1000
DB20000I The SQL command completed successfully.

host1 > db2 "create tablespace TSP2 in NG2 managed by system
using ('/db/cont1') bufferpool BP2"

DB21034E The command was processed as an SQL statement because
it was not a valid Command Line Processor command. During SQL
processing it returned: SQL1761N The nodegroup "NG2" is not
defined for the buffer pool "BP2". SQLSTATE=42735
```

3.5.7.2 Catalog Views Related to Buffer Pools

There are two catalog views related to buffer pools. You can query these views in order to get information about the buffer pools of a database. They are:

- SYSCAT.BUFFERPOOLS: This view contains a row for every buffer pool. The columns defined in this view are:
  - BPNAME. The name of the buffer pool.
  - BUFFERPOOLID. The identifier of the buffer pool.
  - NPAGES. Contains the number of pages in the buffer pool
  - PAGESIZE. The page size for this buffer pool
  - ESTORE. This is a flag with settings Y or N as to whether this buffer pool can use extended storage

- SYSCAT.BUFFERPOOLNODES: This view contains a row for each database partition in the nodegroup where the size of the buffer pool is different from the size given by the PAGESIZE in SYSCAT.BUFFERPOOLS.

There is a column in the SYSCAT.TABLESPACES catalog view called BUFFERPOOLID. This is the identifier of the buffer pool assigned to the table space. A value of 1 in the BUFFERPOOLID denotes the default buffer pool, IBMDEFAULTBP.

3.5.7.3 Performance Improvements Using Multiple Buffer Pools

The use of multiple buffer pools can lead to performance improvements in your system. Here are some actions you can take in order to exploit multiple buffer pools:

- Allocate separate buffer pools for tables and indexes.

  In an environment such as OLTP, where a number of key tables and indexes can be identified, the performance of the application may benefit from assigning the data portion of a table and the index portion of certain tables to different buffer pools. It may then be possible, for example, to provide enough space in the index buffer pool to have a vital index permanently in memory once it has been accessed. Since this is the only object in the database assigned to this area of memory, it will not be flushed out of memory by other application activity.

- Isolate memory for important transaction tables.

  If the application performance in your environment is heavily dependent on the use of one or more key tables, then these tables can be defined in table spaces that are linked to their own exclusive buffer pool. This will provide an area of memory exclusively dedicated to the processing of objects defined within the table space.

- Limit temporary table spaces to prevent ad-hoc queries affecting more critical applications.

  A large ad-hoc query may typically require large temporary work tables for sorting during its processing. This can result in the flushing from the buffer pool of repeatedly used memory pages. By assigning temporary table spaces to their own buffer pools, you can prevent this happening. By isolating the temporary table space from memory used by tables critical to OLTP-type applications, the impact of such ad-hoc activities on the more predictable application activities can be reduced.

- Limit bufferpools on large tables with random access patterns.

In an environment where random access patterns occur, such as a data warehousing application, the benefits of defining a large table to its own buffer pool will be minimal. This is because the likelihood of the buffer pool containing information for reuse without disk I/O are low. In this type of scenario, a smaller buffer pool should be assigned to reduce the impact on other more predictable system activity and conserve memory for other performance gains.

3.6 Tables

A table consists of data logically arranged in columns and rows. Users access the data by referring to its content instead of its location or organization in storage.

As we discussed early in this chapter, nodegroups are created within a database; table spaces are created within nodegroups, and when tables are created, you can specify which table spaces the table will use. The rows of a table are distributed across the database partitions based on the nodegroup's partitioning map via a hashing algorithm (see "Partitioning Maps" on page 154 for details).

Table Rows

Each row of a table is placed on a single database partition.

In DB2 UDB EEE, a table spans the database partitions in its nodegroup. A table can not span more than one nodegroup, but multiple tables can exist in one nodegroup. A DB2 table can contain up to 500 columns, any number of rows, and up to 64 GB of data times the number of database partitions where the table is defined.

Let's look at the relationship between nodegroups, table spaces and tables.

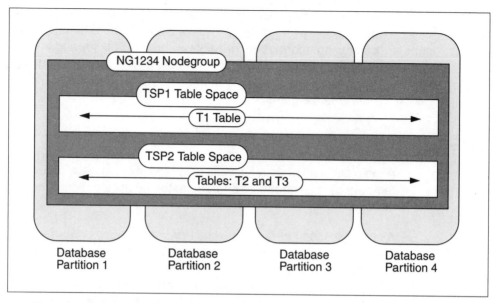

Figure 74. Tables, Table Spaces and Nodegroups

Figure 74 shows that tables T2 and T3 use table space TSP2. Table space TSP2 exists within the NG1234 nodegroup. The TSP1 and TSP2 tables spaces both span all four database partitions. Table T1 is also in the NG1234 nodegroup, but uses the TSP1 table space.

3.6.1 Types of Tables

There are two types of tables:

- System Catalog Tables
- User Tables

3.6.1.1 System Catalog Tables

These are special tables used by DB2 which contain information about all objects within the database (tables, views, indexes, packages and so on) and security information about the type of access users have to these objects.

These tables are updated during the operation of a database, for example when a index is created. You cannot explicitly create or drop these tables, but you can query and view their content. These tables use the SYSCATSPACE table space that belongs to the IBMCATGROUP nodegroup.

The catalog tables have the schema SYSIBM, but it is not recommended to access these tables directly. Instead, you should use specially defined views. There are two kinds of these views:

- A set of read-only views for the system catalog tables created in the SYSCAT schema.
- A set of updateable catalog views created in the SYSSTAT schema. These updateable views allow you to update certain statistical information to investigate the performance of a hypothetical database, or to update statistics without using the RUNSTATS utility. For example, you can make DB2 believe that you have a huge table by updating the *card* column in the SYSSTAT.TABLES view to a high value.

The following table lists all the read-only catalog views:

Table 2. Read-Only System Catalog Views

System Catalog Views	Description
SYSCAT.DBAUTH	Database authorities
SYSCAT.BUFFERPOOLS	Buffer pool configuration for nodegroup
SYSCAT.BUFFERPOOLNODES	Buffer pool size on host
SYSCAT.CHECKS	Check constraints
SYSCAT.DBAUTH	Database authorities
SYSCAT.BUFFERPOOLS	Buffer pool configuration for nodegroup
SYSCAT.BUFFERPOOLNODES	Buffer pool size on host
SYSCAT.CHECKS	Check constraints
SYSCAT.COLAUTH	Column privileges
SYSCAT.COLUMNS	Columns
SYSCAT.COLCHECKS	Columns referenced by check constraints
SYSCAT.KEYCOLUSE	Columns used in keys
SYSCAT.CONSTDEP	Constraint dependencies
SYSCAT.DATATYPES	Data types
SYSCAT.EVENTMONITORS	Event monitor definitions
SYSCAT.EVENTS	Events currently monitored
SYSCAT.FUNCPARMS	Function parameters

System Catalog Views	Description
SYSCAT.INDEXAUTH	Index privileges
SYSCAT.INDEXES	Indexes
SYSCAT.COLDIST	Detailed column statistics
SYSCAT.NODEGROUPS	Nodegroup definitions
SYSCAT.NODEGROUPDEF	Nodegroup hosts
SYSCAT.PARTITIONMAPS	Partitioning maps
SYSCAT.PACKAGEDEP	Package dependencies
SYSCAT.PACKAGEAUTH	Package privileges
SYSCAT.PROCEDURES	Stored procedures
SYSCAT.PROCPARMS	Procedure parameters
SYSCAT.REFERENCES	Referential constraints
SYSCAT.SCHEMAAUTH	Schema privileges
SYSCAT.SCHEMATA	Schemas
SYSCAT.STATEMENTS	Statements in packages
SYSCAT.TABCONST	Table constraints
SYSCAT.TABAUTH	Table privileges
SYSCAT.TABLESPACES	Table spaces
SYSCAT.TRIGDEP	Trigger dependencies
SYSCAT.FUNCTIONS	User-defined functions
SYSCAT.VIEWDEP	View dependencies
SYSCAT.TABLES	Tables
SYSCAT.VIEWS	Views

There are five updateable system catalog views:

Table 3. Updateable System Catalog Views

System Catalog Views	Description
SYSSTAT.COLUMNS	Columns
SYSSTAT.INDEXES	Indexes

System Catalog Views	Description
SYSSTAT.COLDIST	Detailed column statistics
SYSSTAT.TABLES	Tables
SYSSTAT.FUNCTIONS	User-defined functions

Initially, the system catalog views are accessible by all users. After your database has been created, you may wish to limit the access to the system catalog views.

3.6.1.2 User Tables

User tables are the tables created by users (not DB2) with the `create table` SQL statement (see "Creating Tables" on page 192 for more details).

3.6.2 Partitioning Keys

In a DB2 UDB EEE database, the data in each table is distributed among the database partitions. One of the elements that determines how data is allocated among the database partitions is called the *partitioning key*. The partitioning key for a specific table is formed by a subset of the columns of that table.

The partitioning key is defined during the creation of the table. For tables in multi-partition nodegroups, it cannot be changed later. If no partitioning key is specified, the first column that is not a long field is used.

Long Field Columns and Partitioning Keys

Tables containing only long fields cannot have partitioning keys and can only be placed into single-partition nodegroups.

3.6.2.1 Choosing a Partitioning Key

There are some considerations that should be reviewed when choosing a partitioning key for a table:

- Include frequently used join columns.
- Use the smallest number of columns possible.
- The column(s) should have a high proportion of different values.
- Integer columns are more efficient than character columns which are more efficient than decimal.
- Long fields cannot be part of the partitioning key.

• The primary key or a unique index must include the partitioning key.

3.6.2.2 Collocated Tables

Often, in a database, you have tables that are frequently joined. In an environment where the database is physically divided among database partitions, it is preferable to avoid sending data between the hosts to satisfy these joins. This can be achieved by exploiting *table collocation*. Collocation between two joining tables means having the matching rows of the two tables always in the same database partitions. Figure 75 shows an example where tables T1 and T2 are collocated. A join made between these two tables is satisfied in such a way that no row has to be sent from one database partition to another.

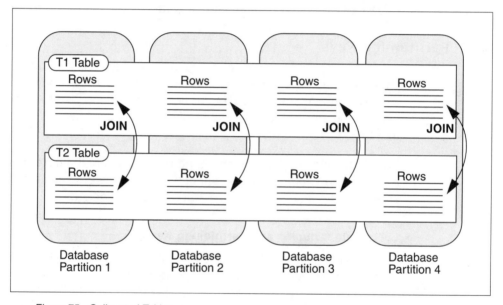

Figure 75. Collocated Tables

Two tables are collocated when they satisfy all of the following conditions:

• For tables in multi-partition nodegroups:

  • The two tables must be in the same nodegroup

• For tables in single-partition nodegroups:

  • The tables can be in different nodegroups, but these nodegroups must include the same (single) database partition.

• The nodegroups of both tables must have the same partitioning map.

• The partitioning key from both tables have the same number of columns.

- Corresponding partitioning key columns must be partition compatible (the same or similar base data type).

A collocated join will occur if:

- Two collocated tables join using all of the columns in the partitioning key.

If two tables join via a collocated join then the query can be performed much more efficiently compared to a join which sends data between the database partitions. For more details about joins in a partitioned database, see "DB2 UDB EEE Join Strategies" on page 335.

3.6.2.3 Changing the Partitioning Key

You can only change the partitioning key of tables residing in single-partition nodegroups. This is done in two steps:

- Drop the existing partitioning key using the **ALTER TABLE** SQL statement.
- Create a new one using the **ALTER TABLE** SQL statement again.

The following SQL statement drops the partitioning key PART_KEY from the DEPARTMENT table:

```
host1 > db2 alter table DEPARTMENT drop partitioning key
DB20000I The SQL command completed successfully.
```

Then you may define a new partitioning key:

```
host1 > db2 "alter table DEPARTMENT add partitioning key
(LASTNAME) using hashing"
DB20000I The SQL command completed successfully.
```

For more information, see the `alter table` statement in the SQL Reference manual.

Adding or Dropping Partitioning Key

You cannot add or drop the partitioning key of a table in a multi-partition nodegroup.

If you try to drop a partitioning key of a table created in a multi-partition nodegroup, an error is returned:

```
host1 > db2 alter table EMPLOYEE drop partitioning key

DB21034E The command was processed as an SQL statement because
it was not a valid Command Line Processor command. During SQL
processing it returned:

SQL0264N Partitioning key cannot be added or dropped because
table resides in a table space defined on the multi-node
nodegroup "IBMDEFAULTGROUP".SQLSTATE=55037
```

The only way to change the partitioning key of a table in a multi-partition
database nodegroup is to export all of the data, drop the table, redefine the
partitioning key, and then import (or load) all of the data. This method is very
time-consuming for large databases; it is therefore essential that you choose
the appropriate partitioning key for each table before loading data into large
databases.

3.6.3 Creating Tables

The CREATE TABLE SQL statement is used to define a table. Before you
create a table, you must accomplish the following:

- Be connected to the database where the table is going to reside

- Have any of the following authorities:

  - SYSADM authority

  - DBADM authority

  - CREATETAB authority and either IMPLICIT_SCHEMA authority or
    CREATEIN privilege

During the creation of the table, the user can:

- Choose a table space for the table's regular data, its indexes and long
  data. These table spaces must all belong to the same nodegroup. The
  nodegroup associates the table with a partitioning map. If you don't
  specify a nodegroup then the IBMDEFAULTGROUP nodegroup is used.

- Choose the partitioning key. The partitioning key is hashed to find an index
  into the partitioning map. The partitioning map entry for the index provides
  the partition number for the hashed row. If you don't specify a partitioning
  key a default one is chosen.

The table definition must include the table name and the names and
attributes of its columns. The definition may include other attributes of the
table, such as which table space should be used for its regular data, indexes

and long columns data. This information is specified when the table is created and can not be changed at a later time.

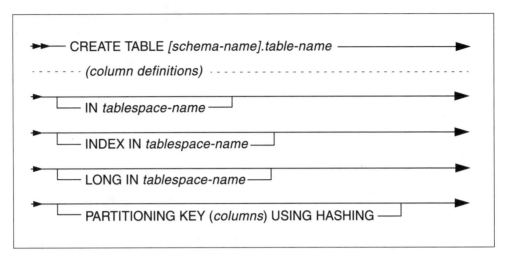

Figure 76. Part of the CREATE TABLE Syntax

Figure 76 shows part of the create table syntax. If no schema name is supplied with the table name, the authorization ID of the user is used as the schema name. The table and column names may be up to 18 characters in length.

You can separate regular data, index and long columns in different table spaces:

- IN identifies the table space in which the table's regular (or non-long) data will be stored. The table space must exist and be a regular table space. If no other table space is specified, then all table parts (regular data, large objects and indexes) will be stored in this table space.

- INDEX IN identifies the table space (that must be a DMS table space), in which any index on the table will be stored. This option is allowed only when the primary table space specified in the IN clause is a DMS table space.

- LONG IN identifies the table space in which the values of any long columns (long varchar, long vargraphic or large object data types) will be stored. This option is allowed only when the primary table space specified in the IN clause is a DMS table space. The table space must exist and be a LONG DMS table space.

If you do not specify any table space when creating a table, it will be created in the first of the following table spaces available:

1. A table space called IBMDEFAULTGROUP. This table space will exist in databases that have been migrated from DB2 Parallel Edition.

2. The user-created table space with the lowest ID. You can see the ID of the tablespace issuing the `LIST TABLESPACES` command.

3. In the USERSPACE1 table space.

4. If none of the above table spaces exist, it will return an error, and the table will not be created.

3.6.4 Indexes

An index is a DB2 object used to make access to data faster and/or to ensure that there are no duplicate rows in a table. Indexes represent a duplication of data within a database. This duplication of data requires extra physical storage. The index is maintained in a specific order (ascending or descending) as data is inserted, updated or deleted.

The uniqueness of the data values can be guaranteed if a *UNIQUE* index has been defined for the column(s) forming the index. The unique index can be used during query processing to perform faster retrieval of data.

A non-unique index can also improve query performance by maintaining a sorted order for the data.

An index key is a column or collection of columns on which an index is defined and which determines the usefulness of an index. Although the order of the columns making up an index key does not make a difference to index key creation, it may make a difference to the optimizer when it is deciding whether or not to use an index for query performance.

An index can be defined by the creator of a table or by a user who knows that certain columns require direct access. Up to 16 columns can be specified for an index. A primary index key is automatically created on the primary key, unless a user-defined index already exists.

Unique Indexes and Partitioning Keys

The columns that form a unique index must contain at least the columns that form the partitioning key of the base table.

Any number of indexes can be defined on a particular base table and they can have a beneficial effect on the performance of queries. However, the more indexes there are, the more the database manager must modify during update, delete, and insert operations. Creating a large number of indexes for a table that receives many updates can slow down processing of requests. Therefore, use indexes only where a clear advantage for frequent access exists.

If the table being indexed is empty, an index is still created, but no index entries are made until the table is loaded or rows are inserted. If the table is not empty, the database manager makes the index entries while processing the `create index` statement.

The indexes of a table are partitioned based on the partitioning key of the table. When you create an index, it will be created in all of the database partitions to which the table belongs. In each database partition, the entries of the index have entries pertaining to the rows of the table that are located on the same database partition.

In Figure 77 shows an example of a table with one index in a partitioned database.

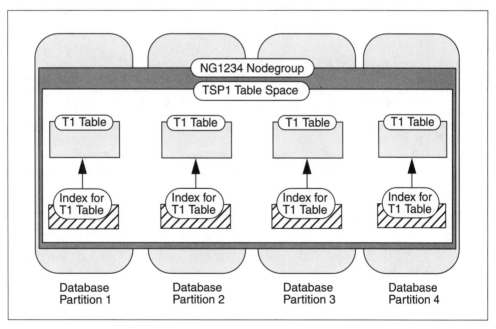

Figure 77. Index for a table

From the figure we see that an index has been created for table T1. The index for table T1 is created in each of the database partitions where table T1 is defined. The entries of the index in database partition 1 will point to the rows of the table in database partition 1; the entries in the indexes for database partition 2 will point to the rows of the table in database partition 2 and so on.

Indexes are maintained after they are created. Subsequently, when application programs use a key value to randomly access and process rows in a table, the index based on that key value can be used to access rows directly. This is important because the physical storage of rows in a base table is not ordered. When a row is inserted, it is placed in the most convenient storage location that can accommodate it. When searching for rows of a table that meet a particular selection condition and the table has no indexes, the entire table is scanned. An index optimizes data retrieval without performing a lengthy sequential search.

The data for your indexes can be stored in the same table space as your table data or in a separate table space containing index data. The table space used to store the index data is determined when the table is created (see "Creating Tables" on page 192 for details).

An index is never directly used by an application program. The decision on whether to use an index and which of the potentially available indexes to use is the responsibility of the optimizer.

3.6.4.1 Creating Indexes
You can use the `create index` SQL statement to create an index:

- To create a unique index, use `create unique index`.
- To create a non-unique index, use `create index`.

The following SQL statement creates a non-unique index called LNAME from the LASTNAME column on the EMPLOYEE table, sorted in ascending order:

```
db2 create index LNAME on EMPLOYEE (LASTNAME asc)
```

The following SQL statement creates a unique index on the phone number column:

```
db2 create unique index PH on EMPLOYEE (PHONENO desc)
```

A unique index ensures that no duplicate values exist in the indexed column or columns. The constraint is enforced at the end of any SQL statement that updates rows or inserts new rows. This type of index cannot be created if the set of one or more columns already has duplicate values.

The keyword ASC puts the index entries in ascending order by column, while DESC puts them in descending order by column. The default is ascending order.

Chapter 4. Loading Data

This chapter discusses various methods for loading data into a DB2 UDB EEE database.

- The LOAD utility moves data into tables, extends existing indexes, and gathers statistics. When loading data into a partitioned database, the input data must first be split using the db2split utility.

- The AutoLoader utility automates the process of splitting large amounts of data and loading the split data into the different partitions of a partitioned database.

- The IMPORT utility can be used to load data into a table. In a partitioned database, its practical usage is limited to small tables.

DB2 Replication is a component of DB2 Universal Database that allows automatic copying of table updates to tables in other DB2 relational databases. We will not discuss DB2 Replication in this book.

4.1 Overview of Loading Data

When you have large volumes of data to load into a table, you will probably prefer to use the load utilities instead of importing the files. IMPORT uses SQL INSERTs on a row-by-row basis. LOAD, on the other hand, writes whole, formatted, 4KB database pages directly into a database, bypassing DB2's usual integrity and recovery mechanisms. The performance of a load is better than IMPORT, which uses SQL INSERTs, especially as the data volumes increase. Some simple precautions must be taken to ensure database integrity.

Loading data into a partitioned database can be done with either several jobs invoking the LOAD utility on each node, or using the AutoLoader utility, which takes care of splitting the input data into several files and invokes a LOAD for each of these files on the individual database partitions. If your data is not split and you want to use only the LOAD utility (not AutoLoader), you will have to first split it into several files and ftp each individual file to each partition.

If the table into which you are loading data is defined in a single-partition nodegroup, you do not have to split the input data. You can use the LOAD utility directly on the input data.

Output from EXPORT can be split and then used as input to LOAD, so using DB2 Connect you can transfer data from a host DB2 database into a DB2 UDB EEE database.

4.1.1 Loading in Parallel

If you want to load a single data file into a table which spans several DB2 UDB EEE database partitions using the LOAD utility, you must first split the input data using the **db2split** utility, which splits data across database partitions in a multi-node environment.

The db2split utility splits one input file into several files, one for each database partition. The LOAD utility then receives this split input data from the db2split utility. These split files are then used as input at each of the database partition.

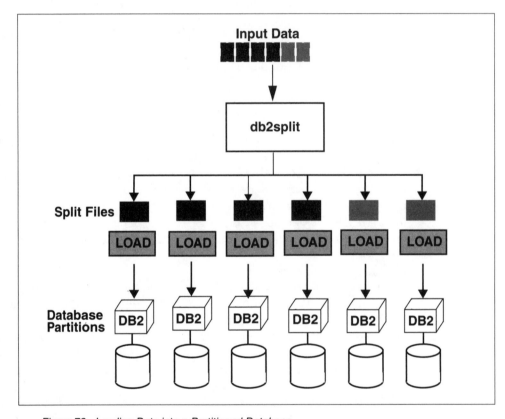

Figure 78. Loading Data into a Partitioned Database

4.2 Splitting Data

If you want to load a single data file into several DB2 UDB EEE database partitions using the LOAD utility, you must first split them with the db2split utility, which splits data across database partitions in a multi-node environment.

4.2.1 db2split Overview

The db2split utility splits an input data file into several split output files, one for each database partition, as shown in Figure 79.

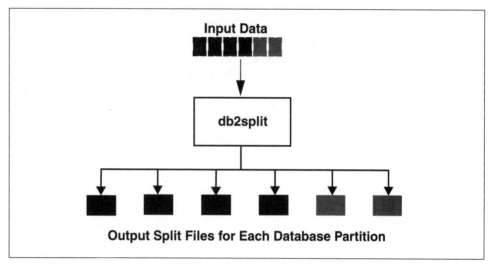

Figure 79. The db2split Utility

You can use db2split in two modes:

- PARTITION mode

  In this mode, db2split will partition the data, and produce a number of split files.

- ANALYZE mode

  In this mode, db2split will analyze the data and determine how many rows would be placed into each partition (without actually producing the output files). You can use this information to determine whether the column selected as the partitioning key will result in an even distribution of the data.

The db2split utility uses partitioning maps to determine how to partition its input data.

4.2.2 Partitioning Maps

Partitioning maps (or pmaps) form an important part of the process used by db2split to divide the lines of its input data into many output files. To understand why db2split uses partitioning maps, we must first understand this process.

4.2.2.1 How db2split Divides its Input Data

The db2split utility uses a hashing algorithm to assign a given line of its input data to particular output file. Each output file is associated with a database partition. In the db2split configuration file, you must specify a partitioning key to be used, which consists of one or many columns of data in the input data file. The db2split utility uses the value of the partitioning key for a given line as the input for the hashing function. The output of this function is a number between 0 and 4095 which is used as a displacement into the partitioning map. We use the term *index* for this displacement. The partitioning map contains a value at this displacement. This value corresponds to the database partition where the row is to be stored. Figure 80 shows an example of this process:

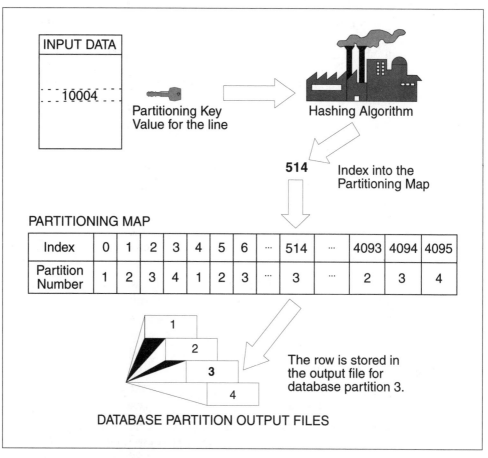

Figure 80. How db2split Divides its Input Data

In order to find out in which database partition output file a given line of input data is stored in, db2split does the following:

- We use the partitioning key value of the row (in this example, 10004) as input for the hashing algorithm. This algorithm transforms the partition key value into a number between 0 and 4095 that is the index into the partitioning map.

- The partitioning map contains a value at that index that indicates the database partition number where the row is to be stored.

4.2.3 Round-Robin Partitioning

If no input pmap is supplied to db2split, then a round-robin partitioning map will be used. In a round-robin partitioning map, the database partition numbers are repeated in ascending order until the end of the map.

Figure 81 shows an example of a round-robin partitioning map for database partition 1,2 and 3.

Index	0	1	2	3	4	5	6	7	...	...	...	4093	4094	4095
Partition Number	1	2	3	1	2	3	1	2	...	...	...	3	1	2

Figure 81. Partitioning Map Examples

In many cases the cardinality of the partitioning key will be high enough so that the default round-robin pmap will be sufficient to achieve an even data distribution. If this is not the case, then you may need to generate a customized partitioning map to achieve even distribution.

4.2.4 Customized Partition Maps

There may be some cases where using a round-robin pmap does not lead to an even distribution of data across the output files. For example, if you use a partitioning key with only a handful of discrete values. These few values may mean that more rows will end up hashing to some output files than others.

Consider the case in Figure 82, where the STORE table has only two locations, identified by store numbers 460 and 223.

Here, partitioning on only the STORE column will, at best, send most of the rows, (those with store number 460) to one partition's output file. The remainder, with store number 223, will be written to the output file of the other partition. In the worst case scenario, they will all hash to the same database partition.

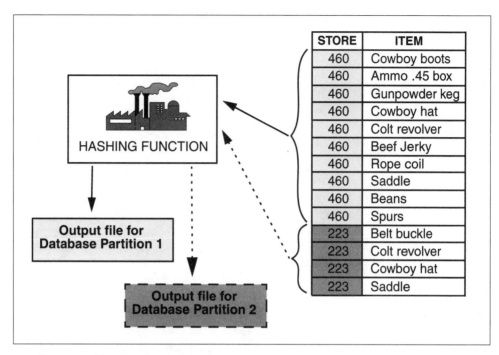

STORE	ITEM
460	Cowboy boots
460	Ammo .45 box
460	Gunpowder keg
460	Cowboy hat
460	Colt revolver
460	Beef Jerky
460	Rope coil
460	Saddle
460	Beans
460	Spurs
223	Belt buckle
223	Colt revolver
223	Cowboy hat
223	Saddle

Figure 82. Choice of Partitioning Key

Note that if we expanded the partitioning key to include the ITEM column, the hashing function would have more distinct values in its input, and would hash the rows more evenly among the two database partitions' output files.

Even if the number of distinct partitioning values is high, you can still end up with an uneven distribution. Consider the example shown in Figure 83.

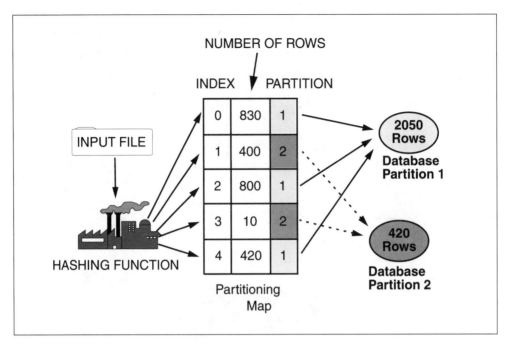

Figure 83. Unbalanced Data Distribution with a Round-Robin Map

For the purposes of this example, imagine that the partitioning map only has five values (instead of 4096). Note that the partitioning map points most of the input lines to database partition 1's output file.

The db2split utility can generate a customized partitioning map to even out this skew. Consider the number of lines that are hashed to each index of the pmap and call this number the hashing total for each index. By using these hashing totals, db2split can generate a new pmap that will result in a more balanced row distribution across all the database partitions' output files.

In Figure 84 we can see the effect of modifying the partition map to assign database partitions to vectors after sorting by weight. DB2 scans the input data file and counts how many records hash into each input vector (4096). The number of rows assigned to each vector is evaluated as the weight for that vector. The pmap vectors are then sorted by weight and the database partitions are then assigned. This will tend to more evenly distribute data among database partitions.

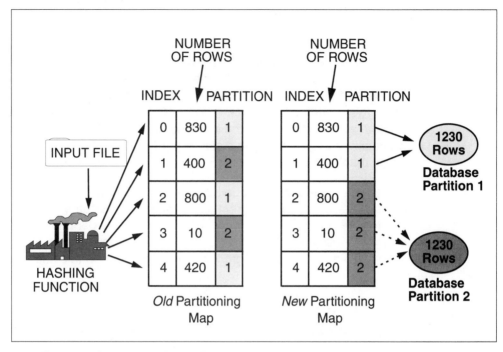

Figure 84. Changing the Default Partitioning Map

4.2.5 How a Partitioning Map Gets Changed and Data Rebalanced

When the default round-robin pmap would lead to skewed distribution among the database partitions, you can load the data anyway and then use the REDISTRIBUTE NODEGROUP command to rebalance your data.

A more efficient method would be to load the data in a balanced way as follows:

1. Invoke the db2split utility in ANALYZE mode to scan your input data files and generate a customized pmap.

2. Invoke db2split in PARTITION mode using the output pmap file from the previous step to split the input data into several files.

3. Use the REDISTRIBUTE NODEGROUP command to replace the default round-robin pmap with the customized pmap.

4. Load the split data files using the new pmap.

The customized pmap is basically the original pmap with the hash buckets (the outputs from the hashing function) sorted according how many rows are assigned to each one. Database partition numbers are then assigned, again in round-robin fashion, but now according to the **sort order** in the hash bucket list. Given the size of the pmap (4096 entries), this should reduce or eliminate data skew.

This process will rebalance most instances of data skew. One exception would be a partitioning key where the data values are clustered among a few values, and those are fewer than your total number of database partitions. Since the hash function hashes rows based on the partitioning key, the clusters will be assigned to the same database partition. In an extreme case, with most of the rows having a single key value, they will all be sent to one single database partition!

If skew is still present, you should consider adding a column to increase cardinality, or look for a different partitioning key altogether. Keep in mind you will only be able to rebalance according to one table per nodegroup at a time. Choose the largest table to generate the pmap from, and the other, smaller, tables would also be split based this pmap, possibly with some measure of skew.

4.2.6 Examples of Splitting Data

Let's consider some examples of splitting data, including when there is data skew.

4.2.6.1 Using the Default Round-Robin PMAP

In this example, shown in Figure 85, db2split is run in PARTITION mode using the default pmap generated when the nodegroup was created. Based on the parameters in the db2split configuration file, the input data file is split into two output files.The pmap is provided either by the MapFili option or generated by db2split using Nodes=(x.x.x...x), where x represents the database partition in the nodegroup.

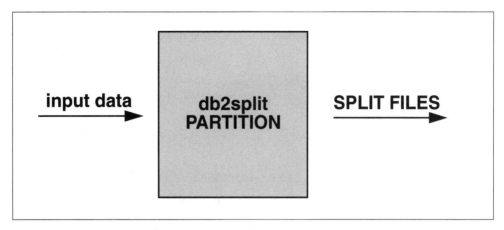

Figure 85. Using db2split in PARTITION Mode

Here is the db2split command:

```
db2split -c order.cfg
```

The following is an excerpt from the order.cfg control file used for this example:

```
      Description=order
(1)   InFile=order.tbl
(2)   RecLen=250
(3)   Nodes=(1,2)
      OutputType=w
      MapFilo=OutMap
      DistFile=DISTFILE
(4)   LogFile=Log,w
      OutFile=order
      CDelimiter=|
      SDelimiter="
(5)   RunType=PARTITION
(6)   Partition=o_orderkey,1,,,NN,integer
(7)   Trace=100
```

In the example:

1. InFile: the input file, here order.tbl, piped output from the TPCD generator program

2. RecLen=250: Maximum allowable record length for the input file

3. Nodes: Which nodes the split output files are meant to. Will be used to name the output files as OutFile.00nnn, with OutFile as prefix, specified below, and nnn ranging from 000 to 999. In our example, the two output files will be order.00001 and order.00002

4. LogFile: The log file name

5. RunType: The type of run we want. Here we specified PARTITION, to split the data rather than analyze it to generate a pmap.

6. Partition: Specifies the column name and other information for the partitioning key. In our example

   - The column name to do the split on is o_ordertype,

   - NN means no nulls are allowed.

   - The "1" is the offset in the record where the key begins, and

   - "integer" means we want the data converted to a 4-byte integer.

7. Trace=100: Will write a trace of 100 records to the Log file. Not required, but useful to visually check the file is in the appropriate format. 100 is a good number to get a feel for what's coming out of db2split.

In this case, db2split will use a round-robin pmap. In the next screen we see part of the Log file:

```
order >Log file opened successfully
order > Start time: Wed Feb 18 09:50:53 1998
order > Input file order.tbl opened successfully
order > Input maximum record length:250
order > Program is running with CHECK level
order > The string delimiter is:<">
order > Tracing 100 delimited (delimiter <|>) record(s)
order > Getting partitioning map...done
order > The Run Type is PARTITION
order > Output map file OutMap opened successfully for writing
order > The message level is NOWARN
order > Distribution file name: DISTFILE
order > Distribution file DISTFILE opened successfully for
writing
order > Working on 1 keys.
order > o_orderkey Start: 0  Len: 0 Position: 1 Type: NN INTEGER
order > Output files will be order.00xxx
order > All output files opened successfully
RECORD:            1
P0> o_orderkey 1 0 0 <1>
Partition number: 0677(x) 1655(d)
RECORD:            2
P0> o_orderkey 1 0 0 <2>
Partition number: 0517(x) 1303(d)
. . . . . . . . . .
RECORD:          100
P0> o_orderkey 1 0 0 <388>
Partition number: 026c(x)  620(d)
order > Processed          50000
order > Processed         100000
order > Processed         150000
order > Writing output map to OutMap
order > Writing distribution map to DISTFILE
order > Total record count:    150000
order > Total record discarded:        0
order > Stop time: Wed Feb 18 09:52:45 1998
order > Elapsed time:  0 hours,  1 minutes, 52 seconds
order > Throughput: 1339 records/sec
order > Record counts for output nodes:
Node: 2: Record count: 74799          ◄─── RECORD COUNT
Node: 1: Record count: 75201
order   > Complete.
Program ran successfully with 0 warning message(s) and 0
discarding record(s)
```

The record count, (shown above), points to a minor skew in the split files, that we will attempt to correct in the following example.

Although there is no exact cut off value to decide when the output data files are skewed, if the discrepancy exceeds 10%, the optimizer may begin to make wrong assumptions about data distribution. Keep in mind the optimizer always bases its decisions on the statistics as maintained in the catalog partition, and expects all database partitions to have essentially the same data distribution.

4.2.6.2 Correcting for Skewed Data

In the previous example, we saw that the default round-robin partitioning map did not hash the same number of rows to each partition. We will try to correct this to balance system load. If one database partition has to process more rows than the others, it will tend to be a performance bottleneck, assuming all database partitions have more or less the same system resources.

In Figure 86, we see how we now first run db2split in ANALYZE mode to generate an output pmap, but no output data files.

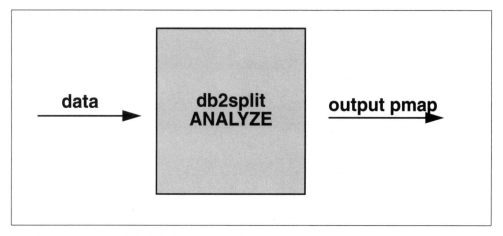

Figure 86. Using db2split in ANALYZE Mode

We again invoke db2split:

```
db2split -c order2.cfg
```

This time, the db2split config file, order2.cfg, is as follows:

```
Description=order
InFile=order.tbl
RecLen=250
Nodes=(1,2)
OutputType=w
MapFilo=OutMap2
DistFile=DISTFILE
LogFile=Log,w
OutFile=order
CDelimiter=|
SDelimiter="
RunType=ANALYZE
Partition=o_orderkey,1,,,NN,integer
Trace=100
```

In the configuration file, the following changes were made:

- MapFilo=OutMap2 for the output pmap filename.
- RunType=ANALYZE to generate the new pmap.

The contents of the output pmap is as follows (only the beginning is shown):

```
1 2 1 1 1 1 2 1 2 1
1 1 1 1 1 2 2 2 2 2
2 1 2 1 2 1 1 2 2 2
2 1 2 2 2 2 1 2 1 2
1 2 2 2 1 1 2 2 2 2
1 2 2 1 2 1 1 2 1 1
. . . . . . . . . . . . . . . . . . . . . . . . . .
```

You can see that this is a customized (not a round-robin) pmap. A round robin pmap would be repeated series of the digits 1 and 2. This is the Log file from the ANALYZE run:

```
order >Log file opened successfully
order > Start time: Fri Feb 27 14:19:06 1998
order > Input file order.tbl opened successfully
order > Input maximum record length:250
order > Program is running with CHECK level
order > The string delimiter is:<">
order > Tracing 100 delimited (delimiter <|>) record(s)
order > Getting partitioning map...done
order > The Run Type is ANALYZE
order > Output map file OutMap2 opened successfully for writing
order > The message level is NOWARN
order > Distribution file name: DISTFILE
order > Distribution file DISTFILE opened successfully for
writing
order > Working on 1 keys.
order > o_orderkey Start: 0 Len: 0 Position: 1 Type: NN INTEGER
order > Output files not used
RECORD: 1
P0> o_orderkey 1 0 0 <1>
Partition number: 0677(x) 1655(d)
RECORD: 2
P0> o_orderkey 1 0 0 <2>
Partition number: 0517(x) 1303(d)
RECORD: 3
P0> o_orderkey 1 0 0 <3>
Partition number: 04e7(x) 1255(d)
RECORD: 4
....
......
P0> o_orderkey 1 0 0 <386>
Partition number: 005e(x)    94(d)
RECORD: 99
P0> o_orderkey 1 0 0 <387>
Partition number: 01f7(x) 503(d)
RECORD: 100
P0> o_orderkey 1 0 0 <388>
Partition number: 026c(x) 620(d)
order > Processed         50000
order > Processed         100000
order > Processed         150000
order > Writing output map to OutMap2
order > Writing distribution map to DISTFILE
order > Total record count:     150000
order > Total record discarded:        0
order > Stop time: Fri Feb 27 14:19:47 1998
order > Elapsed time: 0 hours, 0 minutes, 41 seconds
order > Throughput: 3658 records/sec
order > Record counts for output nodes:
Node: 2: Record count: 75001
Node: 1: Record count: 74999              RECORD COUNT
order    > Complete.
```

The record count on the output files is almost the same. If we run db2split in PARTITION mode using OutMap2 pmap file just generated, then the data should be evenly divided between files.

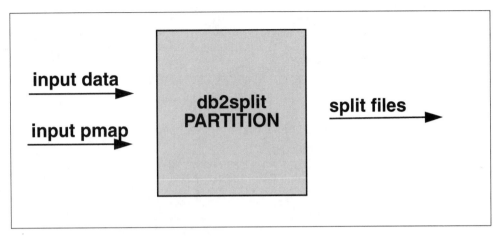

Figure 87. Using db2split in Partition Mode with Input Pmap

Here is the db2split command:

```
db2split -c order3.cfg
```

The configuration file order3.cfg now includes the following:

```
Description=order
InFile=order.tbl
RecLen=250
MapFili=OutMap2
OutputType=w
DistFile=DISTFILE
LogFile=Log,w
OutFile=order
CDelimiter=|
SDelimiter="
RunType=PARTITION
Partition=o_orderkey,1,,,NN,integer
Trace=100
```

In the configuration file, the following changes were made:

- MapFili=OutMap2 for the input pmap filename.

- RunType=PARTITION to generate the output files.

These are the output split files:

```
f01n05:/build/li > ls -l order.0*
-rw-r--r--    1 db2inst1 dbadmin1 8452622 Feb 27 14:31 order.00001
-rw-r--r--    1 db2inst1 dbadmin1 8455712 Feb 27 14:31 order.00002
f01n05:/build/li >
```

The order.00001 and order.00002 files are now almost identical size.

The log file also shows that the files have almost the number of records:

```
order >Log file opened successfully
order > Start time: Fri Feb 27 14:31:04 1998
order > Input file order.tbl opened successfully
order > Input maximum record length :250
order > Program is running with CHECK level
order > The string delimiter is :<">
order > Tracing 100 delimited (delimiter <|>) record(s)
order > Input map file OutMap2 opened successfully for reading
order > Getting partitioning map...done
order > The Run Type is PARTITION
order > Output partitioning map file not used
order > The message level is NOWARN
order > Distribution file name: DISTFILE
order > Distribution file DISTFILE opened successfully for
writing
.....
order > Processed          50000
order > Processed         100000
order > Processed         150000
order > Writing distribution map to DISTFILE
order > Total record count:     150000
order > Total record discarded:        0
order > Stop time: Fri Feb 27 14:31:57 1998
order > Elapsed time:  0 hours,  0 minutes, 53 seconds
order > Throughput: 2830 records/sec
order > Record counts for output nodes:
Node: 2: Record count: 75001
Node: 1: Record count: 74999
order > Complete.
Program ran successfully with 0 warning message(s) and 0
discarding record(s)
```

The next step in the process is to update the nodegroup for the ORDERS2 table with the customized pmap that we have generated. This is done by using the REDISTRIBUTE NODEGROUP statement. The format of this statement is:

```
REDISTRIBUTE NODEGROUP nodegroup USING TARGETMAP targetmap
```

This is the statement we used:

```
f01n05:/build/li > db2 REDISTRIBUTE NODEGROUP WGROUP USING
TARGETMAP OutMap2
DB20000I   The REDISTRIBUTE NODEGROUP command completed
successfully.
f01n05:/build/li >
```

The REDISTRIBUTE NODEGROUP statement will update the entries in the DB2 system catalogs for the WGROUP nodegroup with the customized pmap (OutMap2 in our example). The system catalogs used are SYSCAT. NODEGROUPS and SYSCAT.PARTITIONMAPS.

Now we are ready to load the data into the ORDERS2 table. To complete the example, we will show the steps necessary to perform the load. LOAD is discussed in more detail in "The LOAD Utility" on page 222

The ORDERS2 table is created using the IMPORT command with the CREATE clause:

```
f01n05:/build/li > db2 "import from orders.ixf of ixf create orders2 in
wtemp1"
SQL3150N  The H record in the PC/IXF file has product "DB2    01.00",
date "19980225", and time "145104".
SQL3153N  The T record in the PC/IXF file has name "orders.ixf",
qualifier " ", and source "              ".
SQL3109N  The utility is beginning to load data from file "orders.ixf".
SQL3110N  The utility has completed processing.  "0" rows were read from
the input file.

SQL3221W  ...Begin COMMIT WORK. Input Record Count = "0".

SQL3222W  ...COMMIT of any database changes was successful.

SQL3149N  "0" rows were processed from the input file. "0" rows were
successfully inserted into the table.  "0" rows were rejected.

Number of rows read         = 0
Number of rows skipped      = 0
Number of rows inserted     = 0
Number of rows updated      = 0
Number of rows rejected     = 0
Number of rows committed    = 0

f01n05:/build/li >
```

Next, a LOAD is executed on the first database partition, the catalog partition,
with the newly split order.00001 file:

```
db2 "connect to tpcd100"
db2 "load from order.00001 of del modified by coldel| replace
into orders2 statistics yes with distribution and  detailed
indexes all"
```

The results are as follows:

```
Database Connection Information

Database product        = DB2/6000 5.0.0
SQL authorization ID    = DB2INST1
Local database alias    = TPCD100

SQL3501W  The table space(s) in which the table resides will not
be placed in backup pending state since forward recovery is
disabled for the database.

SQL3109N  The utility is beginning to load data from file
"/build/li/order.00001".

SQL3500W  The utility is beginning the "LOAD" phase at time
"02-27-1998 15:16:51.682210".

SQL3519W  Begin Load Consistency Point. Input record count = "0".
SQL3520W  Load Consistency Point was successful.

SQL3110N  The utility has completed processing.  "74999" rows
were read from the input file.

SQL3519W  Begin Load Consistency Point. Input record count =
"74999".
SQL3520W  Load Consistency Point was successful.

SQL3515W  The utility has finished the "LOAD" phase at time
"02-27-1998 15:17:16.393847".

SQL3500W  The utility is beginning the "BUILD" phase at time
"02-27-1998 15:17:16.564382".

SQL3515W  The utility has finished the "BUILD" phase at time
"02-27-1998 15:17:18.598675".

Number of rows read        = 74999
Number of rows skipped     = 0
Number of rows loaded      = 74999
Number of rows rejected    = 0
Number of rows deleted     = 0
Number of rows committed   = 74999

f01n05:/build/li >
```

Next we have to ftp the order.00002 file to the other database partition, and execute the LOAD utility from there:

```
db2 "connect to tpcd100"
db2 "load from order.00002 of del modified by coldel| replace
into orders2"
```

The results are as follows:

```
Database Connection Information

 Database product     = DB2/6000 5.0.0
 SQL authorization ID  = DB2INST1
 Local database alias  = TPCD100
SQL3501W  The table space(s) in which the table resides will not
be placed in backup pending state since forward recovery is
disabled for the database.
SQL3109N  The utility is beginning to load data from file
"/build/li/order.00002".
SQL3500W  The utility is beginning the "LOAD" phase at time
"02-27-1998 15:29:18.987878".

SQL3519W  Begin Load Consistency Point. Input record count = "0".
SQL3520W  Load Consistency Point was successful.
SQL3110N  The utility has completed processing.  "75001" rows
were read from the input file.
SQL3519W  Begin Load Consistency Point. Input record count =
"75001".
SQL3520W  Load Consistency Point was successful.
SQL3515W  The utility has finished the "LOAD" phase at time
"02-27-1998 15:29:43.360028".

SQL3500W  The utility is beginning the "BUILD" phase at time
"02-27-1998 15:29:43.518895".

SQL3515W  The utility has finished the "BUILD" phase at time
"02-27-1998 15:29:45.410975".

Number of rows read       = 75001
Number of rows skipped    = 0
Number of rows loaded     = 75001
Number of rows rejected   = 0
Number of rows deleted    = 0
Number of rows committed  = 75001
```

If you compare the number of rows loaded into each database partition they
are almost the same.

4.2.6.3 Splitting Additional Tables

Once the data for the largest table in the nodegroup has been split with the customized pmap, you must split the other tables in the same nodegroup using the same pmap. To obtain the partitioning map for nodegroup, you should use the **db2gpmap** utility.

The db2gpmap utility gets the partitioning map for the table or the nodegroup from the catalog partition.

As shown in Figure 88, db2gpmap does the reverse of the REDISTRIBUTE NODEGROUP command: instead of loading a map file into the catalogs, it returns the pmap in a flat file format based on the system catalogs.

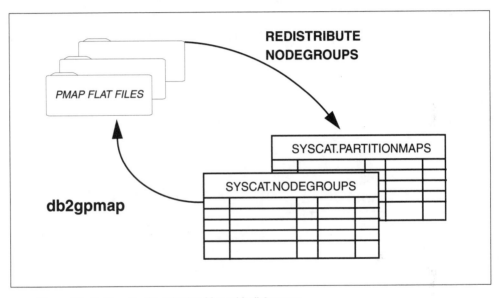

Figure 88. Getting the Partitioning Map with db2gpmap

When executing the db2gpmap utility, you can either set the $DB2DBDFT environment variable to correspond to the database that you want to access, or use the -d option of db2gpmap.

The format to call the db2gpmap utility is:

```
db2gpmap [option ( parameter )]
```

The options can be one or more of the following:

   -d database name (default is $DB2DBDFT)

-m map filename (default is db2split.map)

-g nodegroup name (default is IBMDEFAULTGROUP)

-t table name

-h help message

The following shows an example of the db2gpmap command:

```
f01n05:/build/li > db2gpmap -d TPCD100 -m mymap
Connect to TPCD100.
Successfully connected to database.
Retrieving the partition map ID using nodegroup IBMDEFAULTGROUP.
The partition map has been sent to mymap.
```

Next, execute the db2split utility with the map you have just retrieved as input map file as shown in Figure 89:

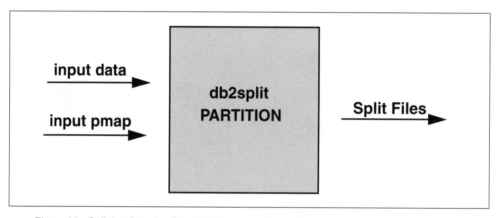

Figure 89. Splitting Data for Other Tables in the Same Nodegroup

4.3 The LOAD Utility

The LOAD utility is intended for the initial load or an append of a table where large amounts of data are moved. There are no restrictions on the data types used by the LOAD utility, including large objects (LOBs) and user-defined types (UDTs). The LOAD utility speeds up the task of loading large amounts of data into a database. LOAD is faster than IMPORT for large volumes of data because it writes formatted pages directly into the database, while IMPORT does SQL INSERTs. The data being loaded must be local to the server (unlike IMPORT and EXPORT, where the input (or output) files can reside at the client).

The LOAD utility can eliminate the logging associated with the loading of data. In place of logging, you have the option of making a copy of the loaded portion of the table. LOAD does *not* fire triggers; and does *not* perform referential and table constraint checking (other than validating the uniqueness of the unique indexes). If you have tables which use a large number of these kinds of constraints, using an IMPORT may be faster than using a LOAD and then applying the constraints.

As logging is not used, one way to guarantee the integrity (and recoverability) of your database is to:

- Explicitly request a copy of the loaded portion of the table be made.
- Take a backup of the table space(s) in which the table resides after the completion of the load.

The LOAD utility can take advantage of a hardware configuration where multiple processors and/or multiple storage devices are used such as in a symmetric multiprocessor (SMP) environment. There are several ways in which parallel processing can take place using the LOAD utility. One way is to use multiple storage devices and enable I/O parallelism during the LOAD process. Another way involves the simultaneous use of the multiple processors in an SMP environment.

4.3.1 LOAD Considerations

There are certain tasks to perform and objects that must exist before executing the LOAD utility:

1. Create table and index.
2. Create exception table.
3. Create (and sort) the input data.
4. Split the input data.
5. Make a table space (or database) backup before running LOAD for recovery purposes, unless you intend to recover the data externally.
6. Run the LOAD utility.
7. Monitor the execution of LOAD with load query.
8. After LOAD completes, examine the message and dump files for any errors.
9. Examine the exception table for any UNIQUE key violations.
10. Take a backup of the table space (if running with COPY NO and using logretain=yes).

11. If the table is left in a check-pending state, run check constraints to fix any RI or check constraints.

12. Update statistics if the statistics were not gathered during the LOAD. Only one of the database partitions in the LOAD can update the statistics. This should be done on a database partition you think has a representative distribution of the data in the table.

For a detailed description of the LOAD command and its parameters and options, see the *DB2 Command Reference*.

4.3.2 The Three Phases of the LOAD Utility

There are three phases in the LOAD:

1. Load: Data is loaded into the tables, index key values are collected.

2. Build: Indexes are built from the key values collected during the LOAD phase.

3. Delete: Indexes are checked for rows that would cause a unique key violation, and the offending rows are removed. The rejected rows can be inserted into the table specified in the FOR EXCEPTION clause.

4.3.2.1 The Load Phase

During the **Load** phase, keys for existing indexes are collected and sorted, and, if STATISTICS YES was specified, statistics will be gathered for the table and for any existing indexes. This option is not possible if the load is in the INSERT or RESTART modes, since it would not be possible to build accurate and representative statistics by scanning only a part of a table. In these modes, a separate execution of RUNSTATS will be necessary

You can also use the SAVECOUNT parameter to establish *save points*, or points of consistency, for recovery purposes. If the LOAD does not complete, and a number of rows have been successfully loaded and committed, LOAD can be restarted at the record specified in the RESTARTCOUNT parameter instead of starting all over again.

Messages are issued by LOAD after each successful save point to let you know how many of the input records have been loaded.

To attempt restarting a LOAD after an error, determine the last saved row and specify a RESTARTCOUNT value 1 record greater than the last SAVECOUNT value. The SAVECOUNT value should be in the messages file or, if you chose not to specify one, displayed in messages to the terminal. If you specify a higher value, some records will not be processed. If you specify a lower value, some records will be processed twice and, unless they violate unique keys, will end up as duplicate rows in your table.

SAVECOUNT will be converted to a page count, and will be rounded up to intervals of the extent size. Should the value selected for SAVECOUNT not be high enough, performance may be impacted because of synchronization of activities performed at each consistency point, such as flushing the buffers.

4.3.2.2 The Build Phase

During the **Build** phase, indexes are created on the index keys that were collected (and sorted) during the Load phase. If the Build phase fails, it must be restarted from the beginning, invoking LOAD with RESTARTCOUNT B. The USING directory clause should be considered because the default sort path is sqllib/tmp.

Rows that violate unique key restrictions are placed in the exception table, if one was specified. More on the exception below. Messages on rejected rows go to the message file, again if one was specified.

4.3.2.3 The Delete Phase

During the **Delete** phase, rows that violate unique key rules are deleted. If a failure occurs, the Delete phase should be restarted from the beginning. Information on the rows that contained invalid keys is stored in a temporary file. The directories to hold the temporary files can be specified with the REMOTE FILE parameter. You must not modify any data in any temporary files. If the temporary file has been modified in any way, you should restart the LOAD command at the build phase. Once the indexes are rebuilt, any invalid keys will be placed in the exception table, if one was specified, and rows with duplicate key entries are deleted. If LOAD fails during the Delete phase, restart it with RESTARTCOUNT D to remove the Delete Pending state.

4.3.3 The Exception Table

The exception table is a table you can create for LOAD to insert copies of the rows that would violate the rules for unique index keys. The exception table does *not* contain invalid data rejected prior to the construction of an index (for example, records with non-matching data types). The exception table is specified in the FOR EXCEPTION option of the LOAD command. The exception table has the same definition as the LOAD table with two extra columns for timestamp and error description.

If rows that would repeat existing unique index key values are encountered and an exception table was not specified in the LOAD command, the LOAD will continue with only a general warning message being issued about the existence of duplicate records. The omitted records will be discarded.

The option **MODIFIED BY DUMPFILE** can be used for positional ASCII (ASC) and delimited ASCII (DEL) files. It writes rows that have been rejected during the load process to a file. For each input record, a maximum of 32K of data will be written to the exception file. This eliminates the need of having an exception table created for the load process.

4.3.4 LOAD Failures

When performing a LOAD into a table, the entire table space for the table is inaccessible except by the LOAD operation itself. Since LOAD copies whole formatted pages into the database bypassing DB2's normal logging and integrity mechanisms, if problems arise, other tables in the table space may not be recoverable.

If a LOAD fails and you choose not to restart it, the table space containing the table will be left in a Load Pending state, since no logging was performed on behalf of the individual rows. To remove this Load Pending state, you will have to either restart the LOAD or recover the table space(s) from the last backup.

If you are restoring on only one partition of a table space from a backup image, you must then perform a roll forward to the end of the logs. If you are restoring across all the database partitions in the table space, you can choose to roll forward to a point-in-time.

You should try as a first option to restart the LOAD specifying a RESTARTCOUNT. Recall that the SAVECOUNT parameter establishes points of consistency. To attempt restarting a LOAD after an error, determine the last saved row and specify a RESTARTCOUNT that is one value greater than the value specified in the last SAVECOUNT. Depending on when a failure occurs during LOAD processing, it may be easier to re-start the LOAD from the beginning and specify the REPLACE option.

If a LOAD fails and cannot be restarted, you will have to restore a backup image for the table space. The backup image and eventually the roll forward procedure must correspond to a point-in-time *before* the load was started, If the table you were loading into was the only one in the table space, it may be easier to drop the table space and re-create it over again, along with the table and indexes.

> **Loading in Parallel**
>
> If executing the LOAD in parallel on several database partitions, you should generate statistics in only one of the LOAD commands. If not, you will receive deadlock errors.

The TERMINATE option of the LOAD command will place all the table spaces in which a table resides in a recovery pending state. The table spaces will not be accessible until a backup image has been restored and a roll forward operation has been performed.

4.3.5 LOAD Performance Considerations

This section offers some general guidelines for performance considerations when using the LOAD utility. We'll explain some of the options available that may be appropriate for your environment.

4.3.5.1 LOAD REPLACE vs. INSERT

Load will normally perform better in REPLACE mode than in INSERT mode, unless you happen to be loading into an empty table. In this case, INSERT will perform better.

4.3.5.2 Data Buffer Size

You can define how many 4K pages of data will be buffered during the load with the DATA buffer parameter.

Each buffer will be at least 16 pages in size, and the minimum number of pages that will be used will be the number of I/O sessions needed for the COPY option, if selected. If COPY YES USE ADSM or COPY YES LOAD lib-name was selected, then the number of I/O sessions can be directly specified. If the number of sessions was not directly specified, it will match the number of devices or directories used.

If the buffer size specified is large enough, more than the minimum size will be used.

Keep in mind the buffers used during the LOAD utility are allocated from the utility heap, which you modify with the *util_heap_sz* database configuration parameter.

4.3.5.3 NOROWWARNINGS

This selection for the MODIFIED BY option suppresses warnings about rejected rows. This may be useful if, for example, you are loading rows from a file with different record formats and you are anticipating a large number of rejected rows that you did not intend to load into this table anyway.

These warnings can cause an important overhead if you only get a few valid rows out of a large file.

4.3.5.4 FASTPARSE

Another file type modification you can specify via the MODIFIED BY option is FASTPARSE. The MODIFIED BY FASTPARSE option enhances performance by omitting data checking on the input files. This is useful if you are *sure* your input files are already in the proper formats.

The utility performs sufficient data checking to prevent a segmentation violation or trap. Data that is in correct form will be loaded correctly.

Data that is *not* in the correct format will be loaded in a variety of odd formats. This means that, even though the table's integrity will not be compromised, you could have a meaningless value(s) loaded for a given row and column. This can in turn affect the result of your queries, particularly scalar functions such as MIN, MAX, AVG, and so on, without any SQL error or warning conditions.

This option does not affect referential integrity checking or constraints checking; it merely reduces syntax checking of the supplied data. For example, if the value 123qwr4 were encountered as a field entry for an integer column in an ASC file, the LOAD utility would ordinarily flag a syntax error, since the value does not represent a valid number. With FASTPARSE, a syntax error is not detected, and an arbitrary number is loaded into the integer field. Care must be taken to use this modifier with clean data only. Performance improvements using this option with ASCII data can be quite substantial. FASTPARSE does not significantly enhance performance with PC/IXF data, since IXF is a binary format, and FASTPARSE affects parsing.

4.3.5.5 PAGEFREESPACE

The MODIFIED BY PAGEFREESPACE=x option specifies the percentage of each page (from 0 to 100) to be reserved as free space.

Any value greater than 0 will, of course, slow your LOAD down a bit, but if you are anticipating UPDATEs on rows with nullable and/or variable length fields, it may help to reduce fragmentation on the table, thus saving you the time from having to perform a REORG.

4.3.5.6 TOTALFREESPACE

Another MODIFIED BY option is TOTALFREESPACE=x, where x is an integer between 0 and 100, and can specify the percentage of the total pages in the table that is to be appended to the end of the table as free space. For example, if x is 20, and the table has 100 data pages, 20 additional empty pages will be appended. The total number of data pages for the table will be 120.

This is only meaningful for SMS tablespaces, and again will slow the performance of the LOAD operation by using more I/O, but will help keep the SMS files defragmented, as DB2 will try to use this space for subsequent INSERTs, or for split overflows during UPDATEs. Although your table data will lose clustering, you will gain from a reduction of fragmentation throughout the disk.

4.3.5.7 NONRECOVERABLE

With the NONRECOVERABLE option, the table space(s) where the table involved in the LOAD operation, will be immediately available after the load operation completes, and not placed in backup pending state, even if no copy of the loaded data was made during the load.

You can specify this option to load several tables into the same table space before performing one final backup of the table space. It can also be used for tables that are always loaded with the LOAD REPLACE option, such as in certain data warehousing applications, where the tables are derived from operational records and are replaced periodically, or when the tables are summarized or derived from other base tables.

If you specify this option in a LOAD, the load transaction will be marked as non-recoverable, meaning that it will not be possible to recover it by a subsequent rollforward action. When processing the log files during recovery, the rollforward utility will skip this transaction, and the table into which data was being loaded will be marked as invalid. The utility will also ignore any further transaction against this table. After the roll forward has been completed, the table can only be loaded into, imported or dropped and created again. The drop and re-create will probably yield better physical clustering of the data on disk.

Use the NONRECOVERABLE option to maximize data availability, and only if the data being loaded can be recovered externally, as when loading from a file. If you are loading through a pipe, for example, be sure you have procedures in place to rebuild the input data.

4.3.5.8 COPY YES vs. COPY NO

COPY YES will reduce the performance of the LOAD, as now a table space copy will have to be taken and completed before the table is ready to use. But, overall performance will improve if a copy had to be made, as a LOAD with COPY YES usually performs better than a LOAD with COPY NO followed by a table space backup: With the latter, by the time the backup is invoked, the amount data in the table requires additional log processing and other overhead to ensure database integrity.

COPY NO should only be used for read only data that can be readily recovered from outside sources, especially if you intend to load several tables into the same table space.

4.3.5.9 Other Parameters

The LOAD utility can take advantage of both CPU and DISK parallelism to improve the speed of loading the data. You can specify CPU and DISK parallelism on the LOAD command. The CPU_PARALLELISM parameter controls the number of sub-agents used for data parsing and sorting. The DISK_PARALLELISM parameter controls the number of I/O writers used to build the table within the table space containers.

LOAD can also take advantage of disk parallelism on its input as it can process input data from multiple locations. If the ANYORDER modifier is used, then the preservation of source data order is not maintained when loading rows, yielding significant additional performance benefit on SMP systems.

4.3.6 LOAD and Table Space States

During the multiple phases of LOAD, regular logging is not carried out for performance reasons, as LOAD builds complete database pages. For this reason, LOAD uses **pending states** to preserve the consistency of the database. The states related to processing a LOAD operation are among the following:

0x0 Normal

0x8 Load pending

0x10 Delete pending

0x20 Backup pending

The load and build phases of the LOAD will place tables spaces associated with the table being loaded into in **load pending** state. The delete pending of the LOAD process places them in **delete pending** state. If you complete a

LOAD without having set either logretain or userexit to on, and you did not specify the COPY YES or the NONRECOVERABLE options, the table spaces involved in the LOAD will be placed in a **backup pending** state. Also, if the current execution of a LOAD operation implies referential integrity (RI) and check constraints, dependent tables may be place in a **check pending state** after a LOAD run. Note that check pending is placed on a table, not a table space.

If you use the NONRECOVERABLE option, there is no requirement for either making a copy with the COPY YES option or taking a backup after the LOAD. The data is assumed to be recoverable by the user.

4.4 The AutoLoader Utility

In a DB2 UDB EEE partitioned database, you usually want to load data across all of the database partitions at the same time. You can use the AutoLoader utility to accomplish this task. This section explains how the utility works and gives a simple example, For a more detailed example in an MDP environment, refer to *Managing VLDB Using DB2 UDB EEE*. Let's start with an overview of how the AutoLoader utility works.

4.4.1 Overview

In a partitioned database, data is distributed among the database partitions in your environment. Partitioning keys are used to determine on which database partition, the data will be stored. The data initially is not split. But to place data, it must pass through a splitting phase before it can be loaded in a database partition.

The entire split and load process can be done by the AutoLoader utility. AutoLoader uses a hashing algorithm to partition the data. Using AutoLoader, you have the option to select a set of database partitions that may be the same or different than the database partitions where data is being loaded, to participate in the parallel split process. The output from these multiple database partitions that are splitting data will also be directed to multiple database partitions in the load. You only need a single configuration file called autoloader.cfg to accomplish the entire parallel split and load process.

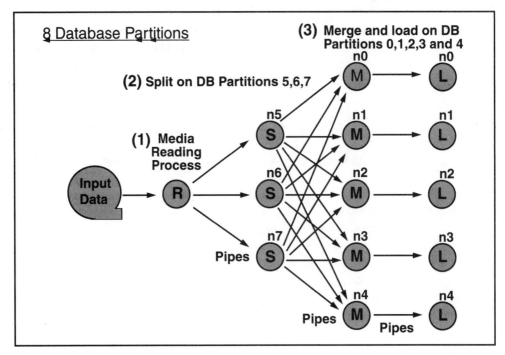

Figure 90. AutoLoader Overview

Figure 90 represents AutoLoader processing in a multi-partitioned environment.

1. First, the media reading process pipes the input data to database partitions running db2split. In our example, the split process (db2split) is running on database partition s n5,n6 and n7. This is done in a round-robin like process with the output being assigned to separate output pipes for each splitting database partition.

2. Next, AutoLoader invokes the db2split utility on each of the database partitions as defined in the configuration file (autoloader.cfg). The input is via a single pipe from the media reader process where the AutoLoader utility was invoked. db2split will then divide the input into a number of output pipes. These is one output pipe for each database partitions that will execute the load. The partition map used for all splits is documented in the autoloader.cfg file.

3. The LOAD utility does not support multiple input streams in parallel. Therefore, the input data pipes from each of the splitting database partitions must be merged together as they arrive at their destination database partition for the load. The single output pipe from this merge

process ensures a constant supply of input records for the load process. This merging will receive many input streams, passing the records out one at a time, but not performing any sort (or merge sort) of the records. This means that the records are passed on with minimal delay, but that the order of the records is not guaranteed as they are passed to the LOAD process.

AutoLoader invokes the LOAD utility on each of the database partitions with the options that are defined in the autoloader.cfg configuration file, using the piped output from the merge process running on the same database partition.

4.4.2 AutoLoader Modes

Figure 91 below illustrates the operation modes of AutoLoader:

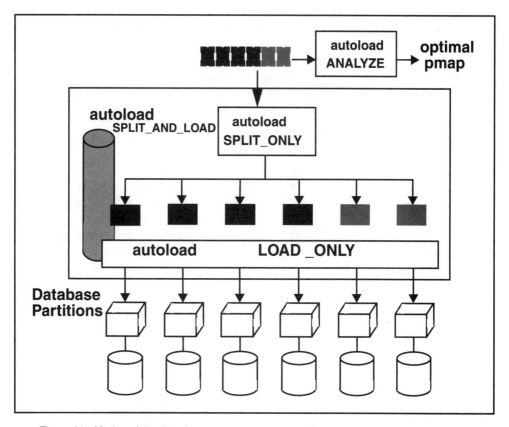

Figure 91. Modes of AutoLoader

AutoLoader can be run in one of the following modes:

SPLIT_AND_LOAD: In this mode, data is split and then loaded on the correct database partitions. Pipes are used for temporary storage and transfer of data between database partitions.

SPLIT_ONLY: With this choice, the data is only split. A set of split data files are generated for the requested output database e partitions. You must have sufficient storage for the original input source and for each of the split data files. The output from the split function writes the files in the location pointed to by the parameter SPLIT_FILE_LOCATION or in the AutoLoader current working directory. Data is split into separate files that are named using the convention filename.xxx where xxx is the node number to which the split file belongs and filename is no longer than eight characters.

LOAD_ONLY: Data is expected to be already split into separate files that are named using the following convention filename.xxx where xxx is the node number to which the split file belongs and filename is no longer than eight characters. AutoLoader expects to find these files in the SPLIT_FILE_LOCATION or in the current AutoLoader working directory. These split files are loaded concurrently on their corresponding nodes.

ANALYZE: This option generates a customized optimal partitioning map for a nodegroup. It is recommended that a data file with a large number of records be specified as input. The output from the ANALYZE mode can be used with the MAP_FILE_INPUT parameter. The larger the number of records used, the better the representation to the actual data that can be analyzed, and the better the resulting new partitioning map. The map will produce a more even distribution of data across each of the database partitions in the nodegroup.

4.4.3 Running the Autoloader Utility

The AutoLoader utility is executed by typing the following command:

```
db2autold [options]
```

with one or more of the following options:

-c Uses the config_file specified as the configuration file for the AutoLoader utility. The default is 'autoloader.cfg'.

-d Cleans up the temporary resources allocated by the AutoLoader utility. In case the AutoLoader utility exits abnormally, it is necessary to run this option to clean up all associated temporary directories, files and processes.

-i Makes the cleanup interactive. By default, cleanup is done without a prompt. This must only be used with the -d option.

The AutoLoader utility creates a file called autoload.log to keep messages returned from the main AutoLoader script. You can check the contents of this file to track the progress of the AutoLoader utility. As well, AutoLoader creates files called load_log.XXX and split_log.XXX, which contain messages from the load and split processes respectively.

4.5 Autoloader Example

In this section we'll look at a multiple database partition configuration with four hosts. Each host has two database partitions. The first database partition is used as the catalog partition.

We'll receive input from a file that was produced by the TPCD data generator (dbgen). The split and load will be done in one run, the split occurring only on database partition 1 and the load on the remaining seven database partitions.

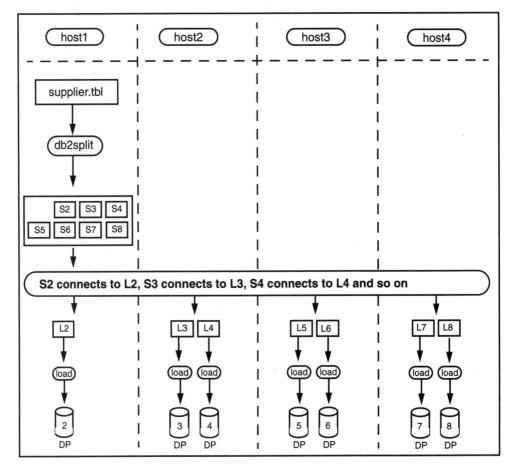

Figure 92. Autoloader Example

In Figure 92, an overview of the autoloader processing is shown. Note that:

- The supplier table has been defined in a 8 database partition nodegroup.

- There are 4 database partitions per host (here an SP node).

- The 4 SP nodes are host1, host2, host3, and host4.

- Database partition 1 is reserved for the System Catalogs.

- S2,S3,S4... S8 represent the 7 output named pipes of the split process. These pipes are named:

  - supplier.tbl2.00n (where n = 2,3,4... 8) and are stored in the /work/db2inst1/psplitload directory.

  - All these pipes exist on host1.

- L2,L3,L4...L8 represent the 7 input named pipes of the 7 load processes. These pipes are named:
  - supplier.tbl.00n (where n = 2,3,4... 8) and are stored in the /work/db2inst1/psplittemp directory
  - The pipe supplier.tbl.002 exists on host1.
  - The pipes supplier.tbl.003 and supplier.tbl.004 exist on host2.
  - The pipes supplier.tbl.005 and supplier.tbl 006 exist on host3,
  - the pipes supplier.tbl.007 and supplier.tbl.008 exist on host4.

4.5.1 Create the Input Data

First, dbgen, the TPCD data generator program, is run to create the input data:

```
dbgen -Ts -v -s1
```

The dbgen tool is run with these flags:

-Ts	Only produce data for the supplier table
-v	Verbose
-s1	Produce supplier data for a 1 GB TPCD database

This will produce this output file:

```
-rw-r--r--   1 db2inst1 sys     supplier.tbl 1409633
```

Note: for reasons of clarity we will run the dbgen into a file and then db2autold will use that file as input. We could also use a named pipe to avoid having to store the supplier.tbl file on disk.

4.5.2 Autoloader Configuration File

This is the autoloader configuration file, supplier.cfg:

```
RELEASE=V5.0

db2 "load from supplier.tbl of del modified by coldel| \
    replace into supplier statistics yes and indexes all using /work"

DATABASE=tpcd30

OUTPUT_NODES=(2,3,4,5,6,7,8)

SPLIT_NODES=(2)

MODE=SPLIT_AND_LOAD

LOGFILE=LOG

NOTNFS_DIR=/work

CHECK_LEVEL=NOCHECK

TRACE=1
```

We must also create a non-nfs directory on each SP node. This directory is used by Autoloader to store the named pipes it uses to channel the output of the splitting processes into the loading processes. In the supplier.cfg file, we have specified NOTNFS_DIR=/work.

The supplier table and all its indexes has been created prior to running db2autold, so during the load processing all the indexes for supplier will be built.

The LOAD utility will:

- Gather statistics during the load (statistics yes and indexes all). As we have not specified a value for RUN_STAT_NODE in the configuration file, statistics will be generated using the data at database partition 2, the first in the list of OUTPUT_NODES. In a EEE database, statistics are only ever generated from the data at a single database partition.

- By specifying "using /work" in the load command, we will use /work (a local non-nfs directory) for sort space when creating indexes. If we don't specify a non-nfs directory here, the default is $INSTHOME/sqllib/tmp which is shared across all database partitions. A local non-nfs directory should be used in place of the default directory as:

  - The sort space will be managed locally on each SP node so all write I/O will be to local disk (not across NFS). This means the performance will be improved as there will be less contention for disk.

- $INSTHOME will fill up very quickly as all 7 load commands will use this one directory for sort space.

4.5.3 Autoloader Command

When we run the db2autold command, we must run it from a directory that is shared across all the SP nodes in the instance. We created a subdirectory in the instance owner's home directory, (in our case /home/host1/db2inst1) as this directory must be shared for EEE to function.

This is the command which drives Autoloader:

```
db2autold -c supplier.cfg
```

4.5.4 Autoloader Output

When we run this command, this is the output:

```
Start reading autoloader configuration file: supplier.cfg.
Start initializing autoloader process.
Start moving data from db2split process(es) to target loading
nodes in background.
Start loading data on "7" node(s) in background.
Start 1 db2split process(es) in background.
Autoloader completed with detailed log message in file
"autoload.LOG".
Cleanup was done!
```

4.5.5 The Phases of AutoLoader Processing

Lets consider each phase in detail:

1. During the phase called "Start initializing autoloader process":

   - The values of NOTNFS_DIR (/work) and the username (db2inst1) are used to make the path /work/db2inst1.

   - In this path directories called psplitload and psplitemp are created (if not already created)

     - psplitload is used to store the named pipes used as the output of the split processing.

     - psplittemp is used to store the named pipes used as the input for the load processing.

- This happens on all SP nodes referenced in the db2nodes.cfg file for this instance.

2. During the phase called "Start moving data from db2split process(es) to target loading nodes in background":

   - The named pipes used for the output of the split processing are connected to the named pipes used for load processing. These latter pipes exist on the SP nodes where the data will be loaded for each of the split output files.

3. During the phase called "Start loading data on "7" node(s) in background."

   - The load processes are started (7 in this case). Each load process:

     - Takes its input from a named pipe and is started in the background.
     - Is run on the SP node where its data belongs.

4. During the phase called "Start 1 db2split process(es) in background."

   - The 1 split process is started. This split process:

     - Takes its input from the file supplier.tbl.
     - Outputs to 7 named pipes.

5. The message "Cleanup was done" indicates that:

   - All the named pipes are removed.
   - All the processes associated with Autoloader are terminated.
   - All the temporary message files used by Autoloader are removed.

Note that the 7 load processes are started in the background, then the single split process is started. For split and load to communicate via pipes, the reader of the pipe (load) must be started before the writer (split) starts.

4.5.6 Log Files

After cleanup has finished, these log files are produced:

- autoload.LOG:

  - This is the log file of the complete autoloader processing.

- load_LOG.<dp>, where dp = 2,3,4.... 8

  - These files, one per value in OUTPUT_NODES, are the messages from each load command.
  - In each file we can see the named pipe used as input. For example, for database partition 2, the named pipe is /work/db2inst1/psplittemp/supplier.tbl.002.

- We can also see the time when the load started and finished, plus the number of rows loaded.
- splt_LOG.2
  - This file contains the messages from the single split process used in this example.
  - In this file, we can see the output data file defined as: /work/db2inst1/psplitload/supplier.tbl2. This means that 7 named pipes called supplier.tbl2.002, supplier.tbl2.003... supplier.tbl2.008 in the /work/db2inst1/psplitload directory will be used as the output of the split process. The "2" after "tbl" indicates that split was run on database partition 2.
  - We can also see the time when the split started and finished, plus the number of processed input lines.

4.5.7 In Case of Problems

If any problems occur during Autoloader processing, cleanup may not take place. In this case you should rerun db2autold with the same configuration file and add the -d flag. Remember that the -d flag cleans up temporary resources allocated by AutoLoader. For example:

```
db2autold -c supplier.cfg -d
```

4.5.8 Common Problems

If you run AutoLoader from a non-NFS directory, you will see output similar to the following:

```
ksh: /work/frame:  not found.
ksh: ./loadscript_supplier.tbl_5:  not found.
```

This messages indicate that the load script for database partition 5 cannot be found. This is because the load process for partition 5 is run on host3. But as the autoloader job was started from a non-nfs directory on host1, this directory is not available on host3.

4.5.9 Considerations and Usage Notes

If you wish to maintain the order of the input data, then only one database partition or logical node should be used for splitting the data. Parallel splitting cannot guarantee that the data will be loaded in its original order.

If your input file contains Large Binary Object files (LOBs), and you are using the LOBSINFILE option of the LOAD utility, all directories containing LOB files must be visible for all the database partitions being loaded.

For best performance, invoke AutoLoader from a database partition that does not take part in either the splitting or loading operations. Also, if the splitting nodes are not the same as the loading database partitions, there will be less contention for CPU resources on any one database partition.

When using multiple database partitions to split the data, an error will be returned if the AutoLoader is used with a savecount greater than zero. This is to ensure AutoLoader can be restarted, since the arrival sequence of the records cannot be determined when splitting with multiple database partitions in parallel.

AutoLoader ignores the *messages* parameter for LOAD, and sends all messages from the LOAD command into load_log.xxx

4.5.10 Autoloader Considerations

If you are loading data into a table in a multiple database partition nodegroup, the LOAD utility requires that the files that are to be loaded were split and contain the correct header information. The LOAD utility verifies the header information that the split operation of AutoLoader writes to each data file to ensure that the data goes to the correct location.

If you are loading data into a table in a single database partition nodegroup, the files do not have to be split, even if the table is defined to have a partitioning key. In this situation, you would specify the NOHEADER option of the LOAD utility.

The LOAD utility checks that the partitioning map used by the split operation of AutoLoader is the same one specified when the table is being loaded. If not, an error is returned. It also checks that the file partition is loaded at the correct database partition, and that the data types of the partitioning key columns specified during splitting match the current definition in the catalog. The nodegroup to which the table is loaded cannot be redistributed between the time that the data file is partitioned and the time that the parts are loaded into the corresponding database table. If redistribution has been done, the utility cannot load the partitioned data.

AutoLoader can only be used to split DEL and ASC files, even though LOAD also supports IXF files. Although IXF files cannot be split, they can be loaded into a single-node nodegroup using the NOHEADER option of the LOAD command.

4.6 The IMPORT Utility

The IMPORT utility inserts data from an input file into a table or view. If the table or view receiving the imported data already contains data, you can either replace the existing data or append new data to the existing data.

Referential Integrity

If the existing table is a parent table containing a primary key that is referenced by a foreign key in a dependent table, you can only use APPEND Mode.

Here is an example using the IMPORT command to load data into the ORDERS table in a database called TPCD100:

```
db2 connect to tpcd100
db2 "import from orderall.del of del commitcount 50000
replace into orders"
```

The output of the above command is:

```
Database Connection Information

  Database product      = DB2/6000 5.0.0
  SQL authorization ID  = DB2INST1
  Local database alias  = TPCD100

SQL3109N The utility is beginning to load data from file "orderall.del".
SQL3221W Begin COMMIT WORK. Input Record Count = "50000".
SQL3222W COMMIT of any database changes was successful.
SQL3221W Begin COMMIT WORK. Input Record Count = "100000".
SQL3222W COMMIT of any database changes was successful.
SQL3221W Begin COMMIT WORK. Input Record Count = "150000".
SQL3222W COMMIT of any database changes was successful.

SQL3110N  The utility has completed processing.  "150000" rows were
read from the input file.
```

The following information is required when importing data to a table or view:

- The fully qualified name of input file where the data to import is stored.

- The name or alias of the table or view into which the data is imported.

- The format of the data in the input file. This format can be IXF, WSF, DEL (ASCII Delimited), or ASC (ASCII Positional).

- Whether the data in the input file is to be inserted or updated.

- Whether a new table is created or replaced.

- A message file name. This is not mandatory but recommended to monitor any errors during the IMPORT, such as unique key, referential integrity or constraint violations.

When importing into large object (LOB) columns, the LOB input data may be either in the same file as the rest of the column data, or in separate files. In the latter case, there is one file for each LOB column. The column data in the file contains either the data to IMPORT into the column, or a file name where the data to IMPORT is stored. The default is the file contains the data to load into the column.

You may also provide the following information in a LOAD command:

- The method to use for importing the data: column location, column name, or relative column position.

- The number of rows to INSERT before committing the changes to the table. If you periodically do a COMMIT, this reduces the number of rows that could need to be re-imported if a failure and a rollback occur during the import. It also reduces the chances of a log full condition.

- The number of records in the file to skip before beginning the import. If an error occurs during an import, you may specify this information to restart the import operation immediately following the last row that was successfully imported and committed.

- The names of the columns within the table or view into which the data is to be inserted.

To import data into a new table, you must have SYSADM or DBADM authority, or CREATETAB privilege for the database. To replace data in an existing table or view, you must have SYSADM or DBADM authority, or CONTROL privilege for the table or view. To append data to an existing table or view, you must have SELECT and INSERT privileges for the table or view.

IMPORT can handle codepage conversions. Such situations could occur with Japanese or Traditional-Chinese Extended UNIX Code (EUC) and double-byte character sets (DBCS) that may have different lengths for the same character. An option, NOCHECKLENGTHS, may be useful in these cases. NOCHECKLENGTHS basically does the following:

1. Compares input data length to target column length before reading in any data. If the input length is larger than the target, NULLs are inserted for that column if it is nullable. Otherwise, the request is rejected. This is the default.

2. No initial comparison is performed and, on a row-by-row basis, an attempt is made to import the data. If the data is too long after translation is complete, the row is rejected.

Otherwise, the data is imported. Specifying NOCHECKLENGTHS will enable this behavior.

The IMPORT utility casts user-defined distinct types (UDTs) to similar base data types automatically. This saves you from having to explicitly cast UDTs to the base data types. Casting allows for comparisons between UDTs and the base data types in SQL.

You can use the IMPORT utility to re-create a table that was saved using the EXPORT utility. The table must have been exported to an IXF file. When creating a table from an IXF file, not all attributes of the original table are preserved. For example, the referential constraints, foreign key definitions, and user-defined data types are not retained. If the IXF file was created with the LOBSINFILE option, then the length of the original LOB data is lost.

4.6.1 IMPORT Performance

This section discusses some of the methods to improve performance during an IMPORT operation.

4.6.1.1 Compound SQL

To improve IMPORT performance, you can use compound SQL by specifying COMPOUND=n in the MODIFIED BY clause of the IMPORT command, with n being the number of SQL statements to be grouped together. The value of n may range from 1 to 100.

The COMPOUND option may help to reduce network overhead and improve response time on remote connections. The statements are grouped and sent together as one unit.

4.6.1.2 Buffered INSERTs

The IMPORT utility can use buffered inserts to improve performance. Buffered inserts are a way to reduce the amount of message passing when performing inserts in a partitioned database.

Non-buffered INSERT processing is serialized across all database partitions. An example of this processing is shown in In Figure 93. Here we see an INSERT being received by database partition 1, the coordinator partition. DB2 UDB EEE uses the partitioning key value to determine that this row should be inserted at database partition 3. Database partition 3 does the INSERT and passes back the SQL return code to the coordinator node, which forwards it to the application.This process will be repeated for each row of data.

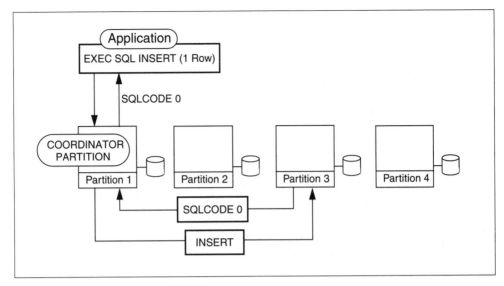

Figure 93. Non-Buffered IMPORT

Buffered INSERTs, shown in Figure 94, are better suited to DB2 UDB EEE. With buffered INSERTs, each row is hashed to a 4KB insert buffer at the coordinator database partition, with one buffer for each database partition where data is being inserted. In Figure 94, there are four database partitions (0 through 3), and hence 4 buffers. As each buffer is filled, it is sent to its target database partition.

In a partitioned database environment, the IMPORT utility can use buffered inserts to reduce the messaging that occurs when data is loaded, resulting in improved performance.

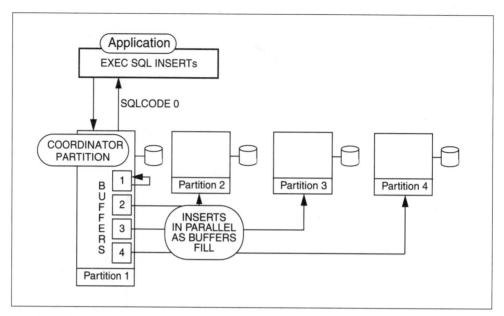

Figure 94. Buffered IMPORT

To select buffered inserts, use the INSERT BUF option of the PREP and BIND commands. (Non-buffered inserts, the default, can also be specified by using INSERT DEF).

You also must rebind the import package. The db2uimpm.bnd bind file (located in the $INSTHOME/sqllib/bnd directory) must be rebound against the database with the INSERT BUF option of the BIND command, as in the following example:

```
cd $INSTHOME/sqllib/bnd
db2 connect to your_database
db2 BIND db2uimpm.bnd INSERT BUF
```

Buffering can significantly improve the performance of an IMPORT. However, if any one record in the input file contains invalid data (for example, a wrong data type, a repeated unique index key, or a referential integrity violation), then the individual record rejected will trigger an SQL ROLLBACK on the whole block. The rollback will be reported asynchronously, and will not identify the individual offending record (or row), as in a non-buffered IMPORT. The ROLLBACK processing will also impact performance, since it must scan the log files sequentially backwards to find the start of the Unit of Work.

Using buffered inserts for IMPORT jobs is a good idea in an DB2 UDB EEE environment, but only if the input data's validity has been checked, or if partial loss of data is not an issue. For a complete list of the options and parameters for IMPORT, please refer to *DB2 UDB Command Reference, S10J-8166*.

Chapter 5. Managing Data

This chapter is divided into two areas: rebalancing data and also backup and recovery.

5.1 Rebalancing Data

The volume of data in your cluster system is more than likely to increase over time. You may find that as the size of your database increases the performance of your system becomes unsatisfactory for your business needs. One way to alleviate this situation is to add new hardware to your system and then rebalance the data to take advantage of the new hardware.

The method DB2 uses to rebalance data is shown in Figure 95.

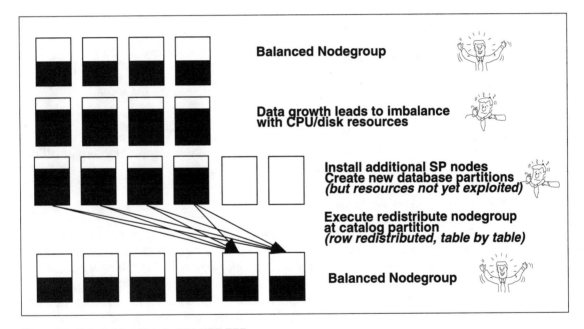

Balanced Nodegroup

Data growth leads to imbalance with CPU/disk resources

Install additional SP nodes
Create new database partitions
(but resources not yet exploited)

Execute redistribute nodegroup
at catalog partition
(row redistributed, table by table)

Balanced Nodegroup

Figure 95. Rebalancing Data in DB2 UDB EEE

In Figure 95, you start with a balanced nodegroup with data distributed evenly among your nodes in your cluster. In this example, data growth leads to a change in your configuration. This change may be the addition of SP nodes, additional CPUs in a SP node, or changing the number of database partitions. The DB2 redistribute nodegroup utility is executed from the catalog partition. The result is a balanced nodegroup.

5.1.1 Scenarios for Scaling

Let's discuss the possible scenarios where a change in the configuration of your cluster system leads you to rebalance your data. This section discusses three possible scenarios that you may cause you to change the number of database partitions:

1. Adding SP node(s) to the cluster system
2. Adding CPUs to an SP node
3. Increasing the number of database partitions (multiple logical nodes)

5.1.1.1 Adding Physical Nodes

This is the case where you have physically added another node to your cluster system (Figure 96). Here there just happens to be two CPUs per node. The number of CPUs is irrelevant to the example.

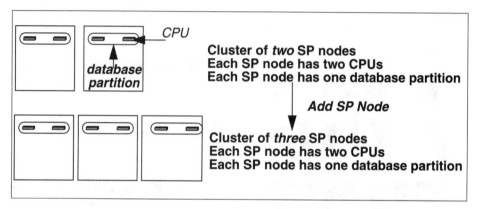

Figure 96. Increasing the Number of SP Nodes

After you add additional SP (physical) nodes, you can then create new database partitions on them. Then using the REDISTRIBUTE NODEGROUP utility, DB2 can rebalance your data to take advantage of the new database partitions. In this scenario you have two SP nodes, each with one database partition. You might increase the number of SP nodes if you experienced an increase in the elapsed response time of your queries. By adding additional SP node(s) and rebalancing the data, you should be able to reduce the query response time.

5.1.1.2 Adding Additional CPUs

In this scenario, the number of CPUs will change. The number of physical nodes remains the same, but CPUs are added to each SP node.

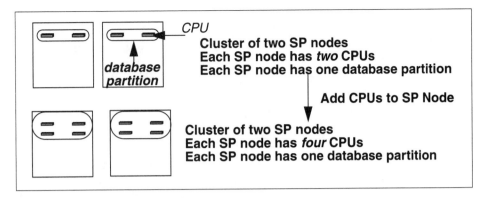

CPU

Cluster of two SP nodes
Each SP node has *two* CPUs
Each SP node has one database partition

database partition

Add CPUs to SP Node

Cluster of two SP nodes
Each SP node has *four* CPUs
Each SP node has one database partition

Figure 97. Increasing the Number of CPUs

If you have Symmetric Multi-Processor (SMP) nodes in your cluster, you can install additional CPUs in each node to take advantage of additional computing capabilities. (The number of CPUs is dependent on your hardware.)

Suppose in Figure 97 we were told that the number of users on the cluster system increased and therefore the number of EEE parallel agent processes executing on each node also increased. By adding additional CPUs, you can take advantage of DB2's inter-query parallelism. Additional parallel agent processes are automatically dispatched to the additional CPU processors by the operating system. A consideration in this case might be adding extra containers to your table spaces to avoid any disk conflicts.

Some of the DB2 utilities, such as `backup`, `restore`, and `load` support CPU parallelism. They also can take advantage of the additional processors.

You can take advantage of additional processors for a single query by adding new logical database partitions which is described in the next section. Intra-partition query parallelism is enabled by setting a parameter. The parameter INTRA_PARALLEL, can be set to either ON or OFF. In a uni-processor environment INTRA_PARALLEL defaults to OFF at install time. If INTRA_PARALLEL flag is ON, intra-partition parallelism is enabled for that DB2 instance. If this parameter is changed, all bound packages will be marked as invalid and will be implicitly rebound on their next execution.

5.1.1.3 Adding Database Partitions

You can add database partitions without changing the hardware configuration. The number of database partitions (logical nodes) may affect the balance of data in your cluster system.

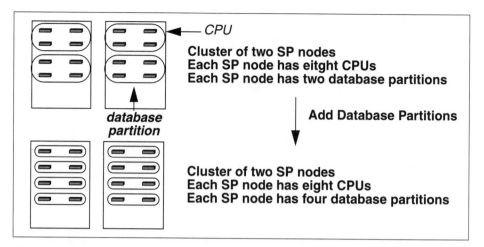

Figure 98. Increasing the Number of Multiple Logical Nodes (MLNs)

You can create new database partitions on existing physical nodes. The database manager processes are started independently for each database partition. You can rebalance your data to include new database partitions with the DB2 REDISTRIBUTE NODEGROUP utility. Figure 98 shows a two-SP node cluster; each SP node is an eight-way SMP (eight CPUs). The original configuration assigned two CPUs to a database partition. On SMP nodes, you can take advantage of additional CPUs and increase the number of database partitions. After the redistribution, each node has four database partitions. As a general rule of thumb, consider assigning two CPUs for each database partition. However, understand that you cannot explicitly assign database partitions in DB2 to CPUs. The operating system controls how the database manager processes are dispatched.

5.1.2 Adding Database Partitions

This section discusses the procedure to add new database partitions. You may have the situation where you are first adding a physical SP host to your cluster and then adding a database partition on the new SP host. If so, there are a number of steps you must do before adding a database partition. This includes some of the following:

- Make the DB2 UDB EEE code available either by using a shared file system mounts or making a local install.

- Synchronize operating system files with those on existing processors.

- Ensure that the sqllib directory is accessible as a shared file system.

- Ensuring that the relevant operating system parameters (such as the maximum number of processes) are set to appropriate values.
- Register the host name with the name server.

Temporary Table Space and Adding Database Partitions

When adding a database partition, you'll need to know some information about the temporary table space containers. To add data to that database partition, a temporary table space for the database partition must exist. There are two methods for adding a database partition in DB2 UDB EEE. This section goes through each method in detail. For each method, however, there are three options, depending on the existing temporary table space, that you need to understand. Understanding the existing temporary table space environment will influence the options of the specific commands you use, regardless of the method for adding database paritions. These options are covered in detail in "Database Partitions and Temporary Table Spaces" on page 262.

Let's look at an overview of the process for adding a database partition.

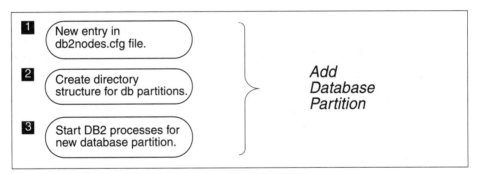

Figure 99. Adding a Database Partition - Overview

Figure 99 is an overview of the steps to add a database partition. There are two methods that you can use to add a database partition. Both of these methods have the same result; a new database partition is added. A new entry is made in the db2nodes.cfg for the database partition. The directory structure for that database partition is created. The temporary table space exists for the database partition. The DB2 processes are started on the newly added database partition. When all these tasks are completed, you may then use the database partition in your database configuration.

There are two methods to adding database partitions in your cluster (Figure 100):

1. Edit the db2nodes.cfg file and manually add the new database partition.

2. Use the `db2start` command with the `ADDNODE` option.

Both of these methods are described in detail in the following sections.

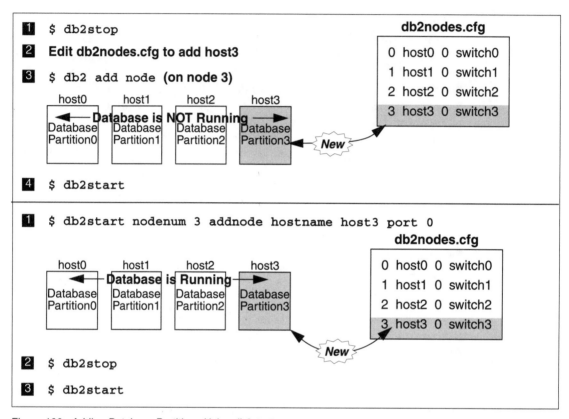

Figure 100. Adding Database Partitions Using db2start

In the first, you must manually edit the db2nodes.cfg file and execute the `ADD NODE` command. The second one involves using the `db2start` command with the `ADDNODE` parameter. Either method will add the database partition. However, if the database manager is running, you can only use the `db2start` command with the `ADDNODE` parameter. This is due to the fact that while the database manager is running, the db2nodes.cfg file is read-only. To edit the file, you must make sure that the database manager is stopped.

Let's look at each method in more detail.

5.1.2.1 Using ADD NODE

This procedure requires that the database manager is stopped. Figure 101 is an overview of the steps to perform. The numbers in the diagram are described as follows:

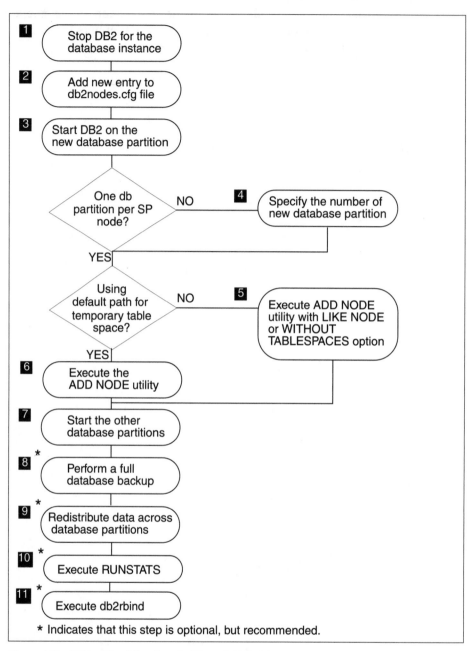

Figure 101. Editing the db2nodes.cfg File to Add Database Partition

1. Stop DB2 for the database instance. Make sure all applications have been disconnected (for example, **db2 force application all**), and then

issue the `db2stop` command. This step is necessary to allow editing to be done to the db2nodes.cfg file. The permissions on the db2nodes.cfg change when the database manager is not active to allow you to edit and save the changes to the file.

2. Edit the db2nodes.cfg file and add the new database partition to it. This is shown in Figure 102.

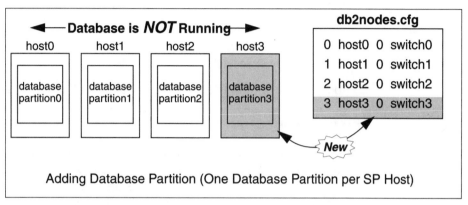

Figure 102. One Database Partition

In Figure 102, we show the example of adding an SP node to the cluster. The new SP node is host3.

3. Issue the following command to start the newly added database partition:

    DB2START NODENUM nodenumber

    Specify the number you are assigning to the new database partition as the value of nodenum. Here, **NODENUM** is 3.

4. If you are configuring multiple database partitions on an SP node, you need to specify the number of the database partition. This step is necessary before using the **ADD NODE** utility and multiple database partitions. To do this task, you can use the **db2set** command with the **DB2NODE** option. Let's consider an example of two SP nodes. We want to add a database partition on one of the SP nodes. Notice how in Figure 103 on page 260, the changes in the db2nodes.cfg. When we edited the file, we added a database partition 3 to host1. In our configuration, we have two database partitions per SP node.

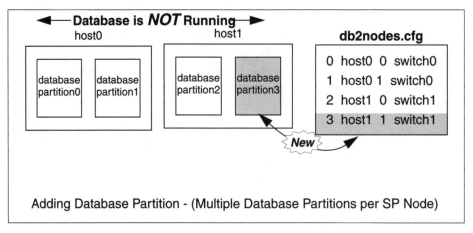

Figure 103. Multiple Database Partitions

If adding a new database partition where multiple database partitions are used, use the `db2set` command to update the DB2NODE registry value, specifying the number of the database partition you are adding. The registry value for DB2NODE is stored in the $HOME/sqllib/profile.env file. In our example (Figure 103):

```
db2set DB2NODE=3
```

To display the current values in the DB2 Profile Registry, execute the `db2set` command with no options.

To see all defined values, at the global and instance level:

```
db2set -all
```

You can also specify the node number by executing the `set client` command. For example:

```
db2 set client attach_node 3
```

If you do not update the DB2 Profile Registry, you will receive an error when executing the `ADD NODE` utility. The `ADD NODE` utility should be executed on the machine where you are adding the database partition. If you do not update the DB2 Profile Registry on that system, the `ADD NODE` utility will use the logical port number that exists on that system. In our example, (Figure 103), we are adding a database partition on host1. You can see from the db2nodes.cfg that the default port number for host1 is 0. If you do not update the DB2 Profile Registry on host1, the `ADD NODE` utility will use logical port 0 by default. You will receive the error the error message saying that database partition already exists (SQLCODE=-1005). Therefore, you must update the DB2 Profile Registry.

5. There are three possibilities to consider for the path for the temporary table space for the database partition you are adding:

   1. You will use the default container path (SMS table space) for the temporary table space. For example, /db/inst1/NODE0000/SQL0001. In this case, you can execute the ADD NODE utility without options.

   2. You must use the LIKE NODE option of the ADD NODE utility.

   3. You must use the WITHOUT TABLESPACES option of the ADD NODE utility.

   The LIKE NODE and WITHOUT TABLESPACES options are discussed in "Temporary Table Space and Multiple DB Partitions (Default)" on page 263.

6. Run the ADD NODE utility on the machine where the you are adding the new database partition.

   ```
   db2 add node
   ```

   The ADD NODE utility creates the directory structure in the database path on the SP node where the new database partition has been created. For example, /dbpath/inst1/NODE0003, where dbpath is the database path, inst1 is the instance name and NODE0003 is the directory for the database partition. The parameters in the database configuration file are set to default values. Also, the ADD NODE utility creates a temporary table space on the newly created database partition. However, only the temporary table space is created. The partition remains empty until you redistribute data.

   If you add another database partition, you must first update the value of DB2NODE in the DB2 Profile Registry before using the ADD NODE utility. To do so, you must terminate your current Command Line Processor session.

   ```
   db2 terminate
   db2set DB2NODE=new_nodenum
   ```

   This is necessary because the value stored in DB2NODE in the DB2 Profile Registry is the last entry. After changing the DB2NODE value in the DB2 Profile Registry, you can execute the ADD NODE utility. Executing the ADD NODE utility starts a new Command Line Processor session which uses the changed value of DB2NODE when determining the database partition to add.

7. When the ADD NODE utility completes, issue the db2start command to start the other existing database partitions in the system.

   ```
   db2start
   ```

You should not attempt to do any system wide activities, such as creating or dropping a database, until all SP nodes are successfully started.

8. Optionally, take a backup of all databases on the new server.

9. Optionally, redistribute data to the new database partition. For details, see "Redistributing Data Across Database Partitions" on page 274.

10. Optionally, execute the RUNSTATS utility to update statistics in the system catalogs. When executing RUNSTATS in DB2 UDB EEE, the statistics that relate to a table and its indexes are done at the database partition level. Because the statistics stored in the catalogs represent table-level information, the database partition-level statistics collected by the DB2 database manager are multiplied where appropriate by the number of partitions.

11. Optionally, rebind all the packages in the database with the db2rbind command.

5.1.2.2 Database Partitions and Temporary Table Spaces

This section discusses the three possible scenarios for temporary table spaces that occur when adding a database partition. We'll show these scenarios in an MDP environment. In either case, you must log into the host where the partition will be added. If adding a database partition in an MDP environment, you must execute the following commands before adding the database partition:

```
$ db2 terminate
$ db2set DB2NODE=new_node_number
```

In the above, new_node_number should be a numeric value. It will be the number of the database partition you are adding as it appears in the db2nodes.cfg file. Alternatively, you can replace the db2set command with the following:

```
db2 set client attach_node new_node_number
```

where new_node_number is the number of the database partition you are adding.

These three scenarios affect both methods of adding a database partition and are basically the same. What is different is the selection of the path for the temporary table space. The options are the following:

1. Using a default path

2. Using a non-default path that is similar to that of an existing database partition

3. Using a non-default path that is unique among the existing partitions

Let's first consider the default path for the temporary table space when using multiple database partitions on a single SP node.

Using a Default Path

When you create a database, the default path for the container of the temporary table space includes the node number of each database partition.

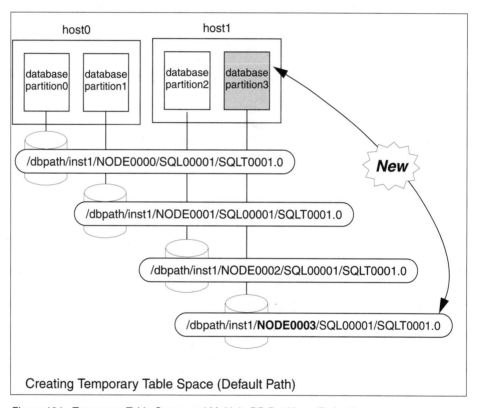

Creating Temporary Table Space (Default Path)

Figure 104. Temporary Table Space and Multiple DB Partitions (Default)

If you execute the ADD NODE utility without any options, the temporary table space definitions are retrieved from the catalog partition, and containers are created in the directory which path for the new node numbers (See Figure 104). Here, we have added database partition 3. The default path for the temporary table space is /dbpath/inst1/NODE0003/SQL00001/SQLT0001.0. NODE0003 was the next number to be assigned because 3 is the first column of the db2nodes.cfg file. If another database partition is added, it will be assigned NODE0004, and so on. This is the default case.

If you are using a different path for the temporary table space that does not include the database partition number, you must use the `ADD NODE` utility either with the `LIKE NODE` parameter or the `WITHOUT TABLESPACES` parameter.

Using a Similar Path (Non-Default)
Suppose we are have created temporary table spaces on our other database partitions so that the path does not include the database partition number. When we execute the `ADD NODE` utility, we receive the following error:

```
$ db2set DB2NODE=3
$ db2 add node
SQL6073N  Add Node operation failed.  SQLCODE = "-294".
```

When executing the `ADD NODE` utility, you receive an error code of -294 indicating that the container is already in use. This is shown in Figure 105.

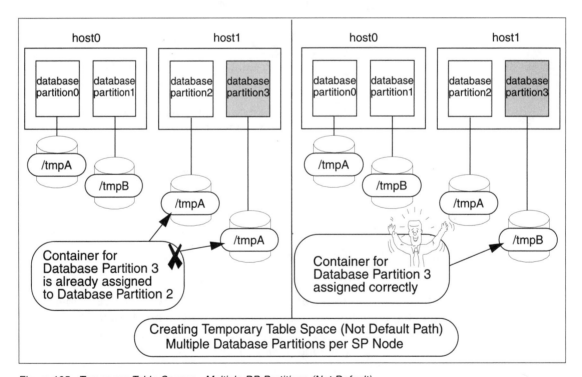

Figure 105. Temporary Table Spaces - Multiple DB Partitions (Not Default)

If you execute the ADD NODE utility without any options, temporary table spaces are assigned according to defaults. If you are using a different path for your temporary table spaces, there are two different options to consider using when executing the ADD NODE utility.

```
$ db2 add node like node 1
DB20000I   The ADD NODE command completed successfully.
```

Using the right-most portion of Figure 105 on page 264 as our example, if we want to add database partition 3, we need to explicitly set the path for the temporary table space. We can do so here with the LIKE NODE parameter of the ADD NODE utility. We want to define the path as it is defined on database partition 1 which is located on host0. Don't be confused by the terminology in the ADD NODE utility. You are adding a database partition. You want to make that database partition definitions similar to those in database partition 1. (The utility uses the term NODE.)

Using a Unique Path (Non-Default)
Another way to accomplish the same result is using the ADD NODE utility with the WITHOUT TABLESPACES parameter.

```
$ db2 add node without tablespaces
DB20000I   The ADD NODE command completed successfully.
$
$ db2 "alter tablespace tmp add ('/tmpB') on node (3)"
$ db2 DB20000I   The SQL command completed successfully.
```

Using the WITHOUT TABLESPACES option will create a database partition without a temporary table space. You must then use the ALTER TABLESPACE SQL statement to correctly add a temporary table space using the container definition you desire.You must issue the ALTER TABLESPACE statement in this case before you use the database partition. If you do not have a temporary table space created when you first use the database partition, you will receive a -1753 error code.

5.1.2.3 Using db2start with ADDNODE Parameter
This method can be used whether the database manager is active or not. However, a newly added database partition does not become available to a database until the database manager is stopped and restarted. When the DB2START command completes, the database partition you are adding is stopped. The db2nodes.cdfg file is not updated with the new information until

a DB2STOP command is executed. This ensures that the ADD NODE utility (which is executed when the ADDNODE parameter is specified with DB2START) executes on the correct database partition.

So any special considerations, such as creating containers for temporary table spaces to be used on the new database partition or multiple database partitions on a host, must be considered before executing the DB2START command.

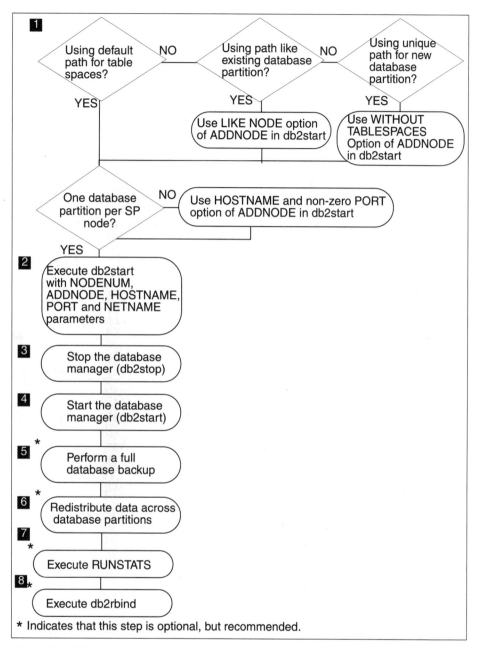

Figure 106. Using db2start to Add Database Partition

When the **ADDNODE** parameter is specified in the **DB2START** utility, the procedure to add the database partition is similar to that using the **ADD NODE** utility; the db2nodes.cfg file is updated, and the ADD NODE utility is executed. To add new database partition using the DB2START utility, use the following steps:

1. You can also optionally specify the containers for temporary table spaces that are used on the database partition you are adding. You need to ask this question before you issue the DB2START command because it will change the options used in the DB2START command. For more detail, see "Database Partitions and Temporary Table Spaces" on page 262.

   You also need to know if multiple database partitions are being used on the host where you are adding the new database partition. You need to supply the database partition number for the PORT option of ADDNODE of the db2start command.

2. Run the DB2START utility on any database partition, specifying the NODENUM, ADDNODE, HOSTNAME, PORT, and NETNAME parameters. The values that you specify for these parameters are used to update the db2nodes.cfg file.

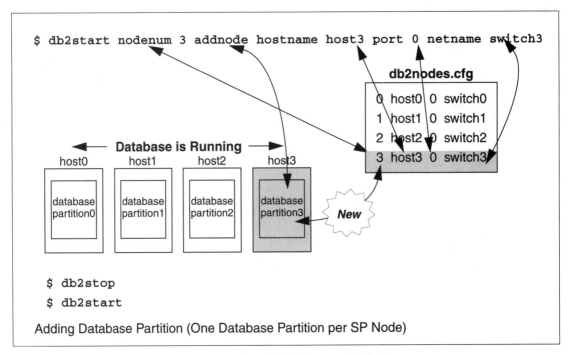

Figure 107. Using db2start to Add DB Partition (One DB Partition per SP Node)

The command used for Figure 108 is as follows:

```
$ db2start nodenum 3 addnode hostname host3 port 0 netname switch3
02-06-1998 08:42:17   3   0   SQL6075W  The Start Database Manager
operation successfully added the node. The node is not active
until all nodes are stopped and started again
```

Figure 107 is an example of using the db2start command to add a database partition. Here, we have one database partition per SP node. The options for the db2start command that we used are the following:

- **NODENUM nodenum** - In an EEE environment, this option is used to tell the database manager that we only want the db2start command to be executed on nodenum. In our example, nodenum is 3, indicating the database partition we are adding. If the nodenum option is not used, db2start is executed on all database partitions as defined in the db2nodes.cfg file.

- **ADDNODE** - This indicates we are adding a database partition to the db2nodes.cfg file. In our example, we are adding database partition 3. The ADDNODE parameter has several options.

  - **HOSTNAME hostname** - The HOSTNAME parameter must always be specified. This is the host name for the database partition we are adding. The value for HOSTNAME is added to the db2nodes.cfg file. Here, HOSTNAME is host3.

  - **PORT logical-port** - As with the HOSTNAME, the PORT must be specified. You cannot use the default values. The HOSTNAME and PORT are necessary to update the db2nodes.cfg file.

  - **NETNAME netname** - If netname is specified, then the hostname is used for db2start, db2stop, and db2_all commands. The netname is used for all other DB2 communication between SP nodes. In our example, NETNAME is switch3, indicating we are using the SP switch for most DB2 communication between machines other than those listed here.

  - **LIKE NODE node-number** - This is the case when we want to specify that the containers for temporary table spaces on the database partition we are adding are like or similar to those specified in LIKE NODE.

  - **WITHOUT TABLESPACES** - When adding a database partition with this parameter, no temporary table spaces will be created for the database partition. You must use the SQL ALTER TABLESPACE statement to add temporary table space containers for the database partition before you can access the database.

For an explanation of the differences between the LIKE NODE and WITHOUT TABLESPACES options of ADDNODE during the DB2START utility, see "Database Partitions and Temporary Table Spaces" on page 262.

3. Stop the database manager by executing the DB2STOP command. When you stop all the nodes in the system, the db2nodes.cfg file is updated to include the new database partition.

```
$ db2stop
02-06-1998 08:47:08   0  0   SQL1064N  DB2STOP processing was successful.
02-06-1998 08:47:08   1  0   SQL1064N  DB2STOP processing was successful.
02-06-1998 08:47:08   2  0   SQL1064N  DB2STOP processing was successful.
SQL1064N  DB2STOP processing was successful.
```

4. Start the database manager by executing the DB2START command. The newly added database partition is now started along with the rest of the system. When all the database partitions in the system are running, system-wide activities, such as creating or dropping a database, can be done.

```
$ db2start
02-06-1998 08:47:11   3  0   SQL1063N  DB2START processing was successful.
02-06-1998 08:47:12   0  0   SQL1063N  DB2START processing was successful.
02-06-1998 08:47:12   1  0   SQL1063N  DB2START processing was successful.
02-06-1998 08:47:12   2  0   SQL1063N  DB2START processing was successful.
SQL1065N  DB2START processing was successful.
```

5. Optionally, take a backup of all databases on the new database partition.

6. Optionally, redistribute data to the new database partition. For details, see "Redistributing Data Across Database Partitions" on page 274.

7. Optionally, execute the RUNSTATS utility.

8. Optionally, execute the db2rbind command.

5.1.3 Dropping A Database Partition

You can drop a database partition by using the DB2STOP command with the DROP NODENUM parameter or the sqlepstp API. Before doing this, you must first ensure that the database partition being dropped is not being used by any database.

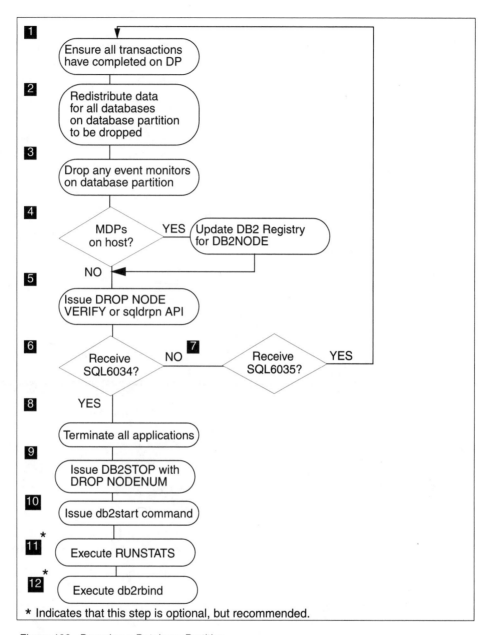

Figure 108. Dropping a Database Partition

Let's look at the steps as outlined in Figure 108.

1. Check to make sure that all transactions where the database partition to be dropped served as the coordinator have committed or rolled back

successfully. This may require you to do a database restart (crash recovery process) on the other database partition server.

For example, if you drop the coordinator database partition where another database partition that was participating in the transaction experienced a failure before the dropping of the database partition, you will not be able to query the coordinator database partition as to the outcome of any indoubt transaction.

2. Redistribute the data for every database using this database partition. The details for this step are discussed in "Update Nodegroup Definition Before Dropping DB Partition" on page 294.

3. Drop any event monitors defined on the database partition.

4. If using MDPs, use the `db2set` command to update the DB2 Registry for the DB2NODE variable, specifying the number of the database partition you are dropping.

```
$ db2 terminate
$ db2set DB2NODE=3
```

5. To ensure that the database partition is not in use, use the **DROP NODE VERIFY** command. Remember that if using multiple database partitions, you must first update the DB2 Profile Registry for the DB2NODE value.

If the database partition is in use, you'll receive the following message:

```
$ db2set DB2NODE=2
$ db2 drop node verify
SQL6035W  Node "2" is being used by database "SAMPLE".
```

6. If you receive SQL6035W indicating that the database partition to be dropped is in use, you must go back to step 1 and repeat the procedure.

If the database partition is not in use, you'll receive the following message:

```
$ db2 terminate
$ db2set DB2NODE=3
$ db2 drop node verify
SQL6034W Node "3" is not being used by any databases.
```

7. If you receive SQL6034W indicating that the database partition to be dropped is not in use, you may proceed to the next step.

8. Terminate all applications for the database. When you issue the `db2stop` command with the `DROP NODENUM` parameter, it will stop the database manager on all database partitions.

9. You can now drop the database partition using the `db2stop` command with the `DROP NODENUM` option.

```
$ db2stop drop nodenum 2
SQL6076W  Warning! This command will remove all database files on the
node for this instance.  Before continuing, ensure that there is no
user data on this node by running the DROP NODE VERIFY command.
Do you want to continue ? (y/n)y
02-09-1998 19:04:19  0  0  SQL1064N  DB2STOP processing was successful.
02-09-1998 19:04:20  2  0  SQL1064N  DB2STOP processing was successful.
02-09-1998 19:04:21  1  0  SQL1064N  DB2STOP processing was successful.
02-09-1998 19:04:23  1  0  SQL1063N  DB2START processing was
successful.
02-09-1998 19:04:25  0  0  SQL1063N  DB2START processing was
successful.
02-09-1998 19:04:26  2  0  SQL1063N  DB2START processing was
successful.
02-09-1998 19:04:32  2  0  SQL6034W  Node "2" is not being used by any
databases.
02-09-1998 19:04:35  2  0  SQL1064N  DB2STOP processing was successful.
02-09-1998 19:04:36  1  0  SQL1064N  DB2STOP processing was successful.
02-09-1998 19:04:37  0  0  SQL1064N  DB2STOP processing was
successful.
02-09-1998 19:04:41  2  0  SQL1064N  DB2STOP processing was
successful.
SQL1064N  DB2STOP processing was successful.
$ db2start
02-09-1998 19:04:50 1  0  SQL1063N  DB2START processing was
successful.
02-09-1998 19:04:50 0  0  SQL1063N  DB2START processing was
successful.
SQL1063N  DB2START processing was successful.
```

Figure 109. Dropping a Database Partition

Figure 109 shows that after executing the `db2stop` command, you will be prompted by DB2 to continue. In our example, we are dropping database partition 2. The first and second columns indicate the date when the command was issued. The third column refers to the database partition. Notice that DB2 stops and starts the database manager for the instance, then issues a `DROP NODE VERIFY` command. This is to check that the partition to be dropped is not in use. If SQL6034W was received, the database manager again is stopped. At this time, DB2 will perform some of the tasks to remove the database partition such as editing the db2nodes.cfg file and stopping DB2 processes on that DP, for example.

10. Upon completion, issue the `db2start` command.

11. Optionally, execute the `RUNSTATS` utility.

12. Optionally, execute the `db2rbind` command.

5.2 Redistributing Data Across Database Partitions

The previous sections dealt with the topics of adding and dropping a database partition. After adding or before dropping a database partition, you must update your nodegroup definition by altering the nodegroup definition and then using the `REDISTRIBUTE NODEGROUP` utility to move the data to the appropriate database partitions.

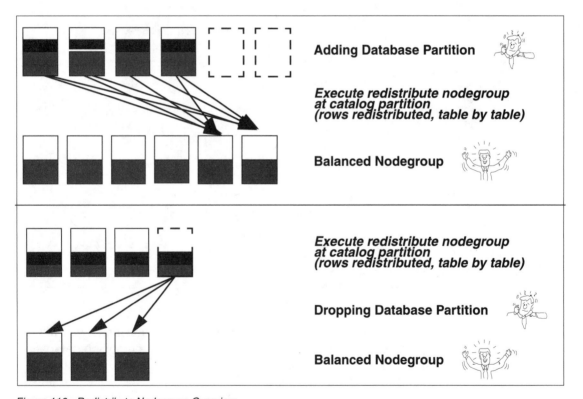

Figure 110. Redistribute Nodegroup Overview

Figure 110 is an overview of the `REDISTRIBUTE NODEGROUP` procedure. Notice that the result is the same, a balanced nodegroup. If you are adding a database partition, you need to be aware of those items that will be added in the event that you have to create objects before performing the redistribution of the nodegroup. Conversely, if dropping a database partition, you need to understand what will be deleted, both automatically by DB2 and manually by you. For example, a file system created for the database partition will no longer be associated with DB2, but will physically remain on the system.

This section focuses on the redistribution process when adding a database partition. The procedure for dropping and redistribution is similar and not covered here.

5.2.1 Update Nodegroup Definition After Adding DB Partition

When a database partition has been successfully added to the db2nodes.cfg file, nodegroup IBMTEMPGROUP's definition has been changed to include the new database partition. However, any user-defined nodegroups remain unchanged. To use the new database partition in all nodegroups, you must:

1. Add the new database partition to user-defined nodegroups.

2. Add containers on the new database partitions for all table spaces in the nodegroup.

   Steps 1 and 2 are performed by executing the SQL `ALTER NODEGROUP` statement with the `ADD NODE` parameter. There are three options for the `ADD NODE` parameter for your table space container definitions. These options are similar to those for the temporary table space when adding a database partition. (See "Database Partitions and Temporary Table Spaces" on page 262 for more information.) These options are:

   1. Use the default container definitions.

      This is when using the `ADD NODE` parameter of the `ALTER NODEGROUP` statement without options. The container definitions are retrieved for the lowest database partition number of the existing partitions in the nodegroup.

   2. Use a container definition that is `LIKE` an existing one in the nodegroup.

      This involves using the `ADD NODE LIKE` parameter of the SQL `ALTER NODEGROUP` statement. You can specify which container definitions for a particular database partition in the nodegroup to use.

   3. Use a unique container definition.

You can use the ADD NODE WITHOUT TABLESPACES parameter of the SQL ALTER NODEGROUP statement. This will alter the nodegroup definition, but not retrieve any container definitions. You must then execute the SQL ALTER TABLESPACES statement to specify the unique definition of the new containers for the table spaces in the nodegroup.

3. Distribute data to the new database partition.

This step redistributes the data to the new database partition. Understand that both the ALTER NODEGROUP and the ALTER TABLESPACE statements do not move data, nor update the partition map for the nodegroup. This is done by the REDISTRIBUTE NODEGROUP command.

There are four possible nodegroup redistribution methods when adding a database partition.

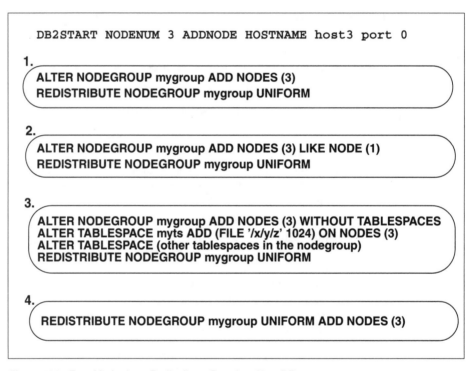

DB2START NODENUM 3 ADDNODE HOSTNAME host3 port 0

1.
ALTER NODEGROUP mygroup ADD NODES (3)
REDISTRIBUTE NODEGROUP mygroup UNIFORM

2.
ALTER NODEGROUP mygroup ADD NODES (3) LIKE NODE (1)
REDISTRIBUTE NODEGROUP mygroup UNIFORM

3.
ALTER NODEGROUP mygroup ADD NODES (3) WITHOUT TABLESPACES
ALTER TABLESPACE myts ADD (FILE '/x/y/z' 1024) ON NODES (3)
ALTER TABLESPACE (other tablespaces in the nodegroup)
REDISTRIBUTE NODEGROUP mygroup UNIFORM

4.
REDISTRIBUTE NODEGROUP mygroup UNIFORM ADD NODES (3)

Figure 111. Four Methods to Redistribute Data in a New DP

Figure 111 shows four possible methods that you can use to redistribute data in a nodegroup after adding a database partition. We look at each method in detail and then give a summary as to when you would use which method. You need to understand how each of these work so that you can decide what method you should use in your cluster environment.

We use basically the same example in each of the four methods. However, we will use both an SDP and MDP environment. Figure 111 shows that database partition 3 is being added to the cluster. Remember that executing the db2start command with the ADDNODE option will make an entry into the db2nodes.cfg file for the database partition. Also, the IBMTEMPGROUP nodegroup definition will be updated, DB2 processes will be started, and so on. Let's discuss each of the four methods.

5.2.1.1 Alter Nodegroup Add Node

In this example, we'll show two scenarios. Both examples use the container definitions that are retrieved from the lowest database partition number of the existing partitions in the nodegroup. The SQL ALTER NODEGROUP statement does the following:

1. Changes the nodegroup definition that is stored in the SYSNODEGROUPS catalog table

2. Creates table spaces on the new database partitions and defines containers

The difference between the two examples is the path defined for the table space. You need to ask yourself the question "Do my table space containers use the database path"? to understand the difference between the next two examples.

Not Using the Database Path

In this example, the ALTER NODEGROUP statement was executed with the ADD NODE parameter. The nodegroup definition was updated and new containers were defined on the new database partitions for all table spaces.

The container definitions of each table space are retrieved from the lowest database partition number of the existing partitions in the nodegroup (see Figure 112).

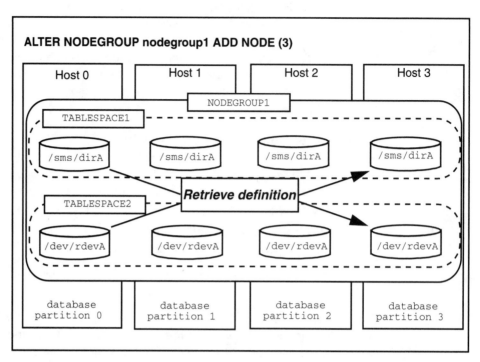

Figure 112. ALTER NODEGROUP ADD NODE (Not Using Database Path)

In Figure 112, database partition 3 is being added to nodegroup1. The container definition for database partition 3 is retrieved from database partition 0. There are two table spaces in NODEGROUP1, TABLESPACE1 and TABLESPACE2. TABLESPACE 1 is an SMS table space. All the containers are directories with an absolute path of /sms/dirA. TABLESPACE2 is a DMS table space using raw devices (logical volumes) with an absolute path /dev/rdevA. If all of your table space containers are in the same file system as the temporary table space, the file system would have been created before executing the ADD NODE command to add the database partition. But if you would like to use a file system other than the one used by the temporary table space or raw devices (logical volumes), you should allocate the storage and change access permissions before executing the ALTER NODEGROUP statement.

Notice how not using the database path for your table space containers as in Figure 112 would not work in an MDP environment.

Using the Database Path
If the your container definition is on the database directory (for example, /dbpath/inst1/NODE0000/SQL00001), the definition of containers retrieved

for the new database partition is not an absolute path, but a relative path (see Figure 113 on page 279).

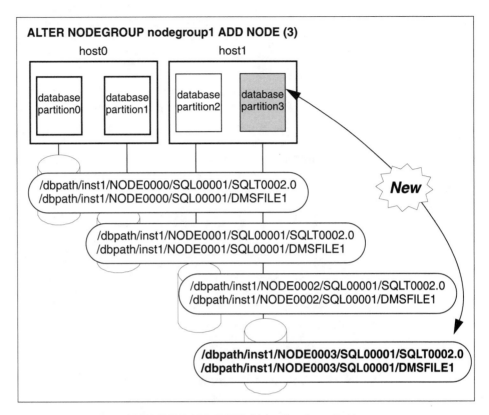

ALTER NODEGROUP nodegroup1 ADD NODE (3)

host0　　　　　　　　host1

database partition0　database partition1　database partition2　database partition3

/dbpath/inst1/NODE0000/SQL00001/SQLT0002.0
/dbpath/inst1/NODE0000/SQL00001/DMSFILE1

/dbpath/inst1/NODE0001/SQL00001/SQLT0002.0
/dbpath/inst1/NODE0001/SQL00001/DMSFILE1

/dbpath/inst1/NODE0002/SQL00001/SQLT0002.0
/dbpath/inst1/NODE0002/SQL00001/DMSFILE1

/dbpath/inst1/NODE0003/SQL00001/SQLT0002.0
/dbpath/inst1/NODE0003/SQL00001/DMSFILE1

New

Figure 113. ALTER NODEGOURP ADD NODE (Using Database Path)

In this case, when the table space container is created on database partition3, the full path is a unique entry, even if the file system, /dbpath/inst1, is shared between database partitions on the same host. For this reason, you could use this type of path (database path) in either an SDP or MDP environment. In this example, our environment is MDP. The syntax for the db2start command in this MDP example is the following:

```
db2start nodenum 3 addnode hostname host1 port 1
```

When the ALTER NODEGROUP statement completes, you might receive the following message:

```
$ db2 "alter nodegroup nodegroup1 add node (3)" SQL1759W
Redistribute nodegroup is required to change data
partitioning for objects in nodegroup "NODEGROUP1" to
include some added nodes or exclude some dropped nodes.
SQLSTATE=01618
```

This message is not an error. It means that data has not been distributed and you need to execute the REDISTRIBUTE NODEGROUP utility. If no tables are defined in the table spaces of that nodegroup, you will not receive the warning message. If you check the SYSNODEGROUPDEF catalog table, you'll see that it has been modified. You can also issue the LIST NODEGROUPS SHOW DETAIL command to obtain the same information.

```
db2 "select * from sysibm.sysnodegroupdef"
NGNAME                NODENUM IN_USE
------------------    ------- ------
IBMCATGROUP                0  Y
IBMDEFAULTGROUP           0  Y
NODEGROUP1                 0  Y
NODEGROUP1                 1  Y
NODEGROUP1                 2  Y
NODEGROUP1                 3  A
```

Added

The IN_USE column of the newly added database partition has the value 'A'. This means that the redistribute utility has not been executed, and this partition is not in the partitioning map; but the containers for the table spaces of the nodegroup have been created.

You can see the table spaces and table space containers that have been created on the new database partition by executing the LIST TABLESPACES and LIST TABLESPACE CONTAINERS commands. These commands list only the information about the current database partition. So if you want to obtain table space information for the new database partition, you have to execute the commands on the host where the new database partition was added. If your cluster system has multiple database partitions, you should update the value of DB2NODE in the DB2 Profile Registry by using the db2set command. The following is sample output for the new database partition:

```
$ db2set DB2NODE=3
$ db2 connect to db1

   Database Connection Information

 Database product       = DB2/6000 5.0.0
 SQL authorization ID   = DB2INST1
 Local database alias   = DB1
$ db2 list tablespaces
Tablespaces for Current Database

 Tablespace ID                          = 1
 Name                                   = TEMPSPACE1
 Type                                   = System managed space
 Contents                               = Temporary data
 State                                  = 0x0000
   Detailed explanation:
     Normal

 Tablespace ID                          = 3
 Name                                   = TABLESPACE1
 Type                                   = System managed space
 Contents                               = Any data
 State                                  = 0x0000
   Detailed explanation:
     Normal

 Tablespace ID                          = 4
 Name                                   = TABLESPACE2
 Type                                   = Database managed space
 Contents                               = Any data
 State                                  = 0x0000
   Detailed explanation:
     Normal
DB21011I  In a partitioned database server environment, only the
table spaces on the current node are listed.

$ db2 list tablespace containers for 3

          Tablespace Containers for Tablespace 3

 Container ID                           = 0
 Name                                   = /sms/dirA

$ db2 list tablespaces containers for 4

          Tablespace Containers for Tablespace 4

 Container ID                           = 0
 Name                                   = /dev/rdevA
```

Three table spaces are displayed. (This matches what is shown in Figure 112 on page 278.) The container for the temporary table space TEMPSPACE1 was created as part of the ADD NODE statement. The containers for TABLESPACE1 and TABLESPACE2 were created as part of the execution of the SQL ALTER NODEGROUP statement. Notice that the table space containers for TABLESPACE1 and TABLESPACE2 have been created with the same names as those obtained from the first database partition defined in db2nodes.cfg (the database partition with the lowest numeric value).

If you now create a new table and load data into it, the new database partition is not used yet. It is used only after the redistribute nodegroup utility has completed. For details on the redistribute nodegroup utility see 5.3 on page 296.

5.2.1.2 Alter Nodegroup Add Node Like Node

This is the second method (see Figure 111 on page 276) that uses container definitions similar to those of existing container definitions. The nodegroup definition is updated, and containers are added on the new database partition for all table spaces. This is same as the method one, but the container definitions of each table space are retrieved from the database partition specified in the LIKE NODE parameter.

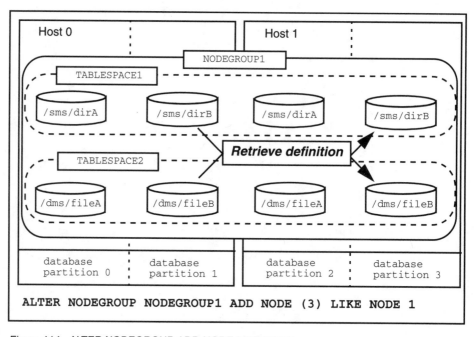

Figure 114. ALTER NODEGROUP ADD NODE LIKE NODE

In Figure 114, multiple database partitions are defined on a single SP host. The path for the containers do not include the database directory. Database partition 3 is being added to nodegroup1. The LIKE NODE parameter is useful in this configuration. If you execute the ALTER NODEGROUP statement without any parameters (default, shown in method one), you'll receive and error stating that the container is already in use because the container definition conflicts with that of database partition 2. You can use the LIKE NODE parameter to specify the database partition number from where the container definition is retrieved. If you would like to use new file systems or raw devices for DMS table spaces, you should allocate them and change access permission before executing the ALTER NODEGROUP statement.

When the ALTER NODEGROUP statement completes, you might receive the following message:

```
$ db2 "alter nodegroup nodegroup1 add node (3) like node 1"
SQL1759W  Redistribute nodegroup is required to change data
partitioning for objects in nodegroup "NODEGROUP1" to include
some added nodes or exclude some dropped nodes. SQLSTATE=01618
```

This message is not an error. It means that data has not been distributed and you need to execute the redistribute nodegroup utility. If no tables are defined in the table spaces of that nodegroup, you will not receive the warning message. If you check the SYSNODEGROUPDEF catalog table, you'll see that it has been modified. You can also issue the LIST NODEGROUPS SHOW DETAIL command to obtain the same information.

```
db2 "select * from sysibm.sysnodegroupdef"
NGNAME                  NODENUM IN_USE
----------------------- ------- ------
IBMCATGROUP                   0 Y
IBMDEFAULTGROUP               0 Y
NODEGROUP1                    0 Y
NODEGROUP1                    1 Y
NODEGROUP1                    2 Y
NODEGROUP1                    3 A
```
Added

You can see the table spaces and table space containers that have been created on the new database partition by executing the LIST TABLESPACES and LIST TABLESPACE CONTAINERS commands. These commands list only the information about the current database partition. So if you want to obtain table space information for the new database partition, you have to execute the commands on the host where the new database partition was added. If your cluster system has multiple database partitions, you should update the value of DB2NODE in the DB2 profile Registry by using the DB2SET command. The following is sample output for the new database partition:

```
$ db2set DB2NODE=3
$ db2 connect to db1

   Database Connection Information
Database product      = DB2/6000 5.0.0
 SQL authorization ID = DB2INST1
 Local database alias = DB1


$ db2 list tablespaces
Tablespaces for Current Database

 Tablespace ID                            = 1
 Name                                     = TEMPSPACE1
 Type                                     = System managed space
 Contents                                 = Temporary data
 State                                    = 0x0000
   Detailed explanation:
      Normal

 Tablespace ID                            = 3
 Name                                     = TABLESPACE1
 Type                                     = System managed space
 Contents                                 = Any data
 State                                    = 0x0000
   Detailed explanation:
      Normal

 Tablespace ID                            = 4
 Name                                     = TABLESPACE2
 Type                                     = Database managed space
 Contents                                 = Any data
 State                                    = 0x0000
   Detailed explanation:
      Normal

DB21011I  In a partitioned database server environment, only the
table spaces on the current node are listed.
$ db2 list tablespace containers for 3

           Tablespace Containers for Tablespace 3

 Container ID                             = 0
 Name                                     = /sms/dirB
 Type                                     = Path
$ db2 list tablespaces containers for 4

           Tablespace Containers for Tablespace 4

 Container ID                             = 0
 Name                                     = /dms/fileB
 Type                                     = File
```

Three tablespaces are displayed. (This matches what is shown in Figure 114 on page 282.) The container for the temporary table space TEMPSPACE1 was created as part of the ADD NODE statement. The containers for TABLESPACE1 and TABLESPACE2 were created as part of the execution of the SQL ALTER NODEGROUP statement. Notice that the table space containers for TABLESPACE1 and TABLESPACE2 have been created with the same names as the database partition specified 1 with the LIKE NODE option.

If you now create a new table and load data into it, the new database partition is not used yet. It is used only after the redistribute nodegroup utility has completed. For details on the redistribute nodegroup utility see 5.3 on page 296.

5.2.1.3 Alter Nodegroup Add Node Without Tablespaces

This method is when the path for the container definition is unique. You execute the ALTER NODEGROUP statement using the WITHOUT TABLESPACES parameter first. This statement updates the nodegroup definition but does not add containers on the new database partition for any user-defined table spaces. You must execute the ALTER TABLESPACE statement for each table space in the nodegroup to specify the container definition (see Figure 115 on page 287).

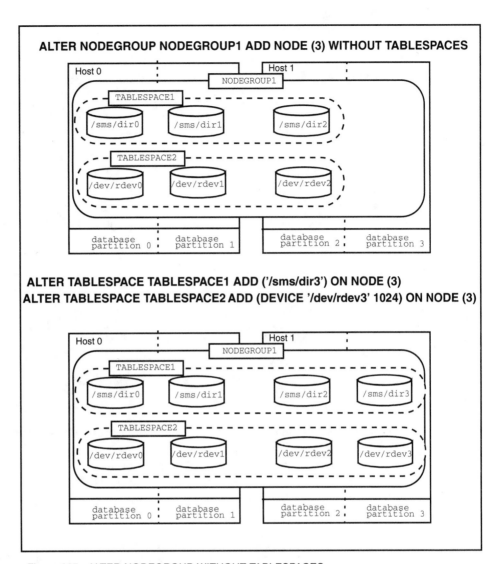

Figure 115. ALTER NODEGROUP WITHOUT TABLESPACES

In Figure 115, database partition 3 is being added to nodegroup1, but when the **ALTER NODEGROUP** statement completes, the containers of the user-defined table spaces in the nodegroup have not been created. The containers for database partition 3 are specified and created by the **ALTER TABLESPACE** statement. You can specify the definition of each table space container by this statement. If you would like to use new file systems or raw devices for DMS table spaces, you should allocate them and change access permission before executing the **ALTER TABLESPACE** statement.

When the `ALTER NODEGROUP` statement completes, you might receive the following message

```
$ db2 "alter nodegroup nodegroup1 add node (3) without tablespaces"
SQL1759W  Redistribute nodegroup is required to change data
partitioning for objects in nodegroup "NODEGROUP1" to include some
added nodes or exclude some dropped nodes. SQLSTATE=01618
```

This message is not an error. It means that data has not been distributed and you need to execute the `REDISTRIBUTE NODEGROUP` utility. If no tables are defined in the table spaces of that nodegroup, you will not receive the warning message. If you check the SYSNODEGROUPDEF catalog table, you'll see that it has been modified. You can also issue the `LIST NODEGROUPS SHOW DETAIL` command to obtain the same information.

```
db2 "select * from sysibm.sysnodegroupdef"
NGNAME                  NODENUM IN_USE
------------------      ------- ------
IBMCATGROUP                 0 Y
IBMDEFAULTGROUP             0 Y          Added
NODEGROUP1                  0 Y          without
NODEGROUP1                  1 Y          Table Spaces
NODEGROUP1                  2 Y
NODEGROUP1                  3 T
```

The IN_USE column for the added database partition has a value of 'T'. This means that this database partition is not in the partition map. It was added using the `WITHOUT TABLESPACES` parameter. If you execute the `redistribute nodegroup` utility when the IN_USE column is marked by 'T', you'll receive the following error message:

```
$ db2 redistribute nodegroup nodegroup1 uniform
SQL1755N  Node "3" does not have containers for all the tablespaces
defined in the nodegroup "NODEGROUP1".
```

You must execute the `ALTER TABLESPACE` statement for all table spaces in this nodegroup and create new containers for this database partition. When creating containers for all table spaces is complete, the IN_USE column becomes an 'A', and you can then execute the `REDISTRIBUTE NODEGROUP` utility.

You can see the table spaces and table space containers that have been created on the new database partition by executing the LIST TABLESPACES and LIST TABLESPACE CONTAINERS commands. These commands list only the information about the current database partition. So if you want to obtain table space information for the new database partition, you have to execute the commands on the host where the new database partition was added. If your cluster system has multiple database partitions, you should update the value of DB2NODE in the DB2 profile Registry by using the DB2SET command. The following is sample output for the new database partition immediately after the ADD NODE WITHOUT TABLESPACES command completed, but before the ALTER TABLESPACE statement has been issued:

```
$ db2set DB2NODE=3
$ db2 connect to db1

   Database Connection Information

 Database product       = DB2/6000 5.0.0
 SQL authorization ID   = DB2INST1
 Local database alias   = DB1

$ db2 list tablespaces

           Tablespaces for Current Database

 Tablespace ID                        = 1
 Name                                 = TEMPSPACE1
 Type                                 = System managed space
 Contents                             = Temporary data
 State                                = 0x0000
   Detailed explanation:
     Normal

DB21011I  In a partitioned database server environment, only the
table spaces on the current node are listed.
```

Notice that only the temporary table space which has been created at the time you executed the ADD NODE utility. You have to execute the ALTER TABLESPACE statement to create table space containers. The following is sample output of the ALTER TABLESPACE statement:

```
$ db2 "ALTER TABLESPACE tablespace1 ADD ('/sms/dir3') ON NODE(2)"
DB20000I  The SQL command completed successfully.
$
$ db2 "ALTER TABLESPACE tablespace2 ADD (FILE '/dev/rdev3' 1024) ON
NODE(2)"
SQL1759W  Redistribute nodegroup is required to change data partitioning
for objects in nodegroup "GROUP1" to include some added nodes or exclude
some dropped nodes.  SQLSTATE=01618
```

When creating the containers for all the table spaces is complete, you might receive an warning message like the above. It is to remind you to execute **REDISTRIBUTE NODEGROUP** utility. You probably received the same message when you executed the **ALTER NODEGROUP** statement. The following is a sample output of the **LIST TABLESPACES** and **LIST TABLESPACE CONTAINERS** command after the **ALTER TABLESPACE** statement has been issued:

```
$ db2set DB2NODE=3
$ db2 connect to db1

   Database Connection Information
Database product       = DB2/6000 5.0.0
 SQL authorization ID   = DB2INST1
 Local database alias   = DB1

$ db2 list tablespaces
Tablespaces for Current Database

 Tablespace ID                           = 1
 Name                                    = TEMPSPACE1
 Type                                    = System managed space
 Contents                                = Temporary data
 State                                   = 0x0000
   Detailed explanation:
     Normal

 Tablespace ID                           = 3
 Name                                    = TABLESPACE1
 Type                                    = System managed space
 Contents                                = Any data
 State                                   = 0x0000
   Detailed explanation:
     Normal

 Tablespace ID                           = 4
 Name                                    = TABLESPACE2
 Type                                    = Database managed space
 Contents                                = Any data
 State                                   = 0x0000
   Detailed explanation:
     Normal

DB21011I  In a partitioned database server environment, only the
table spaces on the current node are listed.
$ db2 list tablespace containers for 3
Tablespace Containers for Tablespace 3
Container ID                             = 0
 Name                                    = /sms/dir3
 Type                                    = Path

$ db2 list tablespaces containers for 4

           Tablespace Containers for Tablespace 4

 Container ID                            = 0
 Name                                    = /dev/rdev3
 Type                                    = Device
```

There are now three table spaces listed. Notice that new table space containers have been created (/sms/dir3 and /dev/rdev3), using the container definitions you specified in the ALTER TABLESPACE statement. Also, the SYSNODEGROUPDEF catalog table has been updated:

```
db2 "select * from sysibm.sysnodegroupdef"
NGNAME                 NODENUM  IN_USE
------------------     -------  ------
IBMCATGROUP                  0  Y
IBMDEFAULTGROUP              0  Y
NODEGROUP1                   0  Y
NODEGROUP1                   1  Y
NODEGROUP1                   2  Y
NODEGROUP1                   3  A
```

Changed from 'T' to 'A'

The IN_USE column of the added database partition has changed from 'T' to 'A'.

When you execute the ALTER TABLESPACE statement and are going to create multiple containers for a system managed table space on the new database partition, you should understand that you can only issue the ALTER TABLESPACE statement once. Therefore, if using multiple containers in an SMS table space, you must include them in the same ALTER TABLESPACE statement. You'll receive an error message if you try to execute the ALTER TABLESPACE statement more than once for the same table space on the same database partition. For example:

```
$ db2 "ALTER TABLESPACE tablespace1 ADD ('/sms/dir3') ON NODE(2)"
DB20000I  The SQL command completed successfully.
$
$ db2 "ALTER TABLESPACE tablespace1 ADD ('/sms/dir4') ON NODE(2)"
DB21034E  The command was processed as an SQL statement because it was
not a valid Command Line Processor command.  During SQL processing it
returned: SQL0281N  Table space "tablespace1" cannot be altered with
additional containers because it is a system managed table space.
SQLSTATE=42921
```

The correct form of the ALTER TABLESPACE statement for multiple containers in an SMS table space is similar to the following:

```
$ db2 "ALTER TABLESPACE tablespace1 ADD
('/sms/dir3','/sms/dir4') ON NODE(2)"
DB20000I  The SQL command completed successfully.
```

You can execute the REDISTRIBUTE NODEGROUP utility to use the new database partition. The details of REDISTRIBUTE NODEGROUP utility is described in "Redistribute Nodegroup Utility" on page 296.

5.2.1.4 Redistribute Nodegroup Add Node

You will not find the ADD NODE parameter in the current command syntax for the REDISTRIBUTE NODEGROUP command. It is provided for backward compatibility with an earlier version of the product, DB2 Parallel Edition Version 1.2. It is recommended that you use the ALTER NODEGROUP statement instead of the REDISTRIBUTE NODEGROUP command with the ADD NODE parameter. If you choose to use this option of the command, it will retrieve the container definition from the lowest database partition number in the nodegroup. Effectively, it executes the ALTER NODEGROUP (using defaults) and the REDISTRIBUTE NODEGROUP command.

```
$ db2 "redistribute nodegroup nodegroup1 uniform add node (3)"
DB20000I  The REDISTRIBUTE NODEGROUP command completed successfully.
```

5.2.2 Summary of Alter Nodegroup

We've discussed four different methods to alter your nodegroup. Let's summarize when you would use which method and why.

1. Using the default path for the container definition.

   ALTER NODEGROUP nodegroup_name ADD NODES (node_num)

   We saw this command used in both an SDP and MDP environment. If you have multiple database partitions, you can only use this method if your container path includes the database directory. For example, /db/inst/NODE0000/SQL00001 and so on would work in both an SDP and MDP environment. If using the same directory name that does not include the database path, you could not use this method because you cannot have the same container path definitions for different database partitions on the same host. For example, if /sms/dirA was the container definition path for every database partition in your table space, you could only use this method if you are in a single database partition environment.

2. Using a path for that container definition that is like those defined for an existing database partition.

   ALTER NODEGROUP nodegroup_name ADD NODE nodes-clause LIKE NODE node_num

   This method works for either an SDP or MDP environment. However, you will be more likely to use it in an MDP environment where you naming convention does not include the database path, but does follow a user-defined sequence.

3. Using a unique path for the container definition.

   `ALTER NODEGROUP node_name ADD NODES (node_num) WITHOUT`
   `TABLESPACES`

   This method can be used in either an SDP or MDP environment. The reason for this method is that your environment uses a container path that is unique for every database partition.

4. Used for backward compatibility with previous version of the product.

   `REDISTRIBUTE NODEGROUP node_name UNIFORM ADD NODES`
   `(node_num)`

   This method can only be used where the database path is included in the container definition. However, whenever possible, one of the other three methods is recommended.

Adding Partition to Single Partition Nodegroup

Remember that when you add a database partition to a single partition nodegroup, all tables in the nodegroup must have a partitioning key.

5.2.3 Update Nodegroup Definition Before Dropping DB Partition

When you try to drop a database partition, you must ensure that the database partition being dropped is not used by any database. This was discussed in "Dropping A Database Partition" on page 270 and will not be discussed here. You will update the nodegroup definition to not use the database partition being dropped, and then move the data from that database partition to remaining partitions.

There are two methods to consider:

1. Execute the SQL `ALTER NODEGROUP DROP NODE` statement and then use the `REDISTRIBUTE NODEGROUP` utility.

   This is the recommended method for updating the nodegroup definition before you redistribute the data.

2. Execute the `REDISTRIBUTE NODEGROUP` utility with the `DROP NODE` parameter.

   This is provided for backwards compatibility with previous versions of the product.

5.2.3.1 Alter Nodegroup Drop Node

The SQL ALTER NODEGROUP statement with the DROP NODE option changes the nodegroup definition, but does not move data. The REDISTRIBUTE NODEGROUP utility is discussed in "Redistribute Nodegroup Utility" on page 296.

Think of this method as a two-step procedure:

1. Execute the SQL ALTER NODEGROUP statement with the DROP NODE parameter.

2. Execute the REDISTRIBUTE NODEGROUP utility.

The example below will update the nodegroup definition by removing database partition 3.

```
$ db2 "alter nodegroup nodegroup1 drop node (3)"
SQL1759W  Redistribute nodegroup is required to change data
partitioning for objects in nodegroup "NODEGROUP1" to include some
added nodes or exclude some dropped nodes. SQLSTATE=01618
```

The warning message that you see in the above example (SQL1759W) means that the data has not be redistributed. You need to execute the REDISTRIBUTE NODEGROUP utility.

Notice that the SYSNODEGROUPDEF catalog table has been modified. You can query the SYSNODEGROUPDEF catalog table or use the LIST NODEGROUPS SHOW DETAIL command.

```
db2 "select * from sysibm.sysnodegroupdef"
NGNAME               NODENUM IN_USE
------------------   ------- ------
IBMCATGROUP              0 Y
IBMDEFAULTGROUP          0 Y
NODEGROUP1               0 Y
NODEGROUP1               1 Y
NODEGROUP1               2 Y
NODEGROUP1               3 D
```

The IN_USE column of database partition 3 is a 'D'. This means that this partition will be dropped when the REDISTRIBUTE NODEGROUP utility has successfully completed.

You should understand that the SQL ALTER NODEGROUP statement does not move data from the database partitions being dropped or delete any of the table space containers for that database partition. This is done by the REDISTRIBUTE NODEGROUP utility. The details of the REDISTRIBUTE NODEGROUP utility is described in "Redistribute Nodegroup Utility" on page 296.

5.2.3.2 Redistribute Nodegroup Drop Node

You can use the DROP NODE option of the REDISTRIBUTE NODEGROUP utility to do the same thing. This will not only change nodegroup definition, but also move the data to the remaining database partitions. The method that uses the SQL ALTER NODEGROUP statement is recommended because the DROP NODE option of the REDISTRIBUTE NODEGROUP utility is not in the command syntax of the current version of DB2 UDB EEE product. It is provided for backward compatibility with DB2 Parallel Edition. When you use the DROP NODE parameter of the REDISTRIBUTE NODEGROUP utility, the SQL ALTER NODEGROUP statement is executed before the data is redistributed. It does both steps, changing the nodegroup definition and redistributing the data in one command.

```
$ db2 "redistribute nodegroup nodegroup1 uniform drop node (3)"
DB20000I  The REDISTRIBUTE NODEGROUP command completed successfully.
```

5.3 Redistribute Nodegroup Utility

The REDISTRIBUTE NODEGROUP utility is used to redistribute data among your database partitions. It must be executed from the catalog partition.

When executing the REDISTRIBUTE NODEGROUP utility in an MDP environment, make sure that the value of DB2NODE in the DB2 Profile Registry is set to the database partition number of your catalog partition. If you change the value of DB2NODE in the DB2 Profile Registry to any other value when you executed the ADD NODE utility, you have to terminate your current Command Line Processor session and set DB2NODE to the catalog database partition. For example, if database partition 1 is where the system catalogs are stored:

```
$ db2 terminate
$ db2set DB2NODE=1
```

There are a number of ways to perform data redistribution using the REDISTRIBUTE NODEGROUP utility. You can:

1. Distribute the data uniformly across all the partitions of the nodegroup. (This is the default option.)

2. Distribute the data using a distribution file.

3. Distribute the data using a target partitioning map.

We'll look at all three ways to help you decide which option is best suited for your environment.

5.3.0.1 Using the UNIFORM Option

The UNIFORM parameter of the REDISTRIBUTE NODEGROUP utility specifies that the data is uniformly distributed across hash partitions (that is, every hash partition is assumed to have the same number of rows), but the same number of hash partitions do not necessarily map to each node. After redistribution, all nodes in the nodegroup have approximately the same number of hash partitions. This can be useful if you know that your tables in the nodegroup have approximately the same number of rows that will hash to each database partition.

The UNIFORM option of the REDISTRIBUTE NODEGROUP utility does not provide skew correction. It assumes that each hash bucket or vector into the partitioning map contains the same amount of data. You would not want to use the UNIFORM option if you had a skew or uneven distribution of data problem. The UNIFORM option simply tries to place the same number of hash buckets on each partition with the minimum amount of data movement.

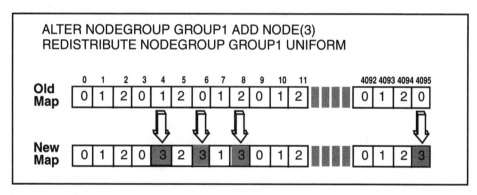

Figure 116. REDISTRIBUTE NODEGROUP (UNIFORM)

Figure 116 is an example of performing data redistribution after adding a database partition to a nodegroup. The database partition has been added by either the ADD NODE command or the db2start command with the ADDNODE option. The ALTER NODEGROUP statement adds database partition 3 to the

GROUP1 nodegroup. The REDISTRIBUTE utility generates a new partitioning map, stores that partitioning map in the system catalogs, and moves the data based on the new map.

In Figure 116, you can see that the database partition numbers are modified from the old map to the new map. Some database partition numbers are changed to reflect the addition of database partition number 3 (Hash bucket value=4,6,8,...,4095). Each row of the data that corresponds to this hash bucket value moves to the new database partition. The LIST NODEGROUPS SHOW DETAIL command can be used to show that database partition 3 is now in nodegroup GROUP1. You can confirm that data redistribution is complete by issuing an SQL SELECT statement using the NODENUMBER function.

Let's look at an example adding a database partition and executing the REDOSTRIBUTE NODEGROUP utility.

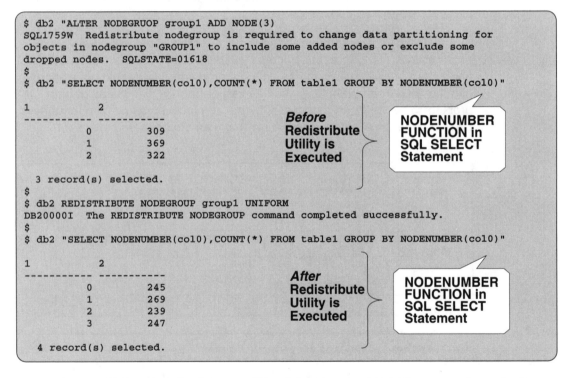

Notice that database partition 3 has been added. The reason you don't see database partition 3 in the first SELECT statement is because of the NODENUMBER function. Database partition 3 has been added and the nodegroup definition has been updated. The REDISTRIBUTE NODEGROUP utility places data on database partition 3. Also, the data is distributed among the four database partitions.

The PMAP_ID column of the SYSNODEGROUPS and the SYSTABLES catalog tables is changed to contain the new partition map ID as part of the execution of the REDISTRIBUTE NODEGROUP utility. The new partitioning map is stored in the SYSPARTITIONMAPS catalog table. You can see the new partitioning map by issuing an SQL statement against these catalog tables or by executing the db2gpmap utility. The syntax for the db2gpmap utility is the following:

```
db2gpmap [-d <database>] [-m <map-file>] [ -g <nodegroup> | -t <tbname>]
```

This utility extracts a partitioning map into a file. Figure 117 is an example of the partitioning map before data redistribution, and Figure 118 is an example of the partitioning map after data redistribution. You can see the new database partition is added in Figure 118. The following command was used to display the contents of the partitioning map.

```
db2gpmap -d tpcd100 -m group1.map -g group1
```

```
0 1 2 0 1 2 0 1 2 0 1 2 0 1 2 0 1 2 0 1 2 0 1 2 0 1 2 0 1 2
0 1 2 0 1 2 0 1 2 0 1 2 0 1 2 0 1 2 0 1 2 0 1 2 0 1 2 0 1 2
0 1 2 0 1 2 0 1 2 0 1 2 0 1 2 0 1 2 0 1 2 0 1 2 0 1 2 0 1 2
0 1 2 0 1 2 0 1 2 0 1 2 0 1 2 0 1 2 0 1 2 0 1 2 0 1 2 0 1 2
0 1 2 0 1 2 0 1 2 0 1 2 0 1 2 0 1 2 0 1 2 0 1 2 0 1 2 0 1 2
..........
0 1 2 0 1 2 0 1 2 0 1 2 0 1 2 0 1 2 0 1 2 0 1 2 0 1 2 0 1 2
0 1 2 0 1 2 0 1 2 0 1 2 0 1 2 0 1 2 0 1 2 0 1 2 0 1 2 0 1 2
0 1 2 0 1 2 0 1 2 0 1 2 0 1 2 0 1 2 0 1 2 0 1 2 0 1 2 0 1 2
0 1 2 0 1 2 0 1 2 0 1 2 0 1 2 0 1 2 0 1 2 0 1 2 0 1 2 0 1 2
0 1 2 0 1 2 0 1 2 0 1 2 0 1 2 0 1 2 0 1 2 0 1 2 0 1 2 0 1 2
```

Figure 117. Partitioning Map Before Data Redistribution

```
0 1 3 3 3 3 3 3 3 3 3 3 3 3 3 3 3 3 3 3 3 3 3 3 3 3 3 3 3 3
3 3 3 3 3 3 3 3 3 3 3 3 3 3 3 3 3 3 3 3 3 3 3 3 3 3 3 3 3 3
3 3 3 3 3 3 3 3 3 3 3 3 3 3 3 3 3 3 3 3 3 3 3 3 3 3 3 3 3 3
3 3 3 3 3 3 3 3 3 3 3 3 3 3 3 3 3 3 3 3 3 3 3 3 3 3 3 3 3 3
3 3 3 3 3 3 3 3 3 3 3 3 3 3 3 3 3 3 3 3 3 3 3 3 3 3 3 3 3 3
. . . . . . . . . .
0 1 2 0 1 2 0 1 2 0 1 2 0 1 2 0 1 2 0 1 2 0 1 2 0 1 2 0 1 2
0 1 2 0 1 2 0 1 2 0 1 2 0 1 2 0 1 2 0 1 2 0 1 2 0 1 2 0 1 2
0 1 2 0 1 2 0 1 2 0 1 2 0 1 2 0 1 2 0 1 2 0 1 2 0 1 2 0 1 2
0 1 2 0 1 2 0 1 2 0 1 2 0 1 2 0 1 2 0 1 2 0 1 2 0 1 2 0 1 2
0 1 2 0 1 2 0 1 2 0 1 2 0 1 2 0 1 2 0 1 2 0 1 2 0 1 2 0 1 2
```

Figure 118. Partitioning Map After Data Redistribution

5.3.1 Using the DISTFILE Option

Understanding the difference between the three options, UNIFORM, using a distfile and using a targetmap is important to your DB2 UDB EEE environment because you will encounter these three options with other utilities such as the `db2split` and `LOAD`.

Let's start with understanding the difference between the two options: UNIFORM and using a distfile. We'll use a non-database example to explain their difference. Let's assume we want to form two soccer teams. There are two team captains, Jon and Calene, and a total of six players to select from for their respective teams.

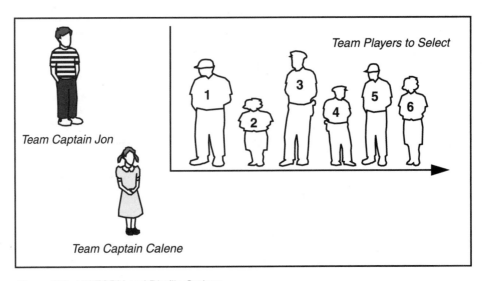

Figure 119. UNIFORM and Distfile Options

Figure 119 shows Jon and Calene and the potential soccer players for their teams. Let's look at how the players are assigned to the team captains if using a round-robin or UNIFORM method.

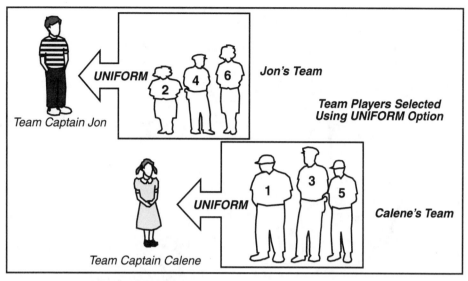

Figure 120. UNIFORM Option of Selection

Calene won the coin toss to select first. By using a round-robin or UNIFORM method of selection, Calene got the tallest men, presumably the better soccer players. This may not have been the desired result, especially if you're on Jon's team.

Let's look at the player selection if we use the DISTFILE option.

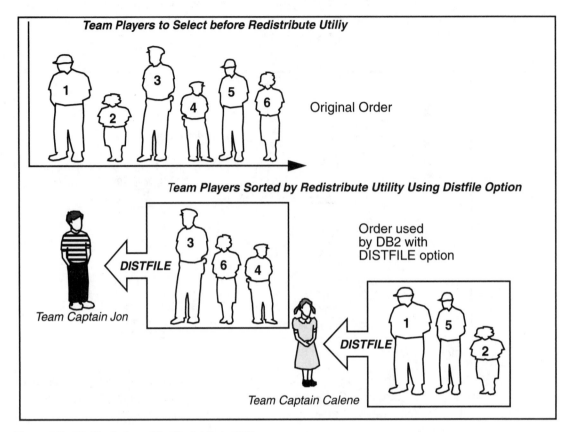

Figure 121. Distfile Option of the Redistribute Utility

Figure 121 shows the same soccer players. If we use the DISTFILE option, DB2 does an internal ordering of the data, here you might assume that height was the factor used for ordering. This would give a more even distribution of soccer players among the two captains.

Even if there were three team captains, the distribution would be similar to using two team captains. This is analogous to having three database partitions. When using the DISTFILE option, you would still have a even distribution of soccer players among team captains.

5.3.1.1 DB2 Example of Using DISTFILE

If your data is skewed, providing a distribution file as input to the redistribution utility (USING DISTFILE) will help achieve an even data distribution across all partitions in the nodegroup. Let's look at a database example showing the effect of using the DISTFILE option. First, we look at the present distribution of data.

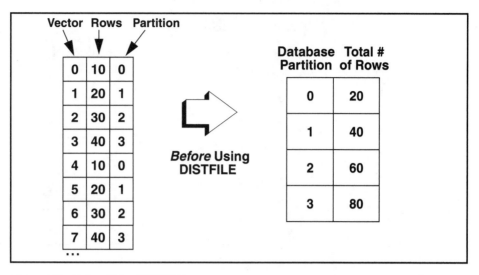

Figure 122. Before Using DISTFILE

Figure 122 shows a portion of the array of vectors (hash buckets), the pmap and the number of rows for that database partition. The vector column represents the array of 4096 integers (0...4095). Each pmap entry represents the database partition associated with the vector or hash bucket. The rows column is the number of rows for that pmap entry that were assigned to the vector number. Even though this example is a small portion (eight entries out of 4096) of the data, you can see that there is an uneven distribution of rows on each database partition. In our example, database partition 3 has the most number of rows (80); database partition 0 has the least number of rows (20), and partitions 2 and 3 fall in between the two extremes with 40 rows and 60 rows respectively.

The DISTFILE parameter can be used to correct data skew. The DISTFILE option will produce a new partitioning map based upon the database distribution file that is provided as input.

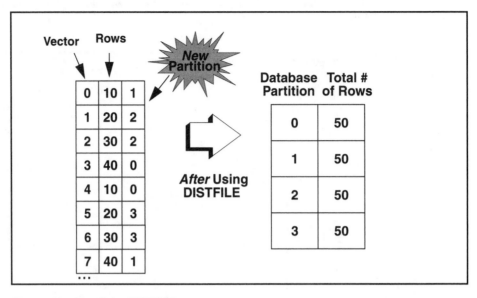

Figure 123. After Using DISTFILE

Figure 123 shows the data distribution if the `DISTFILE` option is used. This distribution file should provide the correct data distribution by bucket weights. The distribution file contains an integer value for each of the 4096 hash partitions. The distribution file is created whenever the db2split utility is executed. This means that if you loaded your table using a customized partitioning map, in most cases, you will probably use the same map when redistributing your data based on adding or dropping a database partition.

The following rules apply to the DISTFILE:

1. The DISTFILE should contain 4096 positive integer values in character format.

2. The sum of the values should be less than or equal to 4294967295.

3. If the path for the DISTFILE is not specified, the current directory is used.

How to Check the Data Distribution
You can use the partition(column-name) and nodenumber(column-name) SQL functions to find out the current data distribution across database partitions:

```
SELECT COUNT(*) FROM tablea GROUP BY PARTITION(partkey) ORDER BY PARTITION(partkey)
```

The result of this SQL **SELECT** statement may be used as the contents of a DISTFILE. However, you should ensure that 4096 records are returned. If the number of rows returned is less than 4096, it means that there are some hash bucket values that do not contain any data. You then have to modify the output of this SQL so that the distfile contains 4096 entries. There are different methods to do that. The following method is one of them.

1. Create a view where the view definition is the same as the **SELECT** statement that used the partition(column-name) and nodenumber(column-name) functions.

```
CREATE VIEW dist (key,weight) AS
    SELECT PARTITION(partkey),COUNT(*) FROM tablea
    GROUP BY PARTITION(partkey) ORDER BY PARTITION(partkey)
```

2. Create a table that has a single column and 4096 rows. Each value is from 0 to 4095.

```
CREATE TABLE allvalue (key smallint)
Insert values from 0 to 4095
```

3. Execute an outer join of the two tables to generate the distfile.

```
SELECT CASE WHEN dist.weight is null then 0
       ELSE dist.weight
       END
    FROM dist RIGHT OUTER JOIN allvalue ON dist.key=allvalue.key
    ORDER BY allvalue.key
```

4. Save the resulting records into a file. The following is an example:

```
1
------------
          0
          0
         42
         27
         45
         25
     ......
         41
         34
         31
          0
          0

  4096 record(s) selected.
```

You can use the records returned by this SQL as a distfile for the REDISTRIBUTE NODEGROUP utility. However, understand that this distfile reflects the data distribution of only one table. If you execute the REDISTRIBUE NODEGROUP utility using this distfile, a new partition map is created to distribute the data of this table evenly, but the data distribution of other tables might be skewed using this distfile. Let's look at an example using DISTFILE:

```
$ db2 "SELECT NODENUMBER(col0),COUNT(*) FROM tablea GROUP BY
NODENUMBER(col0)"
1             2
----------- -----------
          0         512
          1        5861
          2        2866
          3        5761
4 record(s) selected.

$ db2 REDISTRIBUTE NODEGROUP group1 USING DISTFILE tablea.dist
DB20000I  The REDISTRIBUTE NODEGROUP command completed successfully.
$
$ db2 "SELECT NODENUMBER(col0),COUNT(*) FROMf tablea GROUP BY
NODENUMBER(col0)"
1             2
----------- -----------
          0        3408
          1        2965
          2        5662
          3        2965
4 record(s) selected.
```

In this example, database partition 0 has less records than the other database partitions. You can use the REDISTRIBUTE NODEGROUP utility with the USING DISTFILE parameter to achieve an even data distribution. You might think the result this example is not redistributed evenly. But this is a case where each value of the partitioning key is not unique on each row; so it was impossible to distribute more uniformly than this.

5.3.2 Using the TARGETMAP Option

The TARGETMAP option of the REDISTRIBUTE NODEGROUP utility is usually used when doing the initial load of a table or multiple tables into a table space. You can use a TARGETMAP when adding or dropping a database partition, but it is not the recommended method. Let's look at how the TARGETMAP option works in the initial loading of tables in a nodegroup to show why you would not want to use it in the redistribution process.

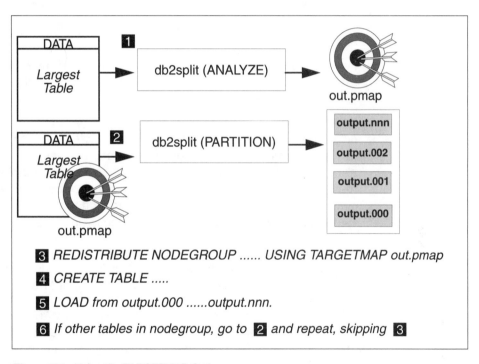

Figure 124. Using the TARGETMAP Option

Figure 124 is an overview of how the TARGETMAP option is used. The numbers in the figure are as follows:

1. You first execute the db2split utility in ANALYZE mode. This will create a partitioning map. The reason for using this option is that you want control

over the assignment of the vector in the partitioning map to a database partition.

2. Next, you execute the `db2split` utility again split the data according to out.pmap, the partitioning map that you created in the step above. In order to load the data, it must be in sequential files. The output from this step are files of data that will be used in the load process. There is one file for every database partition defined in the nodegroup. The files will have an extension beginning with the sequence 001, 002, 003, up to *nnn*, where *nnn* is the last database partition defined in the nodegroup.

3. In this step, you execute the `REDISTRIBUTE NODEGROUP` utility using the `TARGETMAP` option with the partitioning map that was created in step one. In our example, the file is out.pmap. In this scenario, you want to execute this utility only once, when there is no data in the nodegroup. The reason you execute the `REDISTRIBUTE NODEGROUP` utility in this case is that is places the pmap or partitioning map in the system catalogs.

4. You create the table in a table space in the nodegroup that was used in the redistribute nodegroup utility.

5. For every database partition in the nodegroup (001, 002, to 00*n*), you load the data using the input data files that were generated the second time you executed the db2split utility.

6. If there are other tables in the nodegroup, go back to step two to split the data, create output files and then load into tables. Notice that you are using the same target map. You do not want to re-issue the `REDISTRIBUTE NODEGROUP` command because you do not want to redistribute the existing data. If you do issue the redistribute utility, make sure that you use the target map that you used to control the placement of the data. Be aware that executing this step is unnecessary.

To use the TARGETMAP option when adding or dropping a database partition requires you to manually edit the partitioning map. This is a risky venture because there are 4096 entries to control. The risk of error is high.

Let's look at a possible reason for using the TARGETMAP option. Remember that this option is used when you want total control over the amount of data placed on the database partitions. Suppose you had a non-homogeneous cluster environment- that is you have different hardware configurations in your cluster. In such a case, you might want to place more data on one particular host. Even in this situation, you must consider the possibility of system failure of a host in your cluster.

5.3.3 Which Option of Redistribute Nodegroup to Use

This section summarizes the three options that have been discussed and offers suggestions for when to use which of the three options. Remember, the three options of the REDISTRIBUTE NODEGROUP utility are UNIFORM, USING DISTFILE, USING TARGETMAP.

After you add new database partition into your nodegroup, which option should you use to move data into your new database partition? Here are some hints:

UNIFORM

UNIFORM is the default option. DB2 assumes that every hash bucket has the same number of rows, but the same number of database partitions do not necessarily map to each host. The UNIFORM option does not provide skew correction. It tries to place the same number of hash buckets on each database partition with the minimum amount of data movement.

If in your environment, data was constantly being added or deleted before you added or dropped a database partition, it would be useful to check for data skew before assuming that UNIFORM is still the correct option for your environment. How to check for data skew is discussed in "Using the DISTFILE Option" on page 300.

DISTFILE

Using the DISTFILE option when adding or dropping a database partition will use the customized partitioning map and keep the same data distribution for the table. If you want to check the data distribution to check for skew and/or generate a new distfile (see "Using the DISTFILE Option" on page 300). Understand that the DISTFILE option works at the table level, so the data distribution achieved is only for one table.

TARGETMAP

It will probably be a very rare situation that would cause you to consider using the TARGETMAP option for adding or dropping a database partition. Remember that in the case of adding or dropping a database partition when using the TARGETMAP option of the REDISTRIBUTE NODEROUP utility, you would have to manually edit the partitioning map of 4096 entries. The case for using the TARGETMAP option is when there is no data in your nodegroup and you want to create a partitioning map that specifies the database partition for each hash bucket. See "Using the TARGETMAP Option" on page 307 for more details.

5.3.4 How Data is Redistributed Across Database Partitions

The `REDISTRIBUTE NODEGROUP` utility does the following:

1. Obtains a new partitioning map ID for the target partitioning map and inserts it into the SYSPARTITIONMAPS catalog table.

2. Updates the REBALANCE_PMAP_ID column in the SYSNODEGROUPS catalog table for a nodegroup with the new partitioning map ID.

3. Adds any new database partitions to the SYSNODEGROUPDEF catalog table.

4. Sets the IN_USE column in the SYSNODEGROUPDEF catalog table to D for any database partition that is to be dropped.

5. Does a `COMMIT` for the catalog updates.

6. Creates database files for all new database partitions.

7. Redistributes the data in each table for every table in the nodegroup. This is described in "How Data is Redistributed in Tables" on page 310.

8. Deletes database files and deletes entries in the SYSNODEGROUPDEF catalog table for database partitions that were previously marked to be dropped.

9. Updates the nodegroup record in the SYSNODEGROUPS catalog table to set PMAP_ID to the value of REBALANCE_PMAP_ID and REBALANCE_PMAP_ID to NULL.

10. Deletes the old partitioning map from the SYSPARTITIONMAPS catalog table.

11. Does a `COMMIT` for all changes.

5.3.4.1 How Data is Redistributed in Tables

When doing data redistribution on a table, the utility does the following:

1. Locks the row for the table in the SYSTABLES catalog table.

2. Invalidates all plans that involve this table. The partitioning map ID associated with the table will change in the SYSTABLES catalog table because the table is being redistributed. Because the plans are invalidated, the compiler must obtain the new partitioning information for the table and generate plans accordingly.

3. Locks the table in exclusive mode.

4. Redistributes the data in the table.

5. If the redistribution operation succeeds, it:

    1. Issues a `COMMIT` for the table.

2. Continues with the next table in the nodegroup.

If the operation fails before the table is fully redistributed, the utility:

1. Issues a `ROLLBACK` on updates to the table.

2. Ends the entire redistribution operation and returns an error.

Be aware that the `REDISTRIBUTE NODEGROUP` utility operates at the nodegroup level; however, it moves data one table at a time. Collocated tables will temporarily not be collocated during the execution of the `REDISTRIBUTE NODEGROUP` utility. If you create a new table in the nodegroup during the execution of the `REDISTRIBUTE NODEGROUP` utility, the table takes a new partitioning map.

5.3.5 Recovering from Redistribution Errors

If the data redistribution operation fails, some tables may be redistributed while others are not. This occurs because data redistribution is performed one table at a time. You have two options for recovery:

- Use the `CONTINUE` option to continue the operation to redistribute the remaining tables.

- Use the `ROLLBACK` option to undo the redistribution and set the redistributed tables back to their original state. The roll-back operation can take about the same amount of time as the original redistribution operation.

Let's look at a nodegroup redistribution consisting of four tables where an error occurs during processing.

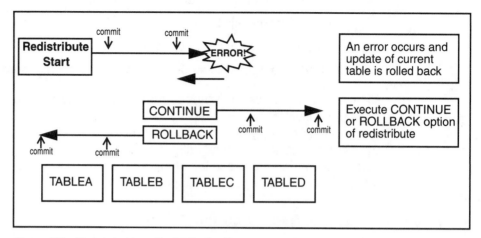

Figure 125. Recovering from Redistribution Errors

When data of the third table (TABLEC) is being moved, a failure occurs, and the database manager performs a rollback to the last commit point (that is the moment when redistribution of the second table completed) and returns error an error message. At this time, data from TABLEA and TABLEB has been redistributed, but the placement data of TABLEC and TABLED has not changed. You can choose the CONTINUE or ROLLBACK option for recovery. The CONTINUE option starts the distribution of TABLEC and TABLED. The ROLLBACK option moves the data of TABLEA and TABLEB back to the state prior to the start of the REDISTRIBUTE NODEGROUP utility.

Before you can use either option, a previous data redistribution operation must have failed such that the REBALANCE_PMID column in the SYSNODEGROUPS catalog table is set to a non-NULL value.

After the redistribution operation begins to execute, a file is written to the redist directory. The redist directory is a subdirectory of the sqllib directory. This file has the following naming convention:

  databasename.nodegroupname.timestamp

This file lists any operations that are done on database partitions, the names of the tables that were redistributed, and the completion status of the operation. If a table cannot be redistributed, its name and the applicable SQLCODE is listed. If the redistribution operation cannot begin because of an incorrect input parameter, the file is not written, and an SQLCODE is returned.

The following is an example. Notice that the error (SQLCODE=-964, Transaction log is full) occurred during the redistribution of TABLEC.

```
                        Data Redistribution Utility
                        _____

    The following options have been specified:
    Nodegroup name                  : GROUP1
    Data Redistribution option      : U
    Redistribute Nodegroup          : uniformly
    No. of nodes to be added        : 1
    List of nodes to be added       :   3
    No. of nodes to be dropped      : 0
    List of nodes to be dropped     :
    The execution of the Data Redistribution operation on:

      Table                                   begun at   ended at
      _____                                   _____   _____

    DB2INST2.TABLEA                           14.38.18
                                                         14.38.20
    DB2INST2.TABLEB                           14.38.20
                                                         14.38.22
    DB2INST2.TABLEC                           14.38.22

    --Data Redistribution cannot be continued.--

    Error: Redistribution failed with SQLCODE=-964 (rc=-30867).
```

If you mistakenly delete this file, you are still able to attempt a CONTINUE operation.

When you fail to execute the REDISTRIBUTE NODEGROUP with the ADD NODE parameter (This option does not only redistribution but also creates the table space containers. See 5.2.1.4 on page 293), you can use the ROLLBACK option to undo the redistribution and set the redistributed tables back to their original state. But understand that table space containers created still exist. So when you execute the REDISTRIBUTE NODEGROUP utility for this nodegroup again, do not specify the add node parameter, use either the DISTFILE or UNIFORM parameter without the ADD NODE parameter. If you do specify the ADD NODE parameter in this case, you will receive an error message similar to the following:

```
SQL0265N  Node "3" is a duplicate node.  SQLSTATE=42728
```

5.3.6 Estimating the Amount of Log Space for Redistribution

When data is being moved by the REDISTRIBUTE NODEGROUP utility, you will be performing numerous insertions and deletions of rows. If 1000 rows of data are moved from one database partition to another, 1000 rows are deleted from the source database partition, and 1000 rows are inserted into the target database partition. As such, the REDISTRIBUTE NODEGROUP utility writes the status of these operations into log files.

As part of the planning considerations for using the REDISTRIBUTE NODEGROUP utility, you must allow for both archive logs and active logs. For archive logs, consider the space requirements for the redistribution of all the tables in the nodegroup. For the active logs, calculate the log space used for the redistribution of the largest table in the nodegroup.

The next sections discuss how you can derive the estimates for the archive logs and the active logs when performing a redistribution of a nodegroup. Our calculations assume that there is little if no data skew, and the UNIFORM option of the redistribute nodegroup utility is being used.

5.3.6.1 Archive Logs for Distribution of All Tables

This section only applies to your environment if you LOGRETAIN=ON or USEREXIT=ON at the database level. Recall that either one or both of these parameters turns on archive logging in the database (circular logging is the default setting). If archive logging is used, log files are saved typically in a file system designated for archived log files. If a user-exit program is used, you need to know how much space is used for the user-exit program. Both of these factors must be considered when you redistribute all the tables in a nodegroup to ensure that you have enough free space to perform the redistribution.

First, you should estimate how many rows will be moved for each table in the nodegroup. Assuming the UNIFORM option with little or no skew of data, you can use following formula to estimate how many rows are deleted from a database partition:

```
Delete row count = Total row count X (1/S - 1/T)
Where:
S = Number of database partitions before redistribution
T = Number of database partitions after redistribution
```

The following formula can be used to estimate how many rows are inserted into the new database partition:

```
Insert row count = Total row count X 1/T
Where:
T = Number of database partitions after redistribution
```

Let's look at an example of increasing the number of database partitions from 8 to 12. We'll assume that a table has 240,000 rows of data before the redistribution. According to our two formulas, each database partition had approximately 30,000 rows. 10,000 rows will be deleted from each of the original eight database partitions. 20,000 rows will be inserted into each of the new four database partitions.

Next, you need to estimate the written log size for each row. You can use the following formula:

```
LOG space for each row = 50 + (Length of Row)
```

The number 50 in the above formula represents the amount of overhead used to identify the log record. You multiply the log space for each row times the number of rows that you have calculated will be moving from each database partition to give you the necessary log space to redistribute this table. Allow an additional 10% for expected data skew. If the table has indexes defined on it, the following formula is used for each index:

```
Log space for each row = 72 to (Key Length)
```

Multiply this with the number of moving rows and get the necessary log space for this index. Again increase this by 10% for the data skew and another 5% for the overhead allowed for an index page split. A better method is to drop the indexes before executing the redistribute nodegroup utility and then re-create them after the redistribution completes. This will reduce the amount of log space and the elapsed time of for the redistribution. You should calculate the log space for all tables and indexes in the nodegroup being distributed and sum them.

Now let's compare the estimated log space with the actual log space.

In our example, we used the ORDERS table for the TPC-D database with 150000 rows initially loaded. The database partition was increased from 1 to 2. We performed this example twice, the first time without indexes on the ORDERS table, the second time an index was created on a integer column.

The database snapshot monitor was used to determine the actual written log space. All applications are terminated before the execution of the `REDISTRIBUTE NODEGROUP` utility to reset each value for the database snapshot monitor. The following is the ORDERS table definition, row length is 55. (Note, assume that the following columns are not null. For nullable columns, add one extra byte per column.)

```
COLNAME              TYPENAME              LENGTH
------------------   -------------------   -----------
O_ORDERKEY           INTEGER                        4
O_CUSTKEY            INTEGER                        4
O_ORDERSTATUS        CHARACTER                      1
O_TOTALPRICE         DOUBLE                         8
O_ORDERDATE          DATE                           4
O_ORDERPRIORITY      CHARACTER                     15
O_CLERK              CHARACTER                     15
O_SHIPPRIORITY       INTEGER                        4
```

The following is the calculation of the estimated log space:

```
Estimated deleted rows = 150000 x (1/1 - 1/2 ) = 75000
Estimated inserted rows = 150000 x 1/2 = 75000
Estimate written Log space for the ORDERS table
= 1.1 x 75000 x (55 + 50) = 8662500 byte = 2155 page
```

The following is the output for the snapshot monitor on the source database partition (database partition 1). It was taken just after redistribute utility was completed. You can see that 75033 rows have been deleted and the written log pages is 1861.

```
$ db2 GET SNAPSHOT FOR DATABASE ON tpcd100
...........
Rows deleted                                = 75033
Rows inserted                               = 0
Rows updated                                = 0
Rows selected                               = 0
Maximum secondary log space used (Bytes)    = 0
Maximum total log space used (Bytes)        = 18460951
Secondary logs allocated currently          = 0
Log pages read                              = 0
Log pages written                           = 1861
...........
```

The following is the output of the snapshot monitor on the target database partition (database partition 2). It was taken just after redistribute utility was completed. You can see that 75033 rows have been inserted, and the written log pages is 1873.

```
$ db2 GET SNAPSHOT FOR DATABASE ON tpcd100
..........
Rows deleted                              = 0
Rows inserted                             = 75033
Rows updated                              = 0
Rows selected                             = 0
Maximum secondary log space used (Bytes)  = 0
Maximum total log space used (Bytes)      = 10771468
Secondary logs allocated currently        = 0
Log pages read                            = 0
Log pages written                         = 1873
..........
```

Next is the calculation of the estimated log space for the table where an index is defined:

```
Estimated deleted rows = 150000 x ( 1/1 - 1/2 ) = 75000 rows
Estimated inserted rows = 150000 x 1/2 = 75000 rows
Estimated written Log space for an index
= 1.1 x 1.05 x 75000 x (4 + 72) = 6583500 bytes

Estimated written Log space for this table
= 1.1 x 75000 x (55 + 50) = 8662500 bytes

Total Log space for this table
= 6583500 + 8662500 = 15246000 bytes = 3723 pages
```

The following is the output from the snapshot monitor for the source partition and the target partition:

```
$ db2 GET SNAPSHOT FOR DATABASE ON tpcd100
. . . . . . . . . .
Rows deleted                                  = 75033
Rows inserted                                 = 0
Rows updated                                  = 0
Rows selected                                 = 0
Maximum secondary log space used (Bytes)      = 0
Maximum total log space used (Bytes)          = 30316179
Secondary logs allocated currently            = 0
Log pages read                                = 0
Log pages written                             = 3261
. . . . . . . . . .
```

```
$ db2 GET SNAPSHOT FOR DATABASE ON tpcd100
. . . . . . . . . .
Rows deleted                                  = 0
Rows inserted                                 = 75033
Rows updated                                  = 0
Rows selected                                 = 0
Maximum secondary log space used (Bytes)      = 0
Maximum total log space used (Bytes)          = 24094882
Secondary logs allocated currently            = 0
Log pages read                                = 0
Log pages written                             = 3485
. . . . . . . . . .
```

Table 4 is the summary of this example. You can see that the estimated log size is large enough for the actual written log pages.

Table 4. Comparison of Estimated and Actual Log Space for Redistribution

Table Name	Insert /Delete	Row Length	Index Key Length	Rows Inserted/ Deleted	Log pages written	Estimated written pages
ORDERS	Delete	55	0	75033	1861	2115
ORDERS	Insert	55	0	75033	1873	2115
ORDERS	Delete	55	4	75033	3261	3646
ORDERS	Insert	55	4	75033	3485	3646

5.3.6.2 Active Log Space for Largest Table

A commit is issued only when the redistribution of each table is completed. If the table being redistributed is large, there is a possibility that you will encounter a situation of transaction log becoming full. You must set the database configuration parameters `LOGFILSIZ`, `LOGPRIMARY` and `LOGSECOND` to appropriate values to keep the log active for the uncommitted transaction of the largest table being redistributed. You only have to calculate this value once for the largest table in the redistribution process.

You have to understand that the active log space for the uncommitted transaction includes the reserved space for roll back. Even if your transaction is not rolled back, this space would be reserved. This space is released when the transaction is committed. See the following output of the database snapshot monitor:

```
$ db2 GET SNAPSHOT FOR DATABASE ON tpcd100
. . . . . . . . . .
Rows deleted                                  = 75033
Rows inserted                                 = 0
Rows updated                                  = 0
Rows selected                                 = 0
Maximum secondary log space used (Bytes)      = 0
Maximum total log space used (Bytes)          = 18460951
Secondary logs allocated currently            = 0
Log pages read                                = 0
Log pages written                             = 1861
. . . . . . . . . .
```

This is the snapshot taken on the source partition after the redistribute of the largest table. Assume that each value of this snapshot was reset before the execution of **REDISTRIBUTE NODEGROUP** utility. The written log pages is 1861 and the maximum total log space used is 18460951 byte (4508 pages). This value shows you the active log space which includes the reserved space for rollback. 1861 pages is the size of the actual written log record. However, if you do not set the database configuration parameters large enough to accommodate a possible 4508 pages of active logs, you will not be able to complete this transaction and will receive an error with the `SQLCODE=-964` (Transaction log is full).

It is not easy to estimating the active log space, including the reserved space for rollback accurately. But you can get the value by using the formulas shown in the previous section and multiply it by 2.4 (for delete), or 1.5 (for insert). Allow for more space than your estimations. It is better to have too much log space, than too little. After your redistribution, you can reduce the log parameters.

Now let's estimate the active log space for the table used in the previous section (see Table 4 on page 318). The following is an example:

```
Estimated Written Log space for this table = 8662500 bytes
Estimated active log space for this table (Delete) = 2.2 x 8662500 = 19057500
bytes
Estimated active log space for this table (Insert) = 1.5 = 8662500 = 12993750
bytes
```

The following is an example for the table where an index is defined:

```
Estimated Written Log space for this table = 15246000 bytes
Estimate active log space for this table (Delete) = 2.2 x 15246000 = 33541200
bytes
Estimated active log space for this table (Insert) = 1.5 x 15246000 =
22869000 bytes
```

Table 5 is the summary of this test. The values of the actual used log space are taken by from the output of the same snapshot monitor as in the previous section.

Table 5. Comparison of Estimated and Actual Log Space for Redistribution

Table Name	Insert /Delete	Row Length	Index Key Length	Rows Inserted/ Deleted	Max total Log space used	Estimated Max log space
ORDERS	Delete	55	0	75033	18460951	19057500
ORDERS	Insert	55	0	75033	10771468	12993750
ORDERS	Delete	55	4	75033	30316179	33541200
ORDERS	Insert	55	4	75033	24094882	22869000

Note that the estimate was low.

5.3.7 Solutions for Redistribution

When you are adding many database partitions that will require substantial movement of data to the new database partitions, you'll need considerable additional log space and time to perform the redistribution. Let's consider an environment of eight database partitions, adding eight more database partitions, for a total of 16.

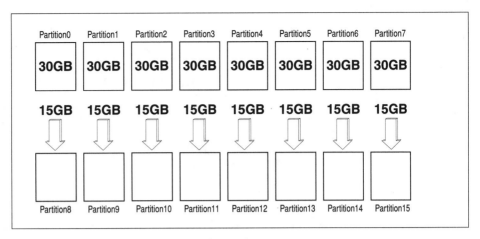

Figure 126. Adding Database Partitions (8 to 16)

In Figure 126, you have eight database partitions and want to add eight more database partitions. The total amount of data on the existing eight database partitions is 240 GB. When you execute the REDISTRIBUTE NODEGROUP utility using the UNIFORM option, 15 GB of data is moved from each of the source database partitions to each of the target database partitions. If you cannot allocate enough reserve active log space or allow enough time for the addition of the eight database partitions in one operation, you can perform the redistribution in phases. See Figure 127 on page 322. Here the adding of database partitions and redistribution of data is done in two phases.

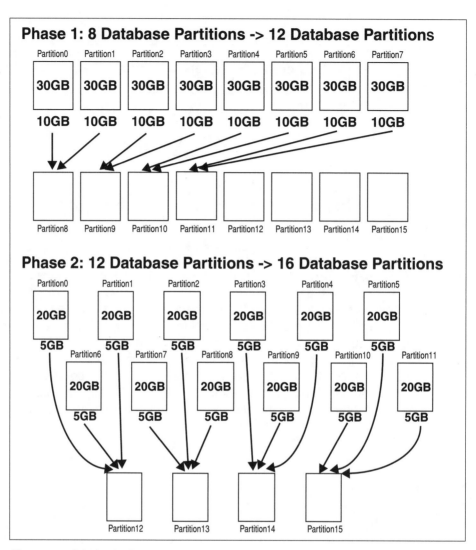

Figure 127. Solution for Redistribution

In the first phase, the amount of data transferred from each database partition is 10 GB. In the second phase, 5 GB. You can reduce the necessary active log space of and elapsed execution time of each phase by breaking down the task into two operations. Overall, the entire task will probably require more time and archive log space, but you can control the redistribution process by taking breaking it down into separate units.

5.3.8 Other Methods to Move Data into New DB Partitions

It has been described that you can use the `REDISTRIBUTE NODEGROUP` utility to move the data into the added new database partition. However, you should understand there are other methods to do that, and understand the advantages and disadvantages of each method. You can choose one of the following methods:

1. `REDISTRIBUTE NODEGROUP` utility (As discussed throughout this chapter.)

   You execute this utility for each nodegroup. This method is simpler than the other methods described in this section. You do have to consider the amount of log space of delete/insert rows incurred by data transfer.

2. Take the data from another environment and re-load

   If your data happens to be duplicated in another environment (MVS host, for example), you can transfer the data, split and load. Before loading you should execute the `ALTER NODEGROUP` statement and drop the table (or table space) and re-create it again. This method is more complicated than the `REDISTRIBUTE NODEGROUP` utility because you have to split and load the data for each table. But if you are adding many database partitions, that is, if the amount of data being transferred is very large, you may want to consider this method because the loading data is very fast and does not require the additional log space.

3. Export the data and load

   If you do not have the data on another machine (MVS host, for example) but you want to use the load utility, you can export the data from each table, and then split and load. To improve the export performance, you should execute the export in parallel on each database partition specifying to use only the data on the local database partition as in the following:

```
db2 "EXPORT TO outfile OF DEL SELECT * FROM tablea \
     WHERE NODENUMBER(cola)=CURRENT NODE"
```

5.3.9 Non-Homogeneous Hardware Environment

As described in "Adding Physical Nodes" on page 252, you can install additional SP nodes in your cluster system and create new database partitions. It is quite possible that you may be mixing your hardware environment. You might install new hardware that has superior performance than the models in your current configuration. To take full advantage of the new hardware, you should consider a different balance among hosts. That is, you may want to place more data on the newer hardware. If you keep the balance of data on the new hardware as it exists in your current configuration, the amount of data assigned to the newer hardware will be the same as that in your existing configuration. You will not be taking advantage of the newer hardware. There are two options to consider for this new hardware:

1. Create more database partitions on the new host(s) than exist on the current hosts.
2. Modify the partitioning map manually and assign more hash buckets to the newer hardware.

The first option is the preferred one. It will be easier to do, plus DB2 works at the database partition level, not at the hardware level. By creating twice the amount of database partitions on this new host, twice the amount of data will be placed there.

5.4 DB2 UDB EEE Backup and Recovery

This section will first cover the backup and recovery features of DB2 UDB EEE. This includes recommendations for implementing a backup and recovery strategy.

5.4.1 Overview of DB2 UDB EEE Backup and Recovery

To begin to create a backup and recovery strategy, the installation must first define the recovery requirements of each database. Once these requirements are determined, the database administrator can develop backup procedures to enable recovery.

Some items to consider when developing a recovery plan follow:

- How critical is the database?
- How large is the database?
- How volatile is the database.
- How current must the database be?
- What about application errors?
- How much space can be allocated for backup copies and archived logs?

Creating a backup and recovery strategy also requires an understanding of the features provided by the product to support backup and recovery. Subsequent sections will explain:

- Methods of recovery. UDB supports crash recovery, restore (or version recovery), and roll-forward recovery.

- Logging. UDB supports two basic types of logging: circular logging and log retention logging.

A couple of items concerning backup and recovery are best considered early in the planning process.

- If the recovery plan requires use of logs, mirroring of the logs is highly recommended. A disk failure causing loss of one or more logs could prevent meeting recovery objectives.

- For a database to be online, UDB requires that its catalog tablespace be available. No catalog table space means no usable database! Consequently, we highly recommend that you configure the catalog database partition to tolerate a disk failure. Allocate both the catalog tablespace and the catalog partition's log files on mirrored or RAID-5 disks.

- Do not place data on the catalog partition for a faster backup and restore time.

5.4.2 Recovery Methods

DB2 UDB supports three methods of recovery: crash recovery, version recovery (also called restore recovery) and roll-forward recovery.

5.4.2.1 Crash Recovery
Transactions or Units of Work against the database may be interrupted unexpectedly. For example, if power fails before all of the changes that are part of a logical unit of work are committed, the database becomes inconsistent and unusable. Crash recovery returns the database to a consistent, usable state.

5.4.2.2 Version (or Restore) Recovery
This recovery method requires loading a backup copy of the database. The database will be restored to exactly the same state that it was in when it was backed up.

5.4.2.3 Roll-Forward Recovery
This recovery method requires loading a backup copy of the database or table space(s) and then re-applying log records to recover changes made after the backup image was created. This method provides recovery from media, hardware, operational, and software failures. The recovery can be up to a point in time after the backup completed or to the last committed unit of work.

If a multi-partition tablespace is to be recovered to a point in time, then the load of the backup image and the application of the logs must be performed on all partitions where the tablespace is defined.

Roll-forward recovery requires enabling log retention. Retention logging is further discussed in the next section.

5.4.3 Logging

Transaction logging records each change to a database to permit recovery of the database to a consistent state. As data in the database buffer pool is modified, log records reflecting these changes are written into the log buffer. At commit, all of the log records reflecting changes to the database during this unit of work MUST be written to the log files on disk. Once the log records are successfully stored to disk, recoverability can be guaranteed. In the parallel database environment, log files must be allocated for each database partition.

After commit, the only certainty is that the log records are written to disk. The modified data in the buffer pool is not written to the database files until some later time. But even if a crash occurs before the database is updated, the log records stored on disk contain all the information needed to rebuild the committed changes.

If you desire a fully recoverable database, allocate the log files on a fault-tolerant disk complex: mirrored, duplexed, or RAID-5 for example. Imagine a situation where your log files are allocated on a disk. The disk is not a member of a RAID configuration. The log files are not mirrored to a separate disk. There is no backup copy of the log file. If you now lose this disk, you cannot recover the database up to the current unit of work. Make an immediate backup of your database!

DB2 UDB supports two basic types of logging: circular logging and archival logging. Archival logging is also referred to as log retention logging

5.4.3.1 Circular Logging

Circular logging initially uses a specified number of log files. The log files reflect changes by in-process transactions. The logs are used sequentially. A log file cannot be reused until all units of work contained within it are either committed or rolled back.

If the database manager requests the next log in sequence and that log is not available for reuse, a secondary log file will be allocated. After the secondary log fills, the database manager again checks if the next sequential primary log is available for reuse. If the primary log is still unavailable, another secondary log file is allocated. This process continues until either the primary log file becomes available for reuse or until the number of secondary logs permitted for allocation is met.

Circular logging supports crash and version/restore recovery. It does not support roll-forward recovery. For more information on the recovery methods (crash, version/restore, and roll-forward) see "Recovery Methods" on page 325.

5.4.3.2 Archival (or Log Retention) Logging

The second type of logging supported by DB2 UDB is archival logging. Archival logging is also called log retention logging. The name log retention logging more accurately reflects the way this type of logging is activated in UDB by setting the **Log retain for recovery enabled** parameter in the database configuration to **on**. Each database partition has its own set of database configuration parameters.

With archival logging, when a log file fills, the database manager allocates another. The database administrator normally configures several primary log files so that the next log file can be allocated before it is needed. The database configuration parameter `Number of primary log files` specifies how many primary log files are allocated when the database is created. UDB will only allocate no more log files than the total of the primary and secondary database configuration parameters. Once that total has been allocated, the need for more logging space will cause the database to halt with a log full condition. Allocate a sufficient number of adequately sized log files to handle the workload. Beware the application that tries to process too large a unit of work. Consider, too, that in-doubt transactions can prevent the freeing of a log file. Be sure to check for in-doubt transactions following a database recovery action. Quickly resolve each that exists to free its log space (and any locks on the database it may hold).

At any point in time, a log file associated with log retention logging will be in one of three classes:

1. **Active**. Such logs contain records for units of work which have not yet committed (or rolled back). Active logs also contain information for transactions which have committed but have not yet had the changes written from the buffer pool in memory to the database files on disk.

   Active log files are used for crash recovery.

2. **Online Archive**. These logs contain information for completed transactions which no longer require protection from crash recovery. All

changes in the log have been written to the database files. They are called online because these logs still reside in the same subdirectory (LOGPATH) as the active logs.

3. **Off-line Archive**. The log files have been moved out of the active log file subdirectory. A manual process or a process invoked through a user exit can be used to move the files.

When archival logging is used, DB2 UDB will truncate and close the current active log when the last application disconnects from the database. This is a positive feature if the database is to be inactive for some period of time. But for a low-activity database where there are short periods when no application will be connected to the database, the overhead of continuously truncating the last active log and then reallocating the primary log files when a new application connects will be costly. In such situations, the DBA should consider the ACTIVATE DATABASE command. The command will keep the database active and log file truncation will not occur. But if log files are not mirrored (or otherwise protected from a disk failure), the administrator must evaluate the impact on recovery. To lose the log through disk failure will make the point of recovery for the database to be less than the current unit of work. The DEACTIVATE DATABASE command can be entered to allow log file truncation to occur for databases on which the ACTIVATE DATABASE command has been used.

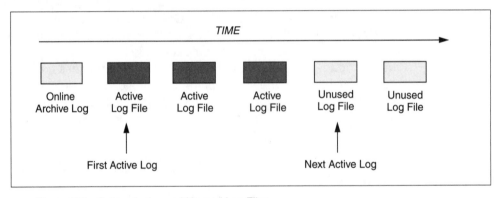

Figure 128. Online, Active and Unused Log Files

DB2 UDB uses a control file to track the status of the log files. The control file identifies the first active log, the oldest or last active log. As shown in Figure 128, this log file is called First active log file. The control file also specifies the name of the next log file to be used. Appropriately enough, this log is called Next active log file.

The values for First active log file and Next active log file can be displayed via the following command:

```
db2_all ';db2 get database configuration for tpcd100' |
grep "active log"
```

where tpcd100 is our database alias. Log files with names that are less (older) than the first active log file are archive files. They are not required for crash recovery and could be moved to different media.

Considering both values, next active and first active, the database administrator can determine the number of active logs that are currently allocated. If this number is abnormally large, an application may not be committing in a timely manner. If the number of allocated active logs is close to the total of primary and secondary logs, the installation may be approaching a log full condition. And when a log full condition occurs, the database partition with the log full condition will come down.

The DB2 UDB log file naming convention starts at S0000000.LOG and sequentially names logs until S9999999.LOG is reached. After S9999999.LOG, the name wraps back to S0000000.LOG, and the sequence starts again. The higher log file numbers will only be used when archive logging is configured for the database. Otherwise, only the numbers corresponding to the actual number of primary and secondary log files (circular logging) will be used.

5.4.4 Recovery History File

The recovery history file resides in the same directory as the database configuration file. There is a file for each database partition. The database manager updates the recovery history file whenever one of the following operations is performed:

- Backup a database or table space
- Restore a database or table space
- Load a table
- Quiesce a table space
- Roll-forward a database or table space

When a recovery action is required, the summary information contained in the file can help the database administrator to create the recovery plan. Information that may be useful includes:

- The part of the database that has been copied by a backup, load, or copy operation

- When the database was copied

- Where the backup or load copy is located

- Time of the last restore

- Quiesce entry with local and CUT timestamps provided

- Table space point-in-time recover information

DB2 UDB provides two commands to extract information from the recovery history file: LIST HISTORY and LIST BACKUP. The commands differ in the amount of information provided. LIST BACKUP retrieves only information pertaining to backups and restores. LIST HISTORY retrieves the full spectrum of records. To maintain this file, the database administrator can control how long history file information is kept before it is purged. The database configuration parameter rec_his_retn can be set to specify the retention period for history file records. The database software automatically prunes records older than the specification, which by default is 366 days. Records can also be removed manually using the PRUNE HISTORY command. The timestamp may be abbreviated to as little as yyyy (4-digit year). All entries with timestamps equal to or less than the timestamp provided are deleted from the file. Using the WITH FORCE option specifies that entries will be pruned according to the specified timestamp even if the command causes entries from the most recent restore set to be deleted.

5.4.5 Choosing A Backup Strategy

Defining a robust backup strategy for your database requires careful consideration of your business requirements, including factors such as the requirements for database availability and the maximum time the database can be down for backups. The Backup Database SmartGuide (included in the DB2 UDB V5 Control Center on Intel platforms) helps you with the decision-making. This section describes the considerations and issues in more detail in order to provide you with a better understanding of this important area.

To begin, you must decide on the types of failure that you are protecting against. The purpose of running a backup is to be able to use it to perform a recovery. Therefore, you must test your processes and procedures to ensure that your backups will be useful in the event of a failure. Backups that cannot be used to restore data are pointless.

The following are general guidelines for planning a recovery strategy:

- The type of data contained in your database is relevant. Databases that contain read-only data do not need to be protected through archive logging if full; off-line backups are run following each new data load activity. The use of circular logging would be sufficient in this case.

- With continuously updated data that is deemed important to your business, you must use archive logging.

- If your database must be continuously available, you must take online backups. This requires the use of archive logs.

- If in the event of a failure your database must be recovered in a short time, you will need to run more frequent backups. In this case, you need to establish how long it would take to recover from a failure (the sum of the time to restore the database from a backup plus the time needed to roll the logs forward).

Beyond transaction failures and system crashes, both of which DB2 will recover from, you should consider application errors. This refers to the general case of data being damaged in some manner. Clearly, there is no way to prevent an authorized user from altering data inappropriately. The best strategy for dealing with this type of problem is to ensure that you have archive logs to roll-forward the database to the point just prior to the corruption of the data. Be sure to factor into your schedule the maximum time the database can be down for backups, and whether these are online or off-line.

Probably the most common type of failure is caused by media problems. This is not limited to disk problems, but can extend to other I/O devices, including disk controllers and tape devices. As a starting point, it is suggested that you do not back up your database to the same disk on which the production version exists: use either a separate disk or external media. The handling of your logs should be similar: consider directing these to a separate physical disk from that of the database. In addition to protecting against a disk failure affecting both, this may also result in performance improvements.

Though unlikely, it is possible that your backup media could suffer a problem just when it is needed to let you recover from a disk failure. Consider the impact of a tape going bad. If your data is absolutely critical, you should consider having duplicate tape media. Another strategy is to minimize the potential for impact caused by a bad disk. This applies to the disks that both the database and logs reside upon. Using disk arrays for your database volumes or logs (or both) is perhaps the best defense against disk media failures. See the *DB2 UDB Administration Guide* for information on disk arrays. If you extend redundancy to disk controllers as well, it is highly unlikely that your database will ever be unavailable or that logs will be lost due to a media failure.

When started, UDB formats primary logs. The more logs to be formatted, the longer UDB requires to initialize. To minimize start-up time, specify no more primary logs than needed to support crash recovery. Use secondary logs to handle the rare times when many logs are required. Let's say UDB starts logging with file S0000000.LOG, and after some time the log fills. UDB allocates the next log and calls the user-exit, db2uexit, to copy the full log to ADSM storage. The full log, though copied, is still active. The full log will remain in active status until every unit of work having changes in that log commits and until every logged (and now committed) change is written to the database disk. Once all the changes are committed and written to the database disk, the log becomes inactive. It is no longer required for crash recovery. At this time, the now inactive log is renamed. It becomes the highest numbered allocated log.

For example, say logprimary equals five. When either the `ACTIVATE DATABASE` command or first connect is issued, UDB will allocate five primary logs. Assume the log file names are S0000017.LOG through S0000021.LOG. UDB starts recording changes in S0000017.LOG. Eventually, the logs fills. UDB starts using the next log, S0000018.LOG, and calls `db2uext2` to archive S0000017.LOG to ADSM storage. Eventually, all the changes reflected in S0000017.LOG will be committed or rolled back. Later still, all the changes will finally be written to the database disk files. At this time, UDB no longer requires S0000017.LOG to support crash recovery. S0000017.LOG is renamed to S0000022.LOG.

Now what if a database partition must be restored? Or worse, what if an application error requires that the entire database be restored and rolled forward to a point just before the errant application ran? Not only must all of the database backups be restored from tape, but the necessary logs must be retrieved as well. This may involve many tape mounts. Bear in mind also that even query-only database systems do their share of logging.

Wouldn't it be nice to have on disk all of the logs needed to roll-forward from the most recent backup? To be able to avoid waiting for log files to be recalled from ADSM tape storage? Wouldn't it be nice if UDB wasn't so quick to rename those inactive log files? To allow some number of log files to remain in the LOGPATH directory. Say just enough to roll-forward from the most recent backup?

A possible solution to this log-on-tape dilemma is to use the sample exit which writes logs to an alternate directory instead of to ADSM. A daemon program could be written to archive the older logs to ADSM. Also you would need to update the database configuration parameter to specify this disk directory as an alternate log path.

Chapter 6. Performance and Tuning

This chapter will focus on understanding how complex queries are processed by DB2 UDB EEE. We'll discuss join strategies, functions and concepts in detail. We'll analyze output from explain statements to understand these join techniques. We'll also discuss some of the performance and tuning items in a DB2 UDB EEE partitioned database environment.

6.1 DB2 UDB EEE Join Strategies

As DB2 has grown as a program product, the variety of join types and methods has expanded to accommodate the growing requirements of the business community. DB2 has grown from just supporting the inner join to now supporting a full complement of outer joins in DB2 UDB EEE. In response to the need to support On-Line Analytical Processing (OLAP) against very large data warehouse tables, DB2 UDB EEE now supports several new SQL functions that allow for the aggregation of data at various levels with only one pass at the data.

The addition of the partitioned database distributed across multiple nodes has added a new level of complexity to the design and implementation of data warehousing and other OLAP databases. When planning for these databases, we must shift our perspective from optimizing data access for On-Line Transaction Processing (OLTP) data retrieval where the user is attempting to access individual rows, to optimizing data access for retrieval of data groupings. Because the data access requirements of an OLTP and OLAP database are so diverse and can negatively impact each other's performance, OLTP and OLAP databases are generally physically separate databases. DB2 UDB EEE is intended for OLAP and data warehousing databases.

The following is an example of an OLTP environment. We have constructed an index over the C_NAME column so that the online end user may perform customer look up on specific customers, as is demonstrated in the following for customer BULLOCK.

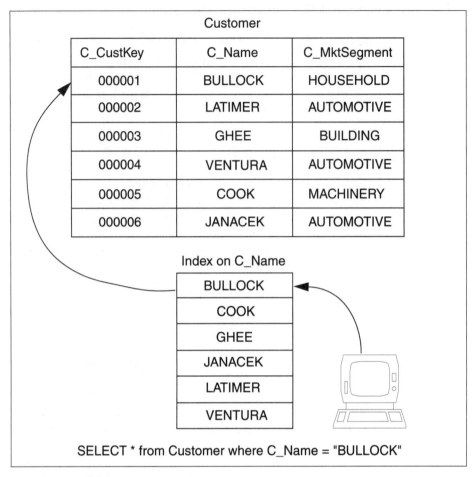

Figure 129. OLTP Environment

In the OLAP following example, we would have little use for an index over C_NAME. In an OLAP environment, our users would be more interested in attributes of groups of customers so that we may more effectively market to our customer base. We have constructed an index over the C_MKTSEGMENT column, so that we can select groups of our customers that are from a specific market segment. In this example, we are locating all of our customers that are in the automotive market segment.

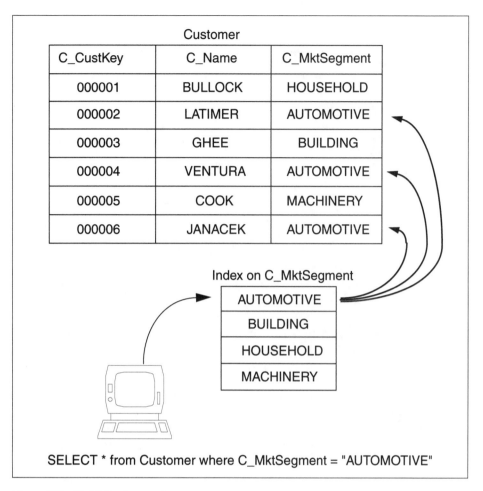

C_CustKey	C_Name	C_MktSegment
000001	BULLOCK	HOUSEHOLD
000002	LATIMER	AUTOMOTIVE
000003	GHEE	BUILDING
000004	VENTURA	AUTOMOTIVE
000005	COOK	MACHINERY
000006	JANACEK	AUTOMOTIVE

Index on C_MktSegment

AUTOMOTIVE
BUILDING
HOUSEHOLD
MACHINERY

SELECT * from Customer where C_MktSegment = "AUTOMOTIVE"

Figure 130. OLAP Environment

6.1.1 Join Concepts

Discussing joins can sometimes be quite confusing. There are *join techniques,* such as *merge join* and *nested loop join* that the database manager invokes to resolve the join criteria. There are *join functions* within SQL syntax such as the implied inner join and the outer joins. There are *join strategies* that are important to consider when designing and implementing a parallel database across multiple database partitions.

Table 6. Join Table

Join Techniques	SQL Join Functions	Parallel DB Join Strategies
Merge Join	Inner Join	Collocated Join
Nested Loop Join	Left Outer Join	Directed Inner Join
	Right Outer Join	Directed Outer Join
	Full Outer Join	Directed Inner and Outer Join
		Broadcast Inner Join
		Broadcast Outer Join

Joining tables is one of the most important concepts within any relational database environment. With the expanded variety of SQL join functions available in DB2 UDB EEE, it is necessary to have a clear, comprehensive understanding of how to properly structure an SQL join predicate and which SQL join function to invoke to obtain the desired results in the most efficient manner. The SQL join functions that are supported in DB2 UDB EEE are *Inner Join*, *Left Outer Join*, *Right Outer Join*, and *Full Outer Join*; each is discussed in section 6.2.2.

In a parallel database environment, it is also important to understand the ways in which the user will most frequently access the data. Understanding which columns are most frequently used to join the tables together is critical in designing the partitioning key. The DB2 UDB EEE parallel database environment supports the join strategies of the *Collocated Join*, the *Directed Inner Join*, *Directed Outer Join*, *Directed Inner and Outer Join*, *Broadcast Inner Join, and Broadcast Outer Join*. Each is discussed in "Join Strategies in a Partitioned Database" on page 355.

The *Star Join* is a new database concept that has become popular in the data warehousing community. This concept is discussed in "DB2 UDB EEE OLAP Features" on page 379.

6.1.1.1 What is an SQL Join?
An SQL join is a relational operation. SQL join clauses enable the retrieval of data from one or more tables in which rows from the specified tables are concatenated together. The concatenation of the rows from the tables should be joined together based on matching column values.

The following figure contains an example of a simple join between the Nation and Region tables. These two tables are joined on the REGIONKEY column of each table. Note that each column from each table is represented in the figure below.

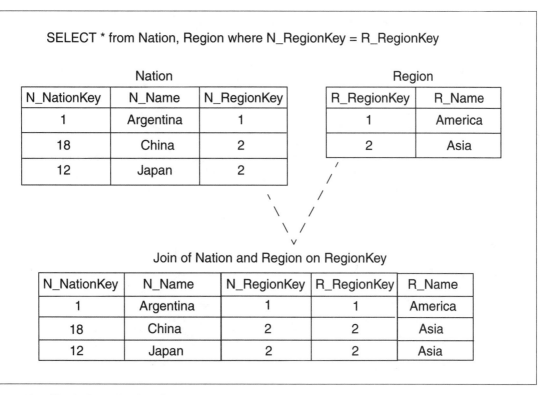

SELECT * from Nation, Region where N_RegionKey = R_RegionKey

Nation

N_NationKey	N_Name	N_RegionKey
1	Argentina	1
18	China	2
12	Japan	2

Region

R_RegionKey	R_Name
1	America
2	Asia

Join of Nation and Region on RegionKey

N_NationKey	N_Name	N_RegionKey	R_RegionKey	R_Name
1	Argentina	1	1	America
18	China	2	2	Asia
12	Japan	2	2	Asia

Figure 131. Simple Example of a Join

6.1.1.2 SQL Join Predicate

The SQL join predicate is the matching of column values between tables being joined.

For example, in the following `select` statement, the portion of the statement that follows the `where` clause is the join predicate. This is an example of an equijoin, or in other words, the value in one column is equal to the value in join column. Equijoin predicates are usually expressed in the form of table1.columna = table2.columnb.

```
SELECT C_NAME,
       O_TOTALPRICE,
       L_SHIPDATE

FROM CUSTOMER,
     ORDERS,
     LINEITEM

WHERE C_CUSTKEY = O_CUSTKEY
  and O_ORDERKEY = L_ORDERKEY
```

6.1.1.3 Cartesian Products

If you do not specify which columns are to be used to establish the mapping
of the data in one table to that of another, each qualifying row of the first table
will be mapped to each qualifying row of the second table forming the
Cartesian product of the two tables. The Cartesian product is a term from
mathematics and represents all possible points along the X and Y axis in the
first quadrant of the Cartesian plane.

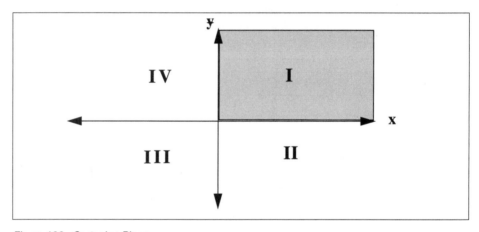

Figure 132. Cartesian Plane

The result of a Cartesian product will usually produce a very large table. In
very large databases, the Cartesian product of two or more very large tables
will consume enormous amounts of virtual memory resulting in high paging
rates. It may also produce a composite table that exceeds the maximum
available disk in the file system and terminate the process abnormally. To
avoid problems of this sort, temporary storage may be assigned to a separate
buffer pool which would protect other processes from the effects of an
abnormal termination.

As a simple example of a Cartesian product, let's use the NATION table with three rows joined to the REGION with two rows. Note that within the SQL sample below, no join criteria is specified so that DB2 may match the appropriate columns in REGION with those in NATION. The resulting composite table contains six rows (3 NATION rows x 2 REGION rows).

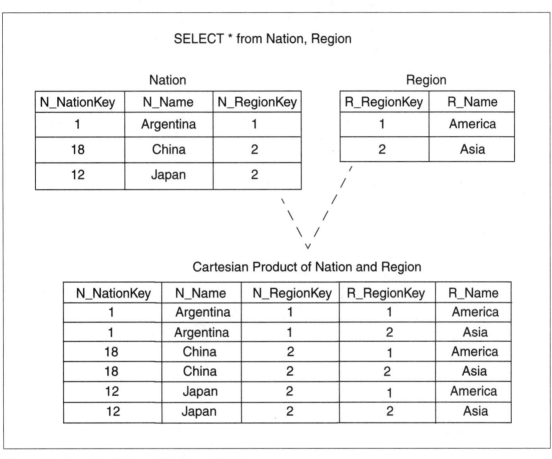

Figure 133. Cartesian Product of Nation and Region

If we use the same SQL statement, but increase the size of the tables to a NATION table which contains 10,000 rows and a REGION table which contains 1,000,000 rows, still do not specify a join predicate, and specify no selection criteria, the number of rows in the output will be 10 billion rows (10,000 x 1,000,000).

In this example, a valid relationship between the concatenated data elements has not been established and would not serve the business purpose of extracting the data. In general, a join that results in a Cartesian product will not return the results that the user desires. Similarly, if the entire join predicate is not specified, the result table may contain invalid or unusable data.

When designing a DB2 UDB EEE table, consider including the most frequently used join columns in the largest tables as the partitioning key. By including the most frequently used join columns in the partitioning key, query performance may be enhanced through the Optimizer's ability to invoke collocated joins on individual nodes and thereby reduce the amount of data being transmitted across the network.

6.1.1.4 Composite Tables

The result of joining a pair of tables is a new table known as a composite.

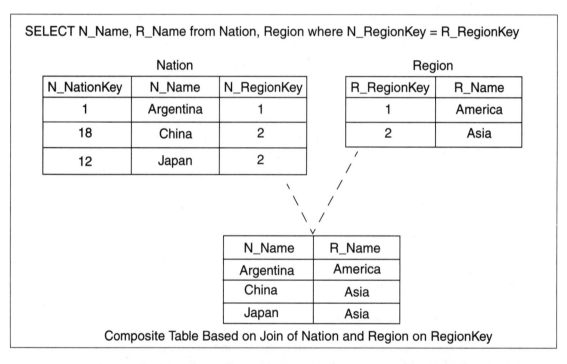

SELECT N_Name, R_Name from Nation, Region where N_RegionKey = R_RegionKey

Nation

N_NationKey	N_Name	N_RegionKey
1	Argentina	1
18	China	2
12	Japan	2

Region

R_RegionKey	R_Name
1	America
2	Asia

N_Name	R_Name
Argentina	America
China	Asia
Japan	Asia

Composite Table Based on Join of Nation and Region on RegionKey

Typically, this resulting composite table becomes the *outer table* of a join with another *inner table*. This is known as a "composite outer". In some situations, particularly when using the greedy join enumeration technique, it is useful to take the result of joining two tables and make that the *inner table* of a later join. When the *inner table* of a join itself consists of the result of joining two or more tables, the resultant table is know as a "composite inner"

6.1.1.5 Join Techniques

Basically, DB2 invokes one of two join techniques to resolve the join request specified in the join predicate of the SQL statement. One technique is known as *Merge Join*, the other is known as *Nested Loop Join*. DB2 will select one of the join techniques based on the existence of a join predicate and the costs that the database manager determines based on various table and index statistics in relationship to the criteria specified.

*Merge join m*ay also be known as *sort merge join* or *merge scan join*. The predicate of a merge join must be in the format of table1.column = table2.column. This is called an equality join predicate. Merge join requires ordered input on the joining columns, either through index access or by sorting. In order for a merge join to be used, the join column cannot be a LONG field column or a large object (LOB) column.

The joined tables are scanned simultaneously. The *outer table* of the merge join is scanned just once. The *inner table* is also scanned once unless there are repeated values in the *outer table*. If there are repeated values in the *outer table*, a group of rows in the *inner table* may be scanned again.

The following is an example of an SQL statement that would result in a merge join. Suppose that we wanted to generate a report of all of our customers whose names begin with the letter B that placed an order on January 20, 1998. In this example, assume that the database is not partitioned and that an index exists over the CUSTOMER table that contains the C_NAME and C_CUSTKEY columns named CUSTIX1. Also assume that an index exists over the ORDER table that contains the O_ORDERDATE and O_CUSTKEY columns named ORDERIX1.

```
Select  C_NAME,
        O_TOTALPRICE,
        O_SHIPDATE

from    CUSTOMER,
        ORDERS
where   C_CUSTKEY = O_CUSTKEY
  and   C_NAME like 'B%'
  and   O_ORDERDATE = 19980120

order by C_NAME
```

The database manager would perform an index scan against CUSTIX1 to locate all customers with a name that begins with the letter B. At the same time, the database manager would be searching the ORDERIX1 index for orderdates of January 20, 1998. The results of each search will be merge joined together and the data returned will be those rows that have matching CUSTKEYs.

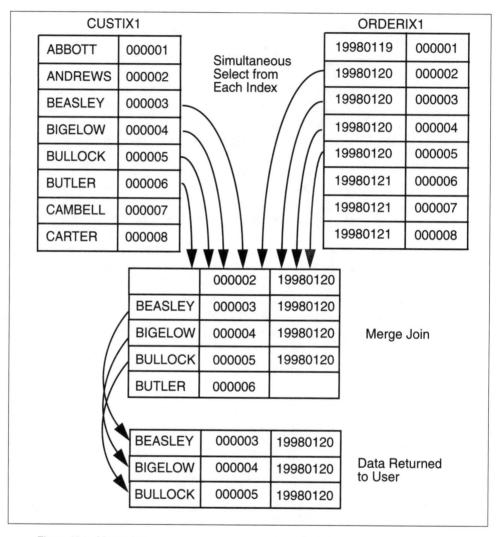

Figure 134. Merge Join

Nested loop joins are performed in one of two ways.

1. For each row of the *outer table* accessed, the *inner table* is scanned for rows that meet the specified criteria.

2. For each row of the *outer table* accessed, *inner table* index look up is invoked in search of rows that meet the specified criteria.

As a simple example of a nested loop join, assume we use the following SQL statement against a database that is not partitioned. We want to report on all customers whose names begin with the letter B and who placed orders on January 20, 1998. In this example, we have no indexes over C_NAME, C_CUSTKEY or over O_ORDERDATE, O_CUSTKEY.

```
SELECT  C_CUSTKEY,
        C_NAME,
        O_ORDERDATE,
        O_ORDERKEY

From    CUSTOMER,
        ORDERS

Where   C_CUSTKEY = O_CUSTKEY
  and   C_NAME like 'B%'
  and   O_ORDERDATE = 19980120

Order by C_NAME
```

The database manager will perform a table scan of the CUSTOMER table in search of C_NAMEs that begin with the character B. For each row found, the database manager will then access the rows in the ORDER table with the matching CUSTKEY and eliminate all but those with an O_ORDERDATE of January 20, 1998. In this example, CUSTOMER is the *outer table,* and ORDERS is the *inner table.*

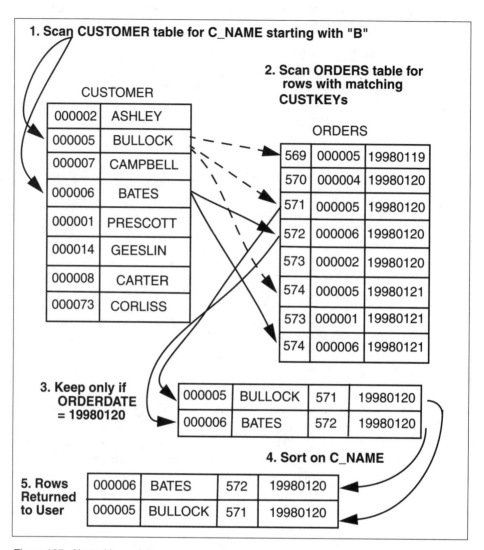

1. Scan CUSTOMER table for C_NAME starting with "B"

2. Scan ORDERS table for rows with matching CUSTKEYs

CUSTOMER

000002	ASHLEY
000005	BULLOCK
000007	CAMPBELL
000006	BATES
000001	PRESCOTT
000014	GEESLIN
000008	CARTER
000073	CORLISS

ORDERS

569	000005	19980119
570	000004	19980120
571	000005	19980120
572	000006	19980120
573	000002	19980120
574	000005	19980121
573	000001	19980121
574	000006	19980121

3. Keep only if ORDERDATE = 19980120

| 000005 | BULLOCK | 571 | 19980120 |
| 000006 | BATES | 572 | 19980120 |

4. Sort on C_NAME

5. Rows Returned to User

| 000006 | BATES | 572 | 19980120 |
| 000005 | BULLOCK | 571 | 19980120 |

Figure 135. Nested Loop Join

As you may have noticed in both the merge join and the nested loop join examples, both were executed against a non-parallel, non-partitioned database. In a parallel, partitioned database environment, the database manager often invokes a combination of both the merge join and nested loop join techniques to resolve the end user request across the database partitions. You will find examples of this in "EXPLAIN" on page 413, where the EXPLAIN facility is discussed in detail.

6.1.2 SQL Join Functions

Next, we discuss the various SQL join functions that are available within DB2 UDB EEE. While the inner join function has always existed in SQL, the outer join functions have only become a requirement for relational databases in the last few years. The outer joins provide the ability to return a row for every qualifying row in the *outer table* even if the *inner table* does not have a match for some of the outer rows selected. Fortunately, DB2 UDB EEE supports these functions fully. Support for these functions has eliminated the need to construct elaborate SQL that contained unions and has simplified SQL coding significantly

6.1.2.1 Inner Join

The *inner join* is the simplest form of a join function. An inner join is a matching of columns between two tables whose resulting composite table contains only rows that have matching join column values. The inner join may be missing rows from either or both of the tables that have been joined together.

You may be wondering if you have ever seen an inner join because you may not recall ever seeing a join predicate that contained the word INNER. After reviewing the following example, you will see that the form of inner join that you are probably most familiar with is equivalent to the explicitly stated inner join.

The following is an example of an explicitly stated inner join SQL statement:

```
SELECT   c_name,
         o_orderdate,
         o_totalprice

FROM     customer INNER JOIN order

WHERE  c_custkey = o_custkey
```

The following is an example of an implicitly stated inner join SQL statement:

```
SELECT   c_name,
         o_orderdate,
         o_totalprice

FROM     customer,
         order

WHERE c_custkey = o_custkey
```

The result of the execution of either the implicit or the explicit join will produce an identical result set. The implicitly stated inner join is the most common form of the inner join SQL statement.

6.1.2.2 Left Outer Join

The *left outer join* is a join between two tables in which all rows meeting the specified selection criteria are returned for the table named to the left of the **LEFT OUTER JOIN** statement. The table to the right of the **LEFT OUTER JOIN** statement returns all specified columns for all rows that have a matching join value and nulls for the columns in all other rows that do not have matching join values.

The following is an example of the SQL syntax required to invoke the *left outer join* SQL function:

```
SELECT c_name,
         o_orderdate,
         o_totalprice

FROM customer LEFT OUTER JOIN order

ON c_custkey = o_custkey
```

The resulting output of this SQL will contain at least one row for each customer row selected even if the customer has never placed an order.

In the following figure, you see two tables. The CUSTOMER table on the left is being joined to the ORDERS table via a *left outer join*. The two tables are being joined on the CUSTKEY column as is specified in the SQL statement above. Note that both customer ELLISON and GHEE have orders in the ORDERS table, but that the third customer, ASHLEY, does not. When the *left outer join* of the CUSTOMER table to ORDERS table is performed, the results contain a row for each customer, order combination and a row for customer Ashley who has not placed an order.

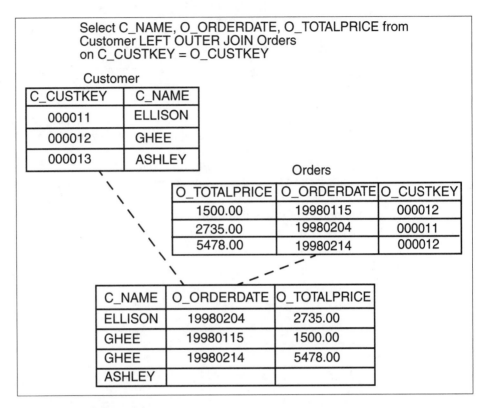

Figure 136. Left Outer Join

6.1.2.3 **Right Outer Join**

The *right outer join* is a join between two tables in which all rows meeting the specified selection criteria are returned for the table named to the right of the `RIGHT OUTER JOIN` statement. The table to the right of the `RIGHT OUTER JOIN` statement returns all specified columns for all rows that have a matching join value and nulls for the columns in all other rows that do not have matching join values.

The following is an example of the SQL syntax required to invoke the *right outer join* SQL function:

```
SELECT c_name,
       o_orderdate,
       o_totalprice

FROM orders RIGHT OUTER JOIN customer

ON c_custkey = o_custkey
```

The resulting output from this SQL statement will contain at least one row for each customer whether the customer has ever ordered from the company.

In the following figure, the *right outer join* is depicted. Once again, we see that customer ELLISON has placed one order and GHEE has placed two orders. Customer ASHLEY has not placed an order. When the *right outer join* of Customer to Orders is performed, the results contain, one row for customer ELLISON, two rows for customer GHEE and one row for customer ASHLEY.

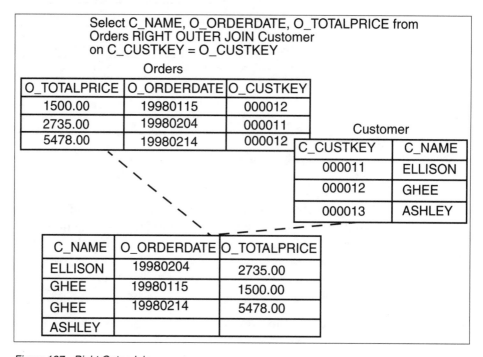

Figure 137. Right Outer Join

As you may have noticed, a *right outer join* is really no different than a *left outer join* with the order of the tables reversed. It is really just a question of which table you designate as the *outer join* table; otherwise, the work of the database manager is identical in resolving the request.

6.1.2.4 Full Outer Join

A full outer join is essentially the union of the *left outer join* results with the *right outer join* results. The full outer join returns all the rows that are matched between the two tables and preserves the unmatched rows from each of the two tables.

The following is an example of the SQL syntax required to invoke the *full outer join* SQL function:

```
SELECT c_name,
       o_orderdate,
       o_totalprice

FROM customer FULL OUTER JOIN orders

ON c_custkey = o_custkey
```

The following figure depicts the full outer join of the CUSTOMER table to the ORDERS table.

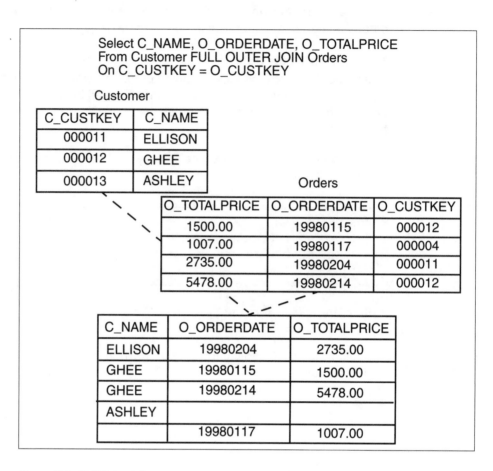

Select C_NAME, O_ORDERDATE, O_TOTALPRICE
From Customer FULL OUTER JOIN Orders
On C_CUSTKEY = O_CUSTKEY

Customer

C_CUSTKEY	C_NAME
000011	ELLISON
000012	GHEE
000013	ASHLEY

Orders

O_TOTALPRICE	O_ORDERDATE	O_CUSTKEY
1500.00	19980115	000012
1007.00	19980117	000004
2735.00	19980204	000011
5478.00	19980214	000012

C_NAME	O_ORDERDATE	O_TOTALPRICE
ELLISON	19980204	2735.00
GHEE	19980115	1500.00
GHEE	19980214	5478.00
ASHLEY		
	19980117	1007.00

Figure 138. Full Outer Join

In the depiction of a *full outer join*, we once again are joining the Customer table to the Orders table. Two of the three customers have orders in the Orders table, and one does not. Note that the order placed on January 17, 1998 does not have a corresponding C_CUSTKEY in the Customer table.

When the *full outer join* of Customer to Orders is performed, the results contain, one row for customer ELLISON, two rows for customer GHEE, one row for customer ASHLEY, and one row for the order placed on January 17, 1998 for $1007.00.

6.1.2.5 Factors that Affect Internal Table Access Order

We have seen how you can use SQL to perform inner as well as outer joins so as to affect the data returned from the SQL request. But to actually access the data, DB2 must perform either the merge join or nested loop join technique to internally resolve the request. While performing either of these two join techniques, DB2 must choose one table to be the *inner table* and one to be the *outer table* during the internal join process. The following are general guidelines for how the optimizer decides on the order in which the tables will be the accessed.

Order of Table Access

The order in which the tables are accessed is particularly important for a nested loop join because the *outer table* is accessed once but the *inner table* is accessed once for each row of the *outer table*. The optimizer chooses the *outer* and *inner tables* based on cost estimates. These cost estimates are influenced by factors such as table size, predicates, buffering, indexes, and ordering.

Table Size

Table size may influence the access plan that the optimizer will choose. The smaller table is often chosen to be the *outer table* to reduce the number of times the *inner table* must be re-accessed. However, prefetch can cause just the opposite to be true. Prefetching can reduce the cost of accessing a large table substantially. Yet, usually prefetching is only effective for the *outer table* of a join. Therefore, the larger table may be accessed first. See "Prefetching Data into the Buffer Pool" in the *DB2 Administration Guide* for more information.

Predicates

Predicates may affect the optimizer's choice as to which table will be selected as the *outer table*. A table is more likely to be chosen as the *outer table* if selective predicates can be applied to it because the *inner table* is only accessed for rows which satisfy the predicates applied to the *outer table*.

In the following SQL example, the optimizer will choose the LINEITEM table as the *outer table*. First, DB2 will select all LINEITEM rows with a ship date of January 20, 1998. Those rows will then be joined to the ORDER table by ORDERKEY, the primary key of the ORDER table. By choosing this access plan, the amount of work that DB2 must do to resolve the request is significantly less than if it chose ORDER as the *outer table* since no selection criteria is explicitly stated for the ORDER table.

```
select  O_ORDERDATE,
        O_TOTALPRICE,
        L_EXTENDEDPRICE,
        L_TAX

from    ORDER,
        LINEITEM

where   L_SHIPDATE = 19980120
  and   O_ORDERKEY = L_ORDERKEY
```

Buffering

Buffering may impact the choice of the optimizer. If the entire *inner table* must be scanned for each row of the *outer table* (that is, an index lookup cannot be performed on the *inner table*), the smaller of the two tables may be chosen as the *inner table* to take advantage of buffering. This will be influenced by table size and buffer pool size.

Note that since join decisions are influenced by buffer pool size, the access plan for your applications may change if you rebind your applications to the database after changing the buffer pool size. Your ability to create more than one buffer pool, change the size of that buffer pool, and control the table spaces that use that buffer pool, can affect when buffering is used within inner and *outer tables*.

Indexes

The existence of indexes may alter the access plan that the optimizer chooses. When appropriate indexes are present, the optimizer will use those indexes if it determines that the cost of accessing the index is less than the other non-index access paths available. If it is possible to do an index look-up on one of the tables, then that table is a good candidate to use as the *inner table*. It could then be accessed with an index key look-up using the *outer table*'s join key predicate as one of the key values. If a table does not have an index, it would not be a good candidate for the *inner table* since in that case the entire *inner table* would have to be scanned for every row of the *outer table*.

Column Ordering

The presence of order requirements may also influence the optimizer's access plan selection in a nested loop join. The table associated with a required order might be accessed first.

In the following SQL example, we are requesting a report of all orders from all customers, and we want the report to be sorted in customer name order.

```
select  C_NAME,
        O_ORDERDATE,
        O_TOTALPRICE

from    CUSTOMER,
        ORDERS

where   C_CUSTKEY = O_CUSTKEY

order by C_NAME
```

Because we have asked to sort the report in customer name order, the optimizer will probably choose CUSTOMER as the *outer table* so that it may perform the customer name sort, then resolve the join to the ORDERS table.

Merge Join Considerations

When the optimizer invokes a merge join, the order in which the tables are accessed is somewhat less important because both the *inner* and *outer tables* are read only once. However, portions of the *inner table* which correspond to duplicate join values in the outer are kept in an in-memory buffer. The buffer is re-read if the next outer row is the same as the previous outer row, otherwise the buffer is reset. If the number of duplicate join values exceeds the capacity of the in-memory buffer, not all of the duplicates are kept. This will only happen when the duplication on any value is large and the value has a matching value in the *outer table*.

6.1.3 Join Strategies in a Partitioned Database

When designing and implementing a partitioned database, we must give careful consideration to the way in which we choose the partitioning keys of the tables within the database. The partitioning key determines how the data is distributed across the database partitions. For further information regarding partitioning keys, please see "Partitioning Keys" on page 189.

When DB2 UDB EEE joins two tables together, the data being joined must be physically located in the same database partition. If the data is not physically located in the same database partition, DB2 must move the data to a database partition by re-locating the data from one partition to another. The movement of data between database partitions can be an enormous effort when the database is very large; therefore, we must examine our largest tables and attempt to choose a partitioning key in such a way as to minimize the amount of data movement. Once the appropriate data is available in the database partition, DB2 may perform either the merge join or a nested loop join techniques to perform the request.

In general, the best join strategy is to have all of your large, frequently accessed tables partitioned in such a way to resolve your most frequent join requests on their database partitions with minimal data movement. The worst join strategy is to have your large, frequently accessed tables partitioned in such a way as to force the movement of the data to the appropriate partitions for the majority of your joins. When choosing your partitioned database join strategy, your primary focus should be on the large and more frequently accessed tables. Tuning the database for access to these large tables will have the greatest impact on performance. Remember the golden rule, the smaller the amount of data that has to be moved to resolve a join, the better the performance of the database.

6.1.3.1 Collocated Table Joins

The collocated join is the best performing partitioned database strategy. For a collocated join to be possible, all the data to perform the join must be located in each of the local database partitions. In this join strategy, no data is relocated to another database partition except to return the answer set to the coordinator database partition. The coordinator database partition assembles the answer set for final presentation to the requestor.

The collocated join strategy will be selected by the DB2 UDB optimizer if the following conditions are true:

- Tables residing in a single node nodegroup

  - If all the tables reside within a single-node nodegroup, then any join may be resolved on that nodegroup. Therefore, all the tables will be collocated.

- Tables residing across multinode nodegroups

  - The joined tables must be defined in the same nodegroup.

- The partitioning key for each of the joined tables must have the same number of columns.

  For example, assume that the CUSTOMER table is partitioned on C_CUSTKEY and the ORDERS table is partitioned on O_CUSTKEY. Each table is partitioned on one column and the column values map together; therefore, they have the potential to participate in a collocated join.

  Now, assume that CUSTOMER is still partitioned on C_CUSTKEY, but the ORDERS table is now partitioned on O_CUSTKEY, O_ORDERKEY. The

CUSTOMER and ORDERS table no longer have the ability to participate in a collocated join. Once the ORDERS table added an additional column, the value that the partitioning key will hash to is now different than when it was just O_CUSTKEY; therefore, there is no guarantee that the rows in the CUSTOMER table on any given partition will directly map to those in the ORDERS table on the same partition.

- For each column in the partitioning key of the joined tables, an equijoin predicate must exist.

For example, assume we have the ORDERS table partitioned on O_ORDERKEY and the LINEITEM column partitioned on L_ORDERKEY. For these two tables to be eligible for a collocated join, the SQL request must specify that the join columns are equal such as ORDERS.O_ORDERKEY=LINEITEM.L_ORDERKEY.

- Corresponding partitioning key columns must be partition compatible.

Suppose that the O_ORDERKEY column is defined as SMALLINT in the ORDERS table and L_ORDERKEY is defined as INTEGER in the LINEITEM table. Even though they are defined as different integer types, they are still compatible and may be used to join the two tables in a collocated join.

Ultimately, the data to complete the join must be found in the local database partition for DB2 to resolve the join. The collocated table join is the best performing because the data already resides on the local database partition. DB2's goal in all the other join strategies is to relocate the data to the appropriate partition so that it may perform a join on each participating database partition.

The following is a diagram of the process flow of a collocated table join. The initial request is sent to the coordinator node. From the coordinator node, the request is split across all appropriate database partitions. Each partition scans the ORDERS table, applies the ORDERS predicates, scans the LINEITEM table, applies the LINEITEM predicates, performs the join locally, and inserts the answer set into a table queue. The table queue is then sent to the coordinator node where it is read and processed. The final answer set is then returned to the originating application.

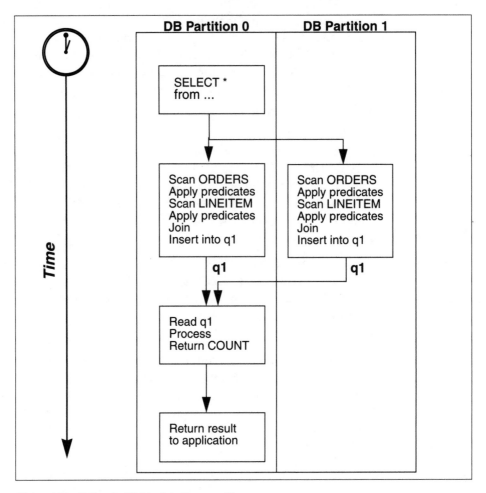

Figure 139. Collocated Table Join Process Flow

Now that we have reviewed the process flow of a collocated join, let's look at the explain output from an SQL statement that invokes a collocated join in a multi-node, multiple partition database.

The following is the SQL statement that caused the DB2 UDB EEE optimizer to choose a collocated table join strategy. Please note that under DB2 UDB EEE Version 5, the explain output no longer explicitly states what type of partitioned join strategy has been chosen by the DB2 UDB EEE optimizer.

```
Select  O_ORDERPRIORITY,
        COUNT(DISTINCT O_ORDERKEY)

From    ORDERS,
        LINEITEM
Where   L_ORDERKEY = O_ORDERKEY
  and   L_COMMITDATE < L_RECEIPTDATE

Group by O_ORDERPRIORITY
```

The two tables involved in this request are ORDERS and LINEITEM, the largest tables in the database. Both tables are defined to the same nodegroup. The partitioning keys for each of these tables are listed below.

Table Name	Partitioning Key	Column Attribute
LINEITEM	L_ORDERKEY	INTEGER
ORDERS	O_ORDERKEY	INTEGER

The optimizer is able to choose a collocated join because all of the requirements for a collocated join have been met.

- The tables reside in the same nodegroup.

- The partitioning keys for both LINEITEM and ORDERS contain 1 column.

- The partitioning key for each table is defined as INTEGER; therefore, they are partition compatible.

- The two tables are joined based on the equijoin L_ORDERKEY = O_ORDERKEY.

Once the collocated join of the tables on each node is completed, the answer sets are returned to the coordinator partition for final assembly and presentation to the requestor.

Now let's look at the explain for the SQL statement above. We will start with the coordinator subsection.

```
Coordinator Subsection:
   Distribute Subsection #1                           ◄──────────  (A)
   |  Broadcast to Node List
   |  |  Nodes = 1, 2
   Access Table Queue  ID = q1   #Columns = 3 ◄──────  (B)
   |  Output Sorted #Key Columns = 2
   Final Aggregation
   |  Group By
   |  Column Function(s)
   Return Data to Application
   |  #Columns = 2
```

The first subsection of each DB2 UDB Explain is the Coordinator Subsection. The Coordinator Subsection tells us the steps that the optimizer intends to take to execute the plan that it has decided will be the most efficient. This subsection is the key to the process flow to resolve the request.

As we can see from the Coordinator Subsection of this Explain, the first step, (designated by an A in the Explain), is to distribute subsection #1 to nodes 1 and 2. Subsection #1 may be found in the next figure. The activities in subsection #1 will occur on each node.

1. In Subsection #1, DB2 will perform a relation scan of the ORDERS table.

2. The output from the scan will be placed in a temp table, t1.

3. The t1 temp table will be merge joined with the LINEITEM table on each database partition. The t1 table is the outer table and LINEITEM is the inner table of the collocated join. Because we are able to resolve the join directly on the partition, we may conclude that the optimizer has chosen a *collocated join* strategy.

4. The output from the merge join of the t1 table and the LINEITEM table will be a new sorted temp table, t2.

5. The t2 temp table will be further processed to resolve any predicates that may be resolved at the node level. The DISTINCT processing will be performed at the node level and duplicate rows will be eliminated, with the final node level answer set placed in temp table t3.

6. The rows in t3 will now be inserted into table queue q1. Table queue q1 will then be sent back to the coordinator node.

We now return to the coordinator subsection. In the second step, *B*, the coordinator reads the table queue, q1. The coordinator node performs the final aggregation of the result set received via table queue q1, and returns the final version of the data to the application requestor.

```
Subsection #1:
  Access Table Name = DB2INST1.ORDERS  ID = 9        ◄─────  ①
  |  #Columns = 2
  |  Relation Scan
  |  |  Prefetch: Eligible
  |  Lock Intents
  |  |  Table: Intent Share
  |  |  Row  : Next Key Share
  |  Insert Into Sorted Temp Table  ID = t1
  |  |  #Columns = 2
  |  |  #Sort Key Columns = 1
  |  |  Sortheap Allocation Parameters:◄──┐
  |  |  |  #Rows     = 75201              │  Amount of
  |  |  |  Row Width = 24                 │  Sortheap
  |  |  Piped                            │  Required!
  Sorted Temp Table Completion  ID = t1
  Access Temp Table  ID = t1        ◄─────  ②
  |  #Columns = 2
  |  Relation Scan
  |  |  Prefetch: Eligible
  Merge Join                        ◄─────  ③
  |  Access Table Name = DB2INST1.LINEITEM  ID = 2
  |  |  #Columns = 3
  |  |  Relation Scan
  |  |  |  Prefetch: Eligible
  |  |  Lock Intents
|  |  |  Table: Intent Share
  |  |  |  Row  : Next Key Share
  |  |  Sargable Predicate(s)
  |  |  |  #Predicates = 1
  |  |  Insert Into Sorted Temp Table  ID = t2
  |  |  |  #Columns = 1
  |  |  |  #Sort Key Columns = 1
  |  |  |  Sortheap Allocation Parameters:
  |  |  |  |  #Rows     = 10023
  |  |  |  |  Row Width = 8
  |  |  |  Piped
  |  Sorted Temp Table Completion  ID = t2
  |  Access Temp Table  ID = t2       ◄─────  ④
  |  |  #Columns = 1
  |  |  Relation Scan
  |  |  |  Prefetch: Eligible
  Insert Into Sorted Temp Table  ID = t3    ◄─────  ⑤
  |  #Columns = 2
  |  #Sort Key Columns = 2
  |  Sortheap Allocation Parameters:◄──┐
  |  |  #Rows     = 10023              │  Amount of
  |  |  Row Width = 24                 │  Sortheap
  |  Piped                            │  Required!
  Access Temp Table  ID = t3
  |  #Columns = 2
  |  Relation Scan
  |  |  Prefetch: Eligible
  |  Partial Predicate Aggregation
  |  |  Group By
  |  |  Column Function(s)
```

In the previous output, you'll notice two indications of the sortheap allocation parameters. The minimum required sortheap size is the maximum of the amounts in the explain statement. In our example, we see two sortheap allocation parameters, one indicating 75201 rows with row width of 24; the other is 10023 rows with row width of 24. The latter value is the one to use when estimating the sortheap size in this example as it is the maximum amount listed in the explain output.

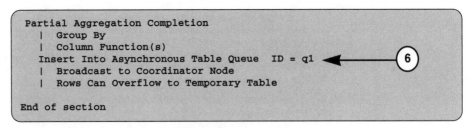

```
Partial Aggregation Completion
    |  Group By
    |  Column Function(s)
Insert Into Asynchronous Table Queue  ID = q1
    |  Broadcast to Coordinator Node
    |  Rows Can Overflow to Temporary Table

End of section
```

Figure 140. Collocated Table Join Explain

6.1.3.2 Directed Outer Table Join Strategy

The directed outer table join strategy may only be selected as the join strategy between two partitioned tables when there are equijoin predicates on all partitioning key columns. With the *Directed Outer Table Join* strategy, rows of the *outer table* are directed to a set of database partitions, based on the hashed values of the joining columns. Once the rows are relocated on the target database partitions, the join between the two tables occurs on these database partitions

The following is a diagram of the process flow for a directed outer table join strategy.

1. The initial request is sent to the coordinator node from the originating application.

2. The coordinator node dispatches the request to all relevant nodes.

3. The nodes scan the table that DB2 has chosen as the outer table and apply any predicates to the interim result set.

4. The nodes hash the join columns of the outer table that correspond to the inner table's partitioning key.

5. Based on the hashing values, the rows are then sent via table queue to the relevant target nodes.

6. The target nodes receive outer table rows via a table queue.

7. The receiving nodes scan the inner table and apply any predicates.

8. The nodes then perform a join of the received outer table rows and inner table.

9. The nodes then send the results of the join back to the coordinator node.

10.The coordinator node performs any final aggregation or other necessary processing and returns the final result set to the originating application.

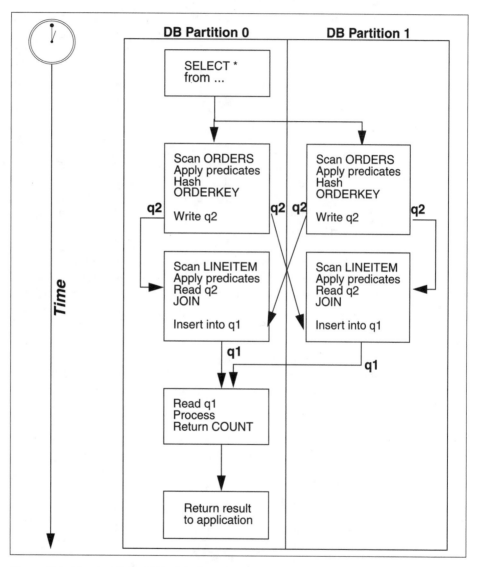

Figure 141. Directed Outer Table Join Strategy

In the *Directed Outer Table Join* strategy, the Explain will always show the *inner table* as a temporary table and the *outer table* as a table queue that has been hashed to the target partitions. As noted in the *collocated table join strategy* section, the Explain output no longer explicitly states what type of partitioned join strategy is being employed to resolve the request.

6.1.3.3 Directed Inner Table Joins

With the *Directed Inner Join* strategy, rows of the *inner table* are directed to a set of database partitions, based on the hashed values of the joining columns. Once the rows are relocated on the target database partitions, the join between the two tables occurs on these database partitions. As before, the directed inner table join may only be chosen as the join strategy when there are equijoin predicates on all partitioning key columns of the two partitioned tables.

In section "Directed Outer Table Join Strategy" on page 362, you will see a diagram of the Directed Outer Table Join Process Flow. This is identical to the process flow for the Directed Inner Table Join except that the table that was directed to the target database partitions based on the hashed value of the joining columns is taken by DB2 as the *inner table* of the join on the database partition.

In the *Directed Inner Table Join* strategy, the Explain will always show the *outer table* as a temporary table and the *inner table* as a table queue that has been hashed to the target partitions. As noted previously, the Explain output no longer explicitly states which join strategy has been chosen by the optimizer.

Now that we have discussed the process flow for directed table join strategies, we will examine the Explain output for a *directed inner table join* strategy. The following SQL statement was used to generate the Explain.

```
Select C_NAME,
       COUNT(DISTINCT O_ORDERKEY)

From CUSTOMER,
     ORDERS

Where C_CUSTKEY = O_CUSTKEY
  and C_ACCTBAL> 0
  and YEAR(O_ORDERDATE) = 1998

Group by C_NAME
```

The two tables involved in this request are the CUSTOMER table and the ORDERS table. The partitioning keys for each of these tables are listed below:

Table Name	Partitioning Key	Column Attribute
CUSTOMER	C_CUSTKEY	INTEGER
ORDERS	O_ORDERKEY	INTEGER

The CUSTOMER and ORDERS tables do not join on their respective partitioning keys; therefore, this join is **not** eligible for the *collocated table join* strategy. The CUSTOMER and ORDERS join predicate as stated in the SQL statement above is C_CUSTKEY = O_CUSTKEY. An equijoin predicate is required for a *directed inner* or *directed outer table join*; therefore, this request is eligible for a directed table join.

Now let's review the Explain output generated from the SQL statement above. We will begin with the coordinator subsection.

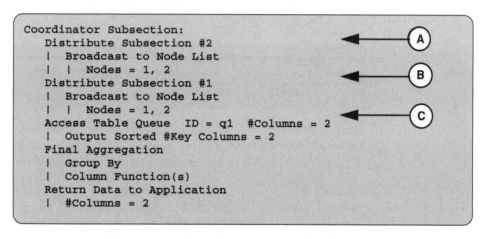

```
Coordinator Subsection:
   Distribute Subsection #2                          ◄──── A
   |   Broadcast to Node List
   |   |   Nodes = 1, 2                               ◄──── B
   Distribute Subsection #1
   |   Broadcast to Node List
   |   |   Nodes = 1, 2
   Access Table Queue   ID = q1   #Columns = 2        ◄──── C
   |   Output Sorted #Key Columns = 2
   Final Aggregation
   |   Group By
   |   Column Function(s)
   Return Data to Application
   |   #Columns = 2
```

The first subsection of each DB2 UDB Explain is the Coordinator Subsection. As always, the coordinator subsection tells us the steps that the optimizer intends to take to obtain the requested results.

The first task (found in letter A above of the Explain), is to distribute subsection #2 to database partitions 1 and 2. Subsection #2 may be found on the following pages. The activities that occur in subsection 2 are described below and occur on both database partition 1 and 2 simultaneously.

1. In subsection #2, DB2 will perform a relation scan of the ORDERS table and apply any predicates.

2. The output from the scan and the application of the predicates will be placed in a temporary table, t3.

3. The t3 table will then be read. Rows from temporary table t3 will be inserted into table queue q2 and distributed to the appropriate target nodes based on the hash value of the column, O_CUSTKEY, that will be used to join to the CUSTOMER table.

We now return to the coordinator subsection, to the second task, *B*. Here the coordinator sends us on to subsection #1 where the request is distributed to both nodes 1 and 2.

4. In subsection #1, DB2 will perform a relation scan of the CUSTOMER table and apply any predicates.

5. The output from the scan and the application of the predicates will be placed in a temporary table, t1.

6. The t1 temporary table will be merge joined to the rows that were hashed to the database partition via the table queue, q2. In this example, CUSTOMER temporary table is the outer table of the join and the hashed rows from ORDERS in table queue, q2, is the inner table of the join. At this point, we may discern that the optimizer has chosen a *directed inner table join*.

    Once the merge join is complete, the result set will be further processed to apply any additional predicates and any possible aggregations.

7. The result set is then written to the q1 table queue and broadcast back to the coordinator node.

We now return once again to the coordinator node, to task *C*. The q1 table queue that has been sent from each participating node is read by the coordinator node, final aggregation is performed and the final result set is returned to the originating application.

```
Subsection #1:
   Access Table Name = DB2INST1.CUSTOMER   ID = 8  ◄──────  ④
   |  #Columns = 3
   |  Relation Scan
   |  |  Prefetch: Eligible
   |  Lock Intents
   |  |  Table: Intent Share
   |  |  Row  : Next Key Share
   |  Sargable Predicate(s)
   |  |  #Predicates = 1
   |  Insert Into Sorted Temp Table  ID = t1
   |  |  #Columns = 2
   |  |  #Sort Key Columns = 1
   |  |  Sortheap Allocation Parameters:
   |  |  |  #Rows      = 6843
   |  |  |  Row Width = 32
   |  |  Piped                              ◄──────  ⑤
   Sorted Temp Table Completion  ID = t1
   Access Temp Table  ID = t1
   |  #Columns = 2
   |  Relation Scan
   |  |  Prefetch: Eligible
Merge Join
   |  Access Table Queue  ID = q2  #Columns = 2  ◄──────  ⑥
   |  |  Output Sorted #Key Columns = 1
   Insert Into Sorted Temp Table  ID = t2
   |  #Columns = 2
   |  #Sort Key Columns = 2
   |  Sortheap Allocation Parameters:
   |  |  #Rows      = 2735
   |  |  Row Width = 32
   |  Piped
   Access Temp Table  ID = t2
   |  #Columns = 2
   |  Relation Scan
   |  |  Prefetch: Eligible
   |  Partial Predicate Aggregation
   |  |  Group By
   Partial Aggregation Completion
   |  Group By
   Insert Into Asynchronous Table Queue  ID = q1  ◄──────  ⑦
   |  Broadcast to Coordinator Node
   |  Rows Can Overflow to Temporary Table
```

```
Subsection #2:
   Access Table Name = DB2INST1.ORDERS   ID = 9    ◄──────(1)
   |  #Columns = 3
   |  Relation Scan
   |  |  Prefetch: Eligible
   |  Lock Intents
   |  |  Table: Intent Share
   |  |  Row  : Next Key Share
   |  Sargable Predicate(s)
   |  |  #Predicates = 1
   |  Insert Into Sorted Temp Table  ID = t3
   |  |  #Columns = 2
   |  |  #Sort Key Columns = 1
   |  |  Sortheap Allocation Parameters:
   |  |  |  #Rows     = 3009
   |  |  |  Row Width = 12
   |  |  Piped
   Sorted Temp Table Completion   ID = t3    ◄──────(2)
   Access Temp Table  ID = t3
   |  #Columns = 2
   |  Relation Scan
   |  |  Prefetch: Eligible
   Insert Into Asynchronous Table Queue  ID = q2  ◄──────(3)
   |  Hash to Specific Node
   |  Rows Can Overflow to Temporary Tables

End of section
```

6.1.3.4 Directed Inner and Outer Table Joins

The *Directed Inner and Outer* table join strategy is basically a combination of a directed inner table join strategy and a directed outer table join strategy. With this strategy, rows of the *outer* and *inner tables* are directed to a set of database partitions, based on the values of the joining columns. The join occurs on these database partitions.

The *directed inner and outer table join* strategy may be chosen by the optimizer when the following situation occurs:

1. The partitioning keys of both tables are different from the join columns.

2. At least one equijoin predicate must exist between the tables being joined in the query.

3. Both tables are relatively large.

The following is a diagram of the process flow of a *directed inner and outer join* strategy. The process flow is explained below. Please note that these activities are being executed simultaneously across multiple database partitions during each step.

1. The initial request is sent to the coordinator database partitions from the originating application.

2. The coordinator database partition dispatches the request to all relevant nodes.

3. The outer table will be scanned on all nodes that contain the table that DB2 has chosen as the outer table of the join. Predicates will be applied where appropriate.

4. The inner table will be scanned on all database partitions that contain the table that DB2 has chosen as the inner table of the join. Predicates will be applied where appropriate.

5. The outer table database partitions will hash each selected row from the outer table using the join columns specified in the query.

6. The inner table database partitions will hash each selected row from the inner table using the join columns specified in the query.

7. Each participating database partition will send the hashed rows to the appropriate database partition via hashed table queues.

8. The selected database partitions will receive the hashed table queues for the outer table rows.

9. The selected database partitions will receive the hashed table queues for the inner table rows.

10. The nodes perform the join of the received outer table rows to the received inner table rows. Predicates will be applied where appropriate.

11. The results of the join are then sent from the database partitions to the coordinator partition.

12. The coordinator partition performs any additional processing and returns the final result to the originating application.

The *directed inner and outer table join* strategy is characterized by the local join of two hashed table queues.

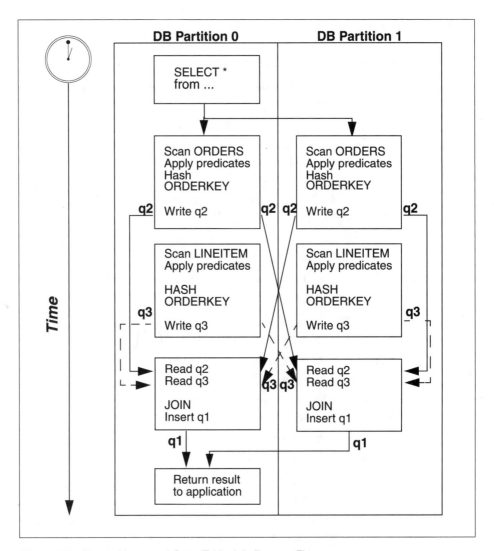

Figure 142. Directed Inner and Outer Table Join Process Flow

6.1.3.5 Broadcast Table Joins - Inner and Outer

The broadcast join strategies are always an option for the optimizer. A broadcast table join will only be chosen when the join is not eligible for any of the other join strategies or in the case where the optimizer determines that a broadcast table join is the most economical solution.

The broadcast parallel join strategies may be chosen in the following situations:

- If there are no equijoin predicates between the joined tables.

- They may also be chosen in situations where the optimizer determines that it is the most cost-effective join method.

- You would usually see this occur when there is one very large table and one very small table, of which neither is partitioned on the join predicate columns. Rather than relocate the data in both tables, it may be cheaper to broadcast the smaller table to all the database partitions where the larger table resides.

- You may also see these join strategies invoked if the result set from applying the predicates to a large table results in a very small table. In this situation we find once again that a broadcast join may be the least expensive method of resolving the request.

The following is a diagram of the process flow of an outer table broadcast join. The process flow is explained below. Please note that these activities are being executed simultaneously across multiple database partitions during each step.

1. The initial request is sent to the coordinator partition from the originating application.

2. The coordinator partition dispatches the request to all relevant nodes.

3. The database partitions scan the table that DB2 has chosen as the outer table and apply any appropriate predicates to the interim result set.

4. The database partitions transmit the full resultant outer table to all relevant database partitions via table queues.

5. The database partitions receive the full resultant outer table via table queue.

6. The receiving database partitions scan the inner table and apply any predicates. The output from this step is placed in a temporary table.

7. The database partitions then perform a join of the received outer table and the local temporary inner table.

8. The database partitions then send the results of the join back to the coordinator partition.

9. The coordinator partition performs any final aggregation or other necessary processing and returns the final result set to the originating application.

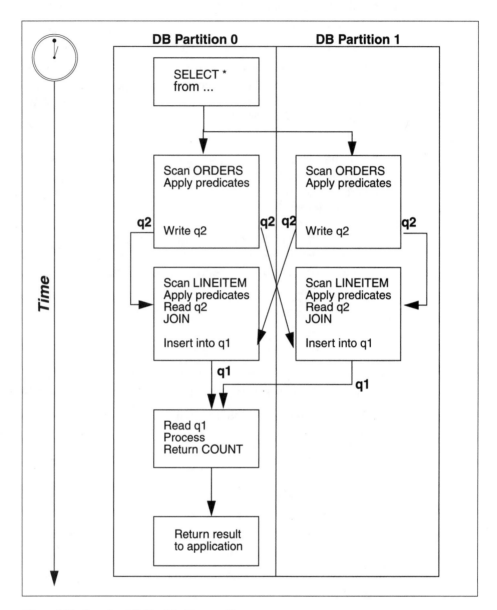

Figure 143. Broadcast Table Join Process Flow

In the *broadcast outer table join strategy*, the rows from the outer table are broadcast to the database partitions where the inner table has rows. In the *broadcast inner table join* strategy, the rows from the inner table are broadcast to the database partitions where the outer table has rows.

Essentially the two broadcast join strategies are equivalent with the inner and outer tables reversed.

Now that we have reviewed the process flow of a broadcast table join, let's look at an Explain from an SQL statement that invokes a broadcast table join on a multi-node, multiple partition database.

The following is the SQL statement that caused the DB2 UDB EEE optimizer to choose a *broadcast inner table join*. Please note that under DB2 UDB EEE Version 5, the Explain output no longer explicitly states what type of join strategy has been chosen by the DB2 UDB EEE optimizer.

```
Select  C_NAME,
        C_ACCTBAL

From    CUSTOMER,
        NATION

Where   C_NATIONKEY> N_NATIONKEY
  and   C_ACCTBAL > 0

Order by C_NAME
```

The two tables involved in this request are CUSTOMER and NATION. The partitioning keys for each of these tables are listed below:

Table Name	Partitioning Key	Column Attribute
CUSTOMER	C_CUSTKEY	INTEGER
NATION	N_NATIONKEY	INTEGER

As we can see from this table, CUSTOMER and NATION are not partitioned on the same key. This join is not eligible for a collocated join. When we examine the SQL statement used to generate this Explain, we see that the two tables are not joined with an equijoin statement (C_NATIONKEY > N_NATIONKEY); therefore, this join is not eligible for any of the directed joins. The only option left to the optimizer is a broadcast join.

Now let's review the Explain for the SQL statement above. As usual, we will start with the coordinator subsection.

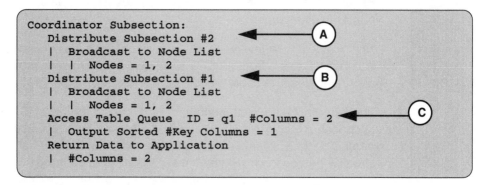

```
Coordinator Subsection:
   Distribute Subsection #2          ◀────────  A
   |  Broadcast to Node List
   |  |  Nodes = 1, 2
   Distribute Subsection #1          ◀────────  B
   |  Broadcast to Node List
   |  |  Nodes = 1, 2
   Access Table Queue  ID = q1  #Columns = 2  ◀────  C
   |  Output Sorted #Key Columns = 1
   Return Data to Application
   |  #Columns = 2
```

The first subsection of each DB2 UDB EEE Explain is the coordinator subsection. The Coordinator Subsection outlines the steps that the optimizer intends to execute to resolve the request. The coordinator subsection is the key to the process flow that occurs to resolve the request.

As we can see from the Coordinator Subsection of this Explain, the first step, *A*, is to distribute subsection #2 to nodes 1 and 2. Subsection #2 may be found on the following pages. You may wish to make a copy of the pages containing the Explain so that you may easily follow the flow as outlined below. The steps in subsection #2 and subsection #1 occur simultaneously across all specified nodes in the Explain.

1. In subsection #2, DB2 will perform a relation scan of the NATION table.

2. The output from the scan will be placed in table queue q2 and broadcast to all nodes named in subsection #1.

We now return to the coordinator subsection to step *B*. The second step, *B*, is to distribute subsection #1 to nodes 1 and 2.

3. In subsection #1, DB2 will perform a relation scan of the CUSTOMER table. Any predicates that may be applied, are applied.

4. The output from the scan is placed in temporary table t1.

5. The temporary table, t1, is nested loop joined to the received broadcast table queue. Any appropriate predicates are applied.

6. The result set is inserted into table queue q1 and broadcast back to the coordinator partition.

We now return to the coordinator subsection and to step *C*. In step C, the coordinator partition receives the q1 table queues sent from database partitions 1 and 2. The data is sorted and returned to the originating application.

```
Subsection #1:
  Access Table Name = DB2INST1.CUSTOMER   ID = 8         ③
  |  #Columns = 3
  |  Relation Scan
  |  |  Prefetch: Eligible
  |  Lock Intents
  |  |  Table: Intent Share
  |  |  Row  : Next Key Share
  |  Sargable Predicate(s)
  |  |  #Predicates = 1
  |  Insert Into Sorted Temp Table  ID = t1
  |  |  #Columns = 3
  |  |  #Sort Key Columns = 1
  |  |  Sortheap Allocation Parameters:
  |  |  |  #Rows      = 6843
  |  |  |  Row Width = 40
  |  |  Piped
  Sorted Temp Table Completion  ID = t1      ④
  Access Temp Table  ID = t1
  |  #Columns = 3
  |  Relation Scan
  |  |  Prefetch: Eligible
  Nested Loop Join                           ⑤
  |  Data Stream 1: Evaluate at Open
  |  |  Not Piped
  |  |  Access Table Queue  ID = q2  #Columns = 1
|  |  Insert Into Temp Table  ID = t2
  |  |  |  #Columns = 1
  |  End of Data Stream 1
  |  Access Temp Table  ID = t2
  |  |  #Columns = 1
  |  |  Relation Scan
  |  |  |  Prefetch: Eligible
  |  |  Sargable Predicate(s)
  |  |  |  #Predicates = 1
  Insert Into Asynchronous Table Queue  ID = q1
  |  Broadcast to Coordinator Node
  |  Rows Can Overflow to Temporary Table     ⑥
```

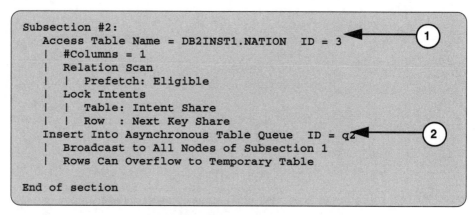

```
Subsection #2:
   Access Table Name = DB2INST1.NATION   ID = 3
   |  #Columns = 1
   |  Relation Scan
   |  |  Prefetch: Eligible
   |  Lock Intents
   |  |  Table: Intent Share
   |  |  Row  : Next Key Share
   Insert Into Asynchronous Table Queue  ID = q2
   |  Broadcast to All Nodes of Subsection 1
   |  Rows Can Overflow to Temporary Table

End of section
```

Figure 144. Broadcast Inner Table Join Explain

6.1.3.6 Partitioned Join Strategies and Performance

Now that we have been through all the detailed descriptions of the various partitioned join strategies, we will now discuss how to easily recognize which join strategy has been chosen. The following table is a summary of the characteristics of the various partitioned database join strategies mentioned above.

Table 7. Join Strategy Characteristics

Join Strategy	Outer Table	Inner Table
Collocated Table Join	Temporary table	Temporary table
Directed Inner Table Join	Temporary table	Table Queue Hashed
Directed Outer Table Join	Table Queue Hashed	Temporary table
Directed Inner and Outer Table Join	Table Queue Hashed	Table Queue Hashed
Broadcast Inner Table Join	Temporary table	Table Queue Broadcast
Broadcast Outer Table Join	Table Queue Broadcast	Temporary table

Using the table of join strategy characteristics, we will now review another Explain. Below you will find a compressed version of the Explain used for the *directed inner join* strategy with numbers in the right column to indicate the steps involved in determining which join strategy has been chosen.

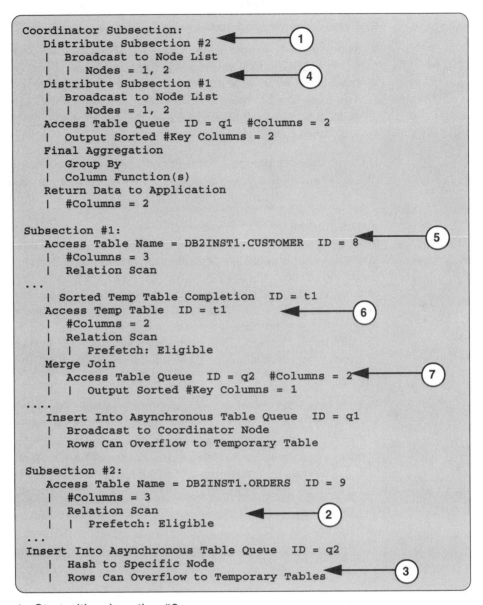

```
Coordinator Subsection:
   Distribute Subsection #2                        (1)
   |   Broadcast to Node List
   |   |   Nodes = 1, 2                             (4)
   Distribute Subsection #1
   |   Broadcast to Node List
   |   |   Nodes = 1, 2
   Access Table Queue   ID = q1   #Columns = 2
   |   Output Sorted #Key Columns = 2
   Final Aggregation
   |   Group By
   |   Column Function(s)
   Return Data to Application
   |   #Columns = 2

Subsection #1:
   Access Table Name = DB2INST1.CUSTOMER   ID = 8  (5)
   |   #Columns = 3
   |   Relation Scan
   ...
   |   Sorted Temp Table Completion   ID = t1
   Access Temp Table   ID = t1                      (6)
   |   #Columns = 2
   |   Relation Scan
   |   |   Prefetch: Eligible
   Merge Join
   |   Access Table Queue   ID = q2   #Columns = 2  (7)
   |   |   Output Sorted #Key Columns = 1
   ....
   Insert Into Asynchronous Table Queue   ID = q1
   |   Broadcast to Coordinator Node
   |   Rows Can Overflow to Temporary Table

Subsection #2:
   Access Table Name = DB2INST1.ORDERS   ID = 9
   |   #Columns = 3
   |   Relation Scan                                (2)
   |   |   Prefetch: Eligible
   ...
Insert Into Asynchronous Table Queue   ID = q2
   |   Hash to Specific Node                        (3)
   |   Rows Can Overflow to Temporary Tables
```

1. Start with subsection #2.

2. Relation scan ORDERS.

3. Output of the scan of ORDERS is placed in hashed table queue and sent to the database partitions specified in the coordinator subsection.

4. Go to subsection #1.

5. Relation scan CUSTOMER.

6. Place output of scan into temp table.

7. Merge join - The table listed in the ACCESS statement immediately before to the MERGE JOIN statement is the outer table. In this case the outer table is the temp table containing the rows selected from CUSTOMER. The table listed in the ACCESS statement immediately after the MERGE JOIN statement is the inner table. In this case the inner table is the hashed table queue created in section #2.

Referring back to the table of partitioned database join strategy characteristics Table 7, we can see that a join between an outer temp table and an inner hashed table queue is a *directed inner join* strategy.

Performance

From a performance point of view, the type of partitioned database join strategy that the optimizer chooses can impact performance. With the exception of the collocated join strategy, all of the parallel join strategies require relocation of data across database partitions before the request may be resolved at the partition level. If you find that your larger tables are frequently being broadcast across database partitions, you may want to reevaluate your choice of the partitioning key. Remember, the larger the amount of data that is moved between database partition, the poorer the performance of the query.

Keep in mind that broadcasting small tables to the database partition where they may be joined with your largest tables is desirable. Placing small tables in a single partition nodegroup is often desirable and will force DB2 to perform a broadcast of the table to the database partitions of the larger tables. The goal in a multi-node, multiple partition database is to perform as much work as possible at the partition level, not at the coordinator partition level.

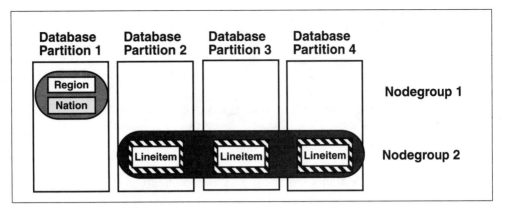

Figure 145. Partitioning to Force Broadcast of Smaller Tables

6.2 DB2 UDB EEE OLAP Features

The OLAP features known as super grouping functions are supported in DB2 UDB EEE V5. These functions are very powerful and are used to analyze data in multiple dimensions. These dimensions may be viewed as various levels of aggregation over a set of one or more tables. The term, *super grouping*, is used to describe the support of the OLAP features because they provide the ability to retrieve multiple aggregation levels in a single access of the data.

OLAP is closely related to the Multi-Dimensional-Analysis and the Star Schema. The Star Schema is used to implement multi-dimensional access in a relational database such as DB2. This section discusses the OLAP SQL features of GROUPING SETS, ROLLUP, CUBE, GROUPING column function as well as the STAR SCHEMA.

6.2.1 Grouping Sets

Grouping sets are the fundamental building block for the OLAP GROUP BY functions. A simple GROUP BY with a single column can be considered a grouping set with one element. The following SQL statement is an example of a simple grouping set. The same result would be obtained by replacing the *group by grouping sets* specification with a simple GROUP BY specification.

```
Select  C_NAME
        COUNT(DISTINCT O_ORDERKEY)

From CUSTOMER,
     ORDERS

Where C_CUSTKEY = O_CUSTKEY

Group By Grouping Sets (C_NAME)
```

A *grouping-sets* specification allows multiple grouping clauses to be specified in a single statement. This can be thought of as the union of two or more groups of rows into a single result set. It is logically equivalent to the union of multiple subselects with the GROUP BY clause in each subselect corresponding to one grouping set. A grouping set can be a single element or can be a list of elements delimited by parentheses, where an element is either a grouping-expression or a super-group. Using grouping-sets allows the groups to be computed with a single access of the base table.

The *grouping-sets* specification allows either a simple grouping-expression to be used, or the more complex forms of super-groups such as ROLLUP and CUBE. The following is the syntax used for grouping sets function

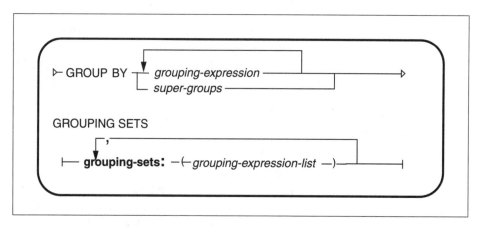

Figure 146. Grouping Sets Syntax

The first step in the use of the GROUPING SETS clause is to determine exactly what the desired output is by describing the expected results in sentence format. This should be done before you attempt to generate your first SQL statement.

Let's use the CUSTOMER table to simulate the use of a GROUPING SETS clause. First we must express the business problem that we wish to resolve in words.

Business Problem: Determine the distribution of customers by country and market segment.

In the following figure, you will find the SQL statement generated to obtain the answer to the business problem stated above. The GROUPING SETS clause causes DB2 to:

1. Count the number of customers in each country.

2. Count the number of customers in each market segment.

3. Union the two result sets to obtain the final result set returned from the execution of the SQL statement.

The result set was obtained via a single access of the CUSTOMER table.

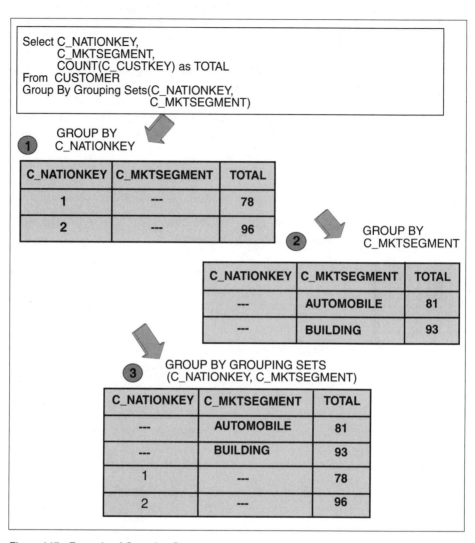

```
Select C_NATIONKEY,
       C_MKTSEGMENT,
       COUNT(C_CUSTKEY) as TOTAL
From  CUSTOMER
Group By Grouping Sets(C_NATIONKEY,
                       C_MKTSEGMENT)
```

① GROUP BY
    C_NATIONKEY

C_NATIONKEY	C_MKTSEGMENT	TOTAL
1	---	78
2	---	96

② GROUP BY
    C_MKTSEGMENT

C_NATIONKEY	C_MKTSEGMENT	TOTAL
---	AUTOMOBILE	81
---	BUILDING	93

③ GROUP BY GROUPING SETS
    (C_NATIONKEY, C_MKTSEGMENT)

C_NATIONKEY	C_MKTSEGMENT	TOTAL
---	AUTOMOBILE	81
---	BUILDING	93
1	---	78
2	---	96

Figure 147. Example of Grouping Sets

6.2.2 Rollup

A ROLLUP grouping is an extension to the GROUP BY clause that produces a result set that contains sub-total rows in addition to the usual grouped rows that were discussed in "Grouping Sets" on page 379. Sub-total rows are super-aggregate rows that contain further totals or aggregates whose values are derived by applying the same column functions that were used to obtain the grouped rows.

ROLLUP produces a series of groupings in the result set that contain different levels of aggregation. The rows containing different levels of aggregation are essentially different levels of sub-total rows based on the order in which the aggregation was specified in the ROLLUP clause.

The following is the syntax for the ROLLUP function:

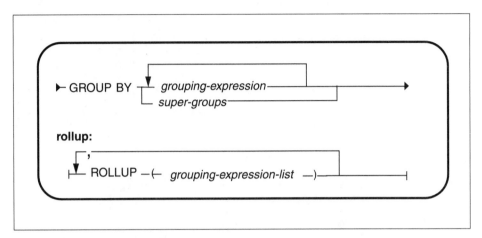

Figure 148. ROLLUP Syntax

The ROLLUP clause is resolved by a single access to the data in the specified tables. The work of aggregating the data at multiple levels is performed by the CPU instead of having the user generate multiple queries that must each access the disk to resolve the request.

As with the grouping sets clause, the first step in the use of the ROLLUP clause of the GROUP BY function in DB2 should not be used without first defining the business problem or question in sentence format.

Let's use the Customer table to demonstrate the use of the ROLLUP grouping expression. As before, we must first state the business problem we are attempting to resolve.

Business Problem: Determine the distribution of customers in each market segment by country, the total number of customers in each country, and the total customer base.

In the following figure, you will find the SQL statement generated to obtain the answer to the business problem stated above. Each of the separate levels of aggregation as well as the final result set is depicted below.

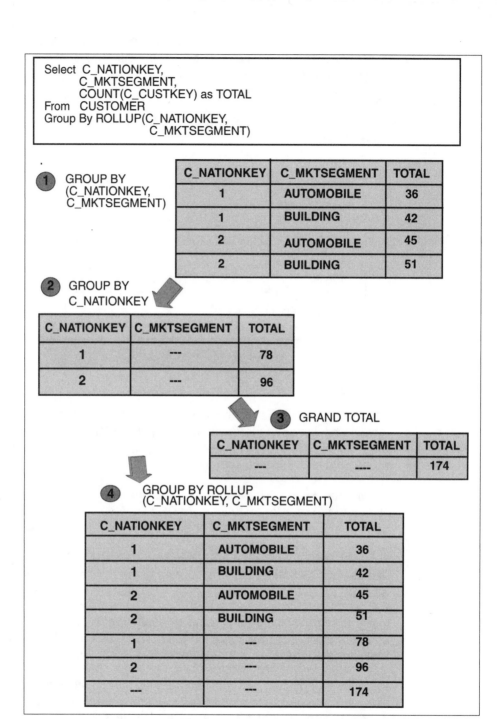

```
Select  C_NATIONKEY,
        C_MKTSEGMENT,
        COUNT(C_CUSTKEY) as TOTAL
From   CUSTOMER
Group By ROLLUP(C_NATIONKEY,
               C_MKTSEGMENT)
```

1 GROUP BY
(C_NATIONKEY,
C_MKTSEGMENT)

C_NATIONKEY	C_MKTSEGMENT	TOTAL
1	AUTOMOBILE	36
1	BUILDING	42
2	AUTOMOBILE	45
2	BUILDING	51

2 GROUP BY
C_NATIONKEY

C_NATIONKEY	C_MKTSEGMENT	TOTAL
1	---	78
2	---	96

3 GRAND TOTAL

C_NATIONKEY	C_MKTSEGMENT	TOTAL
---	----	174

4 GROUP BY ROLLUP
(C_NATIONKEY, C_MKTSEGMENT)

C_NATIONKEY	C_MKTSEGMENT	TOTAL
1	AUTOMOBILE	36
1	BUILDING	42
2	AUTOMOBILE	45
2	BUILDING	51
1	---	78
2	---	96
---	---	174

Figure 149. Example of ROLLUP

The ROLLUP clause in the example ROLLUP SQL statement causes DB2 to:

1. Perform a compound GROUP BY using C_NATIONKEY, C_MKTSEGMENT as the compound column grouping. The result of the compound grouping answers the business request to provide counts of the customers by market segment per country.

2. Perform a GROUP BY C_NATIONKEY to obtain a count of the total customers in each country.

3. Perform a count of all customers to obtain the size of the customer base.

4. Union all three previous intermediate result tables to obtain the final report that answers the business question stated above.

Essentially, the ROLLUP is the equivalent of a grouping sets clause in which each of the levels of aggregation is explicitly expressed. The SQL statement in the figure above could also be expressed using the grouping sets clause in the statement below.

```
Select  C_NATIONKEY,
        C_MKTSEGMENT,
        COUNT(C_CUSTKEY)

From    CUSTOMER

Group By Grouping Sets (
                      (C_NATIONKEY, C_MKTSEGMENT),
                      (C_NATIONKEY),
                      ()
                        )
```

A ROLLUP clause that contains two columns will generate three levels of aggregation. A ROLLUP clause that contains four columns will generate five levels of aggregation. ROLLUP will always generate one more level of aggregation than the number of column elements specified in the ROLLUP clause. In other words if there are n number of column elements specified in the ROLLUP clause, then the ROLLUP clause will generate $n + 1$ levels of grouping set aggregation.

The order of the column elements specified in the ROLLUP grouping expression list is also very important. In the ROLLUP example in the next figure you can see the results of varying the order of the ROLLUP clause. When C_NATIONKEY is specified as the first column element of the ROLLUP clause, the second level aggregation is on the C_NATIONKEY column. When

C_MKTSEGMENT is specified as the first column element of the ROLLUP clause, the second level of aggregation is on the C_MKTSEGMENT column, instead of C_NATIONKEY. The rows in the final result set from each variation of the column ordering in the ROLLUP clause are as depicted below. Note that the fifth and sixth rows of each of the final reports differ based on the first columns specified in the ROLLUP clause.

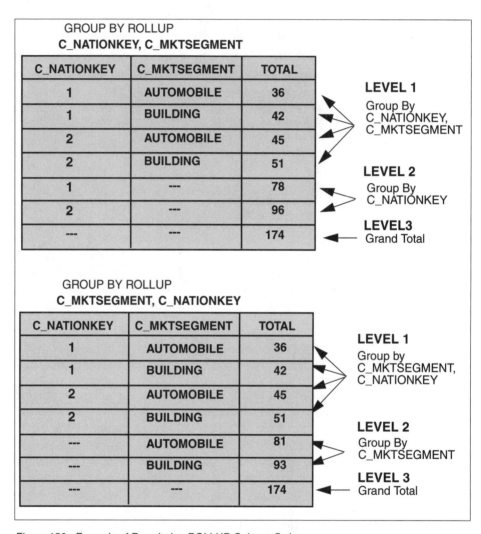

GROUP BY ROLLUP
C_NATIONKEY, C_MKTSEGMENT

C_NATIONKEY	C_MKTSEGMENT	TOTAL
1	AUTOMOBILE	36
1	BUILDING	42
2	AUTOMOBILE	45
2	BUILDING	51
1	---	78
2	---	96
---	---	174

LEVEL 1
Group By
C_NATIONKEY,
C_MKTSEGMENT

LEVEL 2
Group By
C_NATIONKEY

LEVEL3
Grand Total

GROUP BY ROLLUP
C_MKTSEGMENT, C_NATIONKEY

C_NATIONKEY	C_MKTSEGMENT	TOTAL
1	AUTOMOBILE	36
1	BUILDING	42
2	AUTOMOBILE	45
2	BUILDING	51
---	AUTOMOBILE	81
---	BUILDING	93
---	---	174

LEVEL 1
Group by
C_MKTSEGMENT,
C_NATIONKEY

LEVEL 2
Group By
C_MKTSEGMENT

LEVEL 3
Grand Total

Figure 150. Example of Reordering ROLLUP Column Order

All three of the levels of aggregation are obtained by one pass at the data. No additional scans of the CUSTOMER table were required to obtain the various subtotals provided in this report. This report also provides more information than could be obtained by a single GROUP BY clause. Without the OLAP SQL features, multiple queries would have to be executed to obtain all three levels of aggregation provided by the ROLLUP clause.

Now that we have examined the process flow of the ROLLUP grouping expression, let's look at the Explain for an SQL statement that invokes the ROLLUP grouping expression.The following is the SQL statement used to generate the Explain.

```
SELECT C_NATIONKEY,
       C_MKTSEGMENT,
       COUNT(C_CUSTKEY)

From CUSTOMER

Group BY ROLLUP(C_NATIONKEY, C_MKTSEGMENT)
```

As always, we will use the Coordinator Subsection of the Explain output to guide us through the steps that the DB2 UDB optimizer has selected to resolve the SQL request.

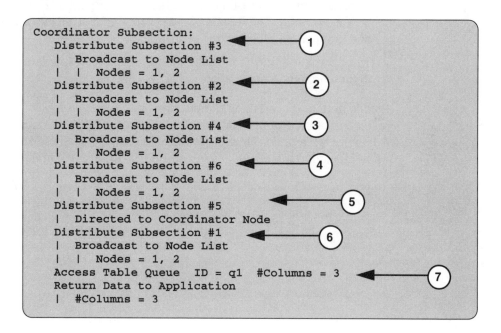

```
Coordinator Subsection:
    Distribute Subsection #3          ◀───── 1
    |  Broadcast to Node List
    |  |  Nodes = 1, 2
    Distribute Subsection #2          ◀───── 2
    |  Broadcast to Node List
    |  |  Nodes = 1, 2
    Distribute Subsection #4          ◀───── 3
    |  Broadcast to Node List
    |  |  Nodes = 1, 2
    Distribute Subsection #6          ◀───── 4
    |  Broadcast to Node List
    |  |  Nodes = 1, 2
    Distribute Subsection #5          ◀───── 5
    |  Directed to Coordinator Node
    Distribute Subsection #1          ◀───── 6
    |  Broadcast to Node List
    |  |  Nodes = 1, 2
    Access Table Queue  ID = q1  #Columns = 3  ◀───── 7
    Return Data to Application
    |  #Columns = 3
```

The following is the flow of the actions that the optimizer has selected to resolve the ROLLUP grouping expression as ordered in the Coordinator Subsection of the Explain

1. Subsection #3 performs the initial relation scan of the Customer table. The results are placed in a temp table. Intermediate aggregation is performed. The results are placed in a table queue, q2, and hashed to specific database partitions.

2. In subsection #2, the table queue distributed in the previous subsection is accessed and final aggregation of one of the grouping sets is completed. The results are inserted into a temp table, t1.

3. In subsection #4, temp table t1 is relation scanned. Aggregation is performed and the results are inserted into temp table t2.

4. In subsection #6, temp table t2 is relation scanned. Partial aggregation is completed. The result set is inserted into table queue, q4, and broadcast to database partitions 1 and 2.

5. In subsection #5, table queue q4 is read. Final aggregation is performed. Conditional predicates are applied. The results are placed in table queue, q3, and hashed to specific database partitions.

6. In subsection #1, a union of temp table t1,temp table t2, and table queue q3 is performed. The results of the union are inserted into table queue, q1, and broadcast to the coordinator partition.

7. The coordinator partition reads the table queue, q1, and returns the data to the originating application.

Please note that even though there are several steps required in the resolution of the ROLLUP grouping expression, DB2 only accessed the Customer table once. All of the information required to resolve the request was obtained in the single access of the Customer table in subsection #3.

```
Subsection #1:
  (
  |   Access Temp Table   ID = t1        ◄──────────  ⑥
  |   |   #Columns = 3
  |   |   Relation Scan
  |   |   |   Prefetch: Eligible
  UNION
  |   Access Temp Table   ID = t2
  |   |   #Columns = 3
  |   |   Relation Scan
  |   |   |   Prefetch: Eligible
  UNION
  |   Access Table Queue   ID = q3   #Columns = 3
  )
  Insert Into Asynchronous Table Queue   ID = q1
  |   Broadcast to Coordinator Node
  |   Rows Can Overflow to Temporary Table

Subsection #2:                              ◄──────────  ②
  Access Table Queue   ID = q2   #Columns = 4
  |   Output Sorted #Key Columns = 2
  Final Aggregation
  |   Group By
  |   Column Function(s)
  Insert Into Temp Table   ID = t1
  |   #Columns = 3
```

```
Subsection #3:
   Access Table Name = DB2INST1.CUSTOMER   ID = 8 ◄─────────────①
   |  #Columns = 3
   |  Relation Scan
   |  |  Prefetch: Eligible
   |  Lock Intents
   |  |  Table: Intent Share
   |  |  Row  : Next Key Share
   Insert Into Sorted Temp Table  ID = t3
   |  #Columns = 4
   |  #Sort Key Columns = 2
   |  Sortheap Allocation Parameters:
   |  |  #Rows     = 2917
   |  |  Row Width = 24
   |  Piped
   |  Partial Aggregation
   Access Temp Table  ID = t3
|  #Columns = 4
   |  Relation Scan
   |  |  Prefetch: Eligible
   |  Intermediate Predicate Aggregation
   |  |  Group By
   |  |  Column Function(s)
   Intermediate Aggregation Completion
   |  Group By
   |  Column Function(s)
   Insert Into Asynchronous Table Queue  ID = q2
   |  Hash to Specific Node
   |  Rows Can Overflow to Temporary Tables

Subsection #4:                       ◄──────────────③
   Access Temp Table  ID = t1
   |  #Columns = 2
   |  Relation Scan
   |  |  Prefetch: Eligible
   |  Predicate Aggregation
   |  |  Group By
   |  |  Column Function(s)
   Aggregation Completion
   |  Group By
   |  Column Function(s)
   Insert Into Temp Table  ID = t2
   |  #Columns = 3
```

```
Subsection #5:
   Access Table Queue  ID = q4   #Columns = 2
   Final Aggregation
   |  Column Function(s)
   Conditional Evaluation
   |  Condition #1:
   |  |  #Predicates = 1
   Insert Into Asynchronous Table Queue  ID = q3
   |  Hash to Specific Node
   |  Rows Can Overflow to Temporary Tables

Subsection #6:
   Access Temp Table  ID = t2
   |  #Columns = 1
   |  Relation Scan
   |  |  Prefetch: Eligible
   |  Partial Predicate Aggregation
   |  |  Column Function(s)
   Partial Aggregation Completion
   |  Column Function(s)
   Insert Into Asynchronous Table Queue  ID = q4
   |  Broadcast to All Nodes of Subsection 5
   |  Rows Can Overflow to Temporary Table

End of section
```

The estimated cost of this query is 5641 CPU seconds against a CUSTOMER table that contains 15,000 rows and has few indexes. This estimate seems rather high; possibly the introduction of a new index over the columns being accessed in the query will improve performance.

After creating an index over C_NATIONKEY, C_MKTSEGMENT, C_CUSTKEY, the estimated CPU time drops to 3303 CPU seconds. This is a 41% reduction in estimated cost.

The difference in the Explain occurs in subsection #3 when the optimizer performs an INDEX ONLY read of the newly created index instead of a table scan of CUSTOMER. If this sort of query was being executed frequently by your users, building this new index could have a significant impact on improving query run-time and user satisfaction.

6.2.3 Cube

A CUBE grouping is an extension to the GROUP BY clause that produces a result set that contains all the rows of a ROLLUP aggregation and also contains what could be referred to as cross-tabulation rows. Cross-tabulation rows are additional "super-aggregate" rows that are not part of the ROLLUP aggregation.

The following is the syntax for the CUBE grouping feature:

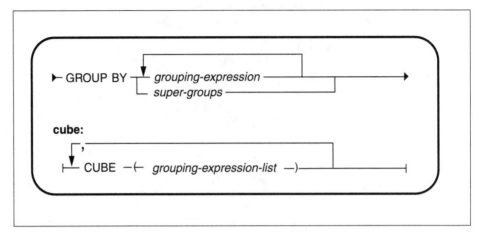

Figure 151. Cube Syntax

Assume that we have want a CUBE grouping that has three column elements in the grouping expression list, for example:

```
Group By CUBE(column1, column2, column3)
```

This translates into the following grouping sets:

```
Group By Grouping Sets((column1, column2, column3),
                       (column1, column2),
                       (column1, column3),
                       (column2, column3),
                       (column1),
                       (column2),
                       (column3),
                       ())
```

The number of grouping sets required to resolve the CUBE grouping of three columns is 8, or 2^3. In general, it will take 2^n grouping sets to resolve a CUBE grouping of n columns.

Basically, CUBE grouping creates grouping sets aggregations of the data in all possible permutations of the column elements listed in the grouping expression list, plus a grand total. When using the CUBE grouping expression, the order of the column elements is not important because all the permutations of the column elements are included in the final result set.

The CUBE grouping expression is resolved via a single pass at the table.

It is important to note that the rows of the final results table may or may not be presented in the order described above. DB2 returns the rows as the grouping sets are resolved; therefore if the table being referenced is reorganized based on a different index, the order in which the rows are returned to the end user may vary.

The only way to ensure that the rows are returned in a consistent order is to specify an ORDER BY clause in the query.

As with all the other grouping set features, the first step in the use of the CUBE grouping is to state the business problem or question in sentence format. Let's use the Customer table to demonstrate the use of the CUBE grouping expression.

Business Problem: Determine the distribution of customers in each market segment by country, the total number of customers by country, the total number of customers by market segment, and the total number of customers.

In the following figure, you will find the SQL statement generated to obtain the answer to the business problem stated above. Each of the separate levels of aggregation as well as the final result set is depicted below.

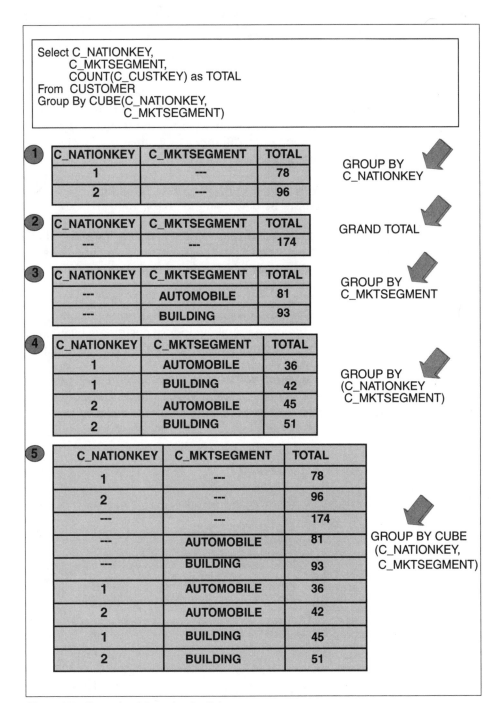

Figure 152. Example of Grouping By Cube

The CUBE clause in the example SQL statement causes DB2 to:

1. Perform a group by C_NATIONKEY to obtain a count of the total customers in each country.

2. Perform a count of all customers to obtain the size of the customer base.

3. Perform a group by C_MKTSEGMENT to obtain a count of the total customers in each market segment.

4. Perform a compound GROUP BY using C_NATIONKEY, C_MKTSEGMENT as the compound column grouping. The result of the compound grouping answers the business request to provide counts of the customers by market segment per country.

5. Union all four previous intermediate result tables to obtain the final report that answers the business problem stated above.

Now that we have examined the process flow of the CUBE grouping expression of the GROUP BY clause, let's look at the Explain for the same query. As always, we begin with the Coordinator Subsection.

```
Coordinator Subsection:
   Distribute Subsection #4
   |   Broadcast to Node List
   |   |   Nodes = 1, 2
   Distribute Subsection #3
   |   Broadcast to Node List
   |   |   Nodes = 1, 2
   Distribute Subsection #2
   |   Broadcast to Node List
   |   |   Nodes = 1, 2
   Distribute Subsection #1
   |   Broadcast to Node List
   |   |   Nodes = 1, 2
   Distribute Subsection #5
   |   Broadcast to Node List
   |   |   Nodes = 1, 2
   (
   |   Access Table Queue   ID = q1   #Columns = 4  ◄─────── 6
   |   |   Output Sorted #Key Columns = 2
   |   Final Aggregation
   |   |   Group By
   |   |   Column Function(s)
   UNION
   |   Access Table Queue   ID = q3   #Columns = 3
   )
   Return Data to Application
   |   #Columns = 3
```

The following is the flow of the actions that the optimizer has selected to resolve the CUBE grouping expression as ordered in the Coordinator Subsection of the Explain.

1. Subsection #4, performs the initial relation scan of the CUSTOMER table. The results are placed in a temp table. Intermediate aggregation is performed. The results are placed in a table queue, q2, and hashed to specific database partitions.

2. In subsection #3, the table queue distributed in the previous subsection is accessed and final aggregation of one of the grouping sets is completed. The results are inserted into a temp table, t3.

3. In subsection #2, temp table t3 is relation scanned. An aggregation is completed. The union of the aggregation and temp table t3 is performed. The results of the union are inserted into temp table t1.

4. In subsection #1, temp table t1 is relation scanned. The results are inserted into temp table t2. Temp table t2 is sorted, then relation scanned and Intermediate aggregation is performed. The results are inserted into table queue q1 and broadcast to the coordinator partition.

5. In subsection #5, temp table t1 is relation scanned. The results are placed in table queue q3 and broadcast to the coordinator partition.

6. In the Coordinator Subsection, final aggregation is performed against table queue q1. A union of the results of the table queue q1 aggregation and table queue t3 is performed.asubsection #1, a union of temp table t1,temp table t2, and table queue q3 is performed. The results are then returned to the originating application.

Please note that even though there are several steps required in the resolution of the CUBE grouping expression, DB2 only accessed the CUSTOMER table once. All of the information required to resolve the request was obtained in the single access of the CUSTOMER table in subsection #4.

```
Subsection #1:
   Access Temp Table   ID = t1                        ◀━━━━━  ④
   |  #Columns = 3
   |  Relation Scan
   |  |  Prefetch: Eligible
   |  Insert Into Sorted Temp Table   ID = t2
   |  |  #Columns = 4
   |  |  #Sort Key Columns = 2
   |  |  Sortheap Allocation Parameters:
   |  |  |  #Rows      = 642
   |  |  |  Row Width = 16
   |  |  Piped
   |  |  Partial Aggregation
   Sorted Temp Table Completion   ID = t2
   Access Temp Table   ID = t2
   |  #Columns = 4
   |  Relation Scan
   |  |  Prefetch: Eligible
   |  Intermediate Predicate Aggregation
   |  |  Group By
   |  |  Column Function(s)
   Intermediate Aggregation Completion
   |  Group By
   |  Column Function(s)
   Insert Into Asynchronous Table Queue   ID = q1
   |  Broadcast to Coordinator Node
   |  Rows Can Overflow to Temporary Table

Subsection #2:                                         ◀━━━━━  ③
   (
   |  Access Temp Table   ID = t3
   |  |  #Columns = 3
   |  |  Relation Scan
   |  |  |  Prefetch: Eligible
   |  |  Predicate Aggregation
   |  |  |  Group By
   |  |  |  Column Function(s)
   |  Aggregation Completion
   |  |  Group By
   |  |  Column Function(s)
   UNION
   |  Access Temp Table   ID = t3
   |  |  #Columns = 5
   |  |  Relation Scan
   |  |  |  Prefetch: Eligible
   )
   Insert Into Temp Table   ID = t1
   |  #Columns = 4
```

```
Subsection #3:
   Access Table Queue  ID = q2  #Columns = 4        ◄──── (2)
   | Output Sorted #Key Columns = 2
   Final Aggregation
   | Group By
   | Column Function(s)
   Insert Into Temp Table  ID = t3
   | #Columns = 5

Subsection #4:                                    ◄──── (1)
   Access Table Name = DB2INST1.CUSTOMER  ID = 8
   | #Columns = 3
   | Relation Scan
   | | Prefetch: Eligible
   | Lock Intents
   | | Table: Intent Share
   | | Row  : Next Key Share
   Insert Into Sorted Temp Table  ID = t4
   | #Columns = 4
   | #Sort Key Columns = 2
   | Sortheap Allocation Parameters:
   | | #Rows       = 2917
   | | Row Width = 24
   | Piped
   | Partial Aggregation
   Access Temp Table  ID = t4
   | #Columns = 4
   | Relation Scan
   | | Prefetch: Eligible
   | Intermediate Predicate Aggregation
   | | Group By
   | | Column Function(s)
   Intermediate Aggregation Completion
   | Group By
   | Column Function(s)
   Insert Into Asynchronous Table Queue  ID = q2
   | Hash to Specific Node
   | Rows Can Overflow to Temporary Tables

Subsection #5:                                    ◄──── (5)
   Access Temp Table  ID = t1
   | #Columns = 4
   | Relation Scan
   | | Prefetch: Eligible
   Insert Into Asynchronous Table Queue  ID = q3
   | Broadcast to Coordinator Node
   | Rows Can Overflow to Temporary Table

End of section
```

The estimated cost of this query is 7659 CPU seconds against a CUSTOMER table that contains 15,000 rows and has few indexes. This estimate seems rather high; possibly the addition of an index over the columns in question may improve the performance of this query.

After creating an index over C_NATIONKEY, C_MKTSEGMENT, C_CUSTKEY, the estimated CPU time drops to 4541 CPU seconds. This is a 41% reduction in estimated cost. The difference in the Explain occurs in subsection #4 when the optimizer performs an INDEX ONLY read of the newly created index instead of a table scan of CUSTOMER. If this sort of query was being executed frequently by your users, building this new index could have a significant impact on improving query runtime and user satisfaction.

```
Subsection #4:
   Access Table Name = DB2INST1.CUSTOMER   ID = 8
   |  #Columns = 3
   |  Index Scan:  Name = DB2INST1.CUSTIX4   ID = 4 ◀━━┓
   |  |  #Key Columns = 0                                ┃
   |  |  Index-Only Access ◀━━━━━━━━━━━━━━━━━━   ( Index Only
   |  |  Index Prefetch: Eligible                          Access )
   |  Lock Intents
   |  |  Table: Intent Share
   |  |  Row  : Next Key Share
   Insert Into Sorted Temp Table   ID = t4
   |  #Columns = 4
   |  #Sort Key Columns = 2
   |  Sortheap Allocation Parameters:
   |  |  #Rows      = 2917
   |  |  Row Width = 24
   |  Piped
   |  Partial Aggregation
   Access Temp Table   ID = t4
   |  #Columns = 4
   |  Relation Scan
   |  |  Prefetch: Eligible
   |  Intermediate Predicate Aggregation
   |  |  Group By
   |  |  Column Function(s)
   Intermediate Aggregation Completion
   |  Group By
   |  Column Function(s)
   Insert Into Asynchronous Table Queue   ID = q2
   |  Hash to Specific Node
   |  Rows Can Overflow to Temporary Tables
```

6.2.4 Grouping Column Function

The purpose of the *grouping column* function is to return a value that can be used to determine whether or not a value is a null as a result of a GROUP BY (column function or extension thereof, such as ROLLUP or CUBE). The possible return values are 0 and 1.

The returned value is an integer of value 1 or 0.

- 1 - The value of the column is a special null value that represents either the set of all values used in an aggregation or the value resulting from the combining together of grouping sets.

- 0 - Otherwise

The primary benefit of this column function is for the interpretation of the answer sets. It allows the user to identify which rows have been generated by a GROUP BY function.

This is of particular value to graphical tools in order to allow the interpretation of answer sets to be displayed in a manner which visualizes the relationships between result set rows.

The following is an example of using the grouping columns function:

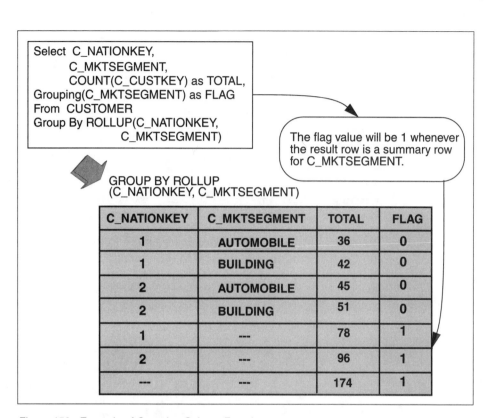

```
Select  C_NATIONKEY,
        C_MKTSEGMENT,
        COUNT(C_CUSTKEY) as TOTAL,
Grouping(C_MKTSEGMENT) as FLAG
From  CUSTOMER
Group By ROLLUP(C_NATIONKEY,
                C_MKTSEGMENT)
```

The flag value will be 1 whenever the result row is a summary row for C_MKTSEGMENT.

GROUP BY ROLLUP
(C_NATIONKEY, C_MKTSEGMENT)

C_NATIONKEY	C_MKTSEGMENT	TOTAL	FLAG
1	AUTOMOBILE	36	0
1	BUILDING	42	0
2	AUTOMOBILE	45	0
2	BUILDING	51	0
1	---	78	1
2	---	96	1
---	---	174	1

Figure 153. Example of Grouping Column Function

Let's take a look at an example using the grouping column function. In the figure, we have used the same SQL statement that we used in the ROLLUP example with the addition of a GROUPING clause. We have specified GROUPING on the C_MKTSEGMENT column and have added a column to the result set for the flag value that is set by the GROUPING clause. In the result set, the flag is set to 1 for every summary row in which all C_MKTSEGMENT data is summarized; or in other words, the flag is set to one when the result set value for C_MKTSEGMENT is null.

The grouping column function may be an appropriate place to use a case expressions. For instance, you could force a column that explicitly marked a row as a summary row by specifying `when grouping(c_mktsegment) = 1 then 'Summary Row'` in a case clause in the SQL statement.

```
Select    C_NATIONKEY,
          C_MKTSEGMENT,
          Count(C_CUSTKEY),
          Grouping(C_MKTSEGMENT) as flag,

Case
    When grouping(C_MKTSEGMENT) = 1 Then 'Summary Row'
    End

From CUSTOMER

Group By Rollup(C_NATIONKEY, C_MKTSEGMENT)
```

The result of the addition of the case clause to the SQL statement will be the creation of an additional column in the output that will mark the rows that are being summarized for C_MKTSEGMENT.

ROLLUP(C_NATIONKEY, C_MKTSEGMENT)

C_NATIONKEY	C_MKTSEGMENT	TOTAL	FLAG	
1	AUTOMOBILE	36	0	
1	BUILDING	42	0	
2	AUTOMOBILE	45	0	
2	BUILDING	51	0	
1	---	78	1	Summary Row
2	---	96	1	Summary Row
---	---	174	1	Summary Row

Figure 154. Example of Using CASE Function with Grouping Columns Function

6.2.5 Star Schema

The *Star Schema* is a relatively new concept in the relational database world and was introduced to support On-Line Analytical Processing (OLAP). OLTP (On Line Transaction Processing) databases are optimized for data entry and the data is highly normalized. OLAP databases, on the other hand, must be optimized for query and analytical processing. In an OLAP environment, the data is generally denormalized to a certain degree so as to allow for faster query access. In an OLTP environment, you frequently have to chain across as many as ten or more tables to obtain the desired collection of associated columns in a report; this becomes a complex process and is frequently error prone and bad for online performance. In an OLAP environment, many of those joins have already been resolved in the design and structure of the OLAP database, thereby, reducing the system resources required to access the data and significantly simplifying the efforts required of the user.

A *Star Schema* consists of a fact table and several dimension tables. Generally, the fact table will be very large and the supporting dimension tables will be small.

The dimension tables usually hold descriptive information about the entities stored in the fact table. Dimension tables characteristically contain only a small number of rows of data. Typically, one of the dimension tables is a period dimension table that describes the time periods for which the data in the fact table is accumulated.

The primary keys of the dimension tables of the *Star Schema* serve as foreign key entries in the fact table. The fact table contains detailed information that is related to the dimension tables. The fact table may contain aggregations of the fact data; if all aggregations are included in the fact table, then either aggregations for all data combinations should be included in the fact table or views of all data combination aggregations should be available. The star schema is intentionally designed to be simple and fast.

The following figure depicts the classic start schema. Note that the keys of each of the dimension tables is part of the compound key of the fact table. It is assumed that the OLAP environment where the *Star Schema* database resides is a quiet environment where no online updates occur. It is important in many OLAP environments that the data remain static for specific time frames so that the analyst may choose to hold some variables constant while altering one or two others so that forecasts may be generated against a static set of data.

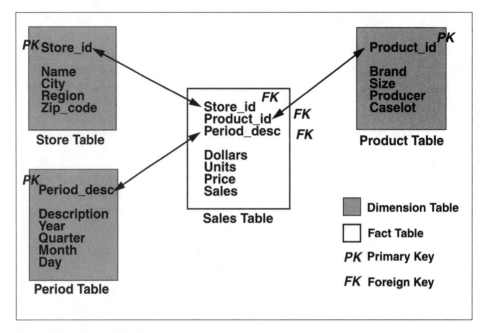

Figure 155. Classic Star Schema Example

6.2.5.1 Dynamic Bitmap Index ANDing (DBIA)

Dynamic Bitmap Index ANDing (DBIA) is a relatively new feature that the optimizer may choose when processing a query. DBIA is chosen if the cost to perform Dynamic Bitmap Index ANDing is considered by the optimizer to be the most cost effective solution.

DBIA improves performance of queries that contain multiple 'AND' predicates in which the columns specified in the 'AND' predicates are contained in one or more indexes.

The steps performed in DBIA are as follows:

1. Perform index scan to identify the qualifying row IDs (RID) for first table.

   - Hash the RIDs to a location in a bitmap.

   - Set the bit in the hashed location of the bitmap to 1.

   - Repeat for all other qualifying RIDs located in the index scan.

2. Proceed to next table

   - Perform an index scan to identify the qualifying row IDs from the current table.

- Probe the bitmap location to which the new RID will be hashed in the previously generated bitmap. If the value in the bitmap location is set to 1, this indicates that the previous scan also found a qualifying RID and that this position in the bitmap may be carried forward to the new bitmap being generated for the current scan. No locations are carried forward that do not have a qualifying bitmap location in both the current and previous bitmaps.

- Repeat this step until all index scans are complete.

3. Retrieve, Validate and Return.

- For each bit set to 1 in the bitmap, respond with the RID so that the qualifying row may be retrieved.

- Validate each retrieved row based on the criteria specified in the predicates.

- Continue until all qualifying rows have been retrieved and validated.

- Return the validated rows to the requesting application.

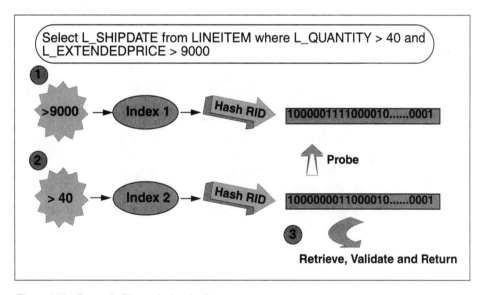

Figure 156. Dynamic Bitmap Index Anding

The following is the Explain output from the query depicted in the figure above. We begin by examining the Coordinator Subsection of the Explain.

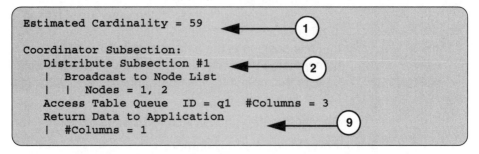

```
Estimated Cardinality = 59        ◄────────  (1)

Coordinator Subsection:
   Distribute Subsection #1       ◄────────  (2)
   |  Broadcast to Node List
   |  |  Nodes = 1, 2
   Access Table Queue  ID = q1   #Columns = 3
   Return Data to Application
   |  #Columns = 1               ◄────────  (9)
```

1. The estimated cardinality of the query is provided. The Estimated Cardinality is 59. With this statement, the optimizer is telling us that it only expects to return 59 rows based on the statistics in the DB2 catalog tables.

2. The Coordinator Subsection distributes subsection #1 to the applicable nodes; in this case, nodes 1 and 2.

3. In Subsection #1, we see that the optimizer has chosen to use Dynamic Bitmap Index ANDing (DBIA) as is evidenced by the `Index ANDing` statement in the Explain output.

4. The DBIA bitmap is created.

5. An index scan of the index over L_EXTENDEDPRICE is performed. The qualifying RIDs will be hashed to a position in the bitmap and that position will be set to 1.

6. Now, the bitmap created for the L_EXTENDEDPRICE qualifying RIDs will be probed based on the qualifying RIDs obtained from the index scan of the index over L_QUANTITY. For those RIDs that occur in both indexes, the bitmap value of 1 will remain the same. For those RIDs that only qualify for the L_QUANTITY predicate, the bitmap value will remain 0.

7. Now that both predicates have been resolved, the bitmap positions must be translated back into RIDs and the corresponding rows retrieved from the LINEITEM table with a final check against the predicates.

8. The results are returned to the coordinator node.

9. The coordinator node returns the final results to the requesting application.

```
Subsection #1:                        ← ③
   Index ANDing
   |  Optimizer Estimate of Set Size: 732    ← ④
   |  Index ANDing Bitmap Build
   |  |  Optimizer Estimate of Set Size: 732
   |  |  Access Table Name = DB2INST1.LINEITEM   ID = 2   ← ⑤
   |  |  |  #Columns = 1
   |  |  |  Index Scan:  Name = DB2INST1.LEXTENDEDPRICE   ID = 6
   |  |  |  |  #Key Columns = 1
   |  |  |  |  |  #Start Keys = 1
   |  |  |  |  |  #Stop Keys  = 0
   |  |  |  |  Index-Only Access
   |  |  |  |  Index Prefetch: Eligible
   |  |  |  Isolation Level: Uncommitted Read
   |  |  |  Lock Intents
   |  |  |  |  Table: Intent None
   |  |  |  |  Row  : None          ← ⑥
   |  Index ANDing Bitmap Probe
   |  |  Optimizer Estimate of Set Size: 732
   |  |  Access Table Name = DB2INST1.LINEITEM   ID = 2
   |  |  |  #Columns = 1
   |  |  |  Index Scan:  Name = DB2INST1.LQUANTITY   ID = 4
   |  |  |  |  #Key Columns = 1
   |  |  |  |  |  #Start Keys = 1
   |  |  |  |  |  #Stop Keys  = 0
   |  |  |  |  Index-Only Access
   |  |  |  |  Index Prefetch: Eligible
   |  |  |  Isolation Level: Uncommitted Read
   |  |  |  Lock Intents
   |  |  |  |  Table: Intent None
   |  |  |  |  Row  : None
   Insert Into Sorted Temp Table  ID = t1
   |  #Columns = 1
   |  #Sort Key Columns = 1
   |  Sortheap Allocation Parameters:
   |  |  #Rows     = 733
   |  |  Row Width = 12
   |  Piped
   List Prefetch RID Preparation         ← ⑦
   Access Table Name = DB2INST1.LINEITEM   ID = 2
   |  #Columns = 2
   |  Fetch Direct
   |  Lock Intents
   |  |  Table: Intent Share
   |  |  Row  : Next Key Share
   |  Residual Predicate(s)
   |  |  #Predicates = 2
   Insert Into Synchronous Table Queue   ID = q1   ← ⑧
   |  Broadcast to Coordinator Node

End of section
```

The optimizer will not select DBIA unless it has enough statistics to evaluate whether or not DBIA will be a good choice for the query. To provide the optimizer with the appropriate level of statistical information, you must at least collect the statistics that are generated by executing the RUNSTATS command with DISTRIBUTION and preferably with index detail.

To determine if any distribution statistics are available, you may want to start by checking SYSSTAT.COLDIST using the following query replacing TABNAME = MY_TABLE with your table name.

```
Select TABNAME,
       COLNAME

From SYSSTAT.COLDIST

Where TABNAME = 'MY_TABLE' ;
```

No lines will be returned from this query if you have not run collected distribution RUNSTATS for the table specified in the query. The following is the format of the RUNSTATS command to obtain basic distribution statistics:

```
RUNSTATS on table MY_TABLE

       With DISTRIBUTION

       And INDEXES ALL
```

If some rows are returned from this query, but you want to know if detailed information on the tables indexes has been collected, you may run the following query.

```
Select TABNAME,
       INDNAME,
       CLUSTERFACTOR

From SYSCAT.INDEXES

Where TABNAME = 'MY_TABLE'
  and CLUSTERFACTOR = -1 ;
```

If detailed statistics have not been collected for some of the indexes on your table, you may want to populate the DB2 catalog with those statistics so that the optimizer may make better decisions. You may use the following query to populate the DB2 catalog with detailed statistics for a specific index:

```
RUNSTATS on table MY_TABLE

    With DISTRIBUTION

    And DETAILED INDEX MY_INDEX ;
```

The DB2 database manager uses the Sort Heap when creating the Dynamic Bitmap. Depending on the cardinality that the optimizer estimates from the existing index statistics for the index scan, the amount of sort heap allocated will vary from 6 KB for a few rows to 24 MB for six million or more rows.

Please note that locking only occurs when the actual qualifying rows are being fetched from the table. If your tables are not updated during the period in which they are available for query, you can be certain that all qualifying rows have been selected during the DBIA process. If you are using Data Propagator Relational or some other software to propagate changes from a legacy application during the period in which the query executes, it is possible that some rows that match the query predicates will be inserted into the tables and will not be detected because the rows were not available at the time of initial predicate DBIA evaluation. This is the nature of a dynamic data warehouse environment. The exception to this situation is setting the isolation level as repeatable read. With repeatable read, locks on the selected rows will be held until the query completes processing. While this may sound like an excellent solution, it will reduce the currency of your data warehouse or OLAP environment and may result in lock escalation and generally poor performance.

6.2.5.2 Star Join

We can apply the star schema concept to our TPCD database. Please keep in mind that if we were doing this in a production environment, we would probably include some additional columns in the ORDERS and SUPPLIER tables to indicate nation and region. We might also include some summary rows in LINEITEM. We might choose to create a period table that could detail the periodic summaries that we will be using in our warehouse or our analytical models. For simplicity and consistency, none of these modifications have been applied to the TPCD database discussed below.

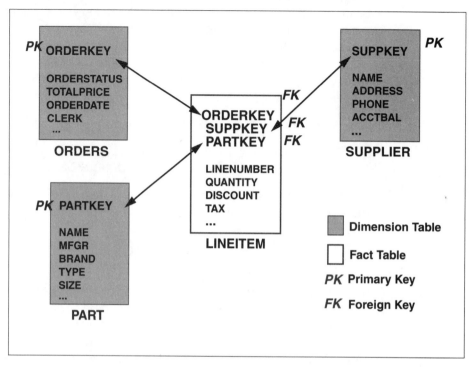

Figure 157. Star Schema Applied to TPCD Database

The *Star Schema* representation of the TPCD database depicted above has been generated by the joining of LINEITEM with ORDERS, LINEITEM with PART, and LINEITEM with SUPPLIER. LINEITEM is at the center of all three joins and resembles a star structure. In this example, LINEITEM serves as the fact table. ORDERS, PART, and SUPPLIER serve as dimension tables containing data related to LINEITEM.

Typically, in a star join, the join predicates are usually based on the primary key of the dimension tables and the foreign keys in the fact table. In this example, P_ PARTKEY, the primary key of PART, joins with LINEITEM on L_PARTKEY. The ORDERS dimension table joins with LINEITEM on ORDERKEY. The SUPPLIER dimension table joins with LINEITEM on SUPPKEY.

The typical data warehouse or OLAP query consists of a multi-table join in which predicates are applied to the dimension tables, and aggregation is performed on the fact table. This sort of join tends to be inefficient even though the result set from the dimension tables may be small, none of them significantly reduce the cardinality of the fact table rows. As the number of dimension tables increase, the possibility of choosing an inefficient access path increases.

The star join technique when coupled with Dynamic Bitmap Index ANDing, is an efficient method of resolving an OLAP or data warehouse query. DBIA used with star join differs slightly from the process described previously.

The difference in DBIA when coupled with the star join technique is that the RIDs are obtained by joining the fact table index with the dimension table. The qualifying fact table RIDs are then hashed to populate the bitmap locations.

As each additional dimension table is joined to the chosen index of the fact table, a new bitmap is generated that contains the qualifying RIDs from the current join after probing the results of the previous bitmap.

The final join of a dimension table to the fact table performs the final probing of the previous bitmaps. The RIDs for the fact table are returned so that the qualifying rows of the fact table may be accessed. The fact table qualifying rows are joined to the dimension table rows. Aggregation of the fact table columns is performed, and the final result set is returned to the requestor.

The following SQL statement and figure depict a star join via DBIA.

```
Select  s_name,,
        p_brand,
        o_orderdate,
        sum(l_extendedprice)

From   ORDERS,
       PART,
       SUPPLIER,
       LINEITEM

Where s_name= 'Ghee'
   and p_brand = 'IBM'
   and year(o_orderdate) in 1997
   and l_orderkey = o_orderkey
   and l_partkey = p_partkey
   and L_suppkey = s_suppkey

Group by s_name, p_brand, o_orderdate

Order by o_orderdate ;
```

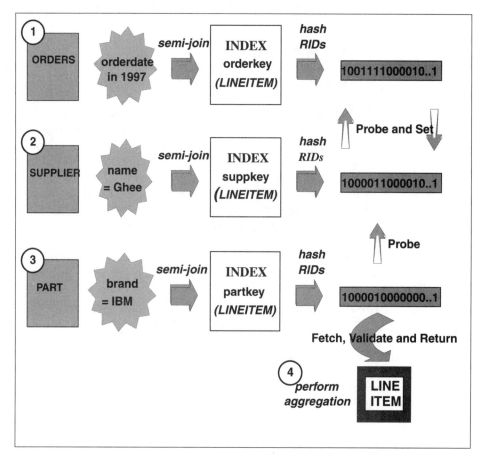

Figure 158. Star Join via Dynamic Bitmap Index ANDing

1. In this example, the ORDERS table is joined to the LINEITEM index over ORDERKEY, the primary key of ORDERS, and a foreign key of LINEITEM. The qualifying RIDs from LINEITEM are hashed to the bitmap.

2. The SUPPLIER table is joined to the LINEITEM index over SUPPKEY, the primary key of SUPPLIER, and a foreign key of LINEITEM. The qualifying RIDs from LINEITEM are hashed to the bitmap after probing the previous bitmap.

3. The PART table is joined to the LINEITEM index over PARTKEY, the primary key of PART, and a foreign key of LINEITEM. The qualifying RIDs from LINEITEM are hashed to the bitmap after probing the previous bitmap.

4. The LINEITEM RIDs are retrieved based on the hashed location in the final bitmap. The corresponding LINEITEM rows are retrieved and joined to the three dimension tables (PART, ORDERS, SUPPLIER). The aggregation of the LINEITEM extended price is performed based on the grouping criteria. The final result set is then returned to the requestor.

6.3 EXPLAIN

The Explain facilities are very powerful tuning tools for your query environment. The Explain facility describes the manner in which DB2 will execute your SQL query. Understanding the steps that the DB2 optimizer has decided to take in resolving your data request, can be quite informative when tuning your database and your queries.

Explain provides information on access path selection, join order, sort usage, locking, prefetch eligibility, DBIA, join technique, data movement between nodes, cost, cardinality, query optimization class, table queue utilization, temp table utilization, piping, predicate application, aggregation, node utilization, blocking, and so on.

This information may be used to create new indexes, modify existing indices, evaluate partitioning key choices, evaluate sort heap requirements, modify SQL statement structure, evaluate level of statistical table data needed, understand how the end user is using the data, and so on.

As you understand more about how the DB2 UDB optimizer accesses your data, you will be better able to tune your environment and assist your users in accessing the data in a more efficient manner. These Explain sections are intended to assist you in utilizing the Explain output in your environment and are not intended as a detailed description of each aspect of the DB2 Explain facilities. Detailed information on the Explain facilities may be found in the *DB2 Universal Database Administration Guide*.

6.3.1 EXPLAIN Tools

6.3.1.1 Explain Facilities

If you want to know how a query will be executed by DB2, you must analyze its access plan. The Explain facilities will provide information about how DB2 will access the data in order to resolve the SQL statements.

Before describing the capabilities and the features of the Explain facilities, you should understand, at a high level, how SQL statements are processed by the DB2 database engine. DB2 creates an executable form of an SQL statement every time a statement is submitted, either during a static bind or when executed dynamically. This executable form of a SQL statement is known as the "access plan". The access plan is the way the database objects will be accessed to solve a query. The component within DB2 that determines the access path to be used is known as the *optimizer*.

During the static preparation of an SQL statement the SQL compiler is called to generate an executable *access plan.* The access plan contains the data access strategy, including index usage, sort methods, locking semantics and join methods. The executable form of the SQL statement is stored in the system catalog tables when the `BIND` command is executed (assuming deferred binding method).

Sometimes, the complete statement is not known at application development time. In this case, the compiler is invoked during program execution to generate an access plan for the query that can be used by the database manager to access the data. The access plans for dynamic SQL statements are **not** stored in the system catalogs. They are temporarily stored in memory (known as the global package cache). The compiler will not be invoked if the access plans for the dynamic SQL statements already exist in the package cache.

6.3.1.2 Query Compilation
The SQL compiler performs a number of tasks during the creation of the compiled form of the SQL statements. These phases are described below and are also shown in Figure 159. As you can see in this figure, the representation of the query is stored in a structure known as a graph called the *Query Graph Model* (QGM).

1. Parse Query

   Parse the SQL statement to validate its syntax. If no error is detected, an initial QGM is created. Otherwise, processing will be stopped and an appropriate SQL error is returned to the calling application.

2. Check Semantics

   Verify that the referenced objects exist and identify any constraints. These constraints could include referential integrity (RI) constraints, table check constraints, triggers, and views. The QGM is modified to include these constraints.

3. Rewrite Query

   Modify the query if necessary (as QGM) to a new form that can be more easily optimized or that produces a shorter access path in the next phase of query processing.

4. Optimize Access Plan

   Use the QGM as input to generate alternative execution plans. The optimizer estimates the execution cost of each alternative plan, using the statistics of tables, indexes, columns and functions to choose the plan with the smallest estimated cost. The output of this task is known as the "access plan".

5. Generate Executable Code

   Create an *executable access plan* for the SQL statement. This access plan will be stored either in the system catalog tables or in memory. Static SQL statements will be stored in the system catalog tables and dynamic SQL statements will be stored in memory. Therefore, the dynamic SQL statements are only available while they remain in memory. The executable access plan is part of a *package*. The amount of memory used to store packages is configurable using the database configuration parameter known as *pckcachesz*.

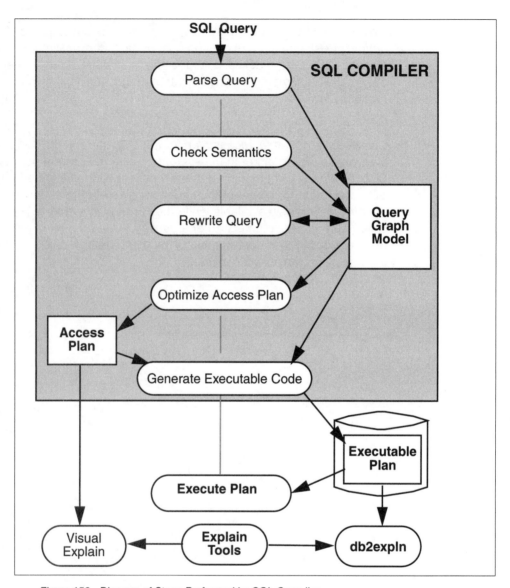

Figure 159. Diagram of Steps Performed by SQL Compiler

6.3.1.3 Explain Tables

DB2 uses Explain tables to store access plan information. These tables are:

- **EXPLAIN_ARGUMENT** — represents the unique characteristics for each individual operator.

- **EXPLAIN_INSTANCE** — main control table for all Explain information. It contains basic information about the source of the SQL statements being explained as well as information about the environment in which the Explain took place.
- **EXPLAIN_OBJECT** — contains data objects required by the access plan generated to satisfy the SQL statement (objects can include tables, indexes, and so on).
- **EXPLAIN_OPERATOR** — contains all the operators needed to satisfy the SQL statement (the operators may include table scans, index scans, and so on)
- **EXPLAIN_PREDICATE** — identifies which predicates are applied by a specific operator.
- **EXPLAIN_STATEMENT** — contains the text of the SQL statement in two forms. The original version entered by the user is stored in addition to as the re-written version.
- **EXPLAIN_STREAM** — contains the input and output streams between individual operators and data objects.

The explain tables have to be created before any explain information can be gathered. The CLP input file called EXPLAIN.DDL, located in the misc subdirectory of the current instance, contains the definition of the Explain tables. To create the explain tables you must connect to the database and use the following command:

```
db2 -tf EXPLAIN.DDL
```

6.3.1.4 The db2expln Utility
The db2expln tool describes the access plan selected for static SQL statements in the packages stored in the system catalog tables. It can be used to obtain a quick explanation of the chosen access plan for packages for which explain data was not captured at bind time.

6.3.1.5 The dynexpln Utility
Dynamic Explain scripts may be created to facilitate the tuning of dynamic SQL. The following is a sample AIX dynamic explain script.

```
dynexpln -d tpcd100 -o example1.exp -s  "
    select o_totalprice,
           o_clerk,
           l_quantity,
           l_shipmode

from orders,
     lineitem

where l_orderkey = o_orderkey
  and  o_totalprice > 220000
  and  l_quantity > 10
  and  l_shipmode = 'AIR'
;
"
```

The following are the key elements of the dynamic Explain syntax:

```
dynexpln
            -d dbname
            -o output file name
            -s SQL statement enclosed in double quotes
```

Figure 160. Dynamic Explain Syntax

In the dynamic Explain syntax

- -d must be followed by the database name

- -o must be followed by the output file where you expect to find the report generated by the dynamic explain utility.

- -s must be followed by the SQL statement. The SQL statement must be terminated with a semicolon and contained within double quotes.

The Dynamic Explain file may be converted to an executable module by changing the file to be executable. Once the file is executable, modifications may be made to the enclosed SQL statement as needed for tuning purposes.

6.3.2 Understanding EXPLAIN Output

The following are several examples of using Explain output to tune queries. Each of the SQL statements is a dynamic SQL statement. All of these Explains were run using the dynexpln utility.

TPCD100 is the database used in all of the SQL statements. The row count for each table is detailed in the table below:

Table 8. TPCD100 Tables and Their Row Counts

Table Name	Number of Rows
CUSTOMER	15,000
LINEITEM	600,572
NATION	25
ORDERS	150,000
PART	20,000
PARTSUPP	80,000
REGION	5
SUPPLIER	1,000

The TPCD100 database is defined across two database partitions. We are using a high speed switch between the two partitions. All of the tables are distributed across both partitions.

You should be aware of information of this sort when attempting to tune queries in your environment. It is very helpful if you have some feel for the number of possible distinct values in the various columns of your database as well as the distribution of those values across each table for the larger tables in your database. In this example we would be most concerned with the distinct values in the columns of LINEITEM, ORDERS, and PARTSUPP because these are the largest tables in the TPCD100 database.

The following is a sample SQL statement to obtain a list of the distinct values and a count of the number of occurrences of each distinct value for the L_DISCOUNT column of the LINEITEM table.

```
Select  DISTINCT L_DISCOUNT,
        Count(*)

From    LINEITEM

Group By L_DISCOUNT

Order By L_DISCOUNT
```

By understanding the distribution of data in your tables, you can more easily evaluate whether or not the plan that the optimizer has selected seems to be the best plan for your environment. Generally speaking, the optimizer will attempt to reduce the size of the result set as early as possible so that the minimum amount of work (such as joining, broadcasting of data, and so forth) will have to be performed. To reduce the result set, the optimizer will typically access the table that will generate the smallest result set once the predicates are applied and will limit the result sets from the other tables specified in the query.

For example, assume that we want all the line items shipped on January 15, 1998 for all suppliers in nationkey 1. In the TPCD100 database described above, there are 38 suppliers in nationkey 1. There are 221 line items shipped on 1/15/1998. You might think that the optimizer should select the SUPPLIER table first because it has the smallest initial result set, but the join of the SUPPLIER result set to LINEITEM results in 22,741 rows in the initial join because there are many LINEITEM rows for each SUPPLIER row. A join from the 221 LINEITEM rows to SUPPLIER will result in a 221 row join prior to the application of the NATIONKEY predicate. In this situation, the optimizer should be choosing LINEITEM first as you can see in the Explain output following. The actual execution of this query had a run time of 2.46 and returned 9 rows.

```
******************** PACKAGE ****************************************

Package Name = DB2INST1.DYNEXPLN
        Prep Date = 1998/03/12
        Prep Time = 10:08:06:084

        Bind Timestamp = 1998-03-12-10.08.06.850100

        Isolation Level            = Cursor Stability
        Blocking                   = Block Unambiguous Cursors
        Query Optimization Class = 5

        Partition Parallel       = Yes
        Intra-Partition Parallel = No

        Function Path              = "SYSIBM", "SYSFUN", "DB2INST1"
-------------------- SECTION --------------------------------------------
Section = 1


SQL Statement:

  select l_shipdate, s_name
  from lineitem, supplier
  where l_suppkey = s_suppkey and l_shipdate = '01/15/1998' and
        s_nationkey = 1

Buffered Insert            = No

Estimated Cost       = 122
Estimated Cardinality = 8

Coordinator Subsection:
  Distribute Subsection #2
  |  Broadcast to Node List
  |  |  Nodes = 1, 2
  Distribute Subsection #1
  |  Broadcast to Node List
  |  |  Nodes = 1, 2
  Access Table Queue  ID = q1  #Columns = 2
  Return Data to Application
  |  #Columns = 2
```

```
Subsection #1:
   Access Table Queue  ID = q2  #Columns = 1
   |  Output Sorted #Key Columns = 1
   Nested Loop Join
   |  Access Table Name = DB2INST1.SUPPLIER  ID = 6
   |  |  #Columns = 3
   |  |  Single Record
   |  |  Index Scan:  Name = DB2INST1.UXS_SKNK  ID = 3
   |  |  |  #Key Columns = 2
   |  |  |  Data Prefetch: None
   |  |  |  Index Prefetch: None
   |  |  Lock Intents
   |  |  |  Table: Intent Share
   |  |  |  Row  : Next Key Share
   Insert Into Asynchronous Table Queue  ID = q1
   |  Broadcast to Coordinator Node
   |  Rows Can Overflow to Temporary Table

Subsection #2:
   Access Table Name = DB2INST1.LINEITEM  ID = 2
   |  #Columns = 2
   |  Index Scan:  Name = DB2INST1.L_SD_EP_DS_SK_PK  ID = 5
   |  |  #Key Columns = 1
   |  |  Index-Only Access
   |  |  Index Prefetch: None
   |  |  |  Insert Into Sorted Temp Table  ID = t1
   |  |  |  |  #Columns = 1
   |  |  |  |  #Sort Key Columns = 1
   |  |  |  |  Sortheap Allocation Parameters:
   |  |  |  |  |  #Rows      = 119
   |  |  |  |  |  Row Width = 8
   |  |  |  |  Piped
   |  Lock Intents
   |  |  Table: Intent Share
   |  |  Row  : Next Key Share
   Sorted Temp Table Completion  ID = t1
   Access Temp Table  ID = t1
   |  #Columns = 1
   |  Relation Scan
   |  |  Prefetch: Eligible
   Insert Into Asynchronous Table Queue  ID = q2
   |  Hash to Specific Node
   |  Rows Can Overflow to Temporary Tables

End of section
```

You should also closely review the estimated cardinality of the request. In general, requests that result in a cardinality of greater than 100,000 should be reviewed to determine if the result set is truly what the user desired. Reports of over 100,000 lines tend to be of no practical use to the recipient.

Of course, there are exceptions to this, such as month-end detail reports that are kept for audit purposes, year-end reports, reports that contain breaks at department levels that are split and distributed after printing, and so on.

When you are reviewing Explain output that has an estimated cardinality that exceeds 100,000 rows, you should contact the person who generated the request and ask what they are attempting to accomplish with the SQL statement. Frequently with a little patience and some time, you will be able to assist the user in adding additional selection criteria so that they receive a reasonable amount of data. This will also generally result in a more efficient query because less data is being move between partitions.

When discussing the SQL statement with the user, discuss the request in business terms that the user can understand. You can gain much insight into how your users are actually using your database if you will discuss their efforts in business terms. Be open to the idea of developing new summary tables if you find that the complexity of the business requests span more tables than the user can easily comprehend and utilize.

6.3.2.1 Before and After RUNSTATS with Distribution and Detail

The ability of the optimizer to choose the most efficient access plan is dependent upon the data that is available to the optimizer for making decisions. That data resides in the DB2 system catalogs. The statistics that populate the DB2 system catalog tables come from the execution of the RUNSTATS command. RUNSTATS may be executed at many different levels.

The following is the syntax for the RUNSTATS command:

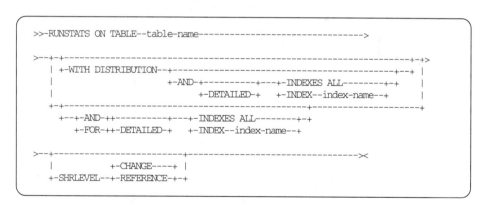

Especially in a large data warehousing or OLAP environments, distribution statistics can make a significant difference in the estimated cost of the query, the actual runtime of the query and the options that the optimizer chooses to resolve the query predicates.

The following table contains a comparison of two executions of the same query against the LINEITEM table. The first execution occurred when the catalog contained only statistics on the LINEITEM table and none of its indexes.

Table 9. Query Execution - with and without RUNSTATS

	Before RUNSTATS	After RUNSTATS	Difference
Estimated Cost	39719	24226	15493
Estimated Cardinality	7411	7411	0
Actual Execution Time	29.37	20.52	8.85
Actual Rows Returned	2601	2601	0
Access Methods	Index Scan	DBIA	Multiple Indexes Accessed

The first execution occurred when the DB2 system catalog contained only statistics on the LINEITEM table and none of its indexes. Note in the first Explain, the optimizer chooses to use an index even though no distribution statistics exist for that index in the DB2 system catalog.

The following items describe the flow of the actions that the optimizer has chosen to perform to resolve the SQL request prior to the execution of the RUNSTATS with distribution and detail command.

1. The estimated cost for the execution of this query is 39719. The estimated cardinality is 7411.

2. The optimizer does know from the catalog that an index exists over the L_EXTENDEDPRICE column of the LINEITEM table and has decided that the LEXTENDEDPRICE index is the best choice given the amount of information available to the optimizer at this time.

3. An index scan is performed against the LEXTENDEDPRICE index using index only access. The result set is placed in a sorted temp table.

4. The data obtained from the index scan is sorted using a piped sort. The optimizer has estimated that 18527 rows will be in the sorted temp table.

5. The rows are then fetched from the LINEITEM table using RID Prefetch.

6. The result set is broadcast to the coordinator node:

```
SQL Statement:

  select l_shipdate
  from lineitem
  where l_quantity > 40 and l_extendedprice > 90000

Buffered Insert          = No

Estimated Cost       = 39719
Estimated Cardinality = 7411                              (1)

Coordinator Subsection:
  Distribute Subsection #1
  |  Broadcast to Node List
  |  |  Nodes = 1, 2
  Access Table Queue  ID = q1  #Columns = 3
  Return Data to Application
  |  #Columns = 1


Subsection #1:
  Access Table Name = DB2INST1.LINEITEM  ID = 2          (2)
  |  #Columns = 1
  |  Index Scan:  Name = DB2INST1.LEXTENDEDPRICE  ID = 3
  |  |  #Key Columns = 1
  |  |  |  #Start Keys = 1
  |  |  |  #Stop Keys  = 0
  |  |  Index-Only Access
  |  |  Index Prefetch: Eligible                         (3)
  |  |  |  Insert Into Sorted Temp Table  ID = t1
  |  |  |  |  #Columns = 1
  |  |  |  |  #Sort Key Columns = 1
  |  |  |  |  Sortheap Allocation Parameters:            (4)
  |  |  |  |  |  #Rows     = 18527
  |  |  |  |  |  Row Width = 12
  |  |  |  |  Piped
  |  Isolation Level: Uncommitted Read
  |  Lock Intents
  |  |  Table: Intent None
  |  |  Row  : None
  Sorted Temp Table Completion  ID = t1
  List Prefetch RID Preparation
  Access Table Name = DB2INST1.LINEITEM  ID = 2          (5)
  |  #Columns = 3
  |  Fetch Direct
  |  Lock Intents
  |  |  Table: Intent Share
  |  |  Row  : Next Key Share  |  Residual Predicate(s)
  |  |  #Predicates = 2
  Insert Into Synchronous Table Queue  ID = q1           (6)
  |  Broadcast to Coordinator Node

End of section
```

The second execution of query occurred after the following RUNSTATS
command was executed:

```
RUNSTATS on table db2inst1.lineitem
             with distribution
             and detailed indexes all ;
```

This RUNSTATS command populates all of the statistics carried in the SYSSTAT.COLDIST table and the SYSSTAT.COLUMNS table. This provides the optimizer with more information upon which to base the access path decision.The following items describe the flow of the actions that the optimizer has chosen to perform to resolve the SQL request.

1. The estimated cost of this query has now been reduced to 24266 from 39719 due to the additional indexing information. The cardinality is still estimated to be 7411.

2. The optimizer has decided to utilize Dynamic Bitmap Index ANDing. The first index scanned is LEXTENDEDPRICE.

3. The second index scanned is LQUANTITY, an index over the L_QUANTITY column. The bitmap generated in the previous index scan is probed and set based on the results of the LQUANTITY index scan. The resulting output is placed in a sorted temp table.

4. The data obtained from the DBIA is sorted using a piped sort. The optimizer has estimated that only 3706 rows will be in the sorted temp table as opposed to 18527 rows.

5. The rows are then fetched from the LINEITEM table using RID Prefetch.

6. The result set is broadcast to the coordinator node.

```
SQL Statement:

  select l_shipdate
  from lineitem
  where l_quantity > 40 and l_extendedprice > 90000

Buffered Insert          = No

Estimated Cost           = 24226
Estimated Cardinality = 7411          ◀────────(1)

Coordinator Subsection:
  Distribute Subsection #1
  |  Broadcast to Node List
  |  |  Nodes = 1, 2
  Access Table Queue  ID = q1  #Columns = 3
  Return Data to Application
  |  #Columns = 1
```

```
Subsection #1:
   Index ANDing
   |   Optimizer Estimate of Set Size: 3705
   |   Index ANDing Bitmap Build
   |   |   Optimizer Estimate of Set Size: 3705        ◀────────( 2 )
   |   |   Access Table Name = DB2INST1.LINEITEM   ID = 2
   |   |   |   #Columns = 1
   |   |   |   Index Scan:  Name = DB2INST1.LEXTENDEDPRICE   ID = 2
   |   |   |   |   #Key Columns = 1
   |   |   |   |   |   #Start Keys = 1
   |   |   |   |   |   #Stop Keys  = 0
   |   |   |   |   Index-Only Access
   |   |   |   |   Index Prefetch: Eligible
   |   |   |   Isolation Level: Uncommitted Read
   |   |   |   Lock Intents
   |   |   |   |   Table: Intent None
   |   |   |   |   Row  : None
   |   Index ANDing Bitmap Probe                       ◀────────( 3 )
   |   |   Optimizer Estimate of Set Size: 3705
   |   |   Access Table Name = DB2INST1.LINEITEM   ID = 2
   |   |   |   #Columns = 1
   |   |   |   Index Scan:  Name = DB2INST1.LQUANTITY   ID = 3
   |   |   |   |   #Key Columns = 1
   |   |   |   |   |   #Start Keys = 1
   |   |   |   |   |   #Stop Keys  = 0
   |   |   |   |   Index-Only Access
   |   |   |   |   Index Prefetch: Eligible
   |   |   |   Isolation Level: Uncommitted Read
   |   |   |   Lock Intents
   |   |   |   |   Table: Intent None
   |   |   |   |   Row  : None
   Insert Into Sorted Temp Table   ID = t1
   |   #Columns = 1
   |   #Sort Key Columns = 1
   |   Sortheap Allocation Parameters:
   |   |   #Rows       = 3706          ◀────────( 4 )
   |   |   Row Width = 12
   |   Piped
   List Prefetch RID Preparation
   Access Table Name = DB2INST1.LINEITEM   ID = 2◀────────( 5 )
   |   #Columns = 3
   |   Fetch Direct
   |   Lock Intents
   |   |   Table: Intent Share
   |   |   Row  : Next Key Share
   |   Residual Predicate(s)
|  |   #Predicates = 2
   Insert Into Synchronous Table Queue  ID = q1 ◀────────( 6 )
   |   Broadcast to Coordinator Node
End of section
```

6.3.2.2 Improving Query Performance by Adding an Index

When working in a database environment that contains large tables, one of the greatest performance degradations is for a query to perform a full table scan because there is no index on a column specified in the predicate. Typically, in an OLAP or data warehousing environment, you will create significantly more indexes than you would in an OLTP environment so as to support the reporting and analytical requirements of the environment.

The following table contains a comparison of two executions of the same query against the LINEITEM and ORDERS tables.

Table 10. Query Statistics - Before and After Adding Index

	Before Index	After Index Added	Difference
Estimated Cost	55857	7274	48583
Estimated Cardinality	17,133	16,626	507
Actual Execution Time	80.55	58.33	22.22
Actual Rows Returned	23.081	23,081	0
Access Methods	Directed Inner Join: Relation Scan of LINEITEM	Directed Inner Join; Index Scan using Index Only Access to LSHIPQUAN	Index Only Access to new index

The first execution occurred when there was no index over L_SHIPMODE or L_QUANTITY in the LINEITEM table. The second execution occurred after the index was created over L_SHIPMODE, L_QUANTITY. The following is the SQL that was executed both before and after the index was created.

```
Select  O_TOTALPRICE,
        O_CLERK,
        L_QUANTITY,
        L_SHIPMODE

From    ORDERS,
        LINEITEM

Where   L_ORDERKEY = O_ORDERKEY
  and   O_TOTALPRICE > 10
  and   L_SHIPMODE = 'AIR'
```

In the Explain example following, we were able to decrease the estimated cost from 55857 to 7274 by adding a new index over the L_SHIPMODE,

L_QUANTITY columns in the LINEITEM table. While the actual runtime is not as dramatic a decrease as the estimated cost, please remember that this is a small database. The results would have been more dramatic if the database had been significantly larger.

The following items describe the flow of the actions that the optimizer has chosen to perform to resolve the SQL request. These actions were chosen prior to the creation of the new index, LSHIPQUAN.

1. The estimated cost for the execution of this query is 55857. The estimated cardinality is 17133. Note that actual cardinality is 23081, or 5948 more rows than estimated.

2. An index scan is performed against the OTOTALPRICE index over the ORDERS table. The results are placed in a sorted temp table.

3. The data obtained from the index scan is sorted using a piped sort. The optimizer has estimated that 14742 rows will be in the sorted temp table.

4. The sorted results are placed in a table queue and hashed to specific nodes.

5. LINEITEM is relation scanned and a Sargable predicated is applied. The results are placed in a sorted temp table.

6. The data obtained from the LINEITEM relation scan is sorted using a piped sort. The optimizer has estimated that 35046 rows will be in the sorted temp table.

7. The piped sort from LINEITEM is then merge joined to the table queue containing data from ORDERS.

8. The result set of the merge join is then broadcast to the coordinator node.

```
SQL Statement:

  select o_totalprice, o_clerk, L_quantity, l_shipmode
  from orders, lineitem
  where l_orderkey = o_orderkey and o_totalprice > 220000 and
        l_quantity > 10 and l_shipmode = 'AIR'
<Buffered Insert          = No

Estimated Cost      = 55857        ◄───────────( 1 )
Estimated Cardinality = 17133

Coordinator Subsection:
  Distribute Subsection #2
  |  Broadcast to Node List
  |  |  Nodes = 1, 2
  Distribute Subsection #1
  |  Broadcast to Node List
  |  |  Nodes = 1, 2
  Access Table Queue  ID = q1  #Columns = 4
  Return Data to Application
  |  #Columns = 4

Subsection #1:
  Access Table Name = DB2INST1.LINEITEM  ID = 2
  |  #Columns = 3
  |  Relation Scan                  ◄──────( 5 )
  |  |  Prefetch: Eligible
  |  Lock Intents
  |  |  Table: Intent Share
  |  |  Row  : Next Key Share
  |  Sargable Predicate(s)
  |  |  #Predicates = 2
  |  Insert Into Sorted Temp Table  ID = t1
  |  |  #Columns = 3
  |  |  #Sort Key Columns = 1
  |  |  Sortheap Allocation Parameters: ◄────( 6 )
  |  |  |  #Rows     = 35046
  |  |  |  Row Width = 28
  |  |  Piped
  Sorted Temp Table Completion  ID = t1
  Access Temp Table  ID = t1
  |  #Columns = 3
  |  Relation Scan
  |  |  Prefetch: Eligible
  Merge Join
  |  Access Table Queue  ID = q2  #Columns = 3 ◄──( 7 )
  |  |  Output Sorted #Key Columns = 1
  Insert Into Asynchronous Table Queue  ID = q1◄──( 8 )
  |  Broadcast to Coordinator Node
  |  Rows Can Overflow to Temporary Table
```

```
Subsection #2:
   Access Table Name = DB2INST1.ORDERS ID = 2
   |  #Columns = 3                                          ← (2)
   |  Index Scan:  Name = DB2INST1.OTOTALPRICE   ID = 2
   |  |  #Key Columns = 1
   |  |  |  #Start Keys = 1
   |  |  |  #Stop Keys  = 0
   |  |  Data Prefetch: Eligible
   |  |  Index Prefetch: Eligible
   |  Lock Intents
   |  |  Table: Intent Share
   |  |  Row  : Next Key Share
   |  Insert Into Sorted Temp Table  ID = t2
   |  |  #Columns = 3
   |  |  #Sort Key Columns = 1
   |  |  Sortheap Allocation Parameters:                    ← (3)
   |  |  |  #Rows       = 14742
   |  |  |  Row Width = 32
   |  |  Piped
   Sorted Temp Table Completion  ID = t2
   Access Temp Table  ID = t2
   |  #Columns = 3
   |  Relation Scan
   |  |  Prefetch: Eligible
   Insert Into Asynchronous Table Queue  ID = q2
   |  Hash to Specific Node
   |  Rows Can Overflow to Temporary Tables    ←           (4)

End of section
```

Now let's look at the Explain output generated after the new index was created.

The following is the SQL statement used to create the new index.

```
Create Index LSHIPQUAN
    on LINEITEM(L_SHIPMODE,L_QUANTITY)
```

After the index was created, RUNSTATS with distribution and detailed index was executed for the new index, LSHIPQUAN.

```
RUNSTATS on Table DB2INST1.LINEITEM
                    with Distribution
                    and detailed Index DB2INST1.LSHIPQUAN ;
```

Once the new index is added, you may want to rebind all of your static packages prior to your users accessing your system. You may use `db2rbind` to rebind all packages within your database. The following in the syntax for `db2rbind`:

```
db2rbind -database -logfile -u userid -p password
```

While it is not necessary to rebind all of your static packages, it may be desirable. The database and logfile parameters are required. User id and password are optional parameters. For further information regarding the `db2rbind` command see the *IBM DB2 Universal Database Command Reference Version 5*.

The following items describe the flow of the actions that the optimizer has chosen to perform to resolve the SQL request as listed in the Explain output. These actions were chosen after the creation of the new index, LSHIPQUAN.

1. The estimated cost for the execution of this query has dropped to 7274 from 55857. The estimated cardinality has dropped to 16626 from 17133. Note that actual cardinality is 23081, or 6455 more rows than estimated.

2. An index scan is performed against the OTOTALPRICE index over the ORDERS table. The results are placed in a sorted temp table.

3. The data obtained from the index scan is sorted using a piped sort. The optimizer has estimated that 14742 rows will be in the sorted temp table.

4. The sorted results are placed in a table queue and hashed to specific nodes.

5. LINEITEM is index scanned on the LSHIPQUAN index using index only access. The results are placed in a sorted temp table.

6. The data obtained from the LINEITEM index scan is sorted using a piped sort. The optimizer has estimated that 34010 rows will be in the sorted temp table. The estimate of 34010 is 1036 rows less than the previous sort rows estimate.

7. The piped sort from LINEITEM is then merge joined to the hashed table queue containing data from ORDERS.

8. The result set of the merge join is then broadcast to the coordinator node.

```
SQL Statement:

  select o_totalprice, o_clerk, L_quantity, l_shipmode
  from orders, lineitem
  where l_orderkey = o_orderkey and o_totalprice > 220000 and
          l_quantity > 10 and l_shipmode = 'AIR'
Buffered Insert             = No

Estimated Cost         = 7274
Estimated Cardinality = 16626                                   ( 1 )
Coordinator Subsection:
  Distribute Subsection #2
  |  Broadcast to Node List
  |  |  Nodes = 1, 2
  Distribute Subsection #1
  |  Broadcast to Node List
  |  |  Nodes = 1, 2
  Access Table Queue  ID = q1  #Columns = 4
  Return Data to Application
  |  #Columns = 4

Subsection #1:
  Access Table Name = DB2INST1.LINEITEM  ID = 2                 ( 5 )
  |  #Columns = 3
  |  Index Scan:  Name = DB2INST1.LSHIPQUAN  ID = 8
  |  |  #Key Columns = 2
  |  |  |  #Start Keys = 2
  |  |  |  #Stop Keys  = 1
  |  |  Index-Only Access
  |  |  Index Prefetch: Eligible
  |  |  |  Insert Into Sorted Temp Table  ID = t1
  |  |  |  |  #Columns = 3
  |  |  |  |  #Sort Key Columns = 1
  |  |  |  |  Sortheap Allocation Parameters:                   ( 6 )
  |  |  |  |  |  #Rows      = 34010
  |  |  |  |  |  Row Width = 28
  |  |  |  |  Piped
  |  Lock Intents
  |  |  Table: Intent Share
  |  |  Row  : Next Key Share
  Sorted Temp Table Completion  ID = t1
  Access Temp Table  ID = t1
  |  #Columns = 3
  |  Relation Scan
  |  |  Prefetch: Eligible
  Merge Join
  |  Access Table Queue  ID = q2  #Columns = 3                  ( 7 )
  |  |  Output Sorted #Key Columns = 1
  Insert Into Asynchronous Table Queue  ID = q1
  |  Broadcast to Coordinator Node                              ( 8 )
  |  Rows Can Overflow to Temporary Table
```

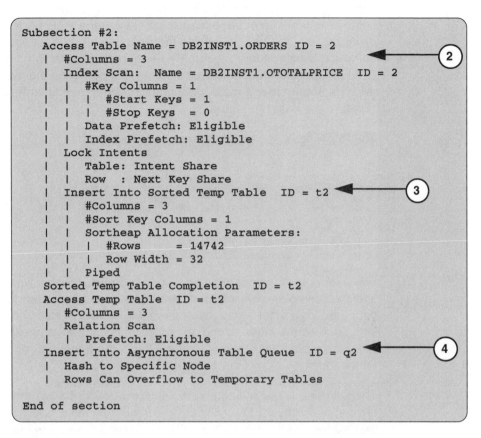

```
Subsection #2:
   Access Table Name = DB2INST1.ORDERS ID = 2                    ◄——— ②
   |  #Columns = 3
   |  Index Scan:  Name = DB2INST1.OTOTALPRICE  ID = 2
   |  |  #Key Columns = 1
   |  |  |  #Start Keys = 1
   |  |  |  #Stop Keys  = 0
   |  |  Data Prefetch: Eligible
   |  |  Index Prefetch: Eligible
   |  Lock Intents
   |  |  Table: Intent Share
   |  |  Row  : Next Key Share
   |  Insert Into Sorted Temp Table  ID = t2        ◄——— ③
   |  |  #Columns = 3
   |  |  #Sort Key Columns = 1
   |  |  Sortheap Allocation Parameters:
   |  |  |  #Rows      = 14742
   |  |  |  Row Width = 32
   |  |  Piped
   Sorted Temp Table Completion  ID = t2
   Access Temp Table  ID = t2
   |  #Columns = 3
   |  Relation Scan
   |  |  Prefetch: Eligible
   Insert Into Asynchronous Table Queue  ID = q2   ◄——— ④
   |  Hash to Specific Node
   |  Rows Can Overflow to Temporary Tables

End of section
```

The use of index scans and index only access are always less costly than performing relation scans against an entire table. As the size of the table grows, the length of actual time to scan the entire table grows exponentially once the size of the table exceeds the amount of memory available to contain pages from the relation scan. The significant increase in time is due to page faulting in memory.

6.3.2.3 Improving Performance by Reorganizing a Table on an Index

In your database environment, you may find that certain tables are most frequently accessed by a certain column or group of columns. Frequently, the database manager is asked to present the results ordered on this column or group of columns. If you have not already generated an index over this column or group of columns, you need to do so. The new index will of course improve your performance. To go a step further, you may also want to reorganize your table based on this index.

Typically, in an OLAP or Data Warehousing environment, the data access patterns to table do not use the primary key to the table because in these environments, the user is looking for groupings or data as opposed to individual pieces of information. By reorganizing the table on a commonly used grouping column or access column, the database manager already has the data in the order it most often needs thereby reducing the effort required to return the data requested.

The following is the syntax of the `REORG TABLE` command:

```
>>-REORG TABLE--table-name---+--------------------+------------->
                             +-INDEX--index-name--+

>--+-----------------------+---------------------------------->< 
   +-USE--tablespace-name--+
```

While reorganizing your table on a specific index, coupled with rebinding your static access plans will improve performance, it is important to also modify your data load program so that the input load data is also sorted in the same sequence as the index. If you do not modify your load process or always reorg the table after the load, you will loose the benefit of reorging the table on the index.

The following is the SQL statement that we use for this example. We already have an index over the O_CLERK column. In this example we are assuming that we frequently access the ORDERS table by the order clerk (O_CLERK) column. The index name is DB2INST1.O_CLERK.

```
Select c_name,
       c_phone,
       o_totalprice,
       o_clerk

From orders,
     customer

Where o_custkey = c_custkey
  and o_clerk = 'Diane '
```

By adding the DB2INST1.O_CLERK index, the estimated cost dropped from 77253 to 3298. The actual runtime for the request also dropped significantly. While this is an excellent improvement, we suspect that we could reduce the runtime even further by reorganizing the ORDERS table on the O_CLERK index.

The following is the SQL statement used to reorganize the ORDERS table on the O_CLERK index.

```
Reorg Table DB2INST1.ORDERS Index DB2INST1.O_CLERK
```

As you can see, the estimated cost was cut almost in half again after the reorganization of the ORDERS table on the O_CLERK index. The actual runtime reduction was 28%. You would expect this reduction to be a greater percentage closer to that in the estimated cost if the database was larger. As noted below, the access methods employed by the optimizer did not change. The execution time reduction was a result of the sorting of the data on the DB2INST1.O_CLERK index.

Table 11. Query Execution Before and After Reorg on Index

	Before Reorg	After Reorg	Difference
Estimated Cost	3298	1722	1576
Estimated Cardinality	948	926	22
Actual Execution Time	6.38	4.62	1.76
Actual Rows Returned	946	946	0
Access Methods	Directed Outer Join; Index Only Access; Fetch Direct	Directed Outer Join; Index Only Access Fetch Direct	None; Data access time is less due to Reorg

The following is a description of the actions that the optimizer has chosen to execute to resolve the SQL request. Please note that the actions that the optimizer chose are identical for both before and after the reorganization on the DB2INST1.O_CLERK index.

1. The estimated cost of the execution of this query is 3298 and the estimated cardinality is 948.

2. The first table to be accessed is the ORDERS table. It is accessed via the O_CLERK index using index only access.

3. The data obtained from the index scan is used to obtain the additional columns specified in the SQL request.

4. Those columns are inserted into a table queue and hashed to the appropriate specific nodes.

5. The hashed table queue containing the selected rows from the ORDERS table is nested loop joined to the CUSTOMER table using the PK_C_CUSTKEY index.

6. The results of the nested loop join of CUSTOMER and ORDERS is broadcast back to the coordinator node and the results are presented to the requestor.

```
SQL Statement:

  select c_name, c_phone, o_totalprice, o_clerk
  from orders, customer
  where o_custkey = c_custkey and o_clerk = 'Diane '
Buffered Insert              = No

Estimated Cost           = 3298           ◄———————(1)
Estimated Cardinality = 948

Coordinator Subsection:
  Distribute Subsection #2
  |  Broadcast to Node List
  |  |  Nodes = 1, 2
  Distribute Subsection #1
  |  Broadcast to Node List
  |  |  Nodes = 1, 2
  Access Table Queue  ID = q1  #Columns = 4
  Return Data to Application
  |  #Columns = 4
Subsection #1:
  Access Table Queue  ID = q2  #Columns = 3
  |  Output Sorted #Key Columns = 1
  Nested Loop Join                          ◄———————(5)
  |  Access Table Name = DB2INST1.CUSTOMER  ID = 8
  |  |  #Columns = 3
  |  |  Single Record
  |  |  Index Scan:  Name = DB2INST1.PK_C_CUSTKEY  ID = 1
  |  |  |  #Key Columns = 1
  |  |  |  Data Prefetch: Eligible
  |  |  |  Index Prefetch: Eligible
  |  |  Lock Intents
  |  |  |  Table: Intent Share
  |  |  |  Row  : Next Key Share
  Insert Into Asynchronous Table Queue  ID =
  |  Broadcast to Coordinator Node         ◄———————(6)
  |  Rows Can Overflow to Temporary Table
```

```
Subsection #2:
   Access Table Name = DB2INST1.ORDERS   ID = 9
   |  #Columns = 1
   |  Index Scan:  Name = DB2INST1.O_CLERK   ID = 2
   |  |  #Key Columns = 1                ◄────────── ②
   |  |  Index-Only Access
   |  |  Index Prefetch: None
   |  |  |  Insert Into Sorted Temp Table  ID = t1
   |  |  |  |  #Columns = 1
   |  |  |  |  #Sort Key Columns = 1
   |  |  |  |  Sortheap Allocation Parameters:
   |  |  |  |  |  #Rows      = 474
   |  |  |  |  |  Row Width = 12
   |  |  |  |  Piped
   |  Isolation Level: Uncommitted Read
   |  Lock Intents
   |  |  Table: Intent None
   |  |  Row  : None
   Sorted Temp Table Completion  ID = t1
   List Prefetch RID Preparation
   Access Table Name = DB2INST1.ORDERS   ID = 9
   |  #Columns = 3
   |  Fetch Direct
   |  Lock Intents
   |  |  Table: Intent Share
   |  |  Row  : Next Key Share
   |  Residual Predicate(s)
   |  |  #Predicates = 1
   Insert Into Sorted Temp Table  ID = t2
   |  #Columns = 3
   |  #Sort Key Columns = 1
   |  Sortheap Allocation Parameters:
   |  |  #Rows      = 474
   |  |  Row Width = 32
   |  Piped
   Access Temp Table  ID = t2
   |  #Columns = 3
   |  Relation Scan                      ◄────────── ③
   |  |  Prefetch: Eligible
   Insert Into Asynchronous Table Queue   ID = q2
   |  Hash to Specific Node              ◄────────── ④
   |  Rows Can Overflow to Temporary Tables

End of section
```

The following is the Explain output generated after the ORDERS table was
reorganized on the DB2INST1.O_CLERK index. The actions that the
optimizer has chosen in this example are the same as in the previous Explain
with the exception of the estimated cost of 1722 and the estimated cardinality

of 926. Please refer to the discussion of the previous Explain for the corresponding details.

```
SQL Statement:

  select c_name, c_phone, o_totalprice, o_clerk
  from orders, customer
  where o_custkey = c_custkey and o_clerk = 'Diane '

Buffered Insert          = No

Estimated Cost      = 1722
Estimated Cardinality = 926                          (1)

Coordinator Subsection:
   Distribute Subsection #2
   |  Broadcast to Node List
   |  |  Nodes = 1, 2
   Distribute Subsection #1
   |  Broadcast to Node List
   |  |  Nodes = 1, 2
   Access Table Queue  ID = q1  #Columns = 4
   Return Data to Application
   |  #Columns = 4

Subsection #1:
   Access Table Queue  ID = q2  #Columns = 3
   |  Output Sorted #Key Columns = 1
   Nested Loop Join
   |  Access Table Name = DB2INST1.CUSTOMER  ID = 8      (5)
   |  |  #Columns = 3
   |  |  Single Record
   |  |  Index Scan:  Name = DB2INST1.PK_C_CUSTKEY  ID = 1
   |  |  |  #Key Columns = 1
   |  |  |  Data Prefetch: Eligible
   |  |  |  Index Prefetch: Eligible
   |  |  Lock Intents
   |  |  |  Table: Intent Share
   |  |  |  Row  : Next Key Share
   Insert Into Asynchronous Table Queue  ID = q1       (6)
   |  Broadcast to Coordinator Node
   |  Rows Can Overflow to Temporary Table
```

```
Subsection #2:
  Access Table Name = DB2INST1.ORDERS  ID = 3
  |  #Columns = 2
  |  Index Scan:  Name = DB2INST1.OCLERK  ID = 3    ◄───②
  |  |  #Key Columns = 1
  |  |  Index-Only Access
  |  |  Index Prefetch: None
  |  |  |  Insert Into Sorted Temp Table  ID = t1
  |  |  |  |  #Columns = 1
  |  |  |  |  #Sort Key Columns = 1
  |  |  |  |  Sortheap Allocation Parameters:
  |  |  |  |  |  #Rows     = 463
  |  |  |  |  |  Row Width = 12
  |  |  |  |  Piped
  |  Isolation Level: Uncommitted Read
  |  Lock Intents
  |  |  Table: Intent None
  |  |  Row  : None
  Sorted Temp Table Completion  ID = t1
  List Prefetch RID Preparation
  Access Table Name = DB2INST1.ORDERS  ID = 3
  |  #Columns = 3
  |  Fetch Direct
  |  Lock Intents
  |  |  Table: Intent Share
  |  |  Row  : Next Key Share
  |  Residual Predicate(s)
  |  |  #Predicates = 1
  Insert Into Sorted Temp Table  ID = t2
  |  #Columns = 3
  |  #Sort Key Columns = 1
  |  Sortheap Allocation Parameters:
  |  |  #Rows     = 463
  |  |  Row Width = 32
  |  Piped
  Access Temp Table  ID = t2
  |  #Columns = 3
  |  Relation Scan                  ◄───③
  |  |  Prefetch: Eligible
  Insert Into Asynchronous Table Queue  ID = q2
  |  Hash to Specific Node
  |  Rows Can Overflow to Temporary Tables  ◄───④

End of section
```

6.3.2.4 Improving Performance by Changing the Partitioning Key

As mentioned earlier, the partitioning key can significantly impact database performance. The optimal situation is for your larger tables to be collocated if at all possible. For details on the requirements of table collocation, see "Collocated Table Joins" on page 356.

If a partitioning key is not specified, DB2 uses the first column as the partitioning key (as long as the first column is not a long or large object data type). To determine the partitioning key for a table in your database, you may execute the following SQL statement substituting your table name for 'ORDERS'.

```
Select tabname,
       colname,
       colno,
       partkeyseq

From syscat.columns

Where tabname = 'ORDERS'
  and partkeyseq <> 0

Order by partkeyseq, colno
```

The results of the request are as follows. The `partkeyseq` contains the numerical position within the table's partitioning key. When the value of `partkeyseq` is 0, or null, the column is not a part of the partitioning key. As we can see in the output below, O_CUSTKEY is the partitioning key for the ORDERS table.

```
TABNAME                 COLNAME                 COLNO    PARTKEYSEQ
------------------- ------------------- ------ ----------
ORDERS                  O_CUSTKEY                 0            1

  1 record(s) selected.
```

ORDERS and LINEITEM are the largest tables in our TPCD100 database. We would like LINEITEM and ORDERS to be collocated. Let's check the partitioning key of LINEITEM. As you can see below, the partitioning key for LINEITEM is L_ORDERKEY.

```
TABNAME                COLNAME              COLNO  PARTKEYSEQ
------------------     --------------------  ------- ----------
LINEITEM               L_ORDERKEY               0         1

  1 record(s) selected.
```

The tables are not partitioned on the same key, ORDERKEY; so the two tables are not collocated. But both tables contain the same column, ORDERKEY and both ORDERKEY columns are partition compatible. Let's check to see if the tables are even in the same tablespace.

To check to be certain that the two tables are in the exist in the same nodegroup, execute the following SQL statement:

```
Select  tabname,
        tbspace,
        a.pmap_id,
        rebalance_pmap_id,
        ngname

from    SYSCAT.TABLES a,
        SYSCAT.NODEGROUPS b

where   a.pmap_id = b.pmap_id
   and  tabname in ('LINEITEM', 'ORDERS') ;
```

After executing this SQL statement, we can see the ORDERS table is in the WTEMP1 table space and LINEITEM is in USERSPACE1. The USERSPACE1 tablespace is in the IBMDEFAULTGROUP node group and the WTEMP1 table space is in the WGROUP node group. Even if the two tables were partitioned on the same column, ORDERKEY, they could not be collocated because they are in different node groups.

```
TABNAME        TBSPACE        PMAP_ID  REBALANCE_PMAP_ID  NGNAME
-------------  -------------  -------  -----------------  ----------------
LINEITEM       USERSPACE1         1                   -1  IBMDEFAULTGROUP

ORDERS         WTEMP1             6                   -1  WGROUP

 2 record(s) selected.
```

Since the two tables the tables were not partitioned on the same column, we will want to drop one of the tables and re-create it in the same nodegroup as the other table. The ORDERS table was chosen because it was smaller than LINEITEM. We could have chosen to repartition LINEITEM, but the possibility of data skew is higher if we repartition LINEITEM on CUSTKEY. There are an average of four rows in LINEITEM for each order. There are an average of 40 rows in LINEITEM for each customer. If a small number of customers place the largest and/or most frequent orders, then the distribution of the data across nodes may be more likely to skew than if we use the ORDERKEY column as the partitioning key.

We want to partition ORDERS on ORDERKEY instead of CUSTKEY so that we can collocate the ORDERS table and the LINEITEM table. The following DDL can be executed to partition the ORDERS table on O_ORDERKEY and to place the ORDERS table in the same tablespace (USERSPACE1), and therefore in the same nodegroup as LINEITEM. While it is not necessary to specify the partitioning key if it is the first column, it is a good practice to always explicitly state the partitioning key. Always make certain that the tables you are attempting to collocate are created in the same nodegroup.

```
CREATE TABLE ORDERS        ( O_ORDERKEY       INTEGER NOT NULL,
                             O_CUSTKEY        INTEGER NOT NULL,
                             O_ORDERSTATUS    CHAR(1) NOT NULL,
                             O_TOTALPRICE     FLOAT NOT NULL,
                             O_ORDERDATE      DATE NOT NULL,
                             O_ORDERPRIORITY  CHAR(15) NOT NULL,
                             O_CLERK          CHAR(15) NOT NULL,
                             O_SHIPPRIORITY   INTEGER NOT NULL,
                           O_COMMENT        VARCHAR(79) NOT NULL)
          Partitioning key (O_ORDERKEY))
          in USERSPACE1 ;
```

Now, let's look at the difference in the Explain's generated when the ORDERS and LINEITEM tables are not collocated and when they are collocated. The following table contains a comparison of two executions of the same query against the LINEITEM and ORDERS tables.

Table 12. Query Execution - Collocated and non-Collocated Tables

	Different Partitioning Key	Same Partitioning Key	Difference
Estimated Cost	63215	59760	3455
Estimated Cardinality	8882	6409	2473

	Different Partitioning Key	Same Partitioning Key	Difference
Actual Runtime	74.80	69.17	5.63
Actual Rows Returned	19,886	19,886	0
Access Methods	Broadcast Outer	Collocated Join	Reduced data movement between partitions

For the first execution of the query, ORDERS and LINEITEM are not collocated. ORDERS partitioning key is different from the partitioning key of LINEITEM as noted earlier. ORDERS and LINEITEM are not defined to the same nodegroup.

1. The estimated cost is 63215 and the estimated cardinality is 8882.

2. The Coordinator Subsection lists two separate subsections that must be executed before the data may be returned to the requesting application. Since there are only two tables referenced in this query, this tells us immediately that this query is not using table collocation. If it was using table collocation, then there would only be one subsection that would have to be executed before the results could be returned to the requesting application.

3. First, the LINEITEM table is accessed via the LSHIPQUAN index and index only access is being used to resolve the first of the shipmode predicates. The LSHIPQUAN index is accessed again to resolve the other of the shipmode predicates. Index ORing is used to resolve predicates further.

4. The output from this section is placed in a table queue and broadcast to the appropriate nodes. We know immediately from this that the join strategy being used is either a broadcast outer or a broadcast inner join.

5. The broadcast table queue is accessed and nested loop joined to the ORDERS table using the O_ORDERKEY index.

6. The results of the nested loop join are broadcast to the coordinator node and returned to the requesting application.

```
SQL Statement:

  select o_orderdate, o_clerk, o_totalprice, l_shipdate
  from orders, lineitem
  where o_orderkey = l_orderkey and l_shipmode in ('TRUCK',
'AIR')
          and year(l_shipdate) in 1998

Buffered Insert          = No

Estimated Cost         = 63215
Estimated Cardinality = 8882                    ◀————————( 1 )

Coordinator Subsection:
  Distribute Subsection #2
  |  Broadcast to Node List
  |  |  Nodes = 1, 2
  Distribute Subsection #1
  |  Broadcast to Node List                     ◀————————( 2 )
  |  |  Nodes = 1, 2
  Access Table Queue  ID = q1  #Columns = 4
  Return Data to Application
  |  #Columns = 4

Subsection #1:
  Access Table Queue  ID = q2  #Columns = 2
  |  Output Sorted #Key Columns = 1
  Nested Loop Join
  |  Access Table Name = DB2INST1.ORDERS ID = 2 ◀————————( 5 )
  |  |  #Columns = 4
  |  |  Index Scan:  Name = DB2INST1.O2_ORDERKEY  ID = 2
  |  |  |  #Key Columns = 1
  |  |  |  Data Prefetch: Eligible
  |  |  |  Index Prefetch: Eligible
  |  |  Lock Intents
  |  |  |  Table: Intent Share
  |  |  |  Row  : Next Key Share
  Insert Into Asynchronous Table Queue  ID = q1
  |  Broadcast to Coordinator Node             ◀————————( 6 )
  |  Rows Can Overflow to Temporary Table
```

```
Subsection #2:
   Access Table Name = DB2INST1.LINEITEM  ID = 2
   |  #Columns = 2
   |  Index Scan:  Name = DB2INST1.LSHIPQUAN  ID = 1
   |  |  #Key Columns = 1
   |  |  Index-Only Access
   |  |  Index Prefetch: Eligible
   |  |  |  Insert Into Sorted Temp Table  ID = t1
   |  |  |  |  #Columns = 1
   |  |  |  |  #Sort Key Columns = 1
   |  |  |  |  Sortheap Allocation Parameters:
   |  |  |  |  |  #Rows      = 86307
   |  |  |  |  |  Row Width = 12
   |  |  |  |  Piped
   |  |  |  |  Duplicate Elimination
   |  Isolation Level: Uncommitted Read
   |  Lock Intents
   |  |  Table: Intent None
   |  |  Row  : None
   Sorted Temp Table Completion  ID = t1
   Access Table Name = DB2INST1.LINEITEM  ID = 2
   |  #Columns = 2
   |  Index Scan:  Name = DB2INST1.LSHIPQUAN  ID = 1
   |  |  #Key Columns = 1
   |  |  Index-Only Access
   |  |  Index Prefetch: Eligible
   |  |  |  Insert Into Sorted Temp Table  ID = t1
   |  |  |  |  #Columns = 1
   |  Isolation Level: Uncommitted Read
   |  Lock Intents
   |  |  Table: Intent None
   |  |  Row  : None
   Sorted Temp Table Completion  ID = t1
   Index ORing RID Preparation
   |  Prefetch: Enabled
   Access Table Name = DB2INST1.LINEITEM  ID = 2
   |  #Columns = 3
   |  Fetch Direct
   |  Lock Intents
   |  |  Table: Intent Share
   |  |  Row  : Next Key Share
|  |  #Predicates = 2
   Insert Into Sorted Temp Table  ID = t2
   |  #Columns = 2
   |  #Sort Key Columns = 1
   |  Sortheap Allocation Parameters:
   |  |  #Rows      = 3205
   |  |  Row Width = 12
   |  Piped
   Access Temp Table  ID = t2
   |  #Columns = 2
   |  Relation Scan
   |  |  Prefetch: Eligible
Insert Into Asynchronous Table Queue  ID = q2
   |  Broadcast to All Nodes of Subsection 1
   |  Rows Can Overflow to Temporary Table
End of section
```

After dropping the ORDERS table, re-creating it with a partitioning key of O_ORDERKEY in the USERSPACE1 tablespace, and running `RUNSTATS`, the following Explain was generated. Now the tables are collocated. There is no longer any need for the broadcast of the LINEITEM results to other partitions, the results may be joined to ORDERS locally, eliminating the need to move data unnecessarily across the network.

1. The estimated cost of this query has dropped to 59760 which is 3455 less than before. The estimated cardinality has dropped to 6409 which is 2473 less than in the non-collocated join. While these do not appear to be large reductions, the size of the result set and the number of columns being returned is relatively small. You should expect to see greater improvements in a larger database.

2. There is only one subsection that must be executed to obtain the results requested. Since we know that two separate tables are involved in this request, we know immediately that the optimizer was able to use a collocated join strategy to resolve this request.

3. First the LINEITEM table is accessed via the LSHIPQUAN index and index only access is being used to resolve the first of the shipmode predicates. The LSHIPQUAN index is accessed again to resolve the other of the shipmode predicates. Index ORing is used to resolve predicates further. The LINEITEM rows selected are placed in a sorted table.

4. The sorted temp table is accessed and nested loop joined to the ORDERS table using the O_ORDERKEY index.

5. The results of the nested loop join are broadcast to the coordinator node and returned to the requesting application.

Essentially, the optimizer chose the same access paths for each of the tables involved in the request without having to broadcast the intermediate LINEITEM results between nodes.

```
SQL Statement:

  select o_orderdate, o_clerk, o_totalprice, l_shipdate
  from orders, lineitem
  where o_orderkey = l_orderkey and l_shipmode in ('TRUCK', 'AIR')
        and year(l_shipdate) in 1998

Buffered Insert            = No

Estimated Cost        = 59760
Estimated Cardinality = 6409              ◀━━━━ ( 1 )

Coordinator Subsection:
  Distribute Subsection #1
  |  Broadcast to Node List
  |  |  Nodes = 1, 2
  Access Table Queue  ID = q1  #Columns = 4
  Return Data to Application
  |  #Columns = 4

Subsection #1:
  Access Table Name = DB2INST1.LINEITEM  ID = 2
  |  #Columns = 2
  |  Index Scan:  Name = DB2INST1.LSHIPQUAN  ID = 1   ◀━━━ ( 2 )
  |  |  #Key Columns = 1
  |  |  Index-Only Access
  |  |  Index Prefetch: Eligible
  |  |  |  Insert Into Sorted Temp Table  ID = t1   ◀━━━ ( 3 )
  |  |  |  |  #Columns = 1
  |  |  |  |  #Sort Key Columns = 1
  |  |  |  |  Sortheap Allocation Parameters:
  |  |  |  |  |  #Rows      = 86307
  |  |  |  |  |  Row Width = 12
  |  |  |  |  Piped
  |  |  |  |  Duplicate Elimination
  |  Isolation Level: Uncommitted Read
  |  Lock Intents
  |  |  Table: Intent None
  |  |  Row  : None
  Sorted Temp Table Completion  ID = t1
  Access Table Name = DB2INST1.LINEITEM  ID = 2
  |  #Columns = 2
  |  Index Scan:  Name = DB2INST1.LSHIPQUAN  ID = 1
  |  |  #Key Columns = 1
  |  |  Index-Only Access
  |  |  Index Prefetch: Eligible
  |  |  |  Insert Into Sorted Temp Table  ID = t1
  |  |  |  |  #Columns = 1
  |  Isolation Level: Uncommitted Read
  |  Lock Intents
  |  |  Table: Intent None
  |  |  Row  : None
  Sorted Temp Table Completion  ID = t1
  Index ORing RID Preparation
  |  Prefetch: Enabled
```

```
Access Table Name = DB2INST1.LINEITEM  ID = 2
 |  #Columns = 3
 |  Fetch Direct
 |  Lock Intents
 |  |  Table: Intent Share
 |  |  Row  : Next Key Share
 |  Residual Predicate(s)
 |  |  #Predicates = 2
Insert Into Sorted Temp Table  ID = t2
 |  #Columns = 2
 |  #Sort Key Columns = 1
 |  Sortheap Allocation Parameters:
 |  |  #Rows     = 3205
 |  |  Row Width = 12
 |  Piped
Access Temp Table  ID = t2
 |  #Columns = 2
 |  Relation Scan
 |  |  Prefetch: Eligible
Nested Loop Join
 |  Access Table Name = DB2INST1.ORDERS  ID = 9  ◄─────── ④
 |  |  #Columns = 4
 |  |  Single Record
 |  |  Index Scan:  Name = DB2INST1.O_ORDERKEY  ID = 1
 |  |  |  #Key Columns = 1
 |  |  |  Data Prefetch: Eligible
 |  |  |  Index Prefetch: Eligible
 |  |  Lock Intents
 |  |  |  Table: Intent Share
 |  |  |  Row  : Next Key Share
Insert Into Asynchronous Table Queue  ID = q1
 |  Broadcast to Coordinator Node
 |  Rows Can Overflow to Temporary Table  ◄─────── ⑤

End of section
```

Please note that you should not drop and re-create tables if the
REDISTRIBUTE NODEGROUP utility is executing or after, if **REDISTRIBUTE
NODEGROUP** utility has failed and not been corrected. If the
REBALANCE_PMAP_ID is -1, then a redistribution is not in process. If a
redistribution is in process or has failed, the REBALANCE_PMAP_ID will be a
positive integer.

The following SQL statement will provide the information as to whether or not
a redistribute is in process:

```
select tbspace,
       pmap_id,
       a.ngname,
       rebalance_PMAP_ID

from syscat.tablespaces a,
     syscat.nodegroups b

where a.ngname = b.ngname.
```

The output from this command on the TPCD100 database is as follows:

TBSPACE	PMAP_ID	NGNAME	REBALANCE_PMAP_ID
SYSCATSPACE	0	IBMCATGROUP	-1
USERSPACE1	1	IBMDEFAULTGROUP	-1
TEMPSPACE1	2	IBMTEMPGROUP	-1
WTEMP1	6	WGROUP	8

If you create a table in the tablespace that is being redistributed, the PMAP_ID assigned will be the PMAP_ID associated with the redistribution. As the redistribution completes for each table, that table's PMAP_ID will be changed to the PMAP_ID for the redistribution. In the example below, the SUPP table has already been changed to the new PMAP_ID of 8. ORDERS2 is still assigned to the old PMAP_ID of 6.

TABNAME	TBSPACE	PMAP_ID	REBALANCE_PMAP_ID	NGNAME
LINEITEM	USERSPACE1	1	-1	IBMDEFAULTGROUP
ORDERS	USERSPACE1	1	-1	IBMDEFAULTGROUP
SUPP	WTEMP1	8	8	WGROUP
AVG_QUANTITY	USERSPACE1	1	-1	IBMDEFAULTGROUP
CUSTOMER	USERSPACE1	1	-1	IBMDEFAULTGROUP
PARTSUPP	USERSPACE1	1	-1	IBMDEFAULTGROUP
SUPPLIER	USERSPACE1	1	-1	IBMDEFAULTGROUP
PART	USERSPACE1	1	-1	IBMDEFAULTGROUP
REGION	USERSPACE1	1	-1	IBMDEFAULTGROUP
NATION	USERSPACE1	1	-1	IBMDEFAULTGROUP
ORDERS2	WTEMP1	6	8	WGROUP

If the redistribute of the IBMDEFAULTGROUP fails and you try to create a new table in that nodegroup without specifying the USERSPACE1 as the tablespace, the table will be placed in the next user tablespace available, not the USERSPACE1 tablespace. This can thwart your efforts to collocate tables and is quite confusing until you wade through all of the details in the database catalogs.

6.3.2.5 Sort Heap Allocation Parameters

The sort heap is where data is sorted. The `sortheap` parameter is set in the database configuration for each database. To determine the amount of sort heap available per sort for your database, issue the following command, replacing TPCD100 with the name of your database.

```
db2 get db cfg for TPCD100 > TPCD100.CFG
```

A portion of the TPCD100 database configuration follows. As you can see, the `sortheap` size is specified in 4 KB blocks. In the case of the TPCD100 database used for this example, the sort heap available is 256 4KB blocks or 1 megabyte per sort.

If the optimizer determines that your sort requires less memory than the amount specified in the `sortheap` parameter, a smaller sort heap will be allocated at sort time.

The value set in the following example is the default setting for `sortheap`. It is probably significantly smaller than what you would like to run in your production environment, especially if you are supporting a large OLAP or data warehousing environment.

```
          Database Configuration for Database tpcd100

......

 Sort list heap (4KB)                             (SORTHEAP) = 256

......
```

The sort heap is used by the optimizer to store sorted output in memory. When the optimizer evaluates a query and determines how it will obtain the data requested, the optimizer develops a sort estimate. The sort estimate includes the number of rows that the optimizer expects to return and the row size. From the row count and the row size, the estimated amount of sort space may be allocated when the request is executed.

The type of sort chosen, piped or non-piped, is effected by the amount of sort heap space available to the database. If the optimizer estimates that the amount of space required to perform the sort exceeds the sort heap value, the optimizer will not pipe the sort, but instead it will write the sorted data to a temporary table. If the optimizer determines there is enough sort heap for the sort to be held in memory, then the optimizer will choose to pipe the sort and retain the sorted data in memory.

Piping is quicker than using non-piped means of communicating the results of the sort. The optimizer chooses to pipe the results of a sort whenever possible.

Independent of whether a sort is piped, the time to sort will depend on a number of factors, including the number of rows to be sorted, the key size and the row width. If the rows to be sorted occupy more than the space available in the sort heap, several sort passes are performed, where each pass sorts a subset of the entire set of rows. Each sort pass is stored in a temporary table in the buffer pool. (As part of the buffer pool management, it is possible that pages from this temporary table may be written to disk.) Once all the sort passes are complete, these sorted subsets must be merged into a single sorted set of rows. If the sort is piped, as the rows are merged, they are handed directly to Relational Data Services.

Sort heaps are allocated at sort time and are freed when sorting is complete. There is a threshold for the amount of sortheap that may be used, and it is set in the database manager configuration in the `sheapthres` parameter. To determine the sort heap threshold for your database manager, issue the following command from one of the database partitions in your configuration.

```
db2 get dbm cfg > databasemgr.cfg
```

The `sheapthres` level prevents the database manager from consuming an inordinate amount of memory for large numbers of sorts.

The following is a portion of the database manager configuration for the TPCD100 database that we have been using for our examples. In this example, the sortheap threshold is 20,000 4KB pages. Our sortheap is defined as 256 4KB pages. If we divide the sortheap threshold value by the sortheap value, you can get 78 full sort heaps allocated before exceeding the threshold depending on the type of sort; shared or private.

```
                    Database Manager Configuration
....
Sort heap threshold (4KB)                    (SHEAPTHRES) = 20000
....
```

Shared sorts are those sorts that result from intra-query parallelism. Shared sorts may be thought of as SMP types of sorts where the memory must be distributed across multiple subagents all sorting simultaneously. Private sorts occur when a single agent within a partition is performing the sort.

With shared sorts, the sort heap threshold is the maximum sort space available within a database partition. The amount of shared memory available is allocated at database start-up based on the value in the **sheapthres** parameter. With each sort heap allocated from the shared sort memory pool, the amount available for subsequent allocations is decreased as long as the subagents retain the sort heap. When the sort heap allocation in shared memory is freed, the memory is returned to the shared sort memory pool.

With private sorts, the threshold is not a hard limit on the amount of memory sort space available. Instead, the sort heap threshold is more of a trigger point for private sorts that causes the database manager to reduce the size of the sort heap allocated for subsequent sort requests.

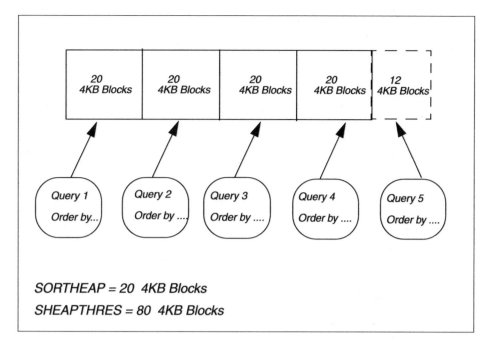

Figure 161. Private Sorts

The following explain contains several piped sort heap allocation statements. We can determine how much sort heap will be allocated for this query by multiplying the number of rows by the bytes per row to obtain the number of bytes of sortheap space that must be allocated to perform the sort in memory. The sortheap space is allocated as needed and freed upon completion of the sort.

1. The first sortheap allocation is for 486 rows with a row width of 12. DB2 will allocate 486 rows x 12 bytes/row = 5832 bytes. This is less than 1 megabyte, so we can pipe this sort. Note that the input to the sort is a temp table and the output is the same temp table; no new temp table was created to contain the piped sort output.

2. The second sortheap allocation is for 486 rows with a row width of 80. DB2 will allocate 486 rows x 80bytes/row = 38880 bytes. This is less than 1 megabyte; so we can pipe this sort. Note that the input to the sort is a temp table, and the output is the same temp table; no new temp table was created to contain the piped sort output.

3. The third sortheap allocation is for 1008 rows with a row width of 32. DB2 will allocate 1008 rows x 32 bytes/row = 32,256 bytes. This is less than 1 megabyte, so we can pipe this sort. Note that the input to the sort is a

temp table and the output is the same temp table; no new temp table was created to contain the piped sort output.

```
******************** PACKAGE
****************************************

Package Name = DB2INST1.DYNEXPLN
        Prep Date = 1998/02/04
        Prep Time = 10:37:40:045

        Bind Timestamp = 1998-02-04-10.37.40.453263

        Isolation Level          = Cursor Stability
        Blocking                 = Block Unambiguous Cursors
        Query Optimization Class = 5

        Partition Parallel       = Yes
        Intra-Partition Parallel = No

        Function Path            = "SYSIBM", "SYSFUN", "DB2INST1"

-------------------- SECTION
----------------------------------------
Section = 1
SQL Statement:

  SELECT S_SUPPKEY, S_NAME, S_ADDRESS, S_PHONE, TOTAL_REVENUE
  FROM SUPPLIER, REVENUE
  WHERE S_SUPPKEY = SUPPLIER_NO AND TOTAL_REVENUE =
     (SELECT MAX(R1.TOTAL_REVENUE)
     FROM REVENUE R1)
Buffered Insert          = No

Estimated Cost        = 8593
Estimated Cardinality = 40

Coordinator Subsection:
   Distribute Subsection #4
   |  Broadcast to Node List
   |  |  Nodes = 1, 2
   Distribute Subsection #3
   |  Broadcast to Node List
   |  |  Nodes = 1, 2
   Distribute Subsection #2
   |  Broadcast to Node List
   |  |  Nodes = 1, 2
   Distribute Subsection #1
   |  Broadcast to Node List
   |  |  Nodes = 1, 2
   Access Table Queue  ID = q1  #Columns = 5
   Return Data to Application
   |  #Columns = 5
```

```
Subsection #1:
  Access Table Name = DB2INST1.SUPPLIER  ID = 6
  | #Columns = 1
  | Index Scan:  Name = DB2INST1.PK_S_SUPPKEY  ID = 1
  | | #Key Columns = 0
  | | Index-Only Access
  | | Index Prefetch: None
  | | | Insert Into Sorted Temp Table  ID = t1
  | | | | #Columns = 1
  | | | | #Sort Key Columns = 1
  | | | | Sortheap Allocation Parameters:
  | | | | | #Rows     = 488          ◄————————————⟨1⟩
  | | | | | Row Width = 12
  | | | | Piped
  | Isolation Level: Uncommitted Read
  | Lock Intents
  | | Table: Intent None
  | | Row  : None
  Sorted Temp Table Completion  ID = t1
  List Prefetch RID Preparation
  Access Table Name = DB2INST1.SUPPLIER  ID = 6
  | #Columns = 4
  | Fetch Direct
  | Lock Intents
  | | Table: Intent Share
  | | Row  : Next Key Share
  Insert Into Sorted Temp Table  ID = t2
  | #Columns = 4
  | #Sort Key Columns = 1
  | Sortheap Allocation Parameters:        ◄————————————⟨2⟩
  | | #Rows     = 488
  | | Row Width = 80
  | Piped
  Access Temp Table  ID = t2
  | #Columns = 4
  | Relation Scan
  | | Prefetch: Eligible
  Merge Join
  | Early Out: Single Match Per Outer Row
  | Access Table Queue  ID = q2  #Columns = 2
  | Final Aggregation
  | | Column Function(s)
  | Nested Loop Join
  | | Piped Inner
  | | Access Temp Table  ID = t3
  | | | #Columns = 2
  | | | Relation Scan
  | | | | Prefetch: Eligible
  | | Residual Predicate Application
  | | | #Predicates = 1
  Insert Into Asynchronous Table Queue  ID = q1
  | Broadcast to Coordinator Node
  | Rows Can Overflow to Temporary Table
```

```
Subsection #2:
  Access Temp Table  ID = t3
  |  #Columns = 1
  |  Relation Scan
  |  |  Prefetch: Eligible
  |  Sargable Predicate(s)
  |  |  #Predicates = 1
  |  Partial Predicate Aggregation
  |  |  Column Function(s)
  Partial Aggregation Completion
  |  Column Function(s)
  Insert Into Asynchronous Table Queue  ID = q2
  |  Broadcast to All Nodes of Subsection 1
  |  Rows Can Overflow to Temporary Table
Subsection #3:
  Access Table Queue  ID = q3  #Columns = 4
  |  Output Sorted #Key Columns = 1
  Final Aggregation
  |  Group By
  |  Column Function(s)
  Insert Into Temp Table  ID = t3
  |  #Columns = 2
Subsection #4:
  Access Table Name = DB2INST1.LINEITEM  ID = 2
  |  #Columns = 4
  |  Index Scan:  Name = DB2INST1.L_SD_EP_DS_SK_PK  ID = 5
  |  |  #Key Columns = 1
  |  |  Index-Only Access
  |  |  Index Prefetch: Eligible
  |  |  |  Insert Into Sorted Temp Table  ID = t4
  |  |  |  |  #Columns = 4
  |  |  |  |  #Sort Key Columns = 1
  |  |  |  |  Sortheap Allocation Parameters:
  |  |  |  |  |  #Rows     = 1008
  |  |  |  |  |  Row Width = 32   ◄──────────  ③
  |  |  |  |  Piped
  |  |  |  |  Partial Aggregation
  |  Lock Intents
  |  |  Table: Intent Share
  |  |  Row  : Next Key Share
  Sorted Temp Table Completion  ID = t4
  Access Temp Table  ID = t4
  |  #Columns = 4
  |  Relation Scan
  |  |  Prefetch: Eligible
  |  Intermediate Predicate Aggregation
  |  |  Group By
  |  |  Column Function(s)
  Intermediate Aggregation Completion
  |  Group By
  |  Column Function(s)
  Insert Into Asynchronous Table Queue  ID = q3
  |  Hash to Specific Node
  |  Rows Can Overflow to Temporary Tables
End of section
```

To determine if you have sorting problems in your environment, you should consult the Snapshot Monitor and Event Monitor from the Control Center. These performance monitors provide information on total sort time.

If you find that sorting is consuming a large portion of your processing time, then you should check the percentage of overflowed sorts. If this is high, then you need to increase the size of the sortheap database configuration parameter.

Post-threshold sorts should also be checked. If the number of post threshold sorts is high, increase the `sheapthres` value specified in the database manager configuration and/or decrease the `sortheap` value specified in the database configuration for your database.

If you find that you are consistently performing sorts on a specific set of columns, you should seriously consider creating indexes over those columns. This will help to minimize the use of the sort heap.

As your database grows, you should re-evaluate the sort heap size. You may find it necessary to increase the sort heap size to accommodate larger sorts.

If you increase the value of the `sortheap` parameter in the database configuration file, you must reevaluate the value of the sheapthres in the database manager configuration file. The `sheapthres` parameter will need to be increased in proportion to the growth of the `sortheap` parameter.

The sortheap value is used by the optimizer to determine access paths. You should consider rebinding applications (using the **REBIND PACKAGE** command) after changing the `sortheap` parameter.

If you add new partitions to your database or new physical nodes to your database, you will need to reevaluate both sort parameters for your environment. If all else fails, add more memory.

6.4 Database Monitoring

The Explain facility provides information to analyze how SQL statements are executed by DB2. However it does not provide detailed resource usage information. Explain tools do not provide runtime information regarding locking, connections, buffer pool usage, table space usage and memory usage.

DB2 Monitors are used to collect detailed resource usage information. Monitoring activity may be performed from a DB2 client or a DB2 server. The monitor interface can be invoked using CLP commands, graphical Performance Monitors or monitoring APIs. DB2 provides different kind of monitoring. They differ in the way monitoring data is gathered. The two ways of monitoring are:

- *Snapshot Monitoring* provides information regarding database activity for a specific point in time. It is a picture of the current state of DB2 activity. The amount of data returned to the user when a snapshot is taken is determined using monitor switches. These switches can be set at instance or application level.

- *Event monitoring* records the occurrence of specific milestones of DB2 events. This can allow you to collect information about transient events, including deadlocks, connections, and SQL statements.

6.4.1 Snapshot Monitoring

The *Snapshot Monitor* provides cumulative information in the form of counters. These counters can be reset using an API. The snapshot information is provided in special data structures that can be examined by the application issuing the snapshot.

The amount of data returned by the *Snapshot Monitor* is set according to switches. The monitor switches, along with the information they provide are shown in Table 13.

Table 13. Available Groups of Information for Taking Snapshots

Group	Information Provided	Monitor Switch	DBM Parameter
Sorts	Number of heaps used, overflows, sort performance	SORT	DFT_MON_SORT
Locks	Number of locks held, number of deadlocks	LOCK	DFT_MON_LOCK
Tables	Measure activity (rows read, rows written)	TABLE	DFT_MON_TABLE
Bufferpools	Number of reads and writes, time taken	BUFFERPOOL	DFT_MON_BUFPOOL
Unit of work	Start times, end times, completion status	UOW	DFT_MON_UOW
SQL Statements	Start time, stop time, statement identification	STATEMENT	DFT_MON_STMT

The monitor switches can be turned on and off at the instance (DBM configuration) level or at the application level (UPDATE MONITOR SWITCHES).

There is also base information provided by the Snapshot Monitor that is gathered regardless of the monitor switches settings.

Setting the instance configuration parameters for monitor switches will affect all databases within the instance. Every application connecting to a database will inherit the default switches set within the DBM configuration.

The DB2 Snapshot Monitors can only be used by users having SYSADM, SYSCTRL or SYSMAINT authority. Event Monitors require SYSADM or DBADM authority.

For example, let's say we want to capture detailed information about the SQL statements executing in DB2. To do this, the appropriate monitor switch must be turned on. You can use either of the following commands.

```
db2 update dbm configuration using DFT_MON_STMT ON
db2 update monitor switches using statement on
```

The **UPDATE DBM CONFIGURATION** command will modify the DBM configuration, and therefore SQL statement information will be captured for applications accessing all databases within the instance. On the other hand, the **UPDATE MONITOR SWITCHES** command will only capture SQL statements for the application that activated the switch (in this example the application is the command line processor).

Even if none of the switches are turned on, there will be some basic information captured by the Snapshot Monitor.

6.4.1.1 Viewing Snapshot Monitor Data

When a monitor switch is turned on, the monitor data starts being collected. To view the monitor data a snapshot must be taken. A snapshot is requested using the DB2 command **GET SNAPSHOT**. This command can be executed in different ways. It can be executed within the Command Center GUI tool, embedded in an application using the appropriate API, executed from the CLP, or executed by the Performance Monitor.

Note that snapshot is performed at the database partition level. There is a minor performance impact when the data is recorded.

There are different levels of monitoring used with the Snapshot Monitor. These levels allow you to focus your analysis in a particular area of interest.

The following snapshot monitor levels are available:

- Database Manager — captures information for an active instance
- Database — captures database(s) information
- Application — captures application(s) information
- Bufferpools —   captures buffer pool information
- Table Space — captures information for table spaces within a database
- Table — captures information for tables within a database
- Lock — captures information for locks held by applications in a database

Snapshot monitor switches and levels are combined to provide different monitoring information when taking a snapshot. The two are very closely related. If the proper monitor switch is not turned on, the snapshot level used may not return any data.

6.4.1.2 Reviewing the Snapshot Monitor Switch Status
At any time, you can determine the current settings of database monitor switches by issuing the following command:

```
GET MONITOR SWITCHES
```

The switch states are shown below. The timestamps correspond to the last time the switches were reset or turned on.

```
                 Monitor Recording Switches

Buffer Pool Activity Information  (BUFFERPOOL) = OFF
Lock Information                       (LOCK) = ON  03-14-1998 15:01:22.624422
Sorting Information                    (SORT) = OFF
SQL Statement Information         (STATEMENT) = ON  03-14-1998 15:01:27.155032
Table Activity Information            (TABLE) = ON  03-14-1998 15:01:09.482143
Unit of Work Information                (UOW) = ON  03-14-1997 15:01:15.340116
```

If you want to know the instance settings for the monitor switches, use the following command:

```
GET DBM MONITOR SWITCHES
```

6.4.1.3 Resetting the Snapshot Monitor Switches

As we have seen, the data returned by a Snapshot Monitor is mostly based on counters. These counters are associated with a monitor switch.

Monitor switches are initialized or reset when one of the following occurs:

- Application level monitoring is used and the application connects to the database.
- Database level monitoring is used and the first application connects
- Table level monitoring is used and the table is first accessed
- Table space level monitoring is used and the table space is first accessed
- Issuing the `RESET MONITOR` command
- Turning on a particular monitor switch

Monitor switches can be reset at any time by issuing the command:

```
RESET MONITOR FOR DATABASE tpcd100
```

Resetting the monitor switches effectively starts all of the counters at zero and further snapshots are based on the new counter values.

To reset the monitor switches for all databases within an instance the `RESET MONITOR ALL` command should be used.

Every application has its own copy of the snapshot monitor values. Resetting the monitor switches, only affects the counters of the application that issues the reset.

6.4.2 Event Monitoring

While Snapshot Monitoring records the state of database activity when the snapshot is taken, an Event Monitor records the database activity when an *event* or *transition* occurs. Some database activities that need to be monitored cannot be easily captured using the Snapshot Monitor. These activities include deadlock scenarios. When a deadlock occurs, DB2 will resolve the deadlock by issuing a `ROLLBACK` for one of the transactions. Information regarding the deadlock event cannot be easily captured using the Snapshot Monitor, since the deadlock has probably been resolved before a snapshot can be taken.

Event Monitors, like other database objects, are created using SQL DDL (Data Definition Language). Event Monitors can be turned on or off, much like the Snapshot Monitor switches. SYSADM or DBADM authority is required to create an Event Monitor.

When an Event Monitor is created, the type of event to be monitored must be stated. The Event Monitor can monitor the following events:

- DATABASE — records an event record when the last application disconnects from the database.

- TABLES — records an event record for each active table when the last application disconnects from the database.

- DEADLOCKS — records an event record for each deadlock event.

- TABLESPACES — records an event record for each active table space when the last application disconnects from the database.

- BUFFERPOOLS — records an event record for buffer pools when the last application disconnects from the database.

- CONNECTIONS — records an event record for each database connection event when an application disconnects from a database.

- STATEMENTS — records an event record for every SQL statement issued by an application (dynamic and static).

- TRANSACTIONS — records an event record for every transaction when it completes (COMMIT or ROLLBACK).

Event Monitors can also be created using the Control Center GUI Tool.

The output of an Event Monitor is stored in a directory or in a named pipe. The existence of the pipe or the file will be verified when the Event Monitor is activated. If the target location for an Event Monitor is a named pipe, then it is the responsibility of the application to read the data promptly from the pipe. If the target for an Event Monitor is a directory, then the stream of data will be written to a series of files. The files are sequentially numbered and have a file extension of evt (such as 00000000.evt, 00000001.evt, and so forth.). The maximum size and number of Event Monitor files is specified when the monitor is defined.

Note that an Event Monitor will turn itself off, if the defined file space has been exceeded.

6.4.2.1 Creating Event Monitors

As mentioned, Event Monitors are database objects created using SQL DDL statements. The Control Center GUI Tool can also be used to create event monitors. Let's create a deadlock Event Monitor that will store its event records in the '/eventmonitors/deadlock/evmon1' directory. The following SQL statement is used to create an Event Monitor. In our example, the Event Monitor is called *evmon1*.

The Event Monitor output directory will *not* be created by DB2. It must be created by the database administrator, and the instance owner must be able to write to the specified directory.

```
CREATE EVENT MONITOR evmon1 FOR DEADLOCKS
WRITE TO FILE '/eventmonitors/deadlock/evmon1' MAXFILES 3
MAXFILESIZE 1000
```

The above monitor is defined to allocate up to 3 files each 4 MB in size, for a total monitor storage area of 12 MB. Other Event Monitor options include specifying the size of the write buffer, synchronous (BLOCKED) writes, asynchronous (UNBLOCKED) writes, APPEND the Event Monitor data to existing records, or REPLACE the Event Monitor data in the directory when the monitor is activated.

Two system catalog tables are used to store Event Monitor definitions:

- SYSCAT.EVENTMONITOR

  Contains a record for each Event Monitor, including the current state of the Event Monitor.

- SYSCAT.EVENTS

  Contains a record for each event being monitored. A single Event Monitor can be defined to monitor multiple events (for example, DEADLOCKS and STATEMENTS).

Event Monitors can be defined to monitor many different types of database activities. A filter can also be specified for an Event Monitor. The filter can be based on the APPL_ID, AUTH_ID or APPL_NAME such as AUTH_ID = 'DB2INST1', APPL_NAME = 'PROGRAM1').

There is no limit in the number of defined Event Monitors, but 32 Event Monitors can be active per DB2 instance.

6.4.2.2 Starting and Stopping Event Monitors

An Event Monitor must be active in order to collect the monitoring data. Once the Event Monitor has been defined using the CREATE EVENT MONITOR statement, it must be activated. The following statement is used to activate an Event Monitor.

```
SET EVENT MONITOR evmon1 STATE = 1
```

When the Event Monitor has been activated, Event Monitor records are written to the files contained in the defined directory or pipe (such as /eventmonitors/deadlocks/evmon1 in our example).

An Event Monitor can be started automatically each time the database is started using the AUTOSTART option. This option is specified at creation time.

The Control Center GUI tool allows you to create and start an Event Monitor in the same operation.

To turn off an Event Monitor, the SET EVENT MONITOR STATE statement is used. Turning off an Event Monitor will also flush all of it contents to disk.

```
SET EVENT MONITOR evmon1 STATE = 0
```

Even when an Event Monitor has been turned off, it is still defined in the system catalog tables. However it is not recording monitor information.

To determine if an Event Monitor is active or inactive, use the SQL function EVENT_MON_STATE. The EVENT_MON_STATE function returns a value of 1 if the Event Monitor is active and 0 if the monitor is not active.

A sample SQL statement using the EVENT_MON_STATE SQL function to query the state of the evmon1 Event Monitor follows:

```
SELECT evmonname, EVENT_MON_STATE(evnomname)
FROM SYSCAT.EVENTMONITORS WHERE evmonname = 'EVMON1'
```

6.4.2.3 Removing an Event Monitor

Just like other database objects, Event Monitors can be dropped from the database. Removing the definition would remove the associated rows in the

SYSCAT.EVENTMONITORS and *SYSCAT.EVENTS* system catalog tables. An example of removing the *evmon1* Event Monitor is shown:

```
DROP EVENT MONITOR evmon1
```

6.4.2.4 Event Monitor Records

Event Monitor files cannot be analyzed directly. An application must be used. There are a few alternatives provided by DB2 for analyzing Event Monitor data that we will discuss, but let's first examine some of the Event Monitor records.

To ensure that all of the event records have been written to disk (some may be buffered), simply turn the Event Monitor off.

Event monitoring is similar to tracing since each event is recorded as it occurs and it is appended to the event record log files. An Event Monitor file will contain a number of event records. Table 14 shows all of the event record types and when they are used.

Table 14. Event Monitor Records.

Record Type	Collected for Event Type
Event Monitor Log Header	All
Event Monitor Start	All
Database Header	All
Database Event	Database
Table Space Event	Table Space
Table Event	Table
Connection Header	Connection
Connection Event	Connection
Connection Header	Transaction
Transaction (Unit of Work) Event	Transaction
Connection Header	Statement
Statement Event	Statement
Dynamic Statement Even	Statement

Record Type	Collected for Event Type
Connection Header	Deadlock
Deadlock Event	Deadlock
Deadlock Connection Even	Deadlock
Event Monitor Overflow	All (if any)

Some event records are created when any application disconnects from the database and others are only created when the *last* application disconnects from the database.

If an Event Monitor is monitoring database, table space, or table events, it will only write event records when the last application using the database disconnects. If database, table space, or table monitoring data is required before the last application disconnects, use the Snapshot Monitor.

6.4.2.5 Analyzing Event Monitor Output

There are two utilities available to analyze Event Monitor data:

- **db2evmon**, a text-based tool which will read the event records and generate a report.

- **db2eva**, a GUI tool that can be invoked from the Control Center interface.

Using an Event Monitor to capture deadlock information is just one of its uses. For example, you can monitor every SQL statement that is issued against a database or every SQL statement issued by a particular application.

6.4.3 Visual Performance Monitors

We have discussed the steps involved in obtaining Snapshot and Event Monitor data. DB2 provides graphical interfaces that allow you to analyze and gather monitoring data for the snapshot and Event Monitors. These tools are:

- *Event Analyzer* - allows you to analyze the Event Monitor files

- *Performance Monitor* - allows you to analyze and view graphical representations of the Snapshot Monitor.

6.4.3.1 Event Analyzer

The *Event Analyzer* is the graphical equivalent to the **db2evmon** tool that we reviewed in previous section.

The *Event Analyzer* displays the Event Monitor records that have been previously collected. To invoke the *Event Analyzer*, you can use the Control Center interface,

6.4.3.2 Performance Monitor

The *Performance Monitor* can be used to display snapshot information at predefined intervals (default interval is 20 seconds). It can be used to analyze the activity of a specific instance, database, table space, table or connection. The *Performance Monitor* is initiated from the Control Center interface.

Performance monitoring in DB2 UDB can be done using the defaults provided when DB2 is first installed, or can be customized to monitor only the parts of UDB which are of interest to you. The *Performance Monitor* is customized using *monitor profiles.* You can think of monitor profiles as separate "instances" of the *Performance Monitor.* For each profile you specify what part of the system you wish to monitor (such as database) and what activity you wish to monitor (such as buffer pool activity).

You can also set alarms in the *Performance Monitor* to trigger when certain characteristics drop below/rise above set values. You can then choose between different monitor profiles and activate the profile which you wish to use.

6.4.4 DB2 Governor

When monitoring DB2 UDB, you can detect where bottlenecks are occurring in the system, where certain types of database activity is occurring, and if DB2 is using all the server's resources to their full extent. You can also analyze the behavior of database applications to see if certain applications are more resource-intensive than others. However, if an application is resource-intensive, or is stopping other applications from obtaining resources, the DBA must first detect the application using monitoring techniques, and then change the behavior of the application, or explicitly force the application off the system. The *DB2 UDB Governor* is a server application that performs such checking automatically. The *Governor* can also force an application that is deemed to be using too much resources on the server.

The *Governor* collects statistics about applications running against a database. It then checks these statistics against rules you have specified for that database. Such rules might include:

- Increase the priority of application *X*, so that it always completes quickly.

- Slow down a subset of applications, namely *A,B* and *C*.

- Don't let any unit of work run for more than 15 minutes.

The *Governor* then enforces these rules by changing the priorities for the specified applications, or by forcing the application off the system. You start and stop the *DB2 Governor* in the same way you might start and stop monitoring DB2 UDB. For example, using a *Governor* configuration file (which contains the governor rules) called *mygov.cfg*, you can start the governor monitoring the TPCD100 database using the `db2gov` utility at the operating system command prompt:

```
db2gov start TPCD100 mygov.cfg gov.log
```

The filename that we specified, *gov.log,* is where the *DB2 Governor* will log any actions that it takes. To stop the *Governor* running against the TPCD100 database:

```
db2gov stop TPCD100
```

You can have multiple "instances" of the *DB2 Governor* running against multiple databases. The *DB2 Governor* does incur a performance impact when running against a DB2 database, since it collects statistics and monitors the activity of database applications at regular intervals. You can examine the logs generated by the *DB2 Governor* using the `db2govlg` tool.

6.5 Performance Issues

Monitoring database activity should be performed with a purpose in mind. The purpose of monitoring may be to achieve greater concurrency or to reduce the amount of disk access wait time. Another key purpose of monitoring database activity is to provide input for configuring various DB2 (instance) and database parameters to optimize memory utilization and improve performance.

Let's examine some of the key DBM and DB configuration parameters and how they relate to each other. Some of these parameters are used to determine the memory allocated for each DB2 instance, database, or application.

Database activity involves disk access (I/O) and memory access (CPU). Each of the DB2 configuration parameters affect either the memory or disk resources. Since disk access is much slower than memory access, the key database performance tuning objective is to decrease the amount of disk activity. If you are able to eliminate I/O wait time, the database requests are CPU bound and increasing performance would then require faster CPUs or multiple CPUs.

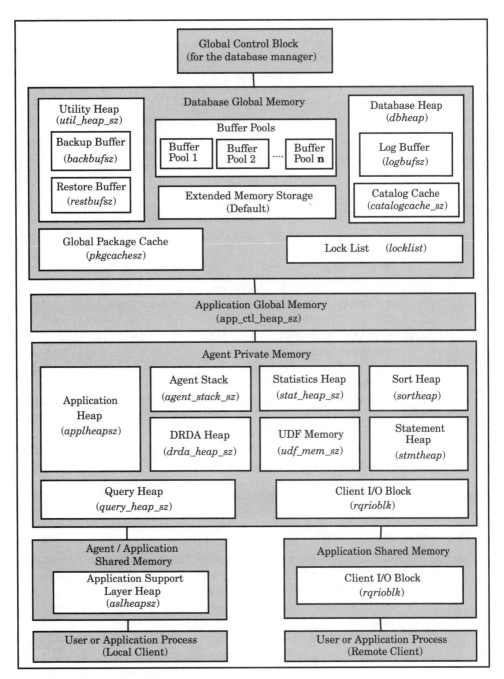

Figure 162. Memory Used by DB2 UDB EEE Database Manager

Figure 162 shows the relationship of the various configurable memory parameters. Memory is allocated on the server or the client. The number of memory segments allocated for the *database global memory* depends on the number of currently active databases.

Each DB2 application has an associated DB2 *coordinating agent*. The database agent accesses the database resources on behalf of the application. Therefore, there are tuning parameters to adjust resource usage of the database agent. The *agent private memory* exists for each application connected to the database and the size is determined by the agent private memory heap. The DBM parameter is called `APPLHEAPSZ`.

In symmetric multiprocessor (SMP) environments, partitioned database environments, and non-partitioned database environments in which the `intra_parallel` database manager configuration parameter is enabled, the coordinator agent distributes database requests to *subagents*, and these agents perform the requests for the application. Once the coordinator agent is created, it handles all database requests on behalf of its application by coordinating the subagents that perform requests on the database. The *application control heap* is used as a global work area for all the agents (coordinating and subordinate) working for the application. The database parameter is `APP_CTL_HEAP_SZ`.

The memory area known as *application shared memory* is used to determine the amount of memory used to communicate between the application and its DB2 coordinating agent. Record blocking occurs within this memory area. The DBM parameter is `ASLHEAPSZ`.

6.5.1 Configuring Database Resources

One of the *most* important factors affecting database performance is the size of each buffer pool in the database. When you create or alter buffer pools, you have to set the size of each one. If you set the size to -1, then the default size is used, which is specified by the `BUFFPAGE` parameter in the database configuration file. Each buffer pool is data *cached* between the applications and the physical database files. You can place your data in separate buffer pools by specifying a buffer pool for a particular table space. Also, it is possible for multiple table spaces to use one buffer pool.

If there were no buffer pools, then all database activity would result in disk access. If the size of each buffer pool is too small, the buffer pool hit ratio will be low and the applications will wait for disk access activity to satisfy SQL queries. If one or more buffer pools are too large, memory on the server may be wasted. If the total amount of space used by all buffer pools is larger than the physical memory available on the server, then operating system paging (disk activity) will occur. Accessing a buffer pool that has been paged out to disk is *very* inefficient.

If you create your own buffer pools, in addition to the default buffer pool IBMDEFAULTBP, you must be careful how you allocate space for each one. There is no point in allocating a large buffer pool to a table space containing a large number of small, rarely used tables and a small buffer pool to a table space containing a large, frequently accessed table. The size of buffer pools should reflect the size of tables in the table space, and how frequently they are updated or queried.

The DB2 optimizer will utilize different buffer pools to achieve the best query performance. There is a parameter that provides the optimizer with information regarding the average number of active applications (AVG_APPLS). This parameter is used by the optimizer to determine how much of each buffer pool may be used for each application.

Another memory block shared at the database level is called the *database heap* (DBHEAP). Most of the database-related resources are allocated out of the dbheap. There are many I/O caches that can be configured, including a log file cache (LOGBUFSZ) and a system catalog table cache (CATALOGCACHE_SZ).

The *log buffer* is used as a buffer for writing log records to disk. Every transaction involves writing multiple log records. To optimize disk write performance, the writes are buffered in memory and periodically flushed to disk.

The *catalog cache* is used to store the system catalog tables in memory. As an SQL statement is compiled or referenced, the database object information needs to be verified. If the information is in memory, then there is no need to perform disk activity to access the data.

Record blocking is a client/server caching technique used to send a group of records across the network to the client instead of a single record at a time. The decrease in network traffic increases application performance and allows for better network throughput.

The records are blocked by DB2 according to the cursor type and bind parameter. If the optimizer decides to return the query output in blocks, then the amount of data in each block is determined by the ASLHEAPSZ parameter.

If the DB2 client is configured with a different value for the RQRIOBLK parameter, the RQRIOBLK parameter is used as the record blocking size.

The *application heap* (`APPLHEAPSZ`) contains a number of memory blocks that are used by DB2 to handle requests for each application. The package cache (`PCKCACHESZ`) is allocated from this heap and is used to reduce the need to reload access plans (sections) of a package. This caching can improve performance when the same section is used multiple times within a program.

The access plans are cached for static and dynamic SQL statements in the *package cache.*

The sort heap (`SORTHEAP`) is allocated from the agent private memory and determines the number of private memory pages that can be used for each sort. This parameter is used by the optimizer to determine if the sorting can be performed in memory or on disk. DB2 will always attempt to perform the sort in memory. The `sheapthres` parameter is used to control the amount of memory that can be allocated for sort heaps in a DB2 server.

Let's modify one of the key performance parameters that affects the amount of memory used on the DB2 server as a data cache (database level). The default buffer pool size is updated.

```
UPDATE DB CONFIG FOR tpcd100 USING BUFFPAGE 5000
```

Allocating at least half of the physical memory on a machine to buffer pool space is usually a good starting point when adjusting the size of buffer pools. This assumes that every dedicated DB2 partitioned database server has the same configuration, and that only a single database active at any given time.

Any modification to the database configuration file will not be effective until all applications using the database are disconnected. The subsequent database connection will use the new database configuration parameters.

If you change the DBM (instance) configuration parameters, the new values will not be effective until the instance has been stopped and restarted.

Let's change the size of the memory used to perform record blocking. The memory area used for record blocking is known as the application support layer heap (`ASLHEAPSZ`). The following command would set the record blocking to be 200 KB in size (the units are 4 KB):

Therefore, when the instance is restarted, records will be sent across the network from the DB2 server to the application in 200 KB blocks (likely more than a single row). If the average row length were 1 KB, then 200 records would be returned in a single block of data (assuming more than 200 records are in the final result table). Record blocking occurs for remote and local DB2 client applications.

Any changes to the database manager configuration (instance) will not take effect until all of the applications have disconnected. The instance must then be stopped (DB2STOP command) and started using the DB2START command.

DB2 Universal Database also provides graphical tools that enable you to configure DB2 easily. The Performance SmartGuide is a tool that asks you to define what you want to use the database for, to define size requirements and certain country-specific information. Then, using your input as a guideline, the SmartGuide tunes certain parameters to better fit your needs in DB2.

6.5.1.1 FCM Requirements

In a DB2 UDB EEE database, most communication between database partitions is done by the Fast Communications Manager (FCM). We discussed in Chapter 2 how to configure the /etc/services file to enable the FCM at a database partition and allow communication with other database partitions.

There are a number of database manager configuration parameters that affect the performance of the FCM. As a general rule of thumb, start with the default values for each parameter and tune from there. The FCM database manager-level parameters are:

- FCM_NUM_BUFFERS - This parameter specifies the number of 4 KB buffers that are used for communication, including messages, between database partitions. If you have multiple database partitions defined on a SP node, you may find it necessary to increase the value of this parameter, if you find that you are running out of message buffers because of the number of users, the number of machines in your DB2 cluster, or the complexity of the applications.

  When using multiple database partitions, there is one pool of FCM_NUM_BUFFERS buffers that is shared by the database partitions on that SP node.

- **FCM_NUM_CONNECT** specifies the number of FCM connection entries. Agents use connection entries to pass data.

- **FCM_NUM_RQB** specifies the number of FCM request blocks. Request blocks are used to pass information between the FCM daemon and an agent or between agents. The size of this parameter will vary according to the number of users, the number of SP nodes, and the complexity of the queries.

Chapter 7. Problem Determination

This chapter discusses the methods and information available within DB2 to quickly and efficiently troubleshoot any problems which may occur. There are a number of different types of problems that may occur, and there are many different techniques you can use in dealing with these problems. In order to resolve any problems as quickly as possible, the ability to determine the cause of the problem is important.

This chapter will discuss the following topics:

- Introduction to problem determination
- What help is available online
- Diagnostic tools available within DB2
- Performing a trace in DB2

7.1 Introduction

In a complex client/server database system, it is important to determine the cause of any problem and to provide a solution to the problem as quickly as possible. In order to determine the cause of a problem, we first must understand what the problem really is.

One method that has been employed by a number of DB2 users is to maintain a log of any problems that they encounter. In this log, it is important to clearly describe the error condition, including **all SQL or system error codes** that occurred. A complete and thorough description of the problem is important to provide a starting point for the investigation.

7.1.1 Problem Description

The ability to accurately describe the error condition is illustrated by the following statements:

1. I cannot connect to the sample database.
2. I receive an SQL 1042 error message every time I attempt to connect to the sample database.

The second description provides much more detail than the first. It provides the SQL error code for the error, as well as an indication that the problem is reproducible.

7.1.2 Error Messages and SQL Codes

DB2 UDB has a number of error codes that explain the various conditions which can occur within the database system. This allows DB2 to report any problem that may occur within a database, or within any of the tools shipped with DB2 UDB. These messages are divided into categories, depending on where they are encountered. Each message includes an error code in which the three first letters of the error code indicate where the error occurs. The error prefixes include:

- **ASN**: DB2 UDB Replication Support messages
- **CCA**: Client Configuration Assistant messages
- **CLI:** ODBC/CLI Application messages
- **DBA:** Control Center or DBA Utility messages
- **DBI:** DB2 UDB Installation messages
- **DB2:** Command Line Processor or Command Center messages
- **SPM:** Syncpoint Manager messages
- **SQL:** SQL messages

When you receive an error message, you can look up the error message description in two different ways.

- Look up the error code in the *DB2 Messages Reference,* which details all of the error codes that may be returned by DB2
- Retrieve the error description using the Command Line Processor or Command Center.

To use the CLP, enter `db2 ? ABCXXXX`

where `ABC` is the error prefix and `XXXX` is the four digit error code. If the error code is only three digits, place a zero(0) before the error code. An example is the following:

```
db2 => ? sql0904

SQL0904N Unsuccessful execution caused by an unavailable
         resource.  Reason code: "<reason-code>", type of
         resource: "<resource-type>", and resource name:
         "<resource-name>".

Cause:  The SQL statement could not be executed because
resource "<resource-name>" of type "<resource-type>" was
not available at the time for the reason indicated by
"<reason-code>".  Refer to the Problem Determination
documentation of DB2 for MVS for an explanation of resource
type codes.

Action:  Verify the identity of the resource that was not
available.  To determine why the resource was unavailable,
refer to the specified "<reason-code>".

sqlcode:  -904

sqlstate:  57011
```

When retrieving the error information, the SQLSTATE will be included. The SQLSTATE is a standard indicator for the error condition that is the same across all DB2 products. For example, SQL0904 may have different meanings between DB2 UDB and DB2 for OS/390. However, the SQLSTATE 57011 has the same meaning for all DB2 platforms.

SQL codes can be positive, negative or zero.

1. **Negative codes** (in the form SQLxxxxN) indicate an error has occurred.

2. **Positive codes** (in the form SQLxxxxW) indicate a warning message.

3. A **zero SQL code** indicates the SQL completed successfully.

Some SQL codes also contain reason codes which further define the error condition. The reason codes provide more detailed information about the actual error condition and are very important in determining the source of the problem.

Note: For more detailed information about Problem Determination and reason codes, refer to *Diagnostic Tips and Techniques for DB2 Common Server.*

7.1.3 Diagnostic and Service Logs

DB2 UDB has built in FFDC (First Failure Data Capture) logging. In the event of an error, DB2 will write diagnostic information to the FFDC log file(s). These logs are written so that the database administrator can examine the logs to determine the cause of any problems that are encountered. The logs are written in an easy to understand manner and contain the information required to determine the source of the problem.

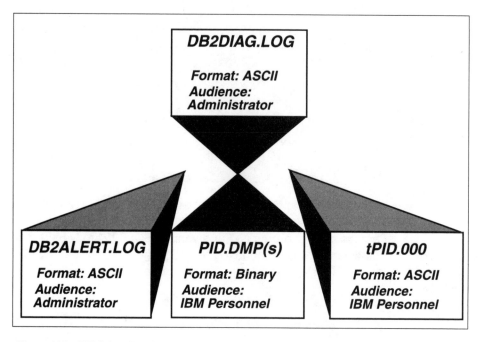

Figure 163. FFDC Log File Structure

The FFDC log files include:

- **db2diag.log:** This is the primary diagnostic log for DB2, and should be the first point of reference for the administrator whenever unexpected error conditions occur. The DIAGLEVEL instance configuration parameter determines the amount and type of information that will be logged.

- **db2alert.log:** If an error is determined by DB2 to be an alert, then an entry is made in the db2alert.log file as well as the operating system error logs. An alert is a severe system error.

- **Dump files (pid.dmp):** When a DB2 process or thread fails, it may log additional information in external binary dump files. These files are unreadable without knowing the format of the information. They are intended only for the DB2 UDB service team.

- **Trap files (tpid.000):** DB2 UDB will create a trap file if an operating system trap/segmentation violation/exception occurs within one of the DB2 processes or threads. It will also create a trap file in the event of deadlocks, lock timeouts, and so on to capture the information about the applications involved.

All of the above information is logged in the directory specified by the DIAGPATH configuration parameter for the instance. Since the SQLLIB directory is shared in a EEE system, all hosts will write to the same directory and by default, to the same db2diag.log file. In a large multi-node system, this can cause the file(s) to grow very large and make problem determination more difficult.

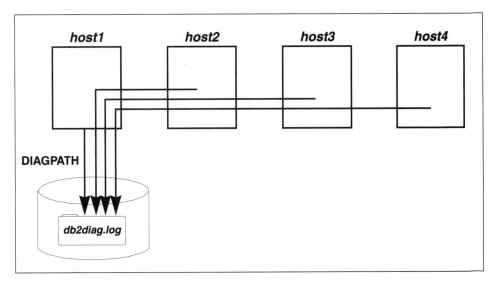

Figure 164. Writing to Same db2diag.log File

You can optionally specify a different DIAGPATH so that each database partition's diagnostic files will be written to a local file. (See "DB2DIAG.LOG in DB2 UDB EEE" on page 488 for more information.)

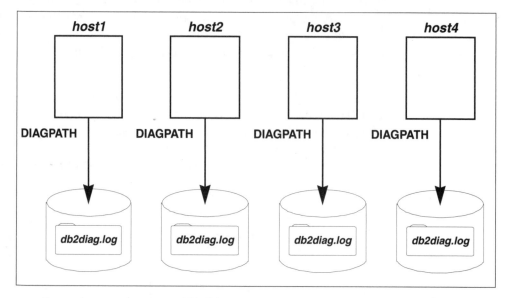

Figure 165. Writing to Local db2diag.log File

When an error is logged and the DIAGLEVEL is set at the proper level, the DB2DIAG.LOG file is updated with information about the error. If an error is determined to be an alert, then an entry will be made in the DB2ALERT.LOG file and in the operating system / native logging facilities:

UNIX: SYSLOG

INTEL: FFST/2

Easily understood structures like an SQLCA will be logged in the db2diag.log file. Extra information, including control blocks, will be logged in an external binary dump files.

The dump files and trap files should be examined by IBM service personnel as they contain binary information which requires knowledge of internal DB2 structures in order to be deciphered.

7.2 DB2 Error Log DB2DIAG.LOG

This section describes the most important diagnostic error log available, the DB2DIAG.LOG file. This file is updated by DB2 and should be the first place that you investigate when a problem has been detected. The DB2DIAG.LOG is a file containing error messages recorded by DB2 as the error is actually occurring. When errors occur within DB2, the component within the DB2 product which is receiving the error will attempt to log any and all information that will help a database administrator fix the problem.

This log is written in an easy-to-read format so that it can be used by database administrators to help them debug their own problems without having to call IBM Service. Its location is specified by the database manager configuration parameter DIAGPATH. If this parameter is null (default value) DB2DIAG.LOG and all the dump files will be created in the sqllib directory under $DB2INSTANCE. This path is specified in the DB2PATH environment variable.

Information is appended to the end of the file as errors or events occur. The DB2DIAG.LOG file will not be truncated. If it grows too large, you can erase the file and a new file will be created as needed.

7.2.1 Setting the DIAGLEVEL Configuration Parameter

You can control the amount of information and type of errors that are recorded in the DB2DIAG.LOG file by setting the database manager configuration parameter DIAGLEVEL to different values:

- 0 - NO diagnostic data captured
- 1 - SEVERE errors only
- 2 - SEVERE and NON-SEVERE errors
- 3 - SEVERE and NON-SEVERE errors, and WARNING messages (Default)
- 4 - SEVERE and NON-SEVERE errors, WARNING, and INFORMATION messages

The default setting for the DIAGLEVEL is 3. A DIAGLEVEL of 4 captures additional information which can be very helpful in debugging problems. Since a DIAGLEVEL of 4 also records informational messages, extra disk space will be used.

A DIAGLEVEL of 3 is sufficient most of the time. If you receive an error and the information provided is not detailed enough, increase DIAGLEVEL to 4 and re-create the problem. If the error is intermittently reported, set DIAGLEVEL to 4 until you are sure the error has been recorded. A DIAGLEVEL of 4 is recommended during the installation and setup of DB2 or during periods of repeated errors.

When investigating an error, you may find that it is helpful to extract only the data from the error situation to reduce the amount of data that is being reviewed. When doing this be careful not to delete any records from the file which are part of the error condition reporting. To ensure you always have the required information it is recommended that you copy the file before removing and records.

7.2.2 DB2DIAG.LOG File Entry Format

Let's look at an example of a DB2DIAG.LOG file to understand its format and the type of information recorded in the file. For our example, our DIAGLEVEL is set to 4. The database is called TPCD100; the SMS tablespace is USERSPACE1, and the table is called TWO.

We issued the commands:

```
db2 connect to TPDC100
db2 select * from TWO
```

This produces an error and the following entries are written to the DB2DIAG.LOG file. (NOTE: Only a portion of the file is shown.)

```
(1) 1998-02-09-15.11.34.869678 (2)Instance:db2inst1 (3)node:001
(4)PID: 24924(db2agntp (TPCD100) 1)
(5)Appid:*LOCAL.db2inst1.980209211108
(6)data_management (7)sqldloadTCB (8)Probe:7 (9)Database:TPCD100
(10)DIA3711C A file "" could not be found.

(11)ZRC=FFFFE60A
Dump file:/homedir/db2inst1/db2dump/24924.000 Data:SQLD_TCB
```

The information contained in every DB2DIAG.LOG entry includes:

1. The time and date that the error occurred.

2. The name of the instance encountering the condition. Here, it is db2inst1.

3. For DB2 Enterprise-Extended Edition systems, the node that generated the diagnostic message.

4. The process ID that generated the message. In this example, the message came from process ID 24924. The application name is db2agentp and it is connected to the database named TPCD100. The coordinator node is node 1 as identified in the db2nodes.cfg file.

5. Identification of the application for which the process is working. In this example, the process generating the messages is working on behalf of an

application running locally on the same machine as DB2 (From the LOCAL part of the application ID).

6. The internal DB2 component that is writing the message.

7. The name of the function that is providing the message. To determine more about the type of activity performed by the particular function, look at the fourth letter of its name. In this example, the letter "d" in the function "sqldloadTCB" indicates the function is part of data management services.

The following list shows the letters used in the function name, and the type of activity they identify

   b: Buffer Pool Services

   c: Client/Server Communications

   d: Data Management Services

   e: The DB2 Engine process

   o: Operating system calls (such as opening and closing files)

   p: Data Protection Services (such as locking and logging).

   r: Relational Database Services, such as optimization

   s: Sorting

   x: Indexing

8. Identification of the internal error that was reported.

9. The database on which the error occurred.

10. Diagnostic messages indicating in this example, that a file could not be found.

11. Hexadecimal representation of the return code. This return code may be an internal return code or an SQL code. To determine what the error code means first try to convert it to decimal. If it converts to decimal then verify whether or not it is a valid SQL Code. If it is a valid SQL code, examine the *DB2 Universal Database Troubleshooting Guide* to get a description of the error condition.

7.2.3 Dump Files

Dump files are created when an error occurs for which additional information, such as internal control blocks, may be required to diagnose the problem. When a dump file is created or appended to, information is also written to the DB2DIAG.LOG file indicating what information was written to the file and what file name was used. For DB2 Enterprise - Extended Edition, the file extension of the dump file identifies the node number which generated the dump file. The following is an example entry where DB2 writes to a dump file:

```
Dump file:/homedir/db2inst1/db2dump/24924.000 Data:SQLD_TCB
```

In this example, `24924.000` is the name of the dump file. The data structure written to the file is the `SQLD_TCB` data structure and it is written to the directory `/homedir/db2inst1/db2dump`.

Under severe error conditions, DB2 may issue a signal (for UNIX-based platforms) or exception (for Intel-based platforms) to itself. All signals or exceptions initiated by DB2 or encountered by DB2 are reported in **trap files.** Trap files contain a flow of the last internal program functions that were executed before the system was stopped.

Trap files are required by DB2 Customer Service personnel. They are located in the directory specified by the `DIAGPATH` database manager configuration parameter. The first letter in their names is "t", followed by a process identifier (pid). The file extension is 000 for single processors, or the node number for multi-node systems.

For example:

- In the above example the error generated the trap file: t24924.000 (Trap file for the process with pid: 24924.).

The trap file t24572.002 is the trap file created by a DB2 process running on node 2.

7.2.4 DB2DIAG.LOG in DB2 UDB EEE

The location of the DB2DIAG.LOG file is specified by the database manager configuration parameter `DIAGPATH`. If this parameter is null (default value) DB2DIAG.LOG and all the dump files will be created in:

$HOME/sqllib/db2dump

In the DB2 UDB EEE case, if the `DIAGPATH` parameter is the default value the DB2DIAG.LOG file will contain information for all nodes, and the error messages for each node will be inter-mixed with the messages for the other nodes.

7.2.4.1 Setting up Local DB2DIAG.LOG Files

To ensure that all the database partitions on each host write to a local DB2DIAG.LOG file, update your DIAGPATH to point to a local file system instead of the `/sqllib/db2dump` directory (which is a shared filesystem).

For a system with multiple database partitions per host, ALL partitions will write to the same DB2DIAG.LOG file since there is only one database manager configuration file.

You can check this parameter with the following command:

```
db2 GET DATABASE MANAGER CONFIGURATION
```

The output of this command would include:

```
DIAGNOSTIC DATA DIRECTORY PATH (DIAGPATH) =
/home/db2inst1/sqllib/db2dump
```

To change the DIAGPATH value to point to a local filesystem, issue the following commands. Note, the instance must be stopped and restarted for the change to take effect.

```
UPDATE DBM CFG USING DIAGPATH /database
```

```
db2stop
```

```
db2start
```

Where `/database` is the local filesystem.

After this change each host will have its own local DB2DIAG.LOG file.

7.3 Using syslogd

The most important diagnostic error log available is the DB2DIAG.LOG file. This file is provided by DB2 and should be one of the first places that you investigate when a problem has been detected. Basically, the DB2DIAG.LOG is a file that logs errors recorded by the DB2 Database manager. However, the error may be severe and the database manager may not be able to write this error to db2diag.log file. In this case, the use of SYSLOG is recommended since the syslog tool can be used to determine and solve the DB2 problem.

7.3.1 Setting up the Syslog

To use the syslog with DB2 on UNIX, you must perform some configuration steps. The following is required to set up the syslog file for use by DB2.

1. Edit /etc/syslog.conf and insert the following line: (you must have system authority to do this).

   <Facility>.<Priority> <Destination> # optional comment

   user.warn fully_qualified_file_name

   where:

   - Facility - User is the facility to log. The DB2 only codes messages under the user facility, so the facility option to manage DB2 messages in syslog is the user option.

   - Priorities - Warn is the priority over which messages are logged. The priorities managed by DB2 are the following:

     - **Alert**: Is the higher priority, this logs severe errors encountered (agent dies, databases damaged).

     - **Error**: This logs internal errors, possibly non severe errors.

     - **Warn**: With this priority warning, error, and alert messages are logged. Any negative SQLCODE with C extension (critical) will be logged in this priority.

     - **Info**: This priority information, warning, error, and alert messages are logged.

   - Destination - The destination is the fully_qualified_file_name where the log information will be written, and the SQLCA will be dumped. This file will not be created by the system, so you must create this file in the specified path.

   For example:

   user.warn /tmp/syslog.out

   When you add this line to the /etc/syslog.conf file, you will have one syslog file per host, regardless of how many database partitions you have configured per host. All messages that are written will be written to the single syslog file /tmp/syslog.out.

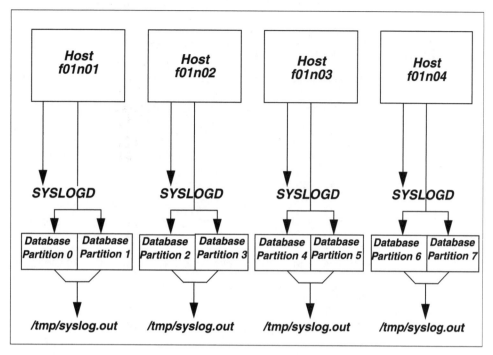

Figure 166. Syslog Example

All the warning messages from user level applications will go into file /tmp/syslog.out. In addition higher priority messages will be dumped. Note that you should start with user.warn, since this captures the most useful information.

2. Touch the fully_qualified_file_name, for example:

```
touch /tmp/syslog.out
```

3. Send a -1 signal to the syslogd process:

kill -1 process.id_syslogd

4. Check to see if information is being logged into SYSLOG by issuing:

```
ps -ef |grep db2sysc
kill -36 db2sysc.process.id
```

5. Check the fully_qualified_file_name (in our example it was /tmp/syslog.out) for messages entries. If there is information in the file, then syslog has been able to capture the information.

Log only to local file system, since if you log to an NFS-mounted filesystem, and the error is due to NFS problems, the error messages will not shown. To log all messages to a local filesystem will take more work in monitoring the syslog files, but it will be easier to debug the error.

7.4 Interpreting syslog Entries

Syslog entries show the error information with the following format:

The following is an example of output from syslog:

```
(1) Jan 30 10:42:50 (2)f01n05 DB2[25676]:DB2
(3)(db2inst1.000)
(4)oper_system_services (5)sqlo_dealloc_sem_po (6)reports:
probe id 3
with (7)error 2055 and (8)alert num 0
Jan 30 10:42:50 f01n05 DB2[25676]:(9)data 00000016
```

The kind of information contained in the syslog is the following:

1. Date and time of entry

2. Hostname

3. Instance name and node number

4. Reporting Component

5. Reporting function

6. Location inside function

7. Error number

8. Alert number

9. Function specific dump information.

The node name may be -1. This indicates that we have not yet set the node number for that process before we dumped information to the syslog. The first entry is usually the root cause of the problem; the subsequent entries may be results of the original cause. Make sure that you are looking at the correct instance, since sometimes error messages from another instance may be mixed with instance that is having the problem.

7.4.1 Return Codes

Error codes written to the syslog should be handled in the same manner as the DB2DIAG.LOG file.

1. Convert the return code to decimal.

2. Check if it is a valid SQL Code

3. If not a valid SQL Code, look up the meaning of the message in the Problem Determination Guide.

   For example, in the syslog we receive the error code `FFFFD60C`. Converting from hex to decimal yields -10740,(`FFFFD60C` = `-10740`). The code `-10740` is not a valid sqlcode. In this case we can see in Appendix C. from *The Troubleshooting Guide,* the internal return code D60C corresponds to:

   /* D60C: -968 Disk Full */

7.5 Using db2trc

The DB2 trace facility (`db2trc`) allows you to trace events, dump the trace data to a file, and format the data into a readable format.

In some cases, the DB2DIAG.LOG file alone may not be enough to completely diagnose the problem. In this case, a trace may be requested by the DB2 customer service team. The DB2 trace information is either stored in memory or written directly to disk. The information gathered by a trace grows rapidly, and you must control the size of the trace you wish to gather.

When limiting the trace file size, it is important to capture only the error situation; otherwise the information you need may be overwritten in the trace. The trace must be run on each node independently. The `db2trc` facility should only used when directed by DB2 customer service. It is recommended that system activity be at a minimum when using this utility, so that the problem can be more easily isolated within the trace information. An example of the steps and commands required to perform a trace is shown in Figure 167 on page 494.

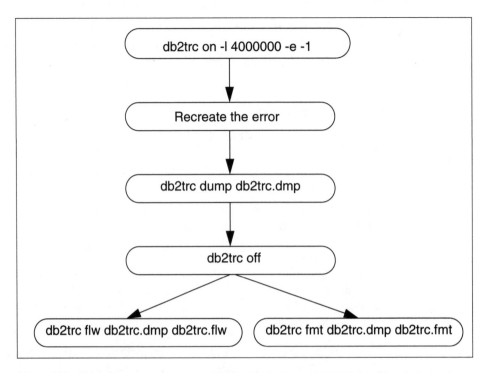

Figure 167. Trace Steps

These commands have the following actions:

1. **db2trc on**: Starts the trace facility. The flag -l 4000000 specifies a trace file of size 4 MB and the -e -1 flags indicate that the trace will continue until it is turned off.

2. **Recreate the error**: The customer must recreate the error that will be logged in the trace

3. **db2trc dmp db2trc.dmp**: This command dumps the trace output to a file.

4. **db2trc off:** Stops the trace facility.

5. **db2trc flw db2trc.dmp db2trc.flw:** Formats flow to an ASCII file.

6. **db2trc fmt db2trc.dmp db2trc.fmt:** Formats to a ASCII file (more detailed).

Appendix A. Test Objectives and Sample Questions

This section contains the test objectives and sample questions for the DB2 Universal Database V5 for Clusters Exam.

A.1 Objectives

The following is a list of the test objectives broken down by category.

A.1.1 DB2 Cluster Concepts

- Identify the components of the DB2 Universal Database Server Product (given a set of requirements)
- Estimate the size of database objects
- Estimate the number of nodes (given a set of requirements)
- Decide the best location for the data to reside
- Identify any re-requisite communication products for DB2 for Clusters
- Use the Command Line Processor
- Estimate the number of required coordinator nodes based on a set of requirements
- Distribute users among the DB2 nodes to distribute coordinator function
- Configure a Loadleveler node to distribute users among the nodes

A.1.2 DB2 Cluster Installation and Configuration

- Create instance owner's group(s)
- Create instance owner's ID
- Decide on DB2 software distribution
- Update software on all nodes using the Control Workstation
- Create/maintain node configuration file (db2nodes.cfg)
- Determine nodegroup requirements
- Configure the server for client communications

A.1.3 DB2 Cluster Administration Tasks

- Create a database
- Create nodegroups
- Add nodes to an existing database system
- Drop nodes from an existing database system
- Execute commands to update data on all nodes simultaneously
- Redistribute nodegroups
- Use the split utility to segment the load data
- Use the LOAD utility to load data
- Create Indexes

- Gather table statistics
- Gather index statistics
- Enable the Buffered Insert option

A.1.4 DB2 Cluster Performance Tuning Tasks

- Obtain database manager configuration information
- Modify key database manager configuration parameters
- Obtain database configuration information
- Modify key database configuration parameters
- Create database buffer pool(s)
- Modify buffer pool sizes
- Decide the best method of distributing the data
- Determine the partition key for a given table
- Define the partitioning key
- Reorganize table data
- Set database monitor switches
- Analyze database monitor information
- Collect explain information
- Interpret explain output, including various join methods
- Use explain to identify poorly written SQL queries within an application

A.1.5 DB2 Cluster Application Considerations

- Create database objects (such as tables, indexes, and so on)
- Disable logging during initial object creation
- Examine system catalog information (to do what)
- Use the DB2 governor to limit database resources
- Use the CURRENT NODE register to direct SQL queries
- Run applications on each node independently using the WHERE NODENUMBER function

A.2 Questions

1. In order to access a database on a DB2 UDB EEE cluster from DB2 for OS/390, which of the following products must be installed on the cluster?

- A. DB2 Connect Personal Edition

- B. DB2 Connect Enterprise Edition

- C. DB2 Universal Database Enterprise Edition

- D. DB2 Universal Database Enterprise-Extended Edition

2. Given the following statement:

```
create table table1 (emp_num into not null, emp_fname
char(30), emp_lname char(30), emp_addr char(30),
constraint emp_uniq unique (emp_num))
```

How much free space must exist in the table space to successfully create the table?

- A. 1 extent
- B. 2 extents
- C. 3 extents
- D. 4 extents

3. Which of the following is the minimum number of partitions to handle a table that contains 55 GB of data using uni-processor nodes?

- A. 2 database partitions
- B. 3 database partitions
- C. 4 database partitions
- D. 5 database partitions

4. A DB2 cluster currently has four database partitions. With ten concurrent queries, the response time is approximately two minutes and CPU usage is 100%. How many database partitions are required to allow one hundred concurrent queries with a response time of four minutes and 100% CPU usage?

- A. 14
- B. 20
- C. 24
- D. 40

5. Which of the following commands will re-start the database mydb1 on all database partitions?

- A. `db2 all restart database mydb1`
- B. `db2_all restart database mydb1`
- C. `db2 -all db2restart database mydb1`
- D. `db2_all db2 restart database mydb1`

6. Given the SAMPLE database with the following defined user table space:

SMS USERSPACE1

SMS MYSPACE1

DMS MYSPACE2

SMS MYSPACE3

DMS MYSPACE4

Which of the following commands will create the Product Table (PRODUCT) so that its data and index objects are in separate table spaces?

- A. `CREATE table PRODUCT (pid int, pdescr char(30), pprice decimal (8,2), invonhand int)`

- B. `CREATE table PRODUCT (pid int, pdescr char(30), pprice decimal (8,2), invonhand int) in MYSPACE2`

- C. `CREATE table PRODUCT (pid int, pdescr char(30), pprice decimal (8,2) invonhand int) in MYSPACE2 index in MYSPACE3`

- D. `CREATE table PRODUCT (pid int, char(30), pprice decimal (8,2), invonhand int) in MYSPACE2 index in MYSPACE4`

7. Which of the following commands creates the Customer table and uses the CustomerID column as the partitioning key?

- A. `CREATE table Customer (CustomerName char(30), CustomerID int, CustomerAddr char(60))`

- B. `CREATE table Customer (CustomerName varchar(30), CustomerID int, CustomerAddr char(60))`

- C. `CREATE table Customer (CustomerName long varchar, CustomerID int, CustomerAddr char(60))`

- D. `CREATE table Customer (CustomerName graphic, CustomerID int, CustomerAddr char(60))`

8. Given 70 users, how many coordinator database partitions must be used in order to evenly balance the workload in a ten database partition database?

- A. 1

- B. 5

- C. 7

- D. 10

9. Which of the following actions must be performed to allow all 10 database partitions in a database to act as coordinator partitions?

- A. Configure the individual clients to connect to separate database partitions.
- B. Configure the server to round robin the connection requests.
- C. Update the database manager configuration on the server using NUM_COORD 10.
- D. Update the database manager configuration on all clients using NUM_COORD 10.

10. Which of the following is the maximum number of partitions that can be configured in a db2nodes.cfg file?

- A. 255
- B. 999
- C. 1000
- D. 65536

11. What is the minimum number of nodegroups required for a database partitioned across four nodes?

- A. 1
- B. 2
- C. 3
- D. 4

12. Given the db2nodes.cfg file:

```
0 node1 0 swnode1
1 node2 0 swnode2
2 node2 1 swnode2
3 node3 0 swnode3
4 node4 0 swnode4
```

A user issues the CREATE DATABASE command on the host node2. The catalog table space will reside on which of the following database partitions?

- A. 0
- B. 1
- C. 2
- D. 3
- E. 4

13. Given the command:

```
CREATE DATABASE testdb
MANAGED BY SYSTEM USING ('patha');
EXTENTSIZE 16 PREFETCHSIZE 32
USER TABLESPACE
MANAGED BY SYSTEM USING ('path1') ON NODE 2
USING ('path2') ON NODE 3
TEMPORARY TABLESPACE
MANAGED BY DATABASE USING (FILE 'filea' 1000)
WITH "EXTENTSIZE 10"
```

How many bufferpools will be assigned to the user TABLESPACE?

- A. 0
- B. 1
- C. 2
- D. 3

14. Which of the following table spaces CANNOT exist on more than one database partition?

- A. LOGSPACE1
- B. SYSCATSPACE
- C. TEMSPACE1
- D. USERSPACE1

15. The results of which TWO of the following catalog views is changed by the "CREATE NODEGROUP ngone" statement?

- A. SYSCAT.DATATYPES
- B. SYSCAT.NODEGROUPS
- C. SYSCAT.PARTITIONMAPS
- D. SYSCAT.TABLES
- E. SYSCAT.TABLESPACES

16. Which of the following commands will update the SORTHEAP parameter for database SAMPLE across all database partitions?

- A. `db2_update database configuration for SAMPLE on all nodes using sortheap 2000`

- B. `db2 all update database configuration for SAMPLE using sortheap 2000`

- C. `db2 update database configuration for SAMPLE on all nodes using sortheap 2000`

- D. `db2_all db2 update database configuration for SAMPLE using sortheap 2000`

17. Which of the following will result when the redistribute nodegroup ng1 uniform command successfully completes?

- A. All nodes in the nodegroup have approximately the same number of hash partitions.

- B. All nodes in the nodegroup have approximately the same number of rows.

- C. All nodes in the nodegroup have a uniform distribution of data.

- D. All table spaces in the nodegroup have a uniform distribution of data.

18. All of the following input file types are supported by db2split EXCEPT

- A. ASC

- B. DEL

- C. IXF

- D. PACK

19. Given the following statement:

```
create table user1.table1 (emp_num int not null,
emp_fname char(30), emp_lname char(30), emp_addr char(30)
constraint emp_uniq unique (emp_num)
```

Which of the following names will be assigned to the system unique index that is used to enforce the unique constraint?

- A. SYSIBM.EMP_UNIQ

- B. USER.EMP_UNIQ

- C. SYSIBM.SYS19980719123456

- D. USER1.SYS19980719123456

20. If nodegroup ng1 is defined on nodes 2, 3, and 4, and RUNSTATS is initiated on node 1 for a table in ng1, statistics will be gathers on which of the following nodes?

- A. 1 only
- B. 2 only
- C. 2, 3, and 4
- D. 1, 2, 3, and 4

21. Which of the following DB2 utilities will collect statistics for DB2 tables and indexes?

- A. REORG
- B. REORGCHK
- C. GETSTATS
- D. GATHER STATISTICS

22. All of the following columns in SYSCAT.INDEXES are updated by the following command EXCEPT

```
runstats on table user1.t1 for indexes all
```

- A. nleaf
- B. density
- C. clusterratio
- D. clusterfactor

23. Which of the following utilities will NOT use the utility heap size (UTIL_HEAP_SZ)?

- A. BACKUP
- B. LOAD
- C. REORG
- D. RESTORE

24. Given the create bufferpool statement run on a three database partition database:

```
create bufferpool BP1 nodegroup NG1 size 5000
```

Which of the following is the size of BP1 on node 4 after it is added to nodegroup NG1?

- A. -1

- B. 1000

- C. 5000

- D. BP1 will not be on this node until alter bufferpool is run.

25. If the current bufferpool bp1 explicitly has a size of 500 pages, which of the following commands will increase the size of bp1 to 1000 pages?

- A. `alter bufferpool bp1 size 500`

- B. `alter bufferpool bp1 size 1000`

- C. `create bufferpool bp1 size 1000`

- D. `update database configuration for sample using buffpage 1000`

26. For the create table statement:

```
db2 create table T1 (c1 blob(10), c2 int, c3 char(4) not
null, c4 int not null) in TS1
```

Which of the following columns is the partitioning key?

- A. c1

- B. c2

- C. c3

- D. c4

27. TS1 is a table space defined across two database partitions. All of the following commands will result in c3 begin the partitioning key EXCEPT

- A. `db2 create table T1 (c1 int not null, c2 char(10), c3
int not null primary key) in TS1`

- B. `db2 create table T1 (c1 dbclob(10) not null, c2
clob(10) not null, c3 int) in TS1`

- C. `db2 create table T1 (c1 real unique, c2 smallint, c3
char not null primary key) in TS1`

- D. `db2 create table T1 (c1 int not null, c2 clob(200), c3
int not null unique) in TS1`

28. Which of the following authorizations is NOT sufficient to perform the command:

```
db2 reorg table T1 index INX1 use TSTEMP1
```

- A. SYSCTRL

- B. SYSMAINT

- C. control privilege on T1

- D. control privilege on INX1

29. Which TWO of the following can be used to obtain snapshot monitor output?

- A. The Alert Center

- B. The Control Center

- C. db2trc facility

- D. The DB2 Event Monitor Tool

- E. The monitor API in an application

30. Which of the following commands will show the number of free FCM buffers for all database partitions?

- A. `db2 get snapshot for fcm`

- B. `db2 get snapshot for fcm for all nodes`

- C. `db2_all "db2 get snapshot for fcm"`

- D. `db2_all "db2 get snapshot for fcm for all nodes"`

31. User1 issues the following commands:

    ```
    create database MYDB1

    connect to MYDB1

    create tablespace TBSP1

    create table TAB1 (col1 int not null primary key)
    ```

    In which of the following table spaces will the primary key index be created?

- A. TBSP1

- B. SYSCATSPACE

- C. SYSINDEXSPCE

- D. USERSPACE1

32. Which of the following commands will NOT log changes to rows in table1?

- A. `import from try.ixf of ixf create into table1`

- B. `import from try.ixf of ixf insert into table1`

- C. `load from try.ixf of ixf replace into table1`
- D. `redistribute nodegroup ng1 uniform`

33. Which of the following catalog schemas can be updated using SQL?

- A. SYSCAT
- B. SYSSTAT
- C. SYSIBM
- D. SYSCTRL

A.3 Answers

1. Correct answer is "D", DB2 Universal Database Enterprise-Extended Edition.
2. Correct answer is "D", four extents
3. The correct answer is "A", 2 database partitions.
4. .The correct answer is "B", 20 database partitions.
5. The correct answer is "D", `db2_all db2 restart database mydb1`
6. .The correct answer is "D".
7. The correct answer is "C".
8. The correct answer is "D".
9. The correct answer is "A".
10. The correct answer is "C", 1000.
11. The correct answer is "B", 2.
12. The catalog table space will reside on database partition 1, answer "B".
13. The correct answer is "B", 1 bufferpool will be assigned to the USER TABLESPACE.
14. The correct answer is "B", SYSCATSPACE.
15. The correct answer is "B" and "C".
16. The correct answer is "D".
17. The correct answer is "B", all nodes in the nodegroup will have approximately the same number of rows.
18. The correct answer is "C", type IXF is not supported by db2split.
19. The correct answer is "B".
20. Statistics will be gathered only on node 2, answer "B".

21. The correct answer is "B", REORGCHK.

22. The correct answer is "C", clusterratio.

23. The REORG utility does not use the utility heap size, answer "C".

24. The correct answer is "C", 5000.

25. The correct answer is "B", alter bufferpool bp1 size 1000.

26. The correct answer is "B", column c2.

27. "D" is the correct answer.

28. Answer "D", control privilege on INX1 is the correct answer.

29. The correct answers are "B" and "E".

30. The correct answer is "D".

31. The primary key index will be created in TBSP1, answer "A".

32. The correct answer is "C".

33. The SYSSTAT catalog schemas can be updated, answer "B".

Appendix B. Related Publications

The publications listed in this section are considered particularly suitable for a more detailed discussion of the topics covered in this redbook.

B.1 International Technical Support Organization Publications

These are related ITSO publications:

- *Managing VLDB Using DB2 UDB EEE,* SG24-5105-00
- *The Universal Connectivity Guide to DB2,* SG24-4894-00
- *Diagnostic Tips and Techniques for DB2 Common Server,* SG24-4759-00

B.2 Other Publications

These publications are also relevant as further information sources:

DB2 Universal Database Ceritifcation Guide, SC09-2465-01

DB2 Universal Database Command Reference, SS20J-8166-00

DB2 UDB EEE for AIX Quick Beginnings, S72H-9620-00

DB2 Universal Database Administration Guide, S10J-8157-00

DB2 Messages References, S10J-8168-00

DB2 Universal Database Troubleshooting Guide, S10J-8169-00

Index

Symbols

A

B

C

D

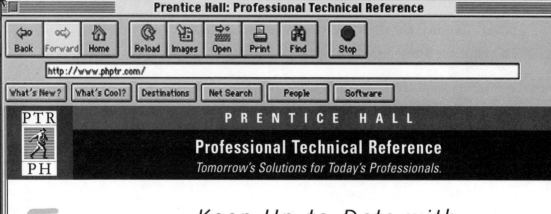